Geometry

Response to Intervention

Houghton Mifflin Harcourt

Contents

Introduction

Tier 2: Prerequisite Skills Module Pre-Tests

Tier 2: Prerequisite Skills Post-Tests

Tier 1: Reteach Worksheets

Tier 2: Strategic Intervention Teacher Guides and Worksheets

UNIT 1 TRANSFORMATIONS AND CONGRUENCE

Student Edition Lessons	Tier 1 Skills	Pre-Tests	Tier 2 Skills Strategic Intervention	Post-Tests	Tier 3 Skills Intensive Intervention
Module 1 Tools of Geometry					
1.1 Segment Length and Midpoints	Reteach 1-1	Module 1	1 Algebraic Representations of Transformations	Skill 1	Building Block (Tier 3) worksheets are available online for students who need additional support on prerequisite skills.
1.2 Angle Measures and Angle Bisectors	Reteach 1-2		2 Angle Relationships	Skill 2	
1.3 Representing and Describing Transformations	Reteach 1-3		9 Distance and Midpoint Formulas	Skill 9	See the teacher page of each Tier 2 Skill lesson for a list of Building Block skills.
1.4 Reasoning and Proof	Reteach 1-4				
Module 2 Transformations and Symmetry					
2.1 Translations	Reteach 2-1	Module 2	17 Properties of Reflections	Skill 17	
2.2 Reflections	Reteach 2-2		18 Properties of Rotations	Skill 18	
2.3 Rotations	Reteach 2-3		19 Properties of Translations	Skill 19	
2.4 Investigating Symmetry	Reteach 2-4				
Module 3 Congruent Figures					
3.1 Sequences of Transformations	Reteach 3-1	Module 3	7 Congruent Figures	Skill 7	
3.2 Proving Figures are Congruent Using Rigid Motions	Reteach 3-2		17 Properties of Reflections	Skill 17	
3.3 Corresponding Parts of Congruent Figures Are Congruent	Reteach 3-3		18 Properties of Rotations	Skill 18	
			19 Properties of Translations	Skill 19	

 ADDITIONAL ONLINE INTERVENTION RESOURCES

Tier 1, Tier 2, Tier 3 Skills

Personal Math Trainer will automatically create a standards-based, personalized intervention assignment for your students, targeting each student's individual needs!

Tier 2 Skills

Students scan QR codes with their smart phones to watch Math on the Spot tutorial videos for every Tier 2 skill.

Response to Intervention

UNIT 2 LINES, ANGLES, AND TRIANGLES

Student Edition Lessons	Tier 1 Skills	Pre-Tests	Tier 2 Skills Strategic Intervention	Post-Tests	Tier 3 Skills Intensive Intervention
Module 4 Lines and Angles					
4.1 Angles Formed by Intersecting Lines	Reteach 4-1	Module 4	2 Angle Relationships	Skill 2	Building Block (Tier 3) worksheets are available online for students who need additional support on prerequisite skills. See the teacher page of each Tier 2 Skill lesson for a list of Building Block skills.
4.2 Transversals and Parallel Lines	Reteach 4-2		12 Parallel Lines Cut by a Transversal	Skill 12	
4.3 Proving Lines are Parallel	Reteach 4-3		17 Properties of Reflections	Skill 17	
4.4 Perpendicular Lines	Reteach 4-4		28 Writing Equations of Parallel, Perpendicular, Vertical, and Horizontal Lines	Skill 28	
4.5 Equations of Parallel and Perpendicular Lines	Reteach 4-5				
Module 5 Triangle Congruence Criteria					
5.1 Exploring What Makes Triangles Congruent	Reteach 5-1	Module 5	7 Congruent Figures	Skill 7	
5.2 ASA Triangle Congruence	Reteach 5-2		12 Parallel Lines Cut by a Transversal	Skill 12	
5.3 SAS Triangle Congruence	Reteach 5-3		17 Properties of Reflection	Skill 17	
			18 Properties of Rotations	Skill 18	
5.4 SSS Triangle Congruence	Reteach 5-4		19 Properties of Translation	Skill 19	
Module 6 Applications of Triangle Congruence					
6.1 Justifying Constructions	Reteach 6-1	Module 6	3 Angle Theorems for Triangles	Skill 3	
6.2 AAS Triangle Congruence	Reteach 6-2		7 Congruent Figures	Skill 7	
6.3 HL Triangle Congruence	Reteach 6-3		12 Parallel Lines Cut by a Transversal	Skill 12	
Module 7 Properties of Triangles					
7.1 Interior and Exterior Angles	Reteach 7-1	Module 7	2 Angle Relationships	Skill 2	
7.2 Isosceles and Equilateral Triangles	Reteach 7-2		3 Angle Theorems for Triangles	Skill 3	
7.3 Triangle Inequalities	Reteach 7-3		9 Distance and Midpoint Formula	Skill 9	
Module 8 Special Segments in Triangles					
8.1 Perpendicular Bisectors of Triangles	Reteach 8-1	Module 8	3 Angle Theorems for Triangles	Skill 3	
8.2 Angle Bisectors of Triangles	Reteach 8-2		9 Distance and Midpoint Formula	Skill 9	
8.3 Medians and Altitudes of Triangles	Reteach 8-3		10 Geometric Drawings	Skill 10	
8.4 Midsegments of Triangles	Reteach 8-4				

UNIT 3 QUADRILATERALS AND COORDINATE PROOF					
Student Edition Lessons	**Tier 1 Skills**	**Pre-Tests**	**Tier 2 Skills Strategic Intervention**	**Post-Tests**	**Tier 3 Skills Intensive Intervention**
Module 9 Properties of Quadrilaterals					
9.1 Properties of Parallelograms	Reteach 9-1	Module 9	7 Congruent Figures 13 Parallelograms	Skill 7 Skill 13	Building Block (Tier 3) worksheets are available online for students who need additional support on prerequisite skills.
9.2 Conditions for Parallelograms	Reteach 9-2				See the teacher page of each Tier 2 Skill lesson for a list of Building Block skills.
9.3 Properties of Rectangles, Rhombuses, and Squares	Reteach 9-3				
9.4 Conditions for Rectangles, Rhombuses, and Squares	Reteach 9-4				
9.5 Properties and Conditions for Kites and Trapezoids	Reteach 9.5				
Module 10 Coordinate Proof Using Slope and Distance					
10.1 Slope and Parallel Lines	Reteach 10-1	Module 10	5 Area of Composite Figures	Skill 5 Skill 9	
10.2 Slope and Perpendicular Lines	Reteach 10-2		9 Distance and Midpoint Formula		
10.3 Coordinate Proof Using Distance with Segments and Triangles	Reteach 10-3		21 Rate of Change and Slope 26 Using Slope and y-intercept	Skill 21 Skill 26	
10.4 Coordinate Proof Using Distance with Quadrilaterals	Reteach 10-4		28 Writing Equations of Parallel, Perpendicular, Vertical, and Horizontal Lines	Skill 28	
10.5 Perimeter and Area on the Coordinate Plane	Reteach 10-5				

 ADDITIONAL ONLINE INTERVENTION RESOURCES

Tier 1, Tier 2, Tier 3 Skills

Personal Math Trainer will automatically create a standards-based, personalized intervention assignment for your students, targeting each student's individual needs!

Tier 2 Skills

Students scan QR codes with their smart phones to watch Math on the Spot tutorial videos for every Tier 2 skill.

Response to Intervention

UNIT 4 SIMILARITY

Student Edition Lessons	Tier 1 Skills	Pre-Tests	Tier 2 Skills Strategic Intervention	Post-Tests	Tier 3 Skills Intensive Intervention
Module 11 Similarity and Transformations					
11.1 Dilations	Reteach 11-1	Module 11	10 Geometric Drawings	Skill 10	Building Block (Tier 3) worksheets are available online for students who need additional support on prerequisite skills.
11.2 Proving Figures are Similar Using Transformations	Reteach 11-2		16 Properties of Dilations	Skill 16	
11.3 Corresponding Parts of Similar Figures	Reteach 11-3		23 Similar Figures	Skill 23	See the teacher page of each Tier 2 Skill lesson for a list of Building Block skills.
11.4 AA Similarity of Triangles	Reteach 11-4				
Module 12 Using Similar Triangles					
12.1 Triangle Proportionality Theorem	Reteach 12-1	Module 12	22 Scale Factor and Scale Drawings	Skill 22	
12.2 Subdividing a Segment in a Given Ratio	Reteach 12-2		23 Similar Figures	Skill 23	
			25 The Pythagorean Theorem	Skill 25	
12.3 Using Proportional Relationships	Reteach 12-3		29 Proportional Relationships	Skill 29	
12.4 Similarity in Right Triangles	Reteach 12-4				

UNIT 5 TRIGONOMETRY

Student Edition Lessons	Tier 1 Skills	Pre-Tests	Tier 2 Skills Strategic Intervention	Post-Tests	Tier 3 Skills Intensive Intervention
Module 13 Trigonometry with Right Triangles					
13.1 Tangent Ratio	Reteach 13-1	Module 13	2 Angle Relationships	Skill 2	Building Block (Tier 3) worksheets are available online for students who need additional support on prerequisite skills.
13.2 Sine and Cosine Ratios	Reteach 13-2		25 The Pythagorean Theorem	Skill 25	
13.3 Special Right Triangles	Reteach 13-3		29 Proportional Relationships	Skill 29	See the teacher page of each Tier 2 Skill lesson for a list of Building Block skills.
13.4 Problem Solving with Trigonometry	Reteach 13-4				
Module 14 Trigonometry with All Triangles					
14.1 Law of Sines	Reteach 14-1	Module 14	23 Similar Figures	Skill 23	
14.2 Law of Cosines	Reteach 14-2		29 Proportional Relationships	Skill 29	
			30 Multi-Step Equations	Skill 30	

Response to Intervention

UNIT 6 PROPERTIES OF CIRCLES

Student Edition Lessons	Tier 1 Skills	Pre-Tests	Tier 2 Skills Strategic Intervention	Post-Tests	Tier 3 Skills Intensive Intervention
Module 15 Angles and Segments in Circles					
15.1 Central Angles and Inscribed Angles	Reteach 15-1	Module 15	2 Angle Relationships	Skill 2	Building Block (Tier 3) worksheets are available online for students who need additional support on prerequisite skills.
15.2 Angles in Inscribed Quadrilaterals	Reteach 15-2		3 Angle Theorems for Triangles	Skill 3	
15.3 Tangents and Circumscribed Angles	Reteach 15-3		13 Parallelograms	Skill 13	See the teacher page of each Tier 2 Skill lesson for a list of Building Block skills.
15.4 Segment Relationships in Circles	Reteach 15-4				
15.5 Angle Relationships in Circles	Reteach 15-5				
Module 16 Arc Length and Sector Area					
16.1 Justifying Circumference and Area of a Circle	Reteach 16-1	Module 16	4 Area of a Circle	Skill 4	
16.2 Arc Length and Radian Measure	Reteach 16-2		6 Circumference	Skill 6	
16.3 Sector Area	Reteach 16-3		20 Quadratic Functions	Skill 20	
Module 17 Equations of Circles and Parabolas					
17.1 Equation of a Circle	Reteach 17-1	Module 17	6 Circumference	Skill 6	
17.2 Equation of a Parabola	Reteach 17-2		9 Distance and Midpoint Formula	Skill 9	
			31 Characteristics of Quadratic Functions	Skill 31	
			32 Solving Quadratic Functions Graphically	Skill 32	

 ADDITIONAL ONLINE INTERVENTION RESOURCES

Tier 1, Tier 2, Tier 3 Skills

Personal Math Trainer will automatically create a standards-based, personalized intervention assignment for your students, targeting each student's individual needs!

Tier 2 Skills

Students scan QR codes with their smart phones to watch Math on the Spot tutorial videos for every Tier 2 skill.

Response to Intervention

UNIT 7 MEASUREMENT AND MODELING IN TWO AND THREE DIMENSIONS

Student Edition Lessons	Tier 1 Skills	Pre-Tests	Tier 2 Skills Strategic Intervention	Post-Tests	Tier 3 Skills Intensive Intervention
Module 18 Volume Formulas					
18.1 Volume of Prisms and Cylinders	Reteach 18-1	Module 18	24 Surface Area	Skill 24	Building Block (Tier 3) worksheets are available online for students who need additional support on prerequisite skills.
18.2 Volume of Pyramids	Reteach 18-2		27 Volume	Skill 27	
18.3 Volume of Cones	Reteach 18-3				
18.4 Volume of Spheres	Reteach 18-4				
Module 19 Visualizing Solids					See the teacher page of each Tier 2 Skill lesson for a list of Building Block skills.
19.1 Cross Sections and Solids of Rotation	Reteach 19-1	Module 19	4 Area of a Circle	Skill 4	
			8 Cross Sections	Skill 8	
19.2 Surface Area of Prisms and Cylinders	Reteach 19-2		24 Surface Area	Skill 24	
19.3 Surface Area of Pyramids and Cones	Reteach 19-3				
19.4 Surface Area of Spheres	Reteach 19-4				
Module 20 Modeling and Problem Solving					
20.1 Scale Factor	Reteach 20-1	Module 20	5 Area of Composite Figures	Skill 5	
20.2 Modeling and Density	Reteach 20-2		22 Scale Factor and Scale Drawings	Skill 22	
20.3 Problem Solving with Constraints	Reteach 20-3		27 Volume	Skill 27	

UNIT 8 PROBABILITY

Student Edition Lessons	Tier 1 Skills	Pre-Tests	Tier 2 Skills Strategic Intervention	Post-Tests	Tier 3 Skills Intensive Intervention
Module 21 Introduction to Probability					
21.1 Probability and Set Theory	Reteach 21-1	Module 21	14 Probability of Compound Events	Skill 14	Building Block (Tier 3) worksheets are available online for students who need additional support on prerequisite skills.
21.2 Permutations and Probability	Reteach 21-2		15 Probability of Simple Events	Skill 15	
21.3 Combinations and Probability	Reteach 21-3				See the teacher page of each Tier 2 Skill lesson for a list of Building Block skills.
21.4 Mutually Exclusive and Overlapping Events	Reteach 21-4				
Module 22 Conditional Probability and Independence of Events					
22.1 Conditional Probability	Reteach 22-1	Module 22	14 Probability of Compound Events	Skill 14	
22.2 Independent Events	Reteach 22-2		24 Surface Area	Skill 24	
22.3 Dependent Events	Reteach 22-3				
Module 23 Probability and Decision Making					
23.1 Using Probability to Make Fair Decisions	Reteach 23-1	Module 23	11 Making Predictions with Probability	Skill 11	
23.2 Analyzing Decisions	Reteach 23-2		15 Probability of Simple Events	Skill 15	

Using HMH Geometry Response to Intervention

RtI — Response to Intervention	Print Resources	Online Resources
TIER 1	**TIER 2 STRATEGIC INTERVENTION**	**TIER 1, TIER 2, AND TIER 3**
Reteach worksheet (one worksheet per lesson) • Use to provide additional support for students who are having difficulty mastering the concepts taught in Geometry.	**Skill Intervention worksheets** (one set per skill) • Use for students who require intervention with prerequisite skills taught in middle school. **Skill Intervention Teacher Guides** (one guide per skill) • Use to provide systematic and explicit instruction, and alternate strategies to help students acquire mastery with prerequisite skills.	 **T1, T2, and T3 skills** • Assign the *Personal Math Trainer,* which will create standards based practice for all students and customized intervention when necessary. **Progress Monitoring** • Use the *Personal Math Trainer* to assess a student's mastery of skills.
Progress Monitoring • Use *Student Edition Ready to Go On? Quizzes* to assess mastery of skills taught in the Modules. Use for all students. • Use *Assessment Resources Module Quizzes* to assess mastery of skills taught in the Modules. For students who are considerably below level, use Modified Quizzes. For all other students, use Level B.	**Progress Monitoring** • Use *Response to Intervention Module Pre-Tests* or the *Student Edition Are You Ready? Quizzes* to assess whether a student has the necessary prerequisite skills for success in each Module. • Use *Response to Intervention Skill Post-Tests* to assess mastery of prerequisite skills.	**T2 skills** • Use *Math on the Spot* tutorial videos to help students review skills taught in middle school. 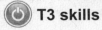 **T3 skills** • Use *Building Block Skills* worksheets for struggling students who require additional intervention.

Recommendations for Intervention

Tier 1	For students who require small group instruction to review lesson skills taught in Geometry.
Tiers 2–3	For students who require strategic or intensive intervention with prerequisite skills needed for success in Geometry.
Tiers 1–3	Intervention materials and the *Personal Math Trainer* are designed to accommodate the diverse skill levels of students at all levels of intervention.

DIAGNOSIS

Tier 2 Module Pre-Tests *(RTI ancillary)*
Tier 2 Are You Ready? Quizzes *(Student Edition)*
Tier 1 Ready to Go On? Quizzes *(Student Edition)*

INTERVENE

Use **Tier 1** Reteach and/or **Tier 2** Skill Worksheets *(RTI ancillary)*.
• Uncluttered with minimum words to help all students, regardless of English acquisition
• Vocabulary presented in context to help English learners and struggling readers
• Multiple instructional examples for students to practice thinking-aloud their solutions

Use **Tier 2** Skill Teacher Guides *(RTI ancillary)*.
• Explicit instruction and key teaching points
• Alternate strategies to address the different types of learners
• Common misconceptions to develop understanding of skills
• Visual representations to make concept connections
• Checks to fine-tune instruction and opportunities for immediate feedback

MONITOR PROGRESS

Tier 2: Skill Post-Tests *(RTI ancillary)*
Tier 1–2: Assessment Readiness *(Student Edition)*
Tier 1–3: Leveled Module Quizzes *(Assessment Resources online)*

Use **Tiers 1–3** online additional intervention, practice, and review materials.

• Personal Math Trainer
• Math on the Spot videos
• Building Block Skills worksheets with Teacher Guides

• Differentiated Instruction with leveled Practice, Reading Strategies, and Success for English Learners worksheets

MODULE 1

Response to Intervention

Pre-Test: Skills 1, 2, 9

Use the information given for 1–2.

A triangle has coordinates of $A(1, 2)$, $B(4, 6)$, and $C(4, -3)$.

1. If the triangle is translated 2 units right, what are the new coordinates?

   _____

2. If $\triangle ABC$ is reflected over the *x*-axis, what are the new coordinates?

   _____

Use the figure for 3–4.

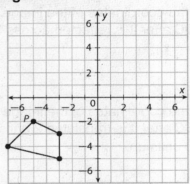

3. If the figure is rotated 90° counterclockwise, in which quadrant will it appear?

   _____

4. After the rotation, what will be the coordinates of P'?

   _____

Use the figure for 5–8.

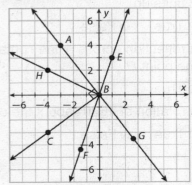

Identify the following pairs of angles as complementary, supplementary, adjacent, and/or vertical angles.

5. $\angle ABH$ and $\angle HBC$

   _____

6. $\angle ABE$ and $\angle FBG$

   _____

7. $\angle ABE$ and $\angle EBG$

   _____

8. $\angle HBF$ and $\angle BFG$

   _____

For 9–10, use the graph below.

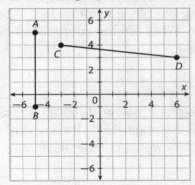

9. What is the length of $\overline{AB}$? Explain your reasoning.

   _____

   _____

   _____

10. What is the midpoint of $\overline{CD}$? Justify your answer.

   _____

   _____

Response to Intervention

Pre-Test: Skills 17, 18, 19

1. Find the image of the point $P(3, 7)$ under the transformation $(x, y) \to (x + 2, y - 1)$.

_____

2. Find the image of $\triangle ABC$ after it is reflected across the y-axis.

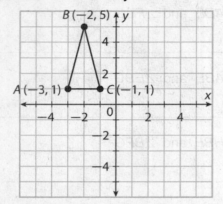

3. Point $P(3, 9)$ counterclockwise in the coordinate plane is rotated 90° about the origin. What are the coordinates of its image?

_____

4. In the graph below, if $ABCD$ is rotated about the origin 180°, then which quadrant would contain its image?

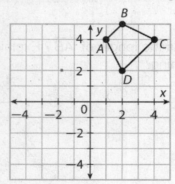

_____

5. Write the rule for an image that is translated 4 units down and 3 units to the right.

_____

For 6–8, use a triangle with vertices at $A(1, 1)$, $B(2, 4)$, and $C(3, 1)$.

6. Find the coordinates of the image of $\triangle ABC$ after it is rotated about the origin 270°.

_____

7. Find the coordinates of the image of $\triangle ABC$ after it is reflected across the line $y = x$.

_____

8. Find the coordinates of the image of $\triangle ABC$ after it is translated 2 units left and 3 units up.

_____

9. Each of the following will map the point P in the coordinate plane onto itself. Choose True or False for each description of a transformation.

A a rotation of 720° about the origin

   ○ True   ○ False

B a reflection across the line $y = -x$

   ○ True   ○ False

C a translation of 2 units down and 2 units up

   ○ True   ○ False

D a reflection across a line containing the point P

   ○ True   ○ False

E a rotation of 1620° about the origin

   ○ True   ○ False

MODULE 3

Response to Intervention

Pre-Test: Skills 7, 17, 18, 19

1. The figures below are congruent.

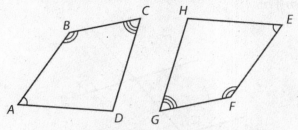

Choose True or False for each statement.

A $\overline{AD} \cong \overline{GF}$ ○ True ○ False

B $\angle B \cong \angle F$ ○ True ○ False

C $\angle C \cong \angle E$ ○ True ○ False

D $\overline{BC} \cong \overline{HE}$ ○ True ○ False

2. Write the rule for the translation that takes point $P(3, 2)$ to its image $P'(2, 6)$.

_____

3. Find the image of ABCD after it is reflected across the line $y = x$.

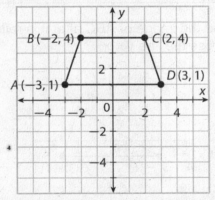

4. If △A′B′C′ in the coordinate plane is the image of △ABC after it is rotated 180° in the coordinate plane, then is it true that △A′B′C′ ≅ △ABC? Explain.

_____

_____

For 5–6, use the point $P(-2, 7)$ in the coordinate plane.

5. What is the image of the point P after it is reflected across a line containing itself?

_____

6. What is the image of the point P after it is rotated about the origin by 270° counterclockwise?

_____

For 7–10, △ABC ≅ △DFE.

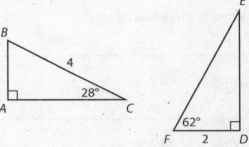

7. What is the measure of $\angle B$?

_____

8. What is the measure of $\angle E$?

_____

9. What is the length of $\overline{FE}$?

_____

10. What is the length of $\overline{AB}$?

_____

MODULE 4

Response to Intervention
Pre-Test: Skills 2, 12, 17, 28

1. Write the equation of a line that is parallel to $y = -5x + 1$ and passes through the *point* (0, 3).

_____

For 2–5, use the figure below where m∠1 = (x − 6)° and m∠2 = (2x)°.

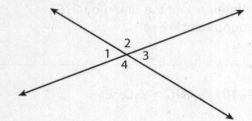

2. What is the value of *x*?

_____

3. What is m∠3?

_____

4. What is m∠4?

_____

5. Classify ∠1 and ∠4 as complementary, supplementary, or neither.

_____

6. Write the equation of a line that is perpendicular to the line $y = -6$ and passes through the *point* (3, 7).

_____

7. Classify the lines represented by the equations $-x + 2y = 8$ and $-3x + y = -1$ as perpendicular, parallel, or neither. Explain.

_____

_____

For 8–10, use the figure below where m ∥ n.

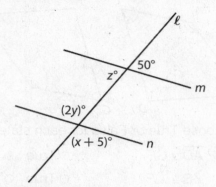

8. What is the value of *y*?

_____

9. What is the value of *x*?

_____

10. What is the value of *z*?

_____

11. Find the image of *ABC* after it is reflected across the line $y = x$.

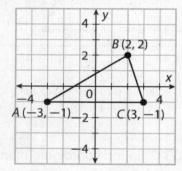

MODULE 5

Response to Intervention

Pre-Test: Skills 7, 12, 17, 18, 19

1. In the figure below, $m \parallel n$.

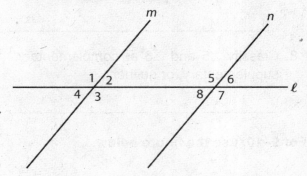

Choose True or False for each statement.

A $\angle 1 \cong \angle 2$ ○ True ○ False

B $\angle 5 \cong \angle 7$ ○ True ○ False

C $\angle 2 \cong \angle 6$ ○ True ○ False

D $\angle 2 \cong \angle 5$ ○ True ○ False

2. Find the image of $\triangle ABC$ after the translation $(x, y) \rightarrow (x + 3, y + 1)$ is applied.

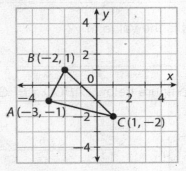

3. What is the image of the point $P(-5, 1)$ after it is rotated about the origin by $180°$?

_____

4. In the figure below, $\triangle ABC \cong \triangle DEF$.

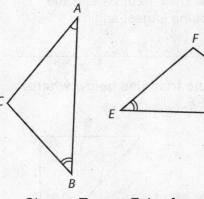

Choose True or False for each statement.

A $\angle A \cong \angle F$ ○ True ○ False

B $\angle B \cong \angle E$ ○ True ○ False

C $\overline{AB} \cong \overline{DE}$ ○ True ○ False

D $\overline{CA} \cong \overline{FD}$ ○ True ○ False

5. Write the rule for a transformation that translates any point 4 units down and 1 unit to the left.

_____

6. A figure ABCD lies completely within quadrant II of the coordinate plane. If the figure is rotated about the origin by 90° counterclockwise, which quadrant does its image $A'B'C'D'$ lie?

_____

7. In the coordinate plane, $\triangle ABC$ is rotated about the origin by 270°. Is it true that $\triangle ABC \cong \triangle A'B'C'$? Why or why not?

_____

_____

_____

MODULE 6 · Response to Intervention

Pre-Test: Skills 3, 7, 12

1. The measures of the angles in a triangle are x, $2x$, and $2x - 20$. What is the measure of the largest angle?

   _____

For 2–4, use the triangles below where △ABC ≅ △DEF.

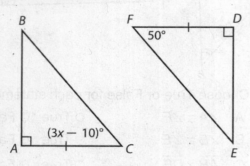

2. What is the value of x?

   _____

3. What is m∠B?

   _____

4. What is m∠E?

   _____

For 5–8, use the figure below where $m \parallel n$ and m∠1 = 20°.

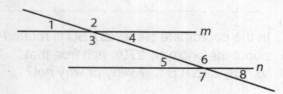

5. What is m∠2?

   _____

6. What is m∠4?

   _____

7. What is m∠6?

   _____

8. Classify ∠5 and ∠6 as complementary, supplementary, or neither.

   _____

For 9–10, use the figure below.

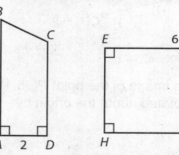

9. What is the value of x?

   _____

10. What is the value of y?

   _____

11. In the figure below, $ABCD \cong EFGH$.

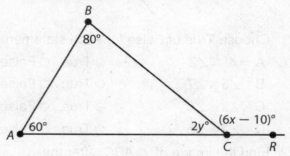

Choose True or False for each statement.

A ∠B ≅ ∠F   ○ True ○ False

B $HG = 2$ ○ True ○ False

C $AB = 6$ ○ True ○ False

D ∠C ≅ ∠G   ○ True ○ False

Name _____ Date _____ Class_____

Response to Intervention
Pre-Test: Skills 2, 3, 9

1. The measures of the angles in a triangle are $2x$, $4x$, and $6x$. What is the measure of the smallest angle?

_____

2. In the figure below, all of the labeled angles lie along the line ℓ. What is the value of x?

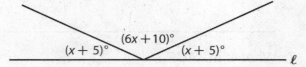

_____

For 3–4, use the graph below.

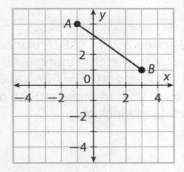

3. What is the length of $\overline{AB}$?

_____

4. If M is the midpoint of $\overline{AB}$, then what are its coordinates?

_____

5. Given the triangle below, choose True or False for each statement.

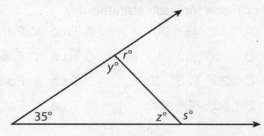

A	$35 + y = 180$	○ True	○ False
B	$r = 35 + z$	○ True	○ False
C	$s = z$	○ True	○ False
D	$z + s = 180$	○ True	○ False

6. In the coordinate plane, what is the distance between the points $(-3, 1)$ and $(-5, -4)$?

_____

7. Is it possible that a triangle has interior angles of 35°, 55°, and 80°? Explain.

_____

_____

8. If C is the midpoint of $\overline{PQ}$ and $CP = 6$, then what is the length of $\overline{PQ}$?

_____

9. Two lines intersect at point P and form four angles: $\angle 1$, $\angle 2$, $\angle 3$, and $\angle 4$. If $\angle 1 = \angle 3 = 48°$, then what is m$\angle 2$?

_____

10. A triangle has two angles with equal measures and one angle with a measure of 70°. What is the measure of the other two angles?

_____

MODULE 8 Response to Intervention

Pre-Test: Skills 3, 9, 10

1. Each of the following represents the interior angles of a triangle. Choose True or False for each statement.

   A 45°, 45°, 90°   ○ True ○ False

   B 110°, 80°, 10°   ○ True ○ False

   C 25°, 125°, 30°   ○ True ○ False

   D 60°, 60°, 60°   ○ True ○ False

For 2–3, use the graph below and provide exact answers.

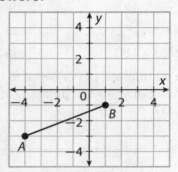

2. What is the length of $\overline{AB}$?

   _____

3. What are the coordinates of the midpoint of $\overline{AB}$?

   _____

4. A triangle has interior angles of $(x+5)°$, $(x-5)°$ and $(2x)°$. What is the measure of the largest interior angle?

   _____

5. If the length of $\overline{QR}$ is 18 units and the midpoint is located at point M, then what is the length of $\overline{MR}$?

   _____

For 6–8, use the figure below.

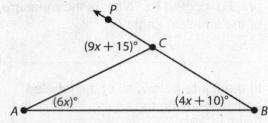

6. What is $m\angle CAB$?

   _____

7. What is $m\angle ACP$?

   _____

8. What is $m\angle ACB$?

   _____

9. In the space below, use a ruler and a protractor to sketch a triangle ABC where $m\angle A = 60°$ and $m\angle B = 80°$. Label the vertices of your triangle and the measure of each angle including $\angle C$.

10. Is the triangle sketched in Number 9 unique? Explain.

    _____

    _____

    _____

MODULE 9

Response to Intervention
Pre-Test: Skills 7, 13

1. Given the parallelogram *ABCD* below, choose True or False for each statement.

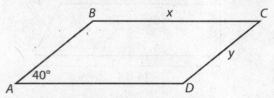

   Choose True or False for each statement.

   A m∠C = 50°   ○ True   ○ False
   B AB = y   ○ True   ○ False
   C m∠B = 140°   ○ True   ○ False
   D AD = y + x   ○ True   ○ False

For 2–3, use the congruent triangles below.

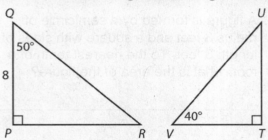

2. What is m∠PRQ?

   _____

3. What is *TU*?

   _____

4. In parallelogram *ABCD*, m∠A = m∠C. If m∠A = 65°, then what is m∠D?

   _____

5. In parallelogram *PQRS*, $\overline{PQ} \parallel \overline{SR}$ and $\overline{PS} \parallel \overline{QR}$. If PQ = 5 and PS = 4, what is the length of $\overline{QR}$?

   _____

For 6–8, use the parallelogram below.

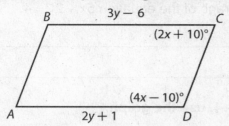

6. What is m∠C?

   _____

7. What is m∠B?

   _____

8. What is *AD*?

   _____

9. Given that △DEF ≅ △MNP, choose True or False for each statement.

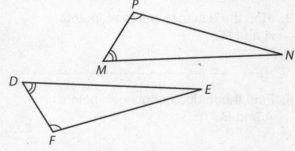

   Choose True or False for each statement.

   A DE = PN   ○ True   ○ False
   B $\overline{DF} \cong \overline{PM}$ ○ True   ○ False
   C m∠D = m∠N   ○ True   ○ False
   D ∠F ≅ ∠P   ○ True   ○ False

10. The diagonals of parallelogram *ABCD* intersect at point *O*. If $\overline{AB}$ is a diagonal and AO = 5, then what is AB?

   _____

MODULE 10

Response to Intervention

Pre-Test: Skills 5, 9, 21, 26, 28

1. Find the slope and *y*-intercept for the graph of the equation $5x + 2y = 4$.

   _____

   _____

For 2–4, use the graph.

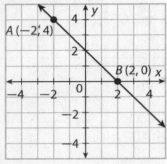

2. Find the slope of the line that passes through points *A* and *B*.

   _____

3. Find the distance between points *A* and *B*.

   _____

4. Find the midpoint between points *A* and *B*.

   _____

5. The graph of the given equation is a vertical line. Select True or False for each given equation.

   A $x = -5$ ○ True ○ False

   B $y = 4$ ○ True ○ False

   C $x + y = -1$ ○ True ○ False

   D $x - 2y = 6$ ○ True ○ False

6. Write the equation of a line that is perpendicular to the line $y = -\dfrac{1}{2}x + 4$ and passes through the point $(0, -1)$.

   _____

7. What is the area of the figure below?

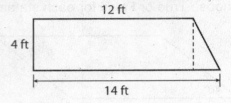

   _____

   _____

8. Write the equation of a line that is parallel to the line $y = -4x + 1$ and passes through the point $(0, 5)$.

   _____

9. A figure is formed by a semicircle of radius 3 feet and a square with sides of length 3 feet. To the nearest tenth of a foot, what is the area of the figure?

   _____

   _____

10. The total monthly cost in dollars, *c*, for a cell phone plan is represented by the equation $c = 0.1m + 12$ where *m* represents the number of minutes of talk time used during the month. Explain what the slope represents in this situation.

   _____

   _____

MODULE 11

Response to Intervention

Pre-Test: Skills 10, 16, 23

1. The triangles below are similar.

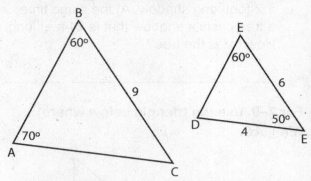

Choose True or False for each statement.

A   m∠C = 50°   ○ True   ○ False

B   AC = 4   ○ True   ○ False

C $\overline{AB} \cong \overline{DE}$ ○ True   ○ False

D   ∠A ≅ ∠D   ○ True   ○ False

2. In the space below, use a ruler and a protractor to sketch a triangle ABC where m∠A = 55° and m∠B = 45°. Label the vertices of your triangle and the measure of each angle including ∠C.

3. Is the triangle sketched in Number 2 unique? Explain.

_____

_____

4. Sketch the image of △ABC after a dilation with a scale factor of $\frac{1}{2}$. Label the vertices of the resulting triangle.

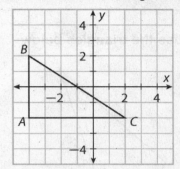

5. In the coordinate plane, A'B'C'D' is the image of the figure ABCD after a dilation by a scale factor of 4. Is it true that A'B'C'D' ~ ABCD? Explain.

_____

6. A right triangle ABC is similar to △PQR such that the hypotenuse BC = 10 and the hypotenuse QR = 4. If AC = 8, then what is the length of $\overline{PR}$? Round your answer to the nearest tenth.

_____

7. Is the transformation $(x, y) \rightarrow \left(\frac{1}{3}x, y\right)$ a dilation? Explain.

_____

_____

8. After a dilation with a scale factor of 2, the image of a vertex of a figure in the coordinate plane is (2, 14). What are the coordinates of the preimage?

_____

Name _____ Date _____ Class_____

1. A right triangle has legs of lengths 2 and 6. What is the exact length of the hypotenuse? Simplify your answer.

   _____

For 2–3, use the triangles below.

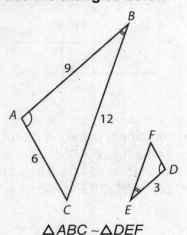

$\triangle ABC \sim \triangle DEF$

2. Find *FD*.

   _____

3. Find *FE*.

   _____

4. Find the value of exact value of *x*. Simplify your answer.

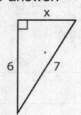

   _____

5. An airplane used for international flights has a length of 242 feet. A scale model is built such that 0.1 inches represents 1 foot. To the nearest tenth of an inch, how long is the scale model?

   _____

6. A 3-foot-tall stake in the ground casts a 1.2-foot-long shadow. At the same time, a tree casts a shadow that is 24 feet long. How tall is the tree?

   _____

For 7–9, use the triangle below where $\overline{MN} \parallel \overline{AC}$.

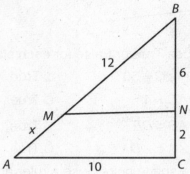

7. What is the value of *x*?

   _____

8. What is the length of $\overline{MN}$?

   _____

9. If $m\angle C = 60°$, then what is $m\angle N$? Explain.

   _____

   _____

10. Is it possible for the side lengths of a right triangle to be 2, 6, 10? Explain.

   _____

   _____

11. On a map, two cities are 14 centimeters apart. If the cities are 21 miles apart, then how many centimeters on the map represent a single mile?

   _____

MODULE 13

Response to Intervention

Pre-Test: Skills 2, 25, 29

1. In the figure below, $\overline{PQ} \parallel \overline{AC}$.

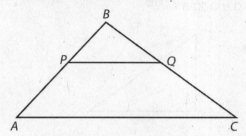

Choose True or False for each statement.

A $\dfrac{PB}{AP} = \dfrac{QB}{CQ}$ ○ True   ○ False

B $\dfrac{PQ}{AC} = \dfrac{QB}{CQ}$ ○ True   ○ False

C $\dfrac{AB}{PB} = \dfrac{AC}{PQ}$ ○ True   ○ False

D $\triangle ABC \sim \triangle PBQ$ ○ True   ○ False

For 2–4, use the figure below.

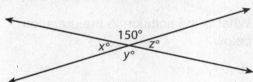

2. What is the value of x?

_____

3. What is the value of y?

_____

4. What is the value of z?

_____

5. A right triangle has two legs of the same length. If its hypotenuse has a length of $3\sqrt{2}$, what is the length of each leg?

_____

6. Find the exact value of x in the triangle below. Simplify your answer completely.

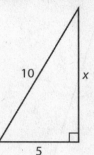

7. Two angles, $\angle 1$ and $\angle 2$ are supplementary. If $m\angle 1 = (6x + 8)^\circ$ and $m\angle 2 = (4x + 12)^\circ$, then what is the value of x?

_____

For 8–10, use the figure below.

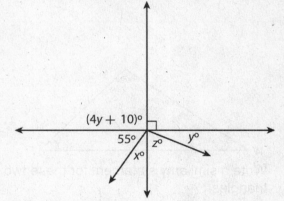

8. What is the value of x?

_____

9. What is the value of y?

_____

10. What is the value of z?

_____

MODULE 14

Response to Intervention

Pre-Test: Skills 23, 29, 30

1. In the figure below, triangle *ABC* is similar to triangle *DEF*.

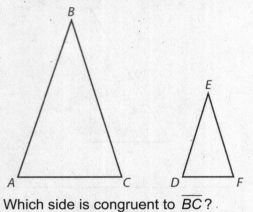

Which side is congruent to $\overline{BC}$?

_____

2. The two triangles below are similar.

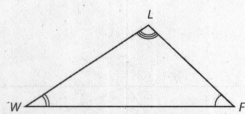

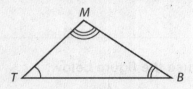

Write a similarity statement for these two triangles.

_____

3. In the figure below, triangle *JKL* is similar to triangle *MNP*.

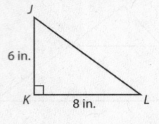

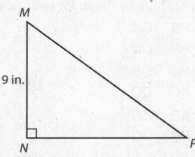

What is *NP*?

_____

4. What is the solution to the equation below?

$$\frac{x}{3} = 2x - 1$$

_____

5. What is the solution to the equation below?

$$3x + 3 = 6(x - 4)$$

_____

MODULE 15

Response to Intervention

Pre-Test: Skills 2, 3, 13

1. Given the figure below,

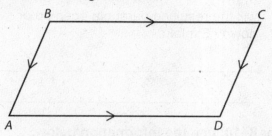

Choose True or False for each statement.

A $\angle A \cong \angle C$ ○ True   ○ False

B $\angle C \cong \angle D$ ○ True   ○ False

C $\overline{BC} \cong \overline{AD}$ ○ True   ○ False

D $m\angle A + m\angle B = 90°$ ○ True   ○ False

2. A right triangle has an interior angle of 50°. What is the measure of the smallest interior angle?

_____

3. In parallelogram $PRQS$, $\overline{PR} \parallel \overline{QS}$ and $\overline{RQ} \parallel \overline{PS}$. If $RQ = 14$, then what is the value of PS? Explain.

_____

_____

For 4–6, use the parallelogram below.

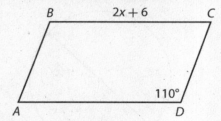

4. What is $m\angle C$?

_____

5. What is $m\angle B$?

_____

6. What is the length of BC?

_____

For 7–8, use the figure below.

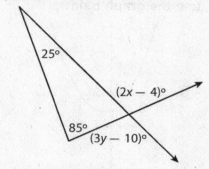

7. What is the value of x?

_____

8. What is the value of y?

_____

9. What is the measure of the unknown angle in the triangle?

_____

10. Explain what it means for two angles to be complementary.

_____

11. What is the value of x in the figure below?

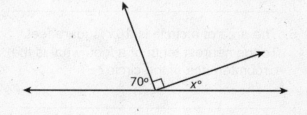

_____

MODULE 16

Response to Intervention

Pre-Test: Skills 4, 6, 20

1. In terms of π, what is the area of a circle with a diameter of 4 meters?

   _____

For 2–4, use the graph below.

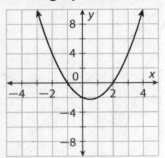

2. What are the zeros of the function? Explain.

   _____

   _____

3. Does the function reach a maximum value? Explain.

   _____

   _____

4. Does the function reach a minimum value? Explain.

   _____

   _____

5. The area of a circle is 16π square feet. To the nearest tenth of a foot, what is the circumference of the circle?

   _____

6. A new logo is being painted at the center of a football field. The first layer of paint must be a circle with a radius of 4.5 feet. To the nearest tenth of a foot, how many square feet of the field will need to be painted?

   _____

7. If the function $f(x) = -2x^2 + 1$ is graphed, will the resulting parabola open up or down? Explain.

   _____

   _____

For 8–10, use the information below.

A quadratic function has a vertex at the point (4, 0). The graph of the function opens up.

8. How many zeros does the function have? Explain.

   _____

   _____

9. What is the equation of the axis of symmetry?

   _____

10. What is the function's minimum value?

   _____

11. The circle below is centered at the point O and $AB = 3$. In terms of π, what is the circumference of the circle?

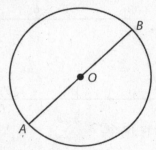

   _____

MODULE
17

Response to Intervention

Pre-Test: Skills 6, 9, 31, 32

1. What is the circumference of this circle? Use 3.14 for π. Round to the nearest tenth of a centimeter.

_____

Use this graph to answer questions 2–3.

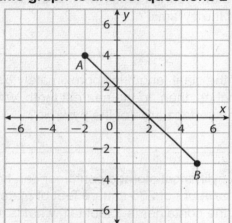

2. What is the midpoint of $\overline{AB}$?

_____

3. What is the length of $\overline{AB}$?

_____

4. Look at the quadratic function below.

$$y = -3x^2 + 4$$

Describe the shape of the graph of this function, and determine whether it has a minimum or maximum value.

_____

_____

5. Look at the quadratic function below.

$$y = 6x^2 - 2x - 4$$

Describe the shape of the graph of this function, and determine whether it has a minimum or maximum value.

_____

_____

6. The graph of the function $y = x^2 - x + 6$ is shown below.

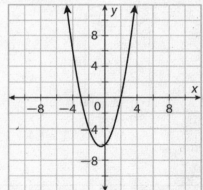

What are the solutions to the equation $x^2 - x + 6 = 0$?

_____

MODULE 18

Response to Intervention
Pre-Test: Skills 24, 27

For 1–2, find the volume and surface area of each figure. Round to the nearest tenth, if necessary.

1.

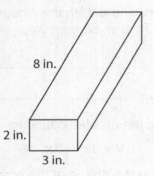

8 in.

2 in.

3 in.

Volume:

_____

Surface area:

_____

2.

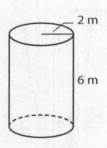

2 m

6 m

Volume:

_____

Surface area:

_____

3. What is the volume of a cube with side lengths of 4 feet?

_____

For 4–5, use the figure below.

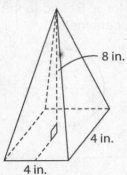

8 in.

4 in.

4 in.

4. To the nearest tenth, what is the volume of the pyramid?

_____

5. If the slant length is approximately 8.9 inches, then, to the nearest tenth, what is the surface area of the pyramid?

_____

6. A cylindrical storage container can hold a maximum of 236 square feet of material. If the container is 3 feet tall, what is its radius? Round your answer to the nearest foot.

_____

7. What is the volume of the figure below?

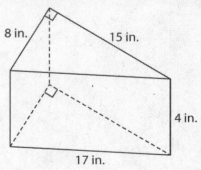

8 in.

15 in.

4 in.

17 in.

_____

MODULE 19

Response to Intervention

Pre-Test: Skills 4, 8, 24

For 1–2, use the figure below.

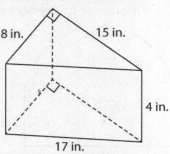

8 in.   15 in.

4 in.

17 in.

1. What shape is the cross section of a horizontal slice of the figure?

   _____

2. What shape is the cross section that results from taking a vertical slice that is parallel to *ABCD*?

   _____

3. A model of a right pyramid with a square base is to be completely painted yellow. The pyramid has a slant length of 5 inches and a base with sides of length 6 inches. What is the area that needs to be painted?

   _____

4. In terms of π, what is the surface area of the cylinder below?

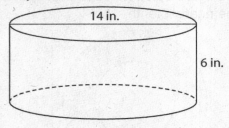

14 in.

6 in.

5. What is the area of the circle centered at point *O* below? Round your answer to the nearest tenth.

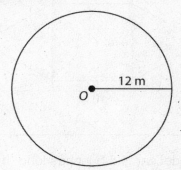

12 m

O

   _____

6. The figure below shows the general shape of a cylindrical pipe. The interior of the pipe is hollow. In the space below, sketch a figure to show the shape of a cross section resulting from a horizontal slice of the pipe.

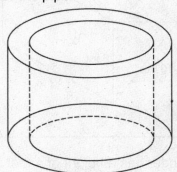

   _____

MODULE 20

Response to Intervention
Pre-Test: Skills 5, 22, 27

1. What is the area of the figure below if the two triangles have the same height?

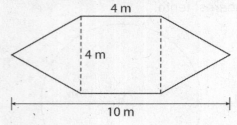

_____

2. A model car is 5.5 inches long. If the model is built such that 1 inch represents 3 feet, then how long is the actual car?

_____

3. What is the volume of the figure below?

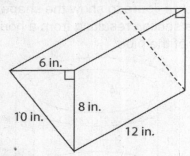

_____

4. A cylinder has a height of 4 feet and a diameter of 6 feet. To the nearest tenth, what is the volume of the cylinder?

_____

5. How many cubic feet of sand can be stored in a rectangular box that is 5 feet long, 3 feet wide, and 2 feet tall?

_____

6. What is the area of the figure below? Round your answer to the nearest tenth.

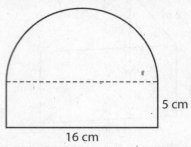

_____

7. An interior designer sketches a 4 inch by 6 inch rectangle to represent the basic shape of a bedroom. If the actual room is 20 feet wide and 30 feet long, what scale factor did the designer use?

_____

8. Hannah and Ellen are taking a road trip. On the first day, they plan to travel 350 miles. On the second day, they plan to travel 125 miles. On their map, 0.8 inches = 15 miles. What is the total distance of their trip on the map?

_____

9. What is the area of the shaded region in the figure below? Round your answer to the nearest tenth.

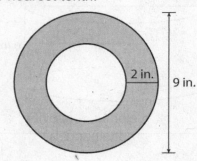

_____

MODULE 21

Response to Intervention

Pre-Test: Skills 14, 15

For 1–4, use the information below. Write each probability as a decimal rounded to three decimal places.

The table below shows the results of a survey of freshmen and sophomore high school students. Each student was asked if he or she prefers to have a study hall for 1st, 2nd, or 3rd period class.

		Year	
		Freshman	**Sophomore**
Preference	1st	18	20
	2nd	5	10
	3rd	25	6

A student is randomly selected from the group.

1. What is the probability that the selected student is a sophomore?

   _____

2. What is the probability that the selected student is a freshman or preferred to have a 3rd period study hall?

   _____

3. What is the probability that the selected student prefers 1st period study hall and is a sophomore?

   _____

4. Are the events "the selected student is a freshman" and "the selected student prefers 2nd period study hall" mutually exclusive? Explain.

   _____

   _____

5. Two coins are flipped and the side on which they land is noted. List the events in the sample space of this experiment.

   _____

For 6–8, use the information below. Write each probability as a simplified fraction.

A number is randomly selected from the set {1, 3, 5, 12, 13, 14, 15, 16, 19, 20}

6. What is the probability the selected number is even?

   _____

7. What is the probability the selected number is greater than 10?

   _____

8. What is the probability the selected number is smaller than 5 or greater than 19?

   _____

For 9–10, use the information below. Write each probability as a percent.

A review of the budgets of several departments in a company finds that 3 of the 15 budgets have errors.

9. If a department's budget is randomly selected, what is the probability it will have an error?

   _____

10. If a department's budget is randomly selected, what is the probability it will NOT have an error?

   _____

11. If a 6-sided number cube is rolled, then, in words, what does the event $E = \{1, 2\}$ represent?

   _____

   _____

Name _____ Date _____ Class _____

Response to Intervention

Pre-Test: Skills 14, 24

For 1–3, find the surface area of each figure. Round to the nearest tenth, if necessary.

1.

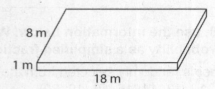

8 m
1 m
18 m

_____

2.

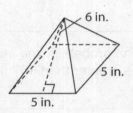

6 in.
5 in.
5 in.

_____

3.

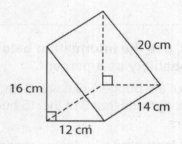

20 cm
16 cm
14 cm
12 cm

_____

4. A jar of marbles contains 14 red, 12 green, and 5 blue marbles. If a marble is randomly selected, what is the probability it is green or blue? Write your answer as a decimal rounded to the nearest hundredth.

_____

For 5–7, use the information below.

A company has two locations and classifies employees as full time or part time. The table below shows the number of employees of each classification at each location.

	Location A	Location B
Full Time	18	10
Part Time	6	14

An employee is randomly selected. Find each probability. Write your answer as a percent. Round to the nearest tenth, if necessary.

5. What is the probability the employee is classified as full time or works at location B?

_____

6. What is the probability the employee is classified as part time and works at location A?

_____

7. Are the events "the employee works full time" and "the employee works at location A" mutually exclusive? Explain.

_____

_____

8. If E and F are events such that $P(E) = 0.1$, $P(F) = 0.3$, and $P(E$ or $F) = 0.2$, then what is $P(E$ and $F)$?

_____

MODULE 23

Response to Intervention

Pre-Test: Skills 11, 15

1. There are 24 ninth-grade and 28 tenth-grade students in a cafeteria. If a student is randomly selected, what is the probability that the student is in the ninth grade? Write your answer as a fraction in simplest form.

_____

_____

For 2–3, use the information and table below.

Customers at a car dealership were surveyed in order to determine how they had learned about the dealership. The results are shown in the table.

Method	Number of Customers
TV Commercial	42
Internet	68
Newspaper	60
Other	20

Suppose a customer is randomly selected from this group. Find each probability as a decimal rounded to the nearest hundredth.

2. Find the probability that the customer learned about the dealership through a TV commercial.

_____

3. Let A represent the event that the selected customer learned about the dealership through the Internet. Find $P(A)$.

_____

4. A jar contains some red marbles and some green marbles. There are 12 marbles in all. If the probability of selecting a green marble is 0.25, how many red marbles are in the jar?

_____

5. A letter is randomly selected from the word "MISSISSIPPI." Select True or False for each of the following statements.

A $P(M) = P(S)$ ○ True   ○ False

B $P(M) = P(I)$ ○ True   ○ False

C $P(P) = \dfrac{2}{11}$ ○ True   ○ False

D $P(S) \approx 36\%$ ○ True   ○ False

6. A weighted coin has two sides: heads and tails. If $P(\text{heads}) = 0.65$, what is $P(\text{tails})$?

_____

7. There are 12 people in a room. 6 of the people speak Spanish, 2 speak English, and the rest speak German. If a person who knows all 3 languages randomly talks to someone in the room, what language should he or she speak? Explain.

_____

_____

8. In a club with 60 members, the probability of selecting a member who works full-time is $\dfrac{4}{5}$. If 30 members are randomly selected, about how many would you expect to work full-time? Explain.

_____

_____

Response to Intervention

Post-Test: Algebraic Representations of Transformations

1. △DEF has vertices D(1, 1), E(2, 4), and F(5, 2). What are the coordinates of the vertices of the image after a translation 3 units right and 2 units down?

_____

2. Describe the translation of point W(3, 1) to W'(−2, 4).

_____

3. Parallelogram ABCD is graphed below.

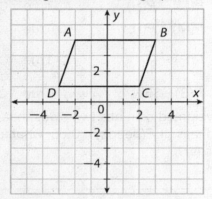

What are the coordinates of the image of point D after a reflection across the y-axis?

_____

4. A triangle has vertices J(0, 4), K(2, −4), and L(−4, −2). The coordinates of the image after a dilation is J'(0, 2), K'(1, −2), and L'(−2, −1). What is the scale factor of the dilation?

_____

5. The following transformation represents a reflection over the x-axis or over the y-axis. Choose True or False for each transformation.

A (0, 2) → (0, −2)   ○ True   ○ False

B (3, 4) → (−3, −4)   ○ True   ○ False

C (−2, 5) → (2, −5)   ○ True   ○ False

D (1, −6) → (−1, −6)   ○ True   ○ False

6. After a reflection across the x-axis, the image of trapezoid HIJK has vertices H'(−5, −2), I'(−3, −2), J'(−3, −6), and K'(−5, −5). What are the coordinates of the preimage?

_____

7. Describe the transformation shown in the graph.

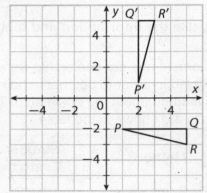

_____

8. Square ABCD has vertices A(2, 3), B(3, −2), C(−2, 3), and D(−3, 2). The square is rotated 90° clockwise about the origin. Which point is located at (−3, 2)?

_____

9. What values for a and b represent a translation 5 units down and 2 units right?

(x, y) → (x + a, y + b)

_____

10. The following scale factor, k, represents a dilation that is an enlargement. Choose True or False for each scale factor.

A k = 3   ○ True   ○ False

B k = $\frac{4}{5}$ ○ True   ○ False

C k = $\frac{3}{2}$ ○ True   ○ False

D k = 1   ○ True   ○ False

Response to Intervention
Post-Test: Angle Relationships

Use the figure for 1–5.

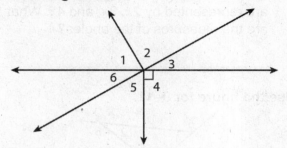

1. Classify ∠2 and ∠5 as *adjacent angles, vertical angles*, or *neither*.

   _____

2. Name a pair of complementary angles.

   _____

3. If m ∠6 = 30°, what is m ∠3?

   _____

4. If m ∠6 = 30°, what is m ∠5?

   _____

5. ∠2 and ∠4 are supplementary angles. What is the measure of ∠2?

   _____

6. ∠J and ∠K are adjacent angles. ∠J and ∠L are vertical angles. The measure of ∠K is 52° and the measure of ∠L is 104°. What is the measure of ∠J?

   _____

7. The following pair of angle measures is the measures of supplementary angles. Choose True or False for each pair of angle measures.

A 42°, 48°	○ True	○ False
B 88°, 92°	○ True	○ False
C 36°, 114°	○ True	○ False
D 75°, 105°	○ True	○ False

8. ∠A and ∠B are complementary angles. The measure of ∠A is 2x° and the measure of ∠B is 48°. What is the value of x?

   _____

9. ∠S and ∠T are vertical angles. The measure of ∠S is (2x – 8)° and the measure of ∠T is 62°. What is the value of x?

   _____

Use the figure for 10–11.

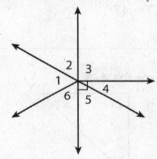

10. The measure of ∠4 is 38°. What is the measure of ∠2?

    _____

11. The measure of ∠1 is 75° and the measure of ∠5 is 52°. What is the measure of ∠6?

    _____

12. ∠X and ∠Y do not share a side. The measure of ∠X is 45° and the measure of ∠Y is 45°. Which of the following terms could describe ∠X and ∠Y. Choose True or False for each term.

A adjacent	○ True	○ False
B vertical	○ True	○ False
C complementary	○ True	○ False
D supplementary	○ True	○ False

SKILL 3 Response to Intervention
Post-Test: Angle Theorems for Triangles

1. What is the value of *x* in the figure?

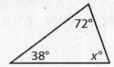

_____

2. The sum of two angles in a triangle is 87°. What is the measure of the third angle?

_____

3. Find the m∠*R* in △*RST* if m∠*S* = 72° and m∠*T* = 47°.

_____

Use the figure for 4–5.

4. What is the value of *x*?

_____

5. What are the measures of the angles in the triangle?

_____

6. What is the measure of the exterior angle whose remote interior angles measure 52° and 70°?

_____

7. The bottom of a lamp is in the shape of a triangle. The base angles of the triangle have equal measures. If the base angles measure 55°, what is the measure of the third angle?

_____

8. The measures of the angles in △*DEF* are represented by 2*x*, 3*x*, and 4*x*. What are the measures of the angles?

_____

Use the figure for 9–11.

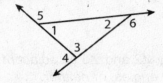

9. What are the two remote interior angles for ∠6?

_____

10. What angle has the same measure as m∠1 + m∠2?

_____

11. If m∠5 = 122° and m∠2 = 34°, what is m∠3?

_____

12. Find the values of *x* and *y* in the figure.

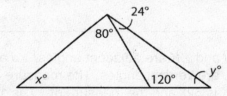

_____

13. The following angle measures are the measures of the interior angles of a triangle. Choose True or False for each set of angle measures.

A 35°, 55°, 90°   ○ True   ○ False

B 60°, 60°, 60°   ○ True   ○ False

C 42°, 72°, 76°   ○ True   ○ False

D 24°, 31°, 125°   ○ True   ○ False

Response to Intervention

Post-Test: Area of a Circle

1. Name the part of a circle that connects two points on the circle and passes through its center.

   _____

2. The diameter of a circle is 8 inches. What is the radius?

   _____

3. A clock has a radius of 7 inches. Find the area of the face of the clock in terms of π.

   _____

4. The area of a circle is 81π square feet.
   a. What is the length of the radius?

   _____

   b. What is the length of the diameter?

   _____

5. Find the area of the circle. Use 3.14 for π.

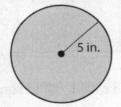

5 in.

   _____

6. Geneva has a circular flower garden in her backyard. The distance from the center of the garden to the edge of the garden is 8 feet. Find the area of the flower garden. Use 3.14 for π.

   _____

7. A semicircle is half of a circle. Find the area of a semicircle with a diameter of 20 centimeters. Leave your answer in terms of π.

   _____

Use the following information for 8–9. Use 3.14 for π. Round answers to the nearest hundredth, if necessary.

The table shows the approximate diameters of several U.S. coins.

Coin	Diameter
Penny	19 mm
Nickel	21 mm
Dime	18 mm
Quarter	24 mm

8. How much greater is the radius of a nickel than the radius of a penny?

   _____

9. How much greater is the area of a quarter than the area of a dime?

   _____

10. A circle is inscribed in a square that has a side length of 12 centimeters.

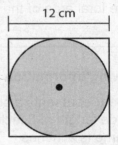

12 cm

   a. What is the diameter of the circle?

   _____

   b. What is the area of the circle? Use 3.14 for π.

   _____

11. A round tablecloth has an area of 50.24° square feet. What is the radius of the tablecloth? Use 3.14 for π.

   _____

SKILL 5

Response to Intervention
Post-Test: Area of Composite Figures

Use the figure for 1–5.

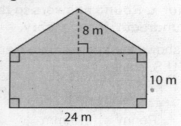

1. What two shapes make up the figure?

_____

2. What is the length of the base of the triangle?

_____

3. Find the area of the triangle.

_____

4. Find the area of the rectangle.

_____

5. What is the total area of the figure?

_____

Use the following information for 6–9.

The shaded area represents a square picture frame with a side length of 8 inches. The width of the frame is 2 inches.

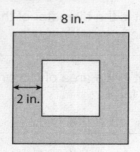

6. What is the length of the side of the unshaded square?

_____

7. Find the area of the unshaded square.

_____

8. Find the area of the large square.

_____

9. What is the area of the frame represented by the shaded region?

_____

Use the following information for 10–14. Use 3.14 for π. Round answers to the nearest hundredth, if necessary.

A window is composed of a rectangle and a semicircle. The height of the window is 7 feet and the width is 4 feet.

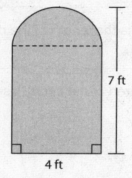

10. What is the radius of the semicircle?

_____

11. Find the area of the semicircle.

_____

12. What is the height of the window without the top semicircle?

_____

13. Find the area of the rectangle.

_____

14. What is the total area of the window?

_____

Name _____ Date _____ Class _____

Response to Intervention

Post-Test: Circumference

For 1–2, find the circumference of the circle with the given measurements. Use 3.14 for π and round to the nearest tenth.

1.

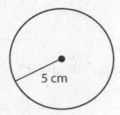

5 cm

_____

2.

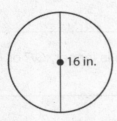

16 in.

_____

For 3–5, find the circumference of the circle with the given measurements. Use $\frac{22}{7}$ for π.

3. radius: 21 m

_____

4. diameter: 70 yd

_____

5. The radius of the semicircle is 4 feet. Find the total distance around the figure. Use 3.14 for π and round to the nearest tenth.

_____

6. The circumference of a hockey puck is exactly 3π inches. What is the diameter?

_____

7. A round tent has a circumference of 32 feet. What is the distance from the center of the tent to the edge of the tent? Use 3.14 for π and round to the nearest tenth.

_____

8. Cassie is decorating a cake with a circumference of 24 inches. Cassie wants to write "Congratulations!" across the center of the cake. If the word is 8 inches long, will it fit on the cake as shown? Explain.

Congratulations!

_____

9. The discus throw is a track and field event in which participants throw a heavy disc, called a discus.

Discus Throw Specifications		
Event	**Diameter**	**Weight**
Men	219 mm	2 kg
Women	180 mm	1 kg

How much greater is the circumference of the discus used in the men's event than the circumference of the discus used in the women's event? Use 3.14 for π and round to the nearest tenth.

_____

Response to Intervention
Post-Test: Congruent Figures

Use the figures for 1–3.

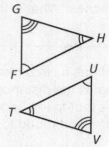

1. List the corresponding angles.

   _____

2. List the corresponding sides.

   _____

3. Write a congruence statement for the triangles.

   _____

For 4–5, use △JKM ≅ △PQR.

4. If m∠P = 86° and m∠R = 21°, what is m∠J?

   _____

5. If JM = 14 inches and MK = 25 inches, what is the length of is RQ?

   _____

6. The following congruence statement represents the corresponding parts of two congruent triangles.

   △BCD ≅ △RST

   Choose True or False for each statement.

   A $\overline{BC} \cong \overline{ST}$ ○ True   ○ False

   B $\overline{CB} \cong \overline{SR}$ ○ True   ○ False

   C $\angle C \cong \angle S$ ○ True   ○ False

   D △DBC ≅ △TRS   ○ True   ○ False

Use the following information for 7–9. The trapezoids below are congruent.

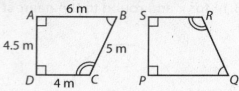

7. What is the length of $\overline{SP}$?

   _____

8. Which angle is congruent to ∠B?

   _____

9. Which side is longer, QR or RS?

   _____

For 10–13, use the figure and the congruence statement △JKM ≅ △PQR.

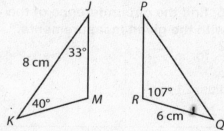

10. What is the measure of ∠Q?

    _____

11. What is the measure of ∠M?

    _____

12. What is the length of $\overline{PQ}$?

    _____

13. If the perimeter of triangle PQR is 20 centimeters, what is the perimeter of triangle JKM?

    _____

SKILL 8

Response to Intervention

Post-Test: Cross Sections

Use the figure for 1–5.

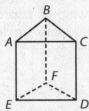

1. What type of solid is the figure?

   _____

2. Name the bases.

   _____

3. Name the faces.

   _____

4. Name the edges.

   _____

5. Name the vertices.

   _____

6. What figure has two parallel bases, no edges, and no vertices?

   _____

Use the figure for 7–8.

7. Is the cross section a result of a horizontal, vertical, or angled slice?

   _____

8. What shape is the cross section?

   _____

9. What is the shape of the cross section that results from a slice through the vertex that is perpendicular to the base of a cone?

   _____

10. What is the shape of the cross section that results from a slice that is parallel to the bases of a cylinder?

   _____

Use the figure for 11–15.

11. What shapes are the faces of the prism?

   _____

12. What shape is the cross section that results from a vertical slice?

   _____

13. What shape is the cross section that results from a horizontal slice?

   _____

14. Name a figure for which the horizontal, vertical, and angled cross sections all result in a triangle.

   _____

15. A vertical, horizontal, or angled slice of the figure results in a cross section that is a rectangle. Choose True or False for each figure.

    A rectangular prism　　○ True　　○ False

    B cylinder　　　　　　　○ True　　○ False

    C cone　　　　　　　　　○ True　　○ False

    D triangular pyramid　　○ True　　○ False

Response to Intervention

Post-Test: Distance and Midpoint Formula

Use the figure for 1–4.

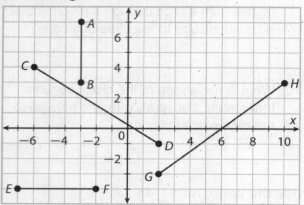

1. What is the midpoint of $\overline{AB}$?

_____

2. What is the midpoint of $\overline{CD}$?

_____

3. What is the midpoint of $\overline{EF}$?

_____

4. What is the midpoint of $\overline{GH}$?

_____

5. A segment has coordinates (−4, 9) and (0, 7). What is the midpoint of the segment?

_____

6. A segment has coordinates (8, −5) and (8, 4). What is the midpoint of the segment?

_____

7. A segment $\overline{ST}$ is graphed on a coordinate plane. The endpoint S is at (−3, 2). The midpoint is at (−3, −2). What are the coordinates of the other endpoint T?

_____

_____

Use the following information for 8–10.

A map is drawn on a coordinate grid. Each unit is equal to 1 mile.

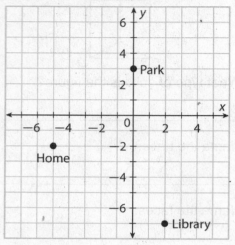

8. David would like to meet a friend at the halfway point between his home and the library. What is the location of the midpoint between David's home and the library?

_____

9. What is the distance between the park and the library?

_____

_____

10. What is the distance between David's home and the park?

_____

_____

11. A segment measures 10 units. One end of the segment has an endpoint at (3, −6). What another possible endpoint to this segment?

_____

SKILL 10

Response to Intervention
Post-Test: Geometric Drawings

1. Use a ruler to draw a triangle with side lengths 5 cm, 5 cm, and 8 cm. Then state whether you can create many triangles with these measures, only one, or none.

_____

2. Can a triangle be formed from side lengths 7 m, 10 m, and 20 m? Explain why or why not.

_____

_____

_____

3. A triangle has angle measures of 30° and 70°. What is the measure of the third angle?

_____

4. Use a protractor and ruler to draw a triangle with angle measures 30° and 70°. Then state whether you can create many triangles with these measures, only one, or none.

_____

5. For each set of side lengths, state whether a triangle exists.

   A 6 cm, 8 cm, 10 cm   ⊙ Yes   ○ No

   B 4 cm, 6 cm, 12 cm   ○ Yes   ○ No

   C 12 cm, 15 cm, 20 cm   ○ Yes   ○ No

6. For each set of angle measures, state whether a triangle exists.

   A 30°, 30°, 30°   ○ Yes   ○ No

   B 60°, 60°, 60°   ○ Yes   ○ No

   C 100°, 10°, 70°   ○ Yes   ○ No

Use the following information for 7–9.

A triangle has side lengths 8 cm and 15 cm.

7. Name a third side length for which no triangle exists.

_____

8. Name a third side length for which only one triangle exists.

_____

9. Name a third side length for which many triangles exist.

_____

10. Use a protractor and ruler to draw a triangle with side length of 5 cm, then a 45 angle, then a side length of 8 cm. Then state whether you can create many triangles with these measures, only one, or none.

_____

Name _____ Date _____ Class_____

Use the information for 1–4. In a board game, the probability of choosing a "Lose a Turn" card is $\frac{2}{15}$.

1. What is a favorable outcome?

   _____

2. What are the possible outcomes?

   _____

3. During a game, 45 cards have been drawn. Predict how many times a "Lose a Turn" card has been drawn.

   _____

4. If the game contains a total of 300 cards, about how many cards are NOT "Lose a Turn" cards?

   _____

5. A manufacturer conducts a quality review of its cell phones and finds that, on average, 3 out of every 250 phones have a defect. Predict how many phones will have a defect in a batch of 2000 phones.

   _____

6. The results of a survey show that 68 out of 100 people participate in a recycling program in a small community. If there are about 3000 people in the community, predict how many people participate in recycling.

   _____

7. A spinner has 5 equal sections numbered 1–5. How many times would you expect to land on an odd number out of 30 spins?

   _____

Use the following information for 8–10. Organizers for a conference conducted a survey that asked attendees about their main source for news. The results are shown in the table.

News Source	Number of Responses
Newspaper	24
Television Newscast	35
Radio Program	11
Internet	30

8. How many people were surveyed?

   _____

9. If a person was randomly chosen from the conference, what is the probability that person's main source of news is the Internet?

   _____

10. If there are 1200 people at the conference, how many people would you expect get their news from the newspaper?

    _____

11. The probability that a basketball player makes a foul shot is $\frac{4}{5}$. During a game, the player had 11 foul shots. Predict how many foul shots the player missed.

    _____

12. A bag of mints contains pink, green, and yellow mints. You randomly take a handful of mints and count 2 green, 5 pink, and 8 yellow mints. If you fill a bowl with 150 mints, predict how many mints of each color will be in the bowl.

    _____

SKILL 12

Response to Intervention

Post-Test: Parallel Lines Cut by a Transversal

For 1–5, use the figure. Classify each pair of angles as *same-side interior, same-side exterior, alternate interior, alternate exterior,* or *corresponding* angles.

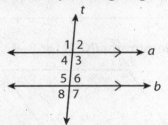

1. ∠1 and ∠5

_____

2. ∠4 and ∠6

_____

3. ∠2 and ∠8

_____

4. ∠1 and ∠8

_____

5. ∠3 and ∠7

_____

Use the figure for 6–7.

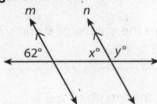

6. What is the value for *x*? Explain your reasoning.

_____

7. What is the value for *y*? Explain your reasoning.

8. In the figure below, classify ∠3 and ∠7. Is ∠3 ≅ ∠7? Explain.

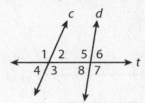

_____

_____

Use the following information for 1–5. In the figure, r‖s and m∠5 = 108°.

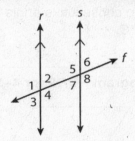

9. Find m∠4.

_____

10. Find m∠3.

_____

11. In the figure, p‖q and lines *r* and *t* are transversals. The lines intersect to form a trapezoid.

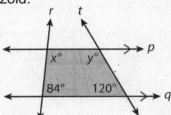

What are the values for *x* and *y*?

_____

SKILL 13

Response to Intervention
Post-Test: Parallelograms

Use the figure for 1–3.

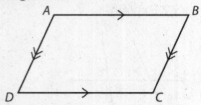

1. List the congruent sides.

   _____

2. List the congruent angles.

   _____

3. Name two consecutive angle pairs that include ∠C.

   _____

Use parallelogram PQRS for 4–5.

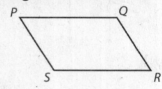

4. If m∠P = 2x°, m∠R = 62°, find the value for x.

   _____

5. If QR = 16 feet and PS = 3y − 5 feet, find the value for y.

   _____

6. Find the unknown angle measures

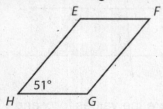

   _____

7. In parallelogram RSTU, $\overline{RS} \parallel \overline{TU}$ and $\overline{ST} \parallel \overline{UR}$. If ST = 9 inches and TU = 4 inches, find RS and UR.

   _____

Use parallelogram JKLM for 8–9.

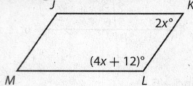

8. What is the value of x?

   _____

9. What are the measures of all of the interior angles of the parallelogram?

   _____

Use the following information for 10–13.

In parallelogram CDEF, AE = 3x + 4, EC = 2x + 8, BE = 4y + 1, and BD = 18.

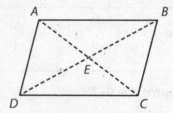

10. What are the values of x and y?

   _____

11. What is the length of $\overline{EC}$?

   _____

12. What is the length of $\overline{AC}$?

   _____

13. What is the length of $\overline{ED}$?

   _____

Response to Intervention

Post-Test: Probability of Compound Events

Use this information for 1–3.

A family has 3 children.

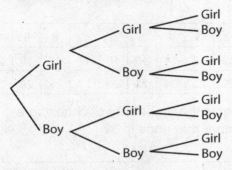

1. What is the probability the family has all girls or all boys?

   _____

2. What is the probability the family has 1 or 2 boys?

   _____

Use this information for 4–5.

A prize machine dispenses prizes one at a time. There are 15 small prizes, 8 medium prizes and 3 large prizes.

3. What is the probability of randomly receiving a large or medium prize?

   _____

4. Are these events mutually exclusive? Explain.

   _____

   _____

5. A student would like to sign up for a class. There are 8 seats open in ceramics, 20 seats in drama, and 9 seats in photography. What is the probability the student randomly receives a seat in drama or photography?

   _____

Use this information for 6–9.

A city polled 100 residents to see whether they would favor building a park or library. The data is shown below.

	Park	Library	Total
18–30 year olds	28	9	37
31–50 year olds	12	21	33
over 50	20	10	30
Total	60	40	100

A resident is selected at random. Determine the following probabilities.

6. *P*(over 50 or favors park)

   _____

7. *P*(18–30 years old or favors library)

   _____

8. *P*(31–50 years old or over 50)

   _____

9. Which compound event is mutually exclusive?

   _____

10. State whether the events are mutually exclusive.

    A Getting odd or prime number on a number cube

    ○ Yes   ○ No

    B Tossing a coin and rolling a number cube

    ○ Yes   ○ No

    C A person has brown hair or blue eyes

    ○ Yes   ○ No

SKILL 15 Response to Intervention
Post-Test: Probability of Simple Events

Use this information for 1–3.

Cards are numbered 15–20. A number is selected at random.

1. List the events in the sample space.

   _____

2. What is the probability of choosing an even number?

   _____

3. What is the probability of choosing a number divisible by 3?

   _____

Use this information for 4–5.

A letter is drawn at random from the letters spelling PROBABILITY.

4. What is the probability of selecting a letter at random and selecting a B?

   _____

5. What is the probability of selecting a letter at random and selecting a vowel (A, E, I, O, U)?

   _____

6. In a class, 2 students rode the bus to school, 16 were in a carpool, 8 walked and 4 rode a bike. Determine the probability of each event if a student is chosen at random.

   A P(student rode the bus)

   _____

   B P(student walked)

   _____

   C P(student rides a bike)

   _____

   D P(student in a carpool)

   _____

Use this information for 7–8.

A game consists of choosing numbers at random.

1	2	3	4	5	6	7	8	9	10
11	12	13	14	15	16	17	18	19	20
21	22	23	24	25	26	27	28	29	30

7. What is the probability of choosing a number that ends in 3?

   _____

8. What is the probability of choosing a number that is divisible by 5.

   _____

Use this information for 9–11.

A company manufactures pens and finds that some are leaking.

9. Batch A has 8 leaky pens out of 100. What is the percent probability a randomly selected pen is leaking?

   _____

10. The company adjusted a machine to try and fix the problem. Batch B has 3 leaky pens out of 60. What is the probability a pen in Batch B will leak?

    _____

11. Did the company's improvements work? Explain.

    _____

    _____

12. State whether each experiment has a probability of $\frac{1}{2}$.

    A Rolling an even number on a number cube

    ○ Yes   ○ No

    B Randomly selecting a boy from a class of 10 boys and 20 girls

    ○ Yes   ○ No

SKILL 16 Response to Intervention

Post-Test: Properties of Dilations

Use the grid for 1–2.

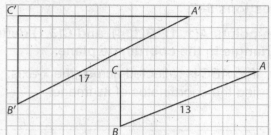

1. Find the ratios of the corresponding side lengths.

_____

2. Is the image a dilation of the preimage? Explain.

_____

_____

3. $\triangle J'K'L$ is the image of $\triangle JKL$. What is the scale factor k of the dilation?

$J\left(0, \dfrac{2}{3}\right)$, $K\left(\dfrac{1}{2}, -2\right)$, $L(-3, -1)$

$J'(0, 2)$, $K'\left(\dfrac{3}{2}, -6\right)$, $L'(-9, -3)$

_____

4. Kylie enlarges a photo that measures 4 in. by 6 in. The new image measures 6 in. by 9 in. Is the new image a dilation of the original photo? Explain.

_____

_____

5. A figure has vertex $A(4, 6)$. The figure is dilated by a scale factor of $\dfrac{1}{2}$. The resulting image is then dilated by a factor of 5. What are the coordinates of vertex A'' of the final image?

_____

Use the following information for 6–8.
Isosceles triangle *FGH* is the preimage of a dilation with a scale factor of $\dfrac{3}{4}$.

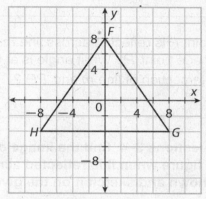

6. What shape is the image?

_____

7. Find the coordinates of the image.

_____

8. Is the dilation an enlargement or a reduction?

_____

9. The coordinates of the image after a dilation with a scale factor of $\dfrac{1}{4}$ are $P'(1, 3)$, $Q'(1, 5)$, $R'(4, 8)$. What are the coordinates of the preimage?

_____

10. The following rule represents a dilation. Choose True or False for each rule.

   A $(x, y) \rightarrow (2x, y)$ ○ True   ○ False

   B $(x, y) \rightarrow \left(\dfrac{3}{8}x, \dfrac{5}{8}y\right)$ ○ True   ○ False

   C $(x, y) \rightarrow (4x, 4y)$ ○ True   ○ False

   D $(x, y) \rightarrow (-x, y)$ ○ True   ○ False

SKILL 17

Response to Intervention

Post-Test: Properties of Reflections

1. If a point *P* lies on line *m*, then what is the image of point *P* when it is reflected across line *m*?

   _____

2. Point *P* is reflected across line *m* to its image point *P′*. What angle is at the intersection of line *m* and $\overline{PP'}$?

   _____

For questions 3–4, find the image of the given figure when it is reflected across the line shown and sketch it on the given graph.

3.

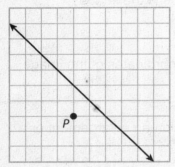

4.

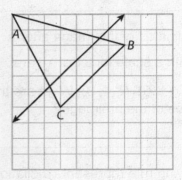

Use the following information to answer questions 5–7.

The points *A*(1, 1), *B*(1, 4), and *C*(3,1) define a triangle in the coordinate plane.

5. If △*ABC* is reflected across the *x*-axis, find the coordinates of its image.

   _____

6. If △*ABC* is reflected across the *y*-axis, find the coordinates of its image.

   _____

7. If △*ABC* is reflected across the line *y* = *x*, find the coordinates of its image.

   _____

8. In the figure below, △*A′B′C′* is the result of reflecting △*ABC* across a line. Find three points on the line of reflection and sketch the line on the figure.

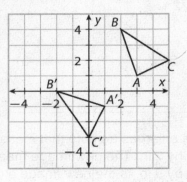

   _____

Response to Intervention
Post-Test: Properties of Rotations

1. Find the image of △*ABC* when it is rotated 100° counterclockwise around point *P*.

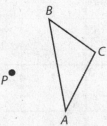

2. Square *ABCD* was rotated counterclockwise around point *P*. What was the angle of rotation?

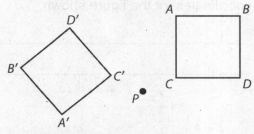

   Angle of rotation: _____

3. Point *A* is rotated around point *P* and its image is point *A'*. If the length of $\overline{AP}$ is 5 units, what is the length of $\overline{A'P}$?

   _____

4. Point *A*(−3, 5) in the coordinate plane is rotated 270° about the origin. What are the coordinates of its image?

   _____

5. Find the image of △*ABC* after it is rotated 180°.

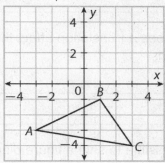

6. Give an example of three rotations in the coordinate plane that would map a figure onto itself.

   _____

   _____

For questions 7 and 8, determine which quadrant would contain the image of the figure.

7. Figure located in Quadrant I and rotated 180°

   _____

8. Figure located in Quadrant IV and rotated 450°

   _____

SKILL
19

Response to Intervention
Post-Test: Properties of Translations

1. What is a translation?

   _____

2. How does a translation affect the figure? Explain.

   _____

   _____

3. Is it possible to shift a figure diagonally? Explain.

   _____

   _____

4. Write the rule for the transformation shown.

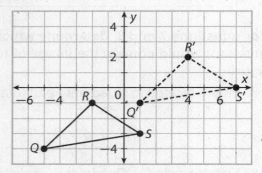

5. Write the rule for an image that is translated 2 units down and 9 units to the left.

   _____

6. Describe in words the translation that is indicated by $(x + 4, y - 7)$.

   _____

   _____

7. Translate the image 4 units left and 1 unit up.

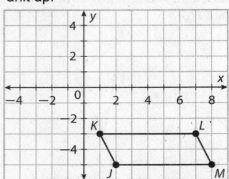

8. Use the rule $(x - 5, y + 7)$ to write new coordinates for the figure shown.

   _____

   _____

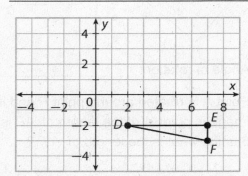

9. Now, graph the translated figure on the graph above.

SKILL 20

Response to Intervention

Post-Test: Quadratic Functions

1. Write an example of a quadratic function.

   _____

2. In the quadratic function $y = -x^2 + 5x + 6$, does the parabola open up or down? How do you know?

   _____

   _____

   _____

Use the graph for 3–7.

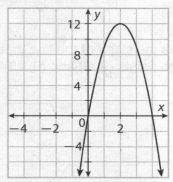

3. Does the graph have a minimum or maximum?

   _____

4. What is the minimum or maximum?

   _____

5. What is the vertex?

   _____

6. Name the zeros, if any.

   _____

7. What is the axis of symmetry?

   _____

8. On the graph, sketch a parabola that opens up and has exactly one zero.

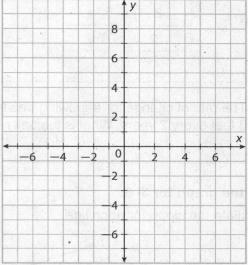

9. A parabola has a vertex at (5, −2). What is the axis of symmetry?

   _____

10. State whether each quadratic function has a maximum or a minimum.

    A $y = 4x^2 + 5x$

       ○ Maximum   ○ Minimum

    B $y = -6x^2 + 2x + 1$

       ○ Maximum   ○ Minimum

    C $y = -x^2 - 2x + 5$

       ○ Maximum   ○ Minimum

    D $y = x^2 + x$

       ○ Maximum   ○ Minimum

11. A quadratic function opens up and has a vertex of (2, 3). Is it possible to determine the number of zeros from this information? Explain.

    _____

    _____

SKILL 21

Response to Intervention

Post-Test: Rate of Change and Slope

1. What is the rate of change in the table?

x	y
0	0
4	2
8	4
12	6

_____

2. The rate of change for a growing tree is 3 feet every 2 years. What is the unit rate?

_____

Use the graph for 3–6.

Calculate the slope for each line.

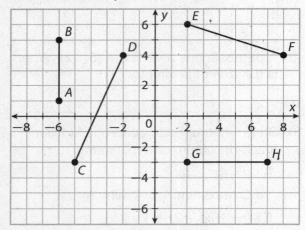

3. What is the slope of $\overline{AB}$?

_____

4. What is the slope of $\overline{CD}$?

_____

5. What is the slope of $\overline{EF}$?

_____

6. What is the slope of $\overline{GH}$?

_____

7. What is the slope of the line that passes through points (−2, 5) and (6, 10)?

_____

_____

_____

8. What is the slope of the line that passes through points (3, 6) and (−8, 2)?

_____

_____

_____

9. What is the slope of the line that passes through points (9, 0) and (9, −3)?

_____

_____

_____

10. Tell whether each statement is true or false.

A Vertical lines have undefined slopes.

   O True   O False

B Slopes must be either positive or negative.

   O True   O False

C A line with slope −3 goes up from left to right.

   O True   O False

D If a line has the same y-coordinates, the slope must be zero.

   O True   O False

E The slopes $\dfrac{-1}{2}$ and $\dfrac{1}{-2}$ are equivalent.

   O True   O False

SKILL 22 Response to Intervention

Post-Test: Scale Factor and Scale Drawings

Use the following information for 1–3.
A map has a scale of 0.5 inch = 25 miles.

1. How many miles do 3 inches represent on the map?

   _____

2. If the distance between two cities on the map is 12 inches, what is the actual distance between the cities?

   _____

3. Two cities are 450 miles apart. What is the distance between the cities on the map?

   _____

4. Two students are making a scale drawing of the school for an art project. One student uses a scale of 1 inch = 10 feet. The other student uses a scale of 1 inch = 12 feet. Which scale will result in a larger drawing of the school?

   _____

5. A basketball coach is making a scale drawing of the basketball court. The length of the actual court is 84 feet and the width is 50 feet. What will be the length and width of the court on the scale drawing if the coach uses a scale of 3 inches = 20 feet?

   _____

   _____

6. The following scales have a scale factor of 1:12. Choose True or False for each scale.

A 1 in. : 1 ft	○ True	○ False
B 0.5 in. : 6 ft	○ True	○ False
C 5 cm : 60 m	○ True	○ False
D 2 ft : 8 yd	○ True	○ False

Use the following information for 7–8.
An artist is making a scale model of a famous sculpture. The height of the sculpture is 60 feet.

7. If the artist wants the scale model to have a height of 12 inches, what scale should the artist use?

   _____

8. What will be the height of the scale model if the artist uses a scale of 1 inch = 4 feet instead?

   _____

9. A model of an ear has a scale of 5:1 to the size of an average ear. The length of the model is 30 centimeters. What is the length of an average ear?

   _____

Use the following information for 10–11.
A model tractor has a length of 6 inches. The actual length of the tractor is 16 feet.

10. What is the scale of the model in feet?

    _____

11. How many times as long as the model is the actual tractor?

    _____

12. A gardener made a sketch of a flower garden on $\frac{1}{4}$ inch grid paper. The garden covers an area that is 8 squares long and 3 squares wide. Use the scale to find the area of the actual flower garden.

    Scale: $\frac{1}{4}$ inch = 5 feet

    _____

SKILL
23

Response to Intervention

Post-Test: Similar Figures

Use △JKL and △RST for 1–3.

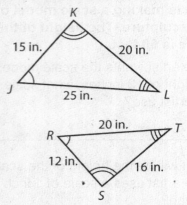

1. Are the corresponding angles congruent? Explain.

   _____

   _____

2. Find the ratios of the corresponding sides.

   _____

   _____

3. Is △JKL ~ △RST? If so, what is the scale factor?

   _____

   _____

4. Parallelogram ABCD is similar to parallelogram PQRS. If AB = 9, BC = 15 and PQ = 3, what is QR?

   _____

5. Triangle EFG has side lengths of 5 feet, 12 feet, and 13 feet. Triangle KLM is similar to triangle EFG with a scale factor of 4. What are the side lengths of triangle KLM?

   _____

   _____

Use the figure below for 6–8.

In the figure, the trapezoids are similar.

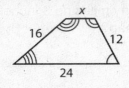

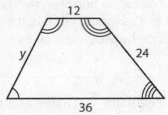

6. What is the scale factor?

   _____

7. Find the missing value of x.

   _____

8. Find the missing value of y.

   _____

9. Rectangle HIJK is similar to rectangle WXYZ. Rectangle HIJK has a length of 12 inches and a perimeter of 36 inches. Rectangle WXYZ has a length of 8 inches.

   What is the perimeter of rectangle WXYZ?

   _____

10. Compare a square with a side length of 5 inches to a square with a side length of 10 inches. Choose True or False for each statement.

    A   The squares are similar.

    ○ True   ○ False

    B   The ratio of the perimeters is 2.

    ○ True   ○ False

    C   The ratio of the areas is 2.

    ○ True   ○ False

SKILL 24 Response to Intervention
Post-Test: Surface Area

For questions 1 and 2, find the surface area of the figure.

1.

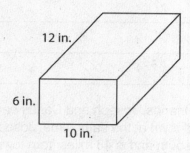

12 in.

6 in.

10 in.

_____

_____

_____

2.

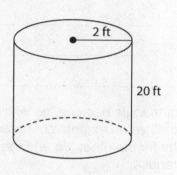

2 ft

20 ft

_____

_____

_____

3. The base of a prism is a right triangle with side lengths of 6, 8, and 10 inches. If the height of the prism is 4 inches, what is its surface area?

_____

_____

_____

4. Find the surface area of the regular pyramid below.

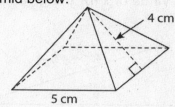

4 cm

5 cm

_____

_____

_____

5. Leah's parents are planning to give her a gift and want to wrap it first. The gift is in a rectangular box with a height of 3 inches, a length of 7 inches, and a width of 4 inches. How many square inches of wrapping paper will they need to wrap the gift?

_____

_____

6. A cylinder is 4 feet tall and its base has a diameter of 8 feet. What is the exact surface area of the cylinder?

_____

_____

_____

7. A regular pyramid has a square base with sides of 12 inches. If the height of the pyramid is 3 inches, what is the surface area of the pyramid to the nearest square inch?

_____

_____

_____

SKILL 25

Response to Intervention
Post-Test: The Pythagorean Theorem

For questions 1 and 2, find the exact, simplified value of x for the given triangle.

1.

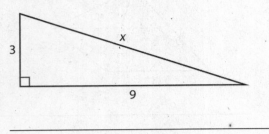

_____

_____

2.

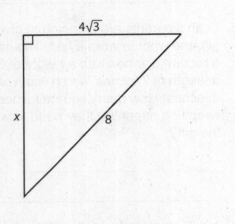

_____

_____

3. Does the Pythagorean Theorem apply to the side lengths of △ABC below? Why or why not?

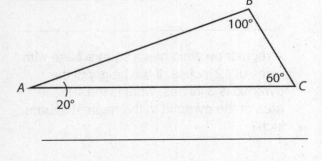

_____

_____

4. Could 16, 30, and 31 be the side lengths of a right triangle? Why or why not?

_____

_____

_____

5. Two friends, Joseph and Darius each drive out of town at the same time. Joseph drives due south and is 48 miles from town after 1 hour. Darius drives due east and is 54 miles from town after 1 hour. To the nearest tenth of a mile, what is the straight line distance between the friends after 1 hour?

_____

_____

_____

6. A right triangle has one leg with a length of two. Give an example of possible lengths for the other leg and the hypotenuse.

_____

_____

7. Find the altitude, h, in the equilateral triangle below.

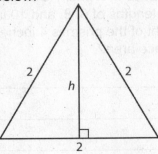

_____

_____

_____

SKILL 26

Response to Intervention

Post-Test: Using Slope and y-intercept

For 1–2, use the graph.

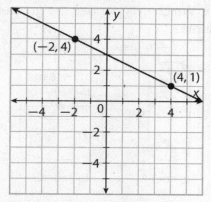

(−2, 4)

(4, 1)

1. Find the slope of the line.

   _____

2. What is the *y*-intercept?

   _____

3. Write an equation in slope-intercept form for the given slope and *y*-intercept.

   slope: 5; *y*-intercept: $-\dfrac{1}{5}$

   _____

4. Find the slope and *y*-intercept for the graph of the equation $y = -x + 4$

   _____

   _____

5. The graph of the following equation has a slope of $\dfrac{3}{2}$. Choose True or False for each equation.

   A $y = x + \dfrac{3}{2}$ ○ True ○ False

   B $y = \dfrac{3}{2}x + 1$ ○ True ○ False

   C $2x + 3y = 12$ ○ True ○ False

   D $-3x + 2y = 4$ ○ True ○ False

6. Write the equation $4x + 2y = 6$ in slope-intercept form.

   _____

7. Find the slope and *y*-intercept for the graph of the equation $-2x + 3y = 1$.

   _____

   _____

8. Graph the equation $y = -\dfrac{3}{4}x + 1$.

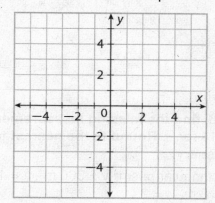

For 9–10, use the following information.

An amusement park charges $15 per ticket for admission and $5 for parking. The equation $y = 15x + 5$ represents the total cost *y* for *x* tickets.

9. What is the slope of the line? Describe its meaning.

   _____

   _____

10. What is the *y*-intercept? Describe its meaning.

   _____

   _____

SKILL 27

Response to Intervention
Post-Test: Volume

For 1–2, find the volume of each figure.

1.

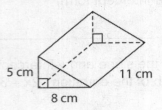

5 cm   11 cm   8 cm

_____

2.

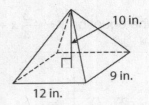

10 in.   9 in.   12 in.

_____

For 3–6, find the missing measurement. Use 3.14 for π. Round to the nearest tenth, if necessary.

3. rectangular prism: $V = 360$ m^3, $\ell = 15$ m, $h = 8$ m, $w = ?$

_____

4. triangular pyramid: $V = 225$ in^3, $B = 30$ in., $h = ?$

_____

5. cone: $r = 2$ ft, $h = 9$ ft, $V = ?$

_____

6. cylinder: $V = 450$ cm^3, $d = 10$ cm, $h = ?$

_____

7. An aquarium is shaped like a rectangular prism. The length of the aquarium is 50 centimeters, the width is 25 centimeters, and the height is 30 centimeters. What is the volume of the aquarium?

_____

8. Find the volume of each cylinder in terms of π. Which cylinder has the greater volume?

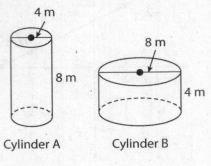

4 m   8 m   8 m   4 m

Cylinder A   Cylinder B

_____
_____

9. A square pyramid and a cube have equal volumes. The side length of the base of each figure is 12 centimeters. What is the height of the pyramid?

_____

10. What is the volume of the figure? Use 3.14 for π. Round to the nearest tenth.

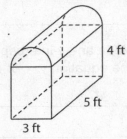

4 ft   5 ft   3 ft

_____

11. A cylinder has a radius of 6 meters and a height of 10 meters. Which of the following measurements will double the volume of the cylinder? Choose True or False for each set of measurements.

A $r = 6$ m, $h = 20$ m   ○ True   ○ False

B $r = 12$ m, $h = 10$ m   ○ True   ○ False

C $r = 12$ m, $h = 5$ m   ○ True   ○ False

D $r = 3$ m, $h = 40$ m   ○ True   ○ False

SKILL 28

Response to Intervention

Post-Test: Writing Equations of Parallel, Perpendicular, Vertical, and Horizontal Lines

1. State whether the following sets of lines are parallel, perpendicular, or neither.

   A $y = 5$ and $y = -2$

   _____

   B $y = 8$ and $x = 8$

   _____

   C $y = 4x + 8$ and $y = -4x - 2$

   _____

   D $y = -x + 6$ and $y = x + 1$

   _____

   E $y = 6x + 2$ and $y = 6x$

   _____

2. What is an equation for the line parallel to $y = 2$ going through the point $(7, -4)$?

   _____

   _____

3. What is an equation for the line parallel to $y = 2x + 4$ going through the point $(1, 1)$?

   _____

   _____

4. What is an equation for the line perpendicular to $y = 5x - 1$ going through the point $(-2, -4)$?

   _____

   _____

5. What is an equation for the line parallel to $y = -x + 2$ going through the point $(-3, -5)$?

   _____

   _____

6. What is an equation for the line perpendicular to $x = -1$ going through the point $(-2, -3)$?

   _____

   _____

7. What is an equation for the line parallel to $x = 0$ going through the point $(6, 5)$?

   _____

   _____

8. What is an equation for the line perpendicular to $y = \frac{1}{3}x + 1$ going through the point $(-2, 3)$?

   _____

   _____

9. Tell whether each statement is true or false.

   A Perpendicular lines have opposite slopes.
   ○ True   ○ False

   B The negative reciprocal of 4 is $-\frac{1}{4}$
   ○ True   ○ False

   C Lines that are parallel have the same slope.
   ○ True   ○ False

   D Horizontal lines are always perpendicular.
   ○ True   ○ False

   E Vertical lines are always parallel.
   ○ True   ○ False

   F Lines with the same slope are always parallel.
   ○ True   ○ False

   G Horizontal and vertical lines are always perpendicular.
   ○ True   ○ False

SKILL 29 Response to Intervention
Post-Test: Proportional Relationships

For questions 1 and 2, fill in the blanks with a side length to make the proportion statements true.

1. $\triangle ABC \sim \triangle DEF$

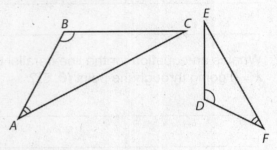

$$\frac{BC}{\underline{\quad}} = \frac{AB}{DF} \qquad \frac{EF}{CA} = \frac{\underline{\quad}}{BA}$$

2. $\overline{MN} \parallel \overline{PR}$

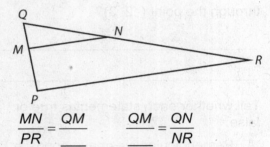

$$\frac{MN}{PR} = \frac{QM}{\underline{\quad}} \qquad \frac{QM}{\underline{\quad}} = \frac{QN}{NR}$$

3. In the triangle below, is it true that $\dfrac{AM}{MB} = \dfrac{CN}{NB}$? Why or why not?

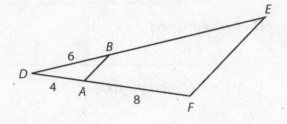

_____

_____

_____

4. A 150 foot tall building casts a shadow that is 330 feet long. At the same time, a nearby flagpole casts a shadow that is 88 feet long. How tall is the flagpole?

_____

_____

_____

5. Given that $\overline{AB} \parallel \overline{EF}$, find BE.

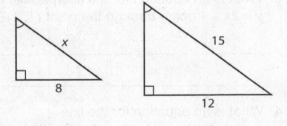

_____

_____

_____

6. Given that $\triangle ABC \sim \triangle PQR$, find the value of x.

_____

7. Triangle ABC has side lengths of 2, 7, and 8. Give an example of the side lengths of a triangle that is similar to ABC.

_____

_____

SKILL
30
Response to Intervention
Post-Test: Multi-step Equations

Find the value for the variable in each equation listed below.

1. $12z + 10z = -22$

   _____

2. $3y + 4 + 9 = 34$

   _____

3. $64 = -n - 7n$

   _____

4. $-9 + 14m = 2m - 9$

   _____

5. $13h + 6 + 2h = 15h - 8$

   _____

6. $4(7x - 6) = 200$

   _____

7. $45 = -5(-4a + 3)$

   _____

8. $-(9k - 4) = -5$

   _____

9. $82 = -2 + 7(r + 3)$

   _____

10. $20 = 3(4 - 5f) - f$

    _____

11. $w - 5(1 - 7w) = -14$

    _____

12. $-9(-3b - 4) = 4b - 33$

    _____

13. $6(2 + 7p) + 7 = 13 + 12p$

    _____

14. $-2(-4g + 5) = -6(9 - g) + 4$

    _____

Response to Intervention

Post-Test: Characteristics of a Quadratic Equation

For questions 1–6, use the equation $y = -x^2 + 4x - 3$.

1. What are the *x*-intercepts of the graph of the equation?

   _____

2. What is the equation for the axis of symmetry?

   _____

3. What are the coordinates of the vertex?

   _____

4. Does the graph of the equation have a maximum or minimum value?

   _____

5. What is the *y*-intercept?

   _____

6. Graph the function.

   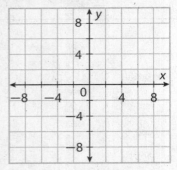

For questions 7–12, use the equation $y = (x + 4)^2 - 9$.

7. What are the *x*-intercepts of the graph of the equation?

   _____

8. What is the equation for the axis of symmetry?

   _____

9. What are the coordinates of the vertex?

   _____

10. Does the graph of the equation have a maximum or minimum value?

    _____

11. What is the *y*-intercept?

    _____

12. Graph the function.

    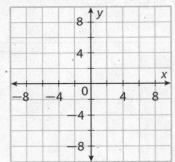

SKILL
32

Response to Intervention

Post-Test: Solving Quadratic Functions

1. The graph of $y = x^2 - x - 6$ is graphed below.

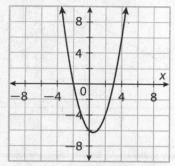

   Use the graph to find the solutions to the equation $x^2 - x - 6 = 0$.

   _____

2. What are the solutions of the equation $2x^2 = 72$?

   _____

3. Solve the equation $4x^2 - 46 = 18$.

   _____

4. What are the solutions of the equation $x^2 - 3x - 18 = 0$?

   _____

5. What are the x-intercepts of the graph of the function $y = 2x^2 - x - 3$?

   _____

6. What are the solutions of the equation $6x^2 + 7x - 20 = 0$?

   _____

7. Solve the equation $24x^2 - 51x + 6 = 0$.

   _____

For 8–9, use the following information. A quadratic equation has solutions $x = 2$ and $x = 7$.

8. What are the factors of the equation?

   _____

9. What is the original equation?

   _____

10. How many solutions does the equation $7x^2 - 5x - 3 = 0$ have?

   _____

11. Use the quadratic formula to solve $-4x^2 + 4x + 2 = 0$. Simplify your answer.

12. A student solves a quadratic equation and finds one of the solutions to be $x = \dfrac{-3 + \sqrt{33}}{2}$. What is the other solution?

   _____

13. Use the quadratic formula to solve $x^2 - 6x - 5 = 0$. Simplify your answer.

LESSON
1-1

Segment Length and Midpoints
Reteach

To find the length of a line segment, use the Pythagorean theorem to calculate the length of the hypotenuse.

$d^2 = 5^2 + 3^2$

$d^2 = 25 + 9$

$d^2 = 34$

$d = \sqrt{34}$ units

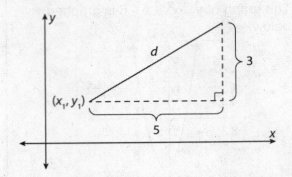

Use the Pythagorean theorem to determine the length of each segment in the figure shown.

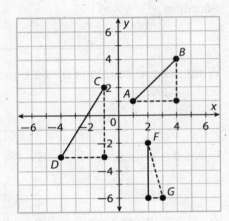

1. $\overline{AB}$

_____

2. $\overline{CD}$

_____

3. $\overline{FG}$

_____

To find the midpoint of a line segment, calculate the average of the x-coordinates and the average of the y-coordinates.

Find the midpoint of $\overline{XY}$ if the endpoints are at $X(-4, 3)$ and $Y(2, 2)$.

The x-coordinates are -4 and 2. The average is $(-4 + 2) \div 2 = -2 \div 2 = -1$.

The y-coordinates are 3 and 2. The average is $(3 + 2) \div 2 = 5 \div 2 = \dfrac{5}{2}$ or 2.5.

The midpoint of $\overline{XY}$ is $\left(-1, \dfrac{5}{2}\right)$.

Find the coordinates of the midpoint of a segment with given endpoints.

4. $A(5, 0)$, $B(3, 4)$

5. $R(-6, 1)$, $S(-3, -3)$

6. $X(2, -7)$, $Y(-1, 7)$

_____ _____ _____

LESSON 1-2

Angle Measures and Angle Bisectors
Reteach

Angles are named
by letters or numbers.

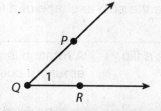

∠PQR
∠RQP
∠Q
∠1

Name each angle in as many ways as you can.

1.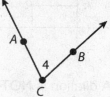

_____

2.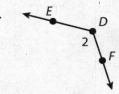

_____

Angles are classified by their measure.	Acute Angle • Between 0° and 90°	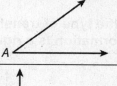
	Right Angle • Exactly 90°	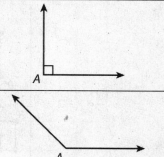
	Obtuse Angle • Between 90° and 180°	
	Straight Angle • Exactly 180°	

Classify each angle.

3.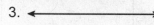

_____

4.

_____

5.

_____

6.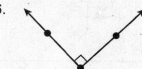

_____

LESSON
1-3

Representing and Describing Transformations

Reteach

A transformation that does NOT change the size or shape of a figure is called a *rigid motion*.

A translation is a slide left or right, up or down.	A reflection is a flip over a line.	A rotation is a turn around a point.	A dilation is a shrink or stretch.
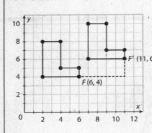	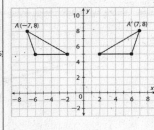	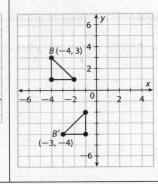	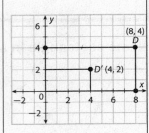

A dilation is NOT a rigid motion.

State the type of transformation. Then determine whether the transformation is a rigid motion.

1.

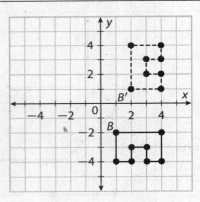

_____

2.

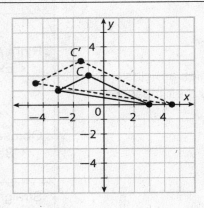

_____

3.

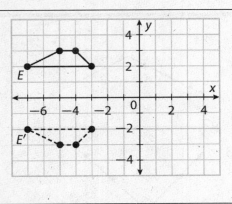

_____

4.

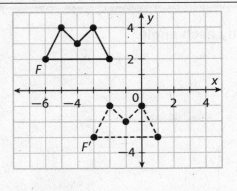

_____

LESSON 1-4

Reasoning and Proof
Reteach

A conditional statement has "if" and "then."	**Example:**
The hypothesis comes after "if."	If the pet is a poodle, then the pet is a dog.
The conclusion comes after "then."	hypothesis conclusion

Write the hypothesis and the conclusion for each conditional statement.

1. Conditional Statement: If angles are vertical angles, then they are congruent angles.

   Hypothesis: _____

   Conclusion: _____

2. Conditional Statement: If an angle measures 90°, then the angle is a right angle.

   Hypothesis: _____

   Conclusion: _____

A counterexample is an example that proves a claim is false.	**Example:** Claim: The sum of all odd numbers is odd. Counterexample: $3 + 3 = 6$ 3 and 3 are odd but their sum, 6, is an even number. So, this claim is false.

Determine if the claim is true or false. If the claim is false, provide a counterexample.

3. Claim: Squaring a number will always make it a greater number.

   _____

   _____

   _____

   _____

Translations

LESSON 2-1

Reteach

Translations can be represented using vectors.

Example:
Translate the preimage along
the vector <3, 5>.

In words:
"Shift the triangle 3 units right
and 5 units up."

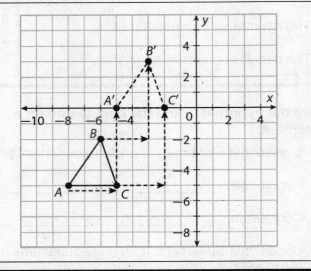

State the meaning of the vector in words.

1. <−3, 1>

2. <6, −2>

_____   _____

3. Draw the image when *ABCD* is translated along <−5, 4>.

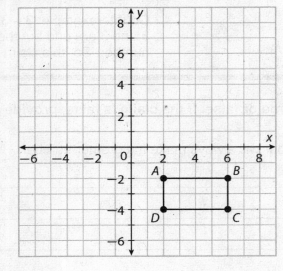

**LESSON
2-2**

Reflections
Reteach

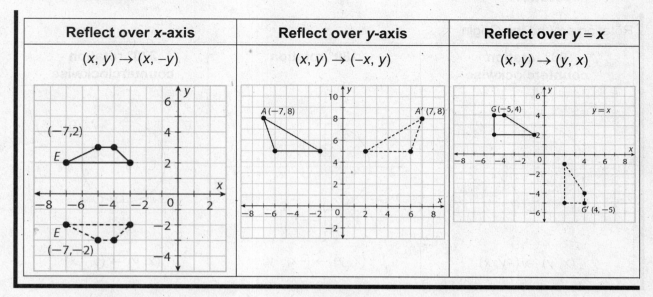

Reflect over *x*-axis	Reflect over *y*-axis	Reflect over *y* = *x*
$(x, y) \rightarrow (x, -y)$	$(x, y) \rightarrow (-x, y)$	$(x, y) \rightarrow (y, x)$

Write the coordinates for the image. Then graph both the preimage and the image.

1. Reflect over the *x*-axis.

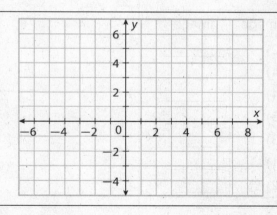

preimage	image
(–4, 5)	_____
(–2, –1)	_____
(2, –2)	_____
(5, 5)	_____

2. Reflect over *y* = *x*.

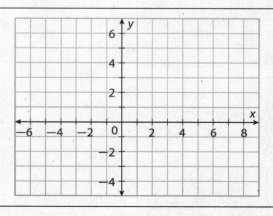

preimage	image
(1, 0)	_____
(3, –4)	_____
(1, –4)	_____

LESSON 2-3

Rotations
Reteach

Rotation around the Origin

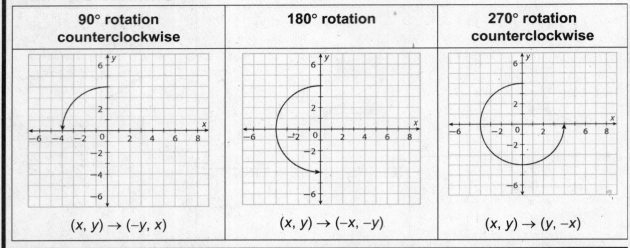

90° rotation counterclockwise	180° rotation	270° rotation counterclockwise
$(x, y) \rightarrow (-y, x)$	$(x, y) \rightarrow (-x, -y)$	$(x, y) \rightarrow (y, -x)$

Write the coordinates for the rotated image. Then graph both figures.

1. Rotate 90° counterclockwise.

preimage	image
(−6, 2)	_____
(−6, 4)	_____
(−4, 4)	_____
(−4, 5)	_____
(−3, 3)	_____
(−4, 1)	_____
(−4, 2)	_____

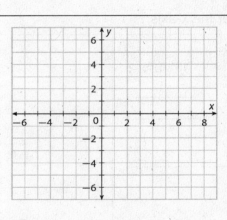

2. Rotate 180°.

preimage	image
(−6, 2)	_____
(−6, 4)	_____
(−4, 4)	_____
(−4, 5)	_____
(−3, 3)	_____
(−4, 1)	_____
(−4, 2)	_____

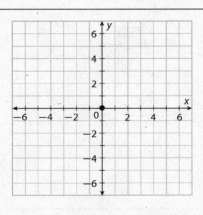

LESSON 2-4

Investigating Symmetry
Reteach

A figure has *line symmetry* if it can be folded in half over a line, and both halves are exactly the same. These lines are called *lines of symmetry*.

A figure can have several different lines of symmetry.

This figure has 2 lines of symmetry.

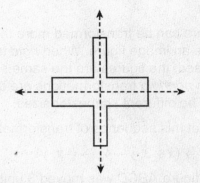

Draw all of the lines of symmetry for each figure.

1.

2.

A figure has *rotational symmetry* if it can be turned between 0° and 180°, and the figure looks exactly the same.

The angle is called an angle of rotational symmetry.

This figure has an angle of rotational symmetry of 90°.

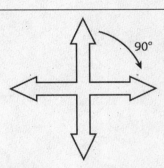

Determine if each figure has rotational symmetry. If so, name the angle of rotational symmetry.

3.

4.

_____

_____

LESSON
3-1

Sequences of Transformations

Reteach

A figure can be transformed more than once to create an image figure. When *rigid* transformations are used, the figures are the same shape and size. When *nonrigid* transformations are used, the figures could be different shapes or sizes.

Look at this sequence of transformations.

$(x, y) \rightarrow (x + 3, y - 4) \rightarrow (-x, y)$

First, figure *ABCD* was moved 3 units right and 4 units down. Then, the image was reflected over the *y*-axis to form figure *A″B″C″D″*.

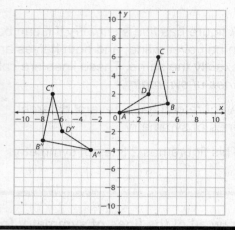

For each figure, draw the image after the given transformations.

1. $(x, y) \rightarrow (x + 2, y) \rightarrow (x, -y)$

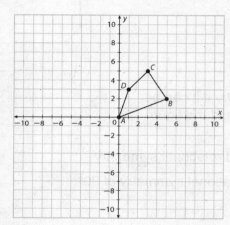

2. $(x, y) \rightarrow (x, y - 8) \rightarrow (2x, y)$

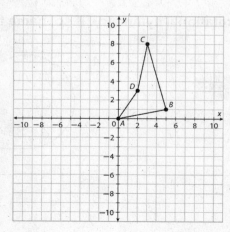

LESSON
3-2

Proving Figures Are Congruent Using Rigid Motions

Reteach

Two figures are congruent if they are exactly the same shape and size. Congruent figures are formed by using rigid transformations (translations, reflections, and rotations).

Figure *FGHJ* was reflected and translated to form figure *F"G"H"J"*, so figure *FGHJ* and figure *F"G"H"J"* are congruent.

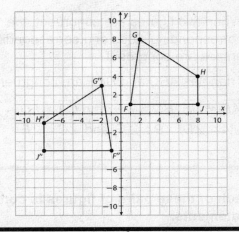

Determine whether each pair of figures is congruent. If so, name the transformations used to form the image figure.

1.

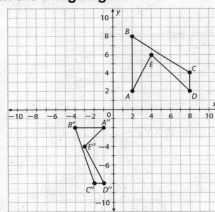

2.

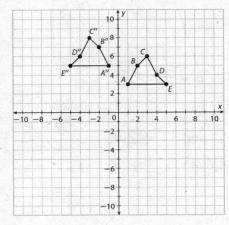

LESSON 3-3

Corresponding Parts of Congruent Figures Are Congruent
Reteach

When two figures are congruent, the corresponding sides and corresponding angles are congruent.

Triangles *ABC* and *DEF* are congruent.

$\overline{AB} \cong \overline{DE}$, $\overline{BC} \cong \overline{EF}$, and $\overline{CA} \cong \overline{FD}$

$\angle A \cong \angle D$, $\angle B \cong \angle E$, and $\angle C \cong \angle F$

Each of these pairs of figures is congruent. Complete the congruence statements.

1. Triangle *FGH* is congruent to triangle *LMN*.

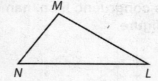

$\overline{FG} \cong$ ___, $\overline{GH} \cong$ ___, and ___ $\cong \overline{NL}$

$\angle F \cong$ ___, ___ $\cong \angle M$, and $\angle H \cong$ ___

2. Figure *STUV* is congruent to figure *WXYZ*.

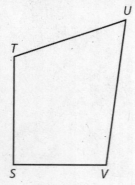 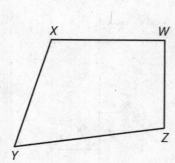

$\overline{ST} \cong$ ___, $\overline{TU} \cong$ ___, ___ $\cong \overline{YZ}$, and ___ $\cong \overline{ZW}$

$\angle S \cong$ ___, $\angle T \cong$ ___, ___ $\cong \angle Y$, and ___ $\cong \angle Z$

LESSON
4-1

Angles Formed by Intersecting Lines

Reteach

Vertical angles have the same measure.
The measures of the angles in a linear
pair add up to 180°.

$m\angle 1 = m\angle 3$ and $m\angle 2 = m\angle 4$

$m\angle 1 + m\angle 2 = 180°$

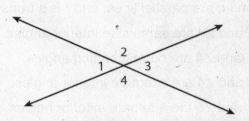

Determine the measure of each angle in the figure shown.

1. m∠a   2. m∠b

3. m∠c

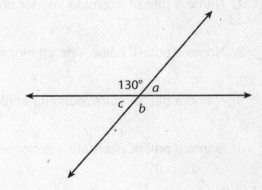

The sum of the measures of complementary angles is 90°. The sum of
the measures of supplementary angles is 180°. Angles that form a linear
pair are supplementary.

If ∠x and ∠y are complementary, and $m\angle x = 40°$, then
$m\angle y = 90 - 40 = 50°$.
If ∠A and ∠B are supplementary, and $m\angle A = 120°$, then $m\angle B = 180 - 120 = 60°$.

Use the figure to answer the following.

4. Name two complementary angles.

5. Name two supplementary angles.

6. If $m\angle AFC = 150°$, what is $m\angle CFD$?

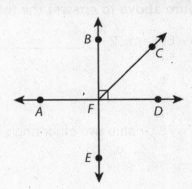

LESSON 4-2 — Transversals and Parallel Lines
Reteach

p and q are parallel lines, and r is a transversal.

∠2 and ∠4 are same side interior angles.

∠1 and ∠4 are corresponding angles.

∠3 and ∠4 are alternate interior angles.

∠1 and ∠5 are alternate exterior angles.

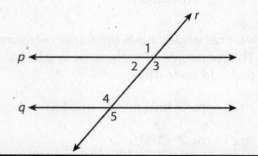

a and b are parallel lines, and c is a transversal.

1. Name a pair of alternate interior angles.

2. Name a pair of same side interior angles.

3. Name a pair of corresponding angles.

4. Name a pair of alternate exterior angles.

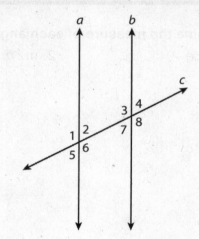

Alternate interior angles are congruent.

Corresponding angles are congruent.

Alternate exterior angles are congruent.

Same side interior angles are supplementary.

Use the figure above to answer the following questions.

5. If m∠5 = 65°, m∠2 = _____.

6. If m∠6 = 100°, m∠7 = _____.

7. If m∠4 = 78°, name two other angles that also measure 78°.

LESSON 4-3

Proving Lines are Parallel
Reteach

To prove that lines cut by a transversal are parallel, show that:
a pair of alternate interior angles are congruent.
a pair of corresponding angles are congruent.
a pair of same side interior angles are supplementary.

f and *g* are parallel lines if:

$\angle 3 \cong \angle 6$ $\angle 4 \cong \angle 5$

$\angle 3 \cong \angle 7$ $\angle 5 \cong \angle 1$

$\angle 2 \cong \angle 6$ $\angle 4 \cong \angle 8$

$m\angle 3 + m\angle 5 = 180°$ or $m\angle 4 + m\angle 6 = 180°$

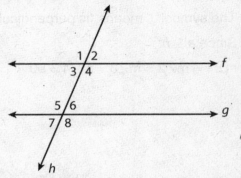

Use the figure to answer questions 1 and 2.

1. Is *m* parallel to *n*? Why or why not?

2. Is *j* parallel to *k*? Why or why not?

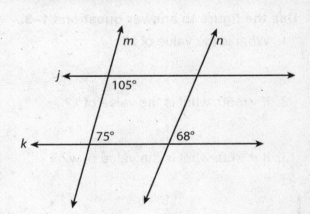

Use the figure to answer questions 3 and 4.

3. For $\overline{AD}$ to be parallel to $\overline{CB}$, the value of

   x must be _____.

4. For $\overline{AC}$ to be parallel to $\overline{DB}$, the value of

   y must be _____.

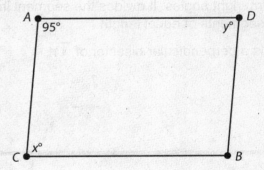

LESSON 4-4

Perpendicular Lines
Reteach

Perpendicular lines intersect to form right angles.

The symbol ⊥ means "is perpendicular to."

Since $a \perp b$:

$m\angle 1 = m\angle 2 = m\angle 3 = m\angle 4 = 90°$

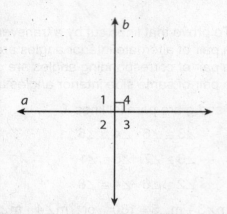

Use the figure to answer questions 1–3.

1. What is the value of z?

2. If $y = 50$, what is the value of x?

3. If $v = 60$, what is the value of w?

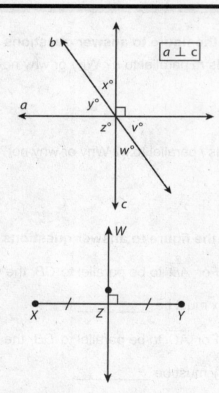

A perpendicular bisector intersects a segment to form right angles. It divides the segment into two segments of equal length.

$\overline{WZ}$ is a perpendicular bisector of $\overline{XY}$.

$\overline{AC}$ is a perpendicular bisector of $\overline{BD}$.

4. What is the measure of $\angle BEC$?

5. If $BD = 8$ cm, $DE = $ _____.

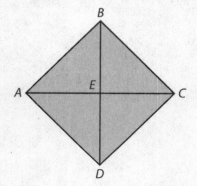

LESSON 4-5

Equations of Parallel and Perpendicular Lines
Reteach

Parallel lines have equal slopes.

The lines $y = -3x + 4$ and $y = -3x - 2$ are parallel.

They both have slopes equal to -3.

Write the equation of the line parallel to the line $y = 2x - 3$ that passes through the point (2, 8).

Use point-slope form $y - y_1 = m(x - x_1)$.

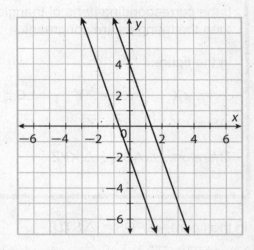

$y - 8 = 2(x - 2)$	Start with point-slope form.
$y - 8 = 2x - 4$	Distribute multiplication.
$y = 2x + 4$	Simplify.

1. What is the slope of a line parallel to the line $y = -5x + 13$? _____

2. Write the equation of the line parallel to the line $y = 5x + 3$ that passes through the point (3, 3).

Perpendicular lines have slopes that multiply to -1.

The lines $y = -3x + 1$ and $y = \frac{1}{3}x - 2$ are perpendicular,

because -3 times $\frac{1}{3}$ equals -1.

Use point-slope form to write equations of lines perpendicular to given lines.

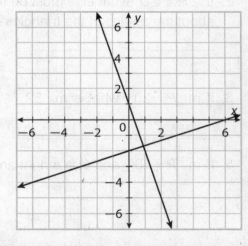

3. What is the slope of a line perpendicular to the line $y = -\frac{2}{3}x + 1$?

_____

4. What is the equation of the line perpendicular to the $y = -\frac{1}{2}x + 5$ that

passes through the point (2, 2)?

LESSON
5-1

Exploring What Makes Triangles Congruent

Reteach

If the corresponding parts of triangles are congruent,
then the triangles are congruent.

In the figure:

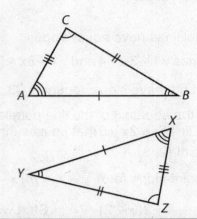

$\angle A \cong \angle X$ $\angle B \cong \angle Y$ $\angle C \cong \angle Z$

$\overline{AB} \cong \overline{XY}$ $\overline{BC} \cong \overline{YZ}$ $\overline{CA} \cong \overline{ZX}$

Therefore, $\triangle ABC \cong \triangle XYZ$.

In the figure, $\triangle PQR \cong \triangle STU$.

1. If $\overline{QR} \cong \overline{TU}$, what else must be true
about the sides of the triangles?

_____ $\cong$ _____

_____ $\cong$ _____

2. If $\angle R \cong \angle U$, what else must be true
about the angles of the triangles?

_____ $\cong$ _____

_____ $\cong$ _____

3. If $m\angle P = 20°$, what is $m\angle S$?

_____

4. If $PQ = 4$ cm, what is ST?

_____

5. If $m\angle P = 30°$, and Q is a right angle, what is $m\angle U$? _____

LESSON 5-2

ASA Triangle Congruence
Reteach

If two angles and the included side of one triangle are congruent to two angles and the included side of another triangle, the triangles are congruent.

In the figure, $\angle R \cong \angle X$, $\angle T \cong \angle Z$,

and $\overline{RT} \cong \overline{XZ}$; therefore,

$\triangle RST \cong \triangle XYZ$.

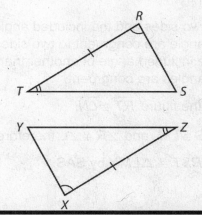

Use the figure to answer questions 1 and 2.

1. If $\angle B$ and $\angle E$ are both right angles, and $\overline{BC} \cong \overline{EF}$, what else must be true if $\triangle ABC \cong \triangle DEF$ by ASA?

   _____

2. If $\angle B$ and $\angle E$ are both right angles, and $\angle A \cong \angle D$, what else must be true if $\triangle ABC \cong \triangle DEF$ by ASA?

   _____

   _____

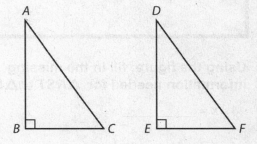

In the figure, $\angle J \cong \angle L$.

3. If $\overline{MK}$ is the perpendicular bisector of $\overline{JL}$, then $\angle$____ $\cong \angle$ ____

   because they are both _____ angles.

4. Since $\overline{MK}$ bisects $\overline{JL}$, the two segments _____ and

   _____ are congruent.

5. Based on the answers to 3 and 4, $\triangle$_____ $\cong \triangle$_____ by

   ____ ____ ____.

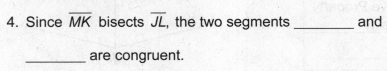

LESSON 5-3

SAS Triangle Congruence
Reteach

If two sides and the included angle of one triangle are congruent to two sides and the included angle of another triangle, the triangles are congruent.

In the figure $\overline{RT} \cong \overline{LN}$,

$\overline{RS} \cong \overline{LM}$, and $\angle R \cong \angle L$; therefore,

$\triangle RST \cong \triangle LMN$ by SAS.

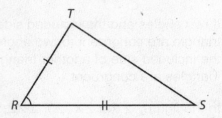

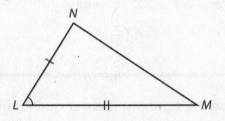

Using the figure, fill in the missing information needed for $\triangle RST \cong \triangle LMN$ by SAS.

1. $x =$ _____

2. $y =$ _____

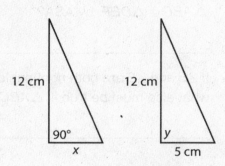

Complete the proof about the figure.

Statements	Reasons
1. $\angle 1 \cong \angle 2$; $\overline{AB} \cong \overline{BC}$	1. Given
2. _____ $\cong$ _____	2. Reflexive Property of Equality
3. $\triangle ABD \cong$ _____	3. _____ _____ _____

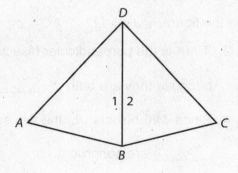

LESSON 5-4
SSS Triangle Congruence
Reteach

If the three sides of one triangle are congruent to three corresponding sides of another triangle, the triangles are congruent.

In the figure, $\overline{AB} \cong \overline{XY}$, $\overline{AC} \cong \overline{XZ}$,

and $\overline{BC} \cong \overline{YZ}$; therefore,

$\triangle ABC \cong \triangle XYZ$ by SSS.

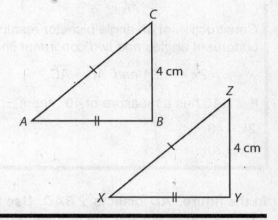

Find the missing values in the figure so that $\triangle PQR \cong \triangle STU$ by SSS.

1. $RQ =$ _____

2. $ST =$ _____

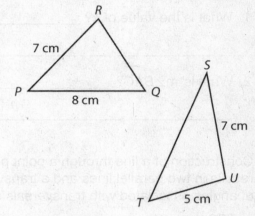

Complete the proof for the figure.

Statements	Reasons
1. $\overline{RU} \cong \overline{TU}$; $\overline{US}$ bisects $\overline{RT}$	1. Given
2. ___ ≅ ___	2. Definition of bisect
3. ___ ≅ ___	3. Reflexive property of equality
4. △___ ≅ △___	4. ____ ____ ____

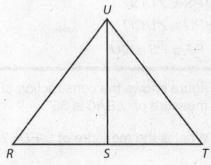

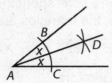

LESSON 6-1

Justifying Constructions
Reteach

Construction of an angle bisector results in two
congruent angles and two congruent line segments.

$x + x = 2x = m\angle A$ and $\overline{AB} \cong \overline{AC}$.

If $\angle BAC$ has a measure of 40°, then:

$2x = 40$

$x = 20$

**In the figure, $\overline{AD}$ bisects $\angle BAC$. Use this
information to answer the following questions.**

1. What is the value of x? _____

_____

2. What is $m\angle BAC$? _____

_____

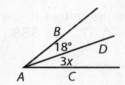

Construction of a line through a point parallel to a given line
results in two parallel lines and a transversal. The properties
of angles associated with transversals apply.

$\angle TPS \cong \angle UQR$

$\angle VPU \cong \angle UQR$

$\overline{PT} \cong \overline{PS} \cong \overline{QU}$

The figure shows the construction of a line m parallel to a line n.
The measure of $\angle BAC$ is 35°.

3. What is the measure of $\angle EDF$? _____

_____

4. What is the measure of $\angle EAC$? _____

_____

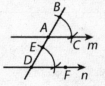

5. If the length of $\overline{DE}$ is 4 units, then what is the radius of a circle
   centered at point A and passing through point B?

_____

LESSON
6-2

AAS Triangle Congruence
Reteach

Given two triangles, it can be shown that they are congruent by showing that two angles and a non-included side are congruent.

Since $\angle A \cong \angle D$, $\angle B \cong \angle E$, and $\overline{AC} \cong \overline{DF}$,
$\triangle ABC \cong \triangle DEF$.

This is called the AAS Congruence Theorem.

 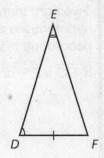

For each pair of triangles, state "yes" if they are congruent by the AAS theorem. Otherwise state "no" and explain why they are not congruent by AAS.

1. _____

2. _____

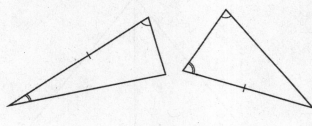 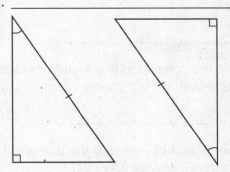

Given the indicated information, what information is needed to show that the two triangles are congruent using the AAS theorem? There may be more than one correct answer.

3. $\angle B \cong \angle E$ _____

4. $\angle A \cong \angle E$ _____

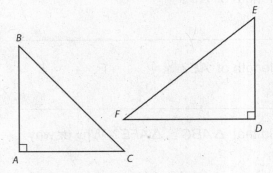 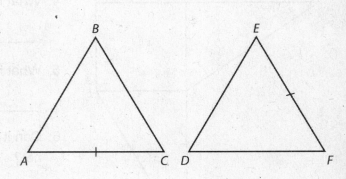

LESSON
6-3

HL Triangle Congruence
Reteach

Two right triangles are congruent if their hypotenuses and one pair of legs are congruent.

If $\overline{BC} \cong \overline{EF}$ and $\overline{AC} \cong \overline{DF}$, then $\triangle ABC \cong \triangle DEF$.

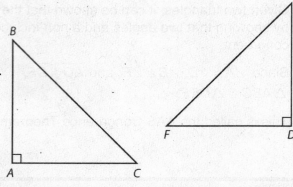

Consider triangles *ABD* and *CBD* in the figure.

1. Which angle is the right angle in triangle *ADB*? Why?

   _____

2. Name the corresponding legs from each triangle that are congruent.

   _____

3. If $AB = 4$ and $BC = 4$, are the triangles congruent? Why or why not?

   _____

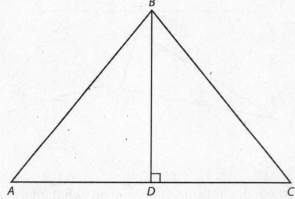

In the figure, *ACDE* is a square and $CD = 5$.

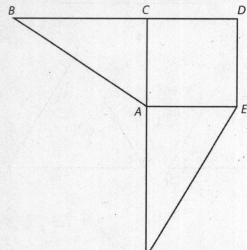

4. What is the length of $\overline{AC}$?

   _____

5. What is the length of $\overline{AE}$?

   _____

6. Can it be said that $\triangle ABC \cong \triangle AFE$? Why or why not?

   _____

LESSON 7-1

Interior and Exterior Angles
Reteach

The sum of the interior angles of a triangle is 180°. For any convex polygon with *n* sides, the sum of the interior angles is $(n - 2)180°$.

In the figure, there are five sides. So, the sum of the interior angles is $(5 - 2)(180°) = 3(180°) = 540°$.

Therefore, to find *x* solve the equation:

$2x + 140 + 106 + 85 + 126 = 540$

$$2x + 457 = 540$$

$$2x = 83$$

$$x = 41.5$$

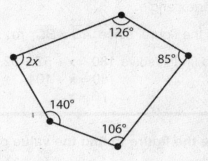

1. The interior angles of a triangle have measures of 55°, 25°, and *x*°. What is *x*?

   _____

2. What is the value of *x* in the figure? _____

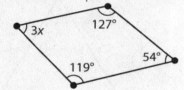

The measure of an exterior angle of a triangle is equal to the sum of the measures of the two remote interior angles.

In the figure,

$62 + x = 145$

$$x = 83$$

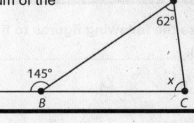

Find the value of *x* in each of the figures below.

3. _____

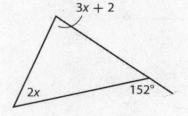

4. _____

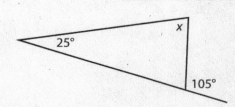

LESSON 7-2

Isosceles and Equilateral Triangles

Reteach

An isosceles triangle has two congruent sides. The angles opposite the congruent sides are also congruent. The remaining angle is called the vertex angle.

In the figure, since $\overline{AB} \cong \overline{BC}$, $m\angle A = 52°$.

To find x, solve $180 = x + 52 + 52$.

$$180 = x + 104$$
$$76 = x$$

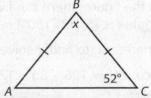

Use the figure to find the value of x.

1. _____

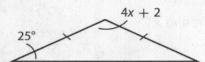

2. _____

All three sides of an equilateral triangle are congruent and the measure of each interior angle is 60°.

If $\triangle ABC$ is an equilateral triangle, then x can be found by solving the equation $2x = x + 4$.

$$2x = x + 4$$
$$x = 4$$

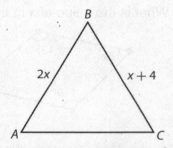

Use the following figures to find the value of x.

3. _____

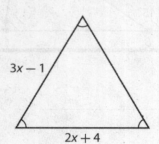

4. _____

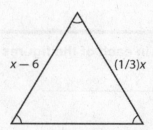

LESSON 7-3

Triangle Inequalities
Reteach

The sum of any two side lengths of a triangle is greater than the third side length. This can be used to determine if three lengths can make the sides of a triangle.

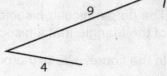

Is it possible for a triangle to have side lengths of 9, 4, and 1?
Check the three possible inequalities.

$9 + 4 > 1$ $9 + 1 > 4$ $4 + 1 < 9$

Since the third inequality does not follow the triangle inequality, a triangle with these side lengths is not possible.

Determine if it is possible for a triangle to have the given side lengths.

1. 8, 4, 7 _____

2. 1, 3, 2 _____

3. 6, 4, 3 _____

4. 18, 12, 9 _____

If two angles of a triangle are not congruent, then the longer side is opposite the larger angle.

Since $m\angle B < m\angle A < m\angle C$,

$AC < BC < AB$.

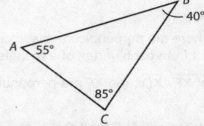

For the given triangles, determine the longest and the shortest sides based on the given angles.

5. _____

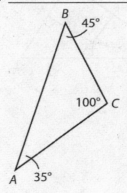

6. _____

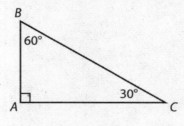

7. _____

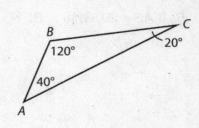

LESSON 8-1
Perpendicular Bisectors of Triangles
Reteach

A perpendicular bisector of triangle is a line or segment that divides a side of a triangle into two equal segments.

The perpendicular bisector forms a right angle with the side of the triangle that it bisects.

In the figure, $\overleftrightarrow{BE}$ is the perpendicular bisector of $\overline{AD}$.

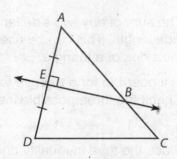

In the figure, $\overline{ZX}$ is the perpendicular bisector of $\overline{WY}$.

1. What is the measure of $\angle YXZ$?

2. If $WY = 24$, what is WX?

3. If $WX = 6$, what is WY?

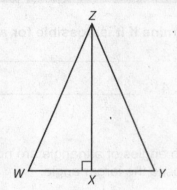

The point where the perpendicular bisectors intersect is equidistant from each vertex of a triangle.

In the figure, $\overline{XE}$, $\overline{XD}$, and $\overline{XF}$ are perpendicular bisectors.

X is equidistant from A, B, and C.

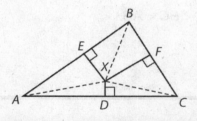

4. If $XA = 8$, what is XC?

5. If $AB = 20$, what is BE?

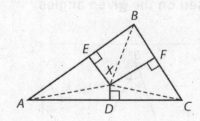

Angle Bisectors of Triangles
Reteach

An angle bisector divides an angle into two congruent angles.

A point on an angle bisector is equidistant from both sides of the angle.

In the figure, $\overrightarrow{BD}$ bisects $\angle ABC$.

D is a point on $\overrightarrow{BD}$ and is the same distance from each of the sides of $\angle ABC$.

$XD = YD$

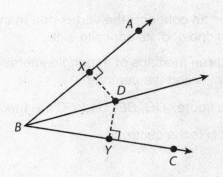

In the figure, $\overrightarrow{WY}$ bisects $\angle XWZ$.

1. $m\angle XWY = m\angle$ _____

2. If $XY = 9$ cm, then $ZY =$ _____.

3. If $m\angle XWY = 25°$, then $m\angle XWZ =$ _____.

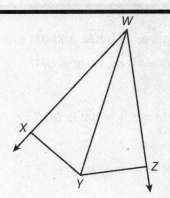

The angle bisectors in a triangle intersect at a point that is equidistant from each of the sides.

In the figure, the angle bisectors intersect at point P.
Point P is the same distance from each side of the triangle.

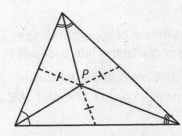

In the figure, $\overline{TS}$ and $\overline{US}$ are angle bisectors and $SR = 3$ cm.

4. $m\angle RUS =$ _____

5. $m\angle VTS =$ _____

6. What is the perpendicular distance from S to $\overline{VT}$?

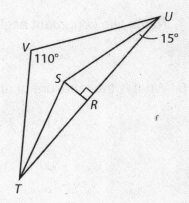

Medians and Altitudes of Triangles
Reteach

A median connects the vertex of a triangle to the midpoint of its opposite side.

The three medians of a triangle intersect at a point called the centroid.

In the figure, $\overline{DG}$, $\overline{BE}$, and $\overline{FC}$ are medians.

Point H is the centroid.

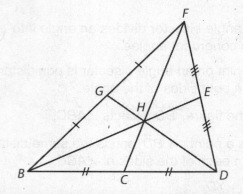

In the figure, $\overline{LP}$, $\overline{KN}$, and $\overline{JM}$ are medians.

1. If $JN = 10$ m, what is JP?

2. If $NM = 8$ ft, what is ML?

3. If $JK = 12$ cm, what is JL?

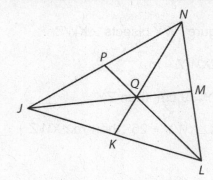

An altitude is a perpendicular segment from a vertex of a triangle to the line that passes through the opposite side.

An altitude can be on, inside, or outside the triangle. In the figure, $\overline{XU}$, $\overline{VY}$, and $\overline{WZ}$ are altitudes.

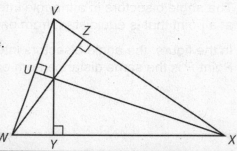

4. Name two congruent angles in the figure.

5. What is the measure of angle VYX?

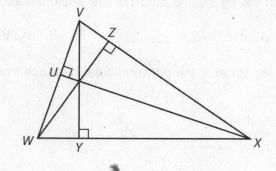

**LESSON
8-4**

Midsegments of Triangles

Reteach

A segment that connects the midpoints of two
sides of a triangle is parallel to the third side.

The length of that segment is half the length of
the third side.

In the figure, X and Y are the midpoints of
$\overline{AC}$ and $\overline{BC}$.

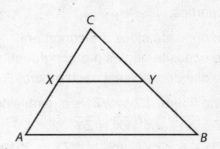

$\overline{XY}$ is parallel to $\overline{AB}$ $\left(\overline{XY} \parallel \overline{AB}\right)$.

$$XY = \frac{1}{2}AB$$

In the figure, R and S are the midpoints of $\overline{QT}$ and $\overline{PT}$.

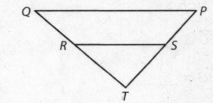

1. $\overline{RS}$ is parallel to _____.

2. If $QP = 16$, then $RS =$ _____.

3. If $RS = 9$, then $QP =$ _____.

In the figure, $\overline{DE} \parallel \overline{BC}$ and $BC = 2\,DE$.

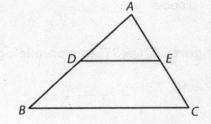

4. If $AB = 8$, then $AD =$ _____.

5. If $CE = 4$, then $CA =$ _____.

LESSON 9-1

Properties of Parallelograms
Reteach

A parallelogram is a quadrilateral (four-sided figure) with the following properties:

The opposite sides are congruent.
The opposite angles are congruent.
The diagonals bisect each other.

In the figure, $\square WXYZ$ is a parallelogram.

$\overline{WZ} \cong \overline{XY}$ and $\overline{WX} \cong \overline{ZY}$

$\angle ZWX \cong \angle XYZ$ and $\angle WZY \cong \angle WXY$

$\overline{WY}$ and $\overline{XZ}$ bisect each other.

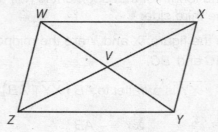

In the figure, $\square EFGH$ is a parallelogram. Complete the following statements.

1. $\angle HEF \cong$ _____.

2. $\overline{ED} \cong$ _____.

3. $\overline{HG} \cong$ _____.

4. $\overline{HF}$ bisects _____.

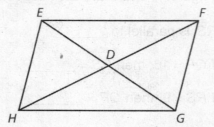

In the figure, $\square QRST$ is a parallelogram. Complete the following statements.

5. $QR = 16$, $TS =$ _____

6. $m\angle QTS = 95°$, $m\angle SRQ =$ _____

7. $QU = 4$, $SU =$ _____

8. $TR = 20$, $TU =$ _____

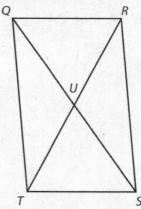

Conditions for Parallelograms
Reteach

There are a number of ways to prove that a quadrilateral is
a parallelogram:

- If the opposite sides are congruent.
- If the opposite angles are congruent.
- If the diagonals bisect each other.

Then the quadrilateral must be a parallelogram.

The given figure, *EFGH*, is a quadrilateral. *EFGH* must be a
parallelogram if: $\overline{EF} \cong \overline{HG}$ and $\overline{EH} \cong \overline{FG}$, or ∠HEF, or ∠HGF and
∠EHG ≅ ∠EFG, or $\overline{HF}$ and $\overline{EG}$ bisect each other.

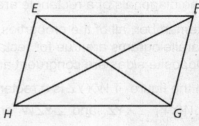

Fill in the missing information that would prove that *WXYZ* is a parallelogram.

1. ∠WZY ≅ _____ and ∠ZWX ≅ _____

2. $\overline{WX} \cong$ _____ and $\overline{WZ} \cong$ _____

3. $\overline{WY}$ and $\overline{XZ}$ _____.

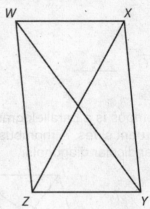

Fill in the missing information that would prove that *WXYZ* is a parallelogram.

4. *EH* = 12 and *GF* = _____; *EF* = 24 and _____ = 24.

5. m∠HEF = 100° and m∠HGF = _____;

   m∠EHG = 80° and m∠ _____ = 80°

LESSON 9-3
Properties of Rectangles, Rhombuses, and Squares
Reteach

A rectangle is a parallelogram that contains four right angles.
The diagonals of a rectangle are congruent.

Remember, all of the properties of
parallelograms are true for rectangles.
Opposite sides are congruent and parallel.

In the figure, if *WXYZ* is a rectangle, then: $\angle ZWX$,
$\angle WXY$, $\angle XYZ$, and $\angle YZW$ are right angles, and $\overline{WY} \cong \overline{XZ}$.

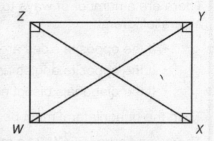

EFGH is a rectangle. Complete the statements that must be true about EFGH.

1. $\overline{EG} \cong$ _____

2. $m\angle EHG =$ _____

3. $\overline{EH} \parallel$ = _____

A rhombus is a parallelogram with four congruent sides. A rhombus has perpendicular diagonals.

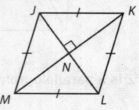

A square is a rhombus with four congruent sides and four right angles. A square is, therefore, also a parallelogram and a rectangle.

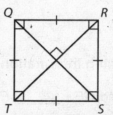

JKLM is a rhombus. Fill in the missing information. Use the figure shown above.

QRST is a square. Fill in the missing information. Use the figure shown above.

4. If *ML* = 32, *LK* = _____

5. $m\angle MNL =$ _____

6. $\overline{QT} \cong$ ____ $\cong$ _____ $\cong$ _____

LESSON 9-4

Conditions for Rectangles, Rhombuses, and Squares
Reteach

Certain conditions of a parallelogram are enough to prove that a parallelogram is a rectangle, a rhombus, or a square.

If one angle of a parallelogram is a right angle, the parallelogram is a rectangle.

If two consecutive sides are of a parallelogram are congruent, the parallelogram is a rhombus.

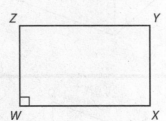

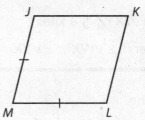

If the diagonals of a parallelogram are perpendicular, it is a rhombus.

If one diagonal of a parallelogram bisects a pair of opposite angles, it is a rhombus.

If a parallelogram can be proven to be a rectangle and a rhombus, it is a square.

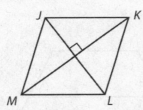

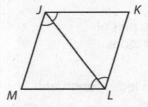

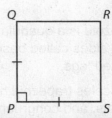

State whether the figure is a rectangle, rhombus, or square. Explain your reasoning. There may be more than 1 answer.

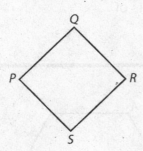

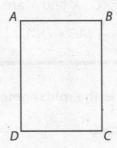

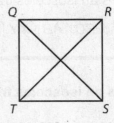

1. $\overline{PQ} \cong \overline{QR}$

2. $m\angle D = 90°$

3. $\overline{QS} \perp \overline{TR}$; $\overline{TQ} \cong \overline{QR}$

_____

_____

_____

_____

_____

_____

Properties and Conditions for Kites and Trapezoids

Reteach

A kite is a quadrilateral with two distinct sets of congruent sides.

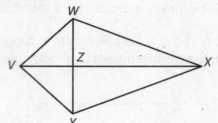

The diagonals of a kite are perpendicular.
One pair of opposite angles are congruent.

In the figure *WXYZ* is a kite.

$\overline{WY} \perp \overline{VX}$ and $\angle VWX \cong \angle VYX$

ABCD is a kite.

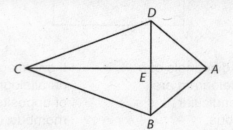

1. m∠*DEA* = _____

2. If *CD* = 9 and *DA* = 5, *BC* = _____.

A trapezoid is a quadrilateral with one pair of
parallel sides called bases. The other sides
are called legs.

An isosceles trapezoid has congruent legs, congruent
diagonals, and congruent base angles.

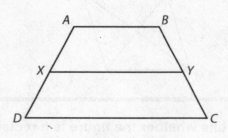

The midsegment connects the midpoints of the legs.
Its length is half the sum of the lengths of the bases
and is parallel to the bases.

ABCD is an isosceles trapezoid. ∠*D* ≅ ∠*C*; *X* and *Y* are the midpoints of

$\overline{AD}$ and $\overline{BC}$. $\overline{AB} \parallel \overline{XY} \parallel \overline{DC}$ and $XY = \dfrac{1}{2} (AB + DC)$.

ABCD is an isosceles trapezoid. $\overline{XY}$ is the midsegment.

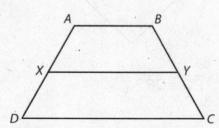

3. Name the base angles of the trapezoid.

4. What three segments are parallel to each other?

5. If *AB* = 6 and *DC* = 14, what is *XY*?

LESSON 10-1	**Slope and Parallel Lines**
	Reteach

Parallel lines have the same slope.

In the figure, the slope of lines *a* and *b* is $\frac{2}{3}$.

Slope can be used to classify quadrilaterals.

If only one set of opposite sides have the same slope, the quadrilateral is a trapezoid.

If both pairs of opposite sides have the same slope, the quadrilateral is a parallelogram.

Remember, the slope (*m*) of a line that passes through the points

(x_1, y_1) and (x_2, y_2) is computed using the formula $m = \dfrac{y_2 - y_1}{x_2 - x_1}$

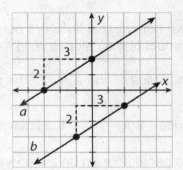

Prove that *ABCD* is a parallelogram.

1. *ABCD* is a parallelogram if _____ || _____, and

    _____ || _____.

2. Names the coordinates of *A, B, C,* and *D.*

    _____

3. Find the slope of $\overline{AB}$. _____

4. Find the slope of $\overline{BC}$. _____

5. Find the slope of $\overline{CD}$. _____

6. Find the slope of $\overline{DA}$. _____

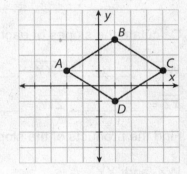

7. Do you have enough information to prove that *ABCD* is a parallelogram? Why or why not?

    _____

Slope and Perpendicular Lines
Reteach

Two non-vertical lines are perpendicular to each other if the product of their slopes is –1.

The slope of line *a* is –2. The slope of line *b* is $\frac{1}{2}$.

Since $-2 \times \frac{1}{2} = -1$, the lines are perpendicular.

If a parallelogram on the coordinate plane has four right angles, that parallelogram is a rectangle.

To prove this, show the consecutive sides of the parallelogram are perpendicular. So, show the product of the slopes is –1.

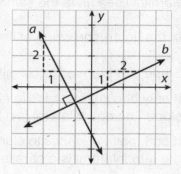

Prove that ☐*WXYZ* is a rectangle.

1. Name the coordinates of *W*, *X*, *Y*, and *Z*.

   W _____ *X* _____ *Y* _____ *Z* _____

2. Calculate the slopes of each side of the parallelogram.

   $\overline{WX}$ = _____ $\overline{XY}$ = _____

   $\overline{YZ}$ = _____ $\overline{ZW}$ = _____

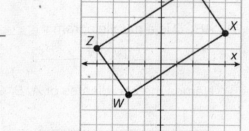

3. Find the products of the slopes of these segments:

   $\overline{WX}$ and $\overline{XY}$ = _____ $\overline{XY}$ and $\overline{YZ}$ = _____

   $\overline{YZ}$ and $\overline{ZW}$ = _____ $\overline{ZW}$ and $\overline{YZ}$ = _____

4. Is *WXYZ* a rectangle? Why or why not?

   _____

LESSON 10-3

Coordinate Proof Using Distance with Segments and Triangles
Reteach

The coordinate plane can be used to prove theorems about geometric figures.

The distance formula can be used to find the length of segments with endpoints (x_1, y_1) and (x_2, y_2).

$$d = \sqrt{(y_2 - y_1) + (x_2 - x_1)}$$

The midpoint formula can be used to find the midpoint of a segment with endpoints (x_1, y_1) and (x_2, y_2).

$$\text{Midpoint} = \left(\frac{x_1 + x_2}{2}, \frac{y_1 + y_2}{2} \right)$$

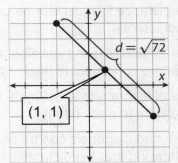

$d = \sqrt{72}$

$(1, 1)$

Use the distance formula to prove that $\angle C \cong \angle Z$.

Find the lengths of the sides of $\triangle ABC$ and $\triangle XYZ$ by using the distance formula.

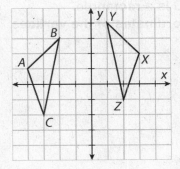

1. $AB = $ _____

2. $BC = $ _____

3. $CA = $ _____

4. $XY = $ _____

5. $YZ = $ _____

6. $ZX = $ _____

7. Which sides of $\triangle ABC$ are congruent to which sides of $\triangle XYZ$?

_____ $\cong$ _____   _____ $\cong$ _____   _____ $\cong$ _____

8. $\triangle ABC \cong \triangle XYZ$ by _____.

9. What can you conclude from 1–8? Why? _____

_____

Coordinate Proof Using Distance with Quadrilaterals

LESSON 10-4

Reteach

The distance formula can be used to prove theorems about quadrilaterals.

A quadrilateral is a parallelogram if both pairs of opposite sides are congruent to each other.

A parallelogram is a rectangle if its diagonals are congruent to each other.

Sides and diagonals can be proven congruent by showing that the distances between their endpoints are equal.

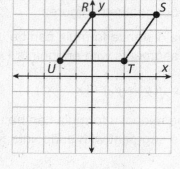

In the figure, if it can be shown that the distance from *R* to *U* equals the distance from *S* to *T*, and the distance from *R* to *S* equals the distance from *U* to *T*, then *RSTU* is a parallelogram.

Prove that *DEFG* is a rectangle.
What are the coordinates of the vertices of *DEFG*?

1. *D* _____

2. *E* _____

3. *F* _____

4. *G* _____

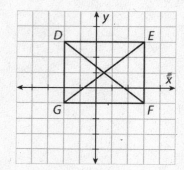

Using the distance formula, calculate the lengths of the diagonals of *DEFG*.

5. *DF* = _____

6. *EG* = _____

7. Is *DEFG* a rectangle? Why or why not?

_____

Perimeter and Area on the Coordinate Plane
Reteach

The *perimeter* of a figure can be found by adding the lengths of the sides of the figure.

The *area* of any parallelogram can be found by multiplying the length of the base times by the length of the height.

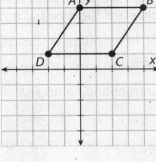

The area of a triangle can be found by multiplying the length of the base times the length of the height and multiplying that product by ½.

The perimeter of *ABCD* can be found by using the distance formula and calculating the lengths of $\overline{AB}$, $\overline{BC}$, $\overline{CD}$, and $\overline{DA}$, and adding those lengths together.

The base of *ABCD* is the length of $\overline{CD}$. The height can be found by calculating the perpendicular length from *A* to $\overline{CD}$. The area is the product of these lengths.

Calculate the perimeter and area of the parallelogram *ABCD* and the triangle *RST*. Use the distance formula to find side and height lengths as needed.

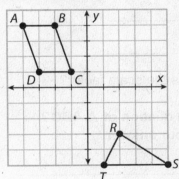

1. Length of *AB* and *DC* = _____

2. Length of *AD* and *BC* = _____

3. Height of *ABCD* = _____

4. Perimeter of *ABCD* = _____

5. Area of *ABCD* = _____

6. Lengths of sides of *RST* = _____ _____ _____

7. Height of *RST* = _____

8. Perimeter of *RST* = _____

9. Area of *RST* = _____

<table>
</table>

LESSON	Dilations
11-1	*Reteach*

A dilation is a transformation of a figure that changes the size but not the shape of the figure.

△DEF is a dilation of △ABC.

△DEF is the same shape as △ABC.

The corresponding angles of △ABC and △DEF are congruent.

$\angle A \cong \angle D$, $\angle B \cong \angle E$, and $\angle C \cong \angle F$

The ratios of the corresponding side lengths are equal.

Each side of △DEF has a length that is twice the length of the corresponding side in △ABC. So, the *scale factor* of the dilation is 2.

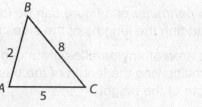

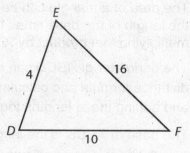

WXYZ is a dilation of PQRS.

1. m∠P = 80°, m∠W = _____

2. WZ = _____

3. WX = _____

4. What is the scale factor? _____

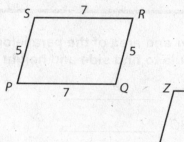

**Is △DEF a dilation of △ABC?
Explain your answer.**

5. _____

   _____

   _____

   _____

   _____

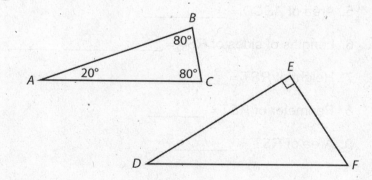

LESSON
11-2
Proving Figures are Similar Using Transformations
Reteach

A similarity transformation is a transformation in which an image can be mapped to a new image that has the same shape.

△*ABC* is similar to △*WXY* if it can be shown that one of the triangles can be transformed to the other through a series of reflections, translations, rotations, or dilations.

If △*ABC* is translated 3 units up and 2 units right, and is dilated by a scale factor of 2, it will become △*WXY*. So, △*ABC* ~ △*WXY*.

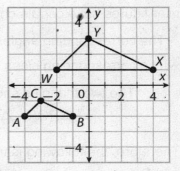

Complete the following transformations that prove that rectangle *ABCD* is similar to rectangle *SVUT*.

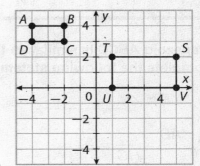

1. *ABCD* is reflected across the _____.

2. *ABCD* is translated _____ units down

   and _____ units _____.

3. *ABCD* is dilated by a scale factor of _____.

Triangle *FGH* is transformed into similar triangle *JKL* using the given transformations.

4. Draw *JKL* on the coordinate plane.

   • Translate *FGH* 3 units down and 2 units left.

   • Rotate *FGH* counterclockwise 90 degrees.

   • Dilate *FGH* by a scale of 2 to 1.

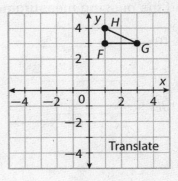

LESSON
11-3

Corresponding Parts of Similar Figures

Reteach

Similar figures have certain characteristics:

- The corresponding angles are congruent.
- The corresponding sides are in proportion.

     The two triangles shown are similar.

$$\triangle PQR \sim \triangle UVW$$

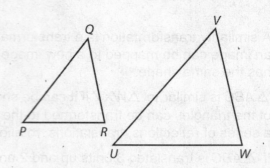

Therefore, the following is true:

$$\angle P \cong \angle U \qquad \angle Q \cong \angle V \qquad \angle R \cong \angle W$$

$$\frac{PQ}{UV} = \frac{QR}{VW} = \frac{PR}{UW}$$

Trapezoid *ABCD* is similar to trapezoid *EFGH*.
Complete the following statements.

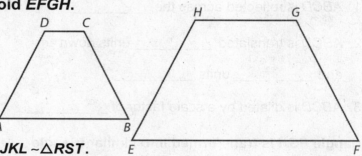

1. $\angle B \cong \angle$ _____

2. $\dfrac{AB}{HG} = \dfrac{}{} = \dfrac{CB}{} = -$

Find the missing measurements if $\triangle JKL \sim \triangle RST$.

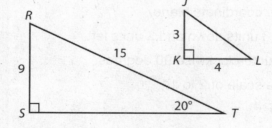

3. $m\angle J =$ _____

4. $ST =$ _____

5. $JL =$ _____

LESSON 11-4

AA Similarity of Triangles
Reteach

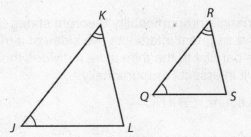

If two angles of one triangle are congruent
to two corresponding angles of another triangle,

then the triangles are similar to each other.

Since $\angle J \cong \angle Q$ and $\angle K \cong \angle R$,

$$\triangle JKL \sim \triangle QRS.$$

In the figure, $\overline{AB} \parallel \overline{DE}$.
Prove that $\triangle ACB \sim \triangle ECD$.

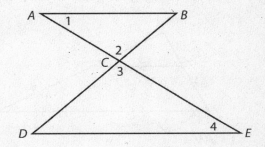

Statements	Reasons
1.	1. Given
2.	2. Vertical $\angle$s $\cong$
3.	3. Alternate Interior $\angle$s $\cong$
4. $\triangle ACB \sim \triangle ECD$	4.

If the corresponding sides of two triangles
are proportional, then the triangles are similar.

In the figure, $\triangle ACB \sim \triangle ECD$ since all
of the corresponding sides are in the ratio
3 to 2.

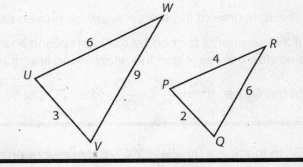

$\triangle WXY \sim \triangle LMN$. Find the missing
measures in the figure.

5. $WY =$ _____

6. $LM =$ _____

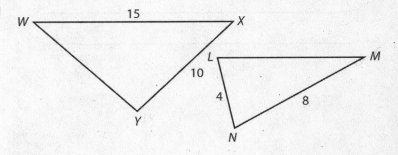

Triangle Proportionality Theorem

LESSON 12-1

Reteach

The triangle proportionality theorem states that if a segment intersects two sides of a triangle and is parallel to the third side, it divides the two sides it intersects proportionally.

In the figure, $\overline{EB} \parallel \overline{DC}$.

According to the theorem: $\dfrac{AE}{ED} = \dfrac{AB}{BC}$.

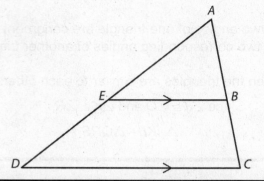

Find the missing lengths in each of the figures.

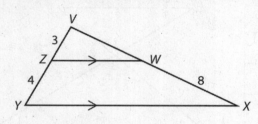

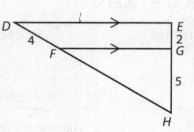

1. $VW =$ _____

2. $HF =$ _____

The converse of the theorem can be proven as well.

If the segments formed by the intersecting line are proportional, then the third side and the intersecting line must be parallel.

In the figure, since $\dfrac{PT}{TS} = \dfrac{PQ}{QR}$, then $\overline{TQ} \parallel \overline{SR}$.

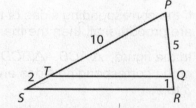

3. In the figure, is $\overline{ZW} \parallel \overline{YX}$? Explain your answer.

_____

_____

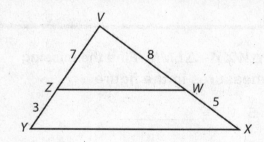

LESSON 12-2 **Subdividing Segment in a Given Ratio**
Reteach

A line segment on the coordinate plane can
be divided into smaller segments. To *partition*
a segment means to divide it into 2 segments
with a given ratio.

The figure shows the segment $\overline{XY}$ partitioned
into a ratio of 2 to 1. The segment $\overline{XZ}$ is $\dfrac{2}{2+1}=\dfrac{2}{3}$
of the way from X to Y.

To get from X to Y, the rise is 6 and the run is 3.

From X, move $\dfrac{2}{3}$ of the rise $\left(\dfrac{2}{3}\times 6 = 4\right)$ units,

and move $\dfrac{2}{3}$ of the run $\left(\dfrac{2}{3}\times 3 = 2\right)$ units.

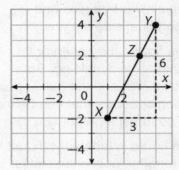

Partition $\overline{CD}$ into a 2 to 1 ratio.

1. The coordinates of C are _____.

2. The coordinates of D are _____.

3. The rise from C to D is _____ units.

4. The run from C to D is _____ units.

5. With a 2 to 1 ratio, move _____ of the rise

   and _____ of the run to get to the point of partition.

6. Add _____ to the x-coordinate of C and _____

   to the y-coordinate of C to get to the point of partition.

7. The coordinates of the point of partition are _____.

8. Plot the point of partition and label it X.

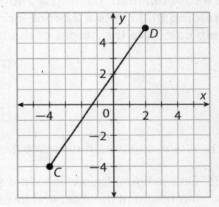

LESSON 12-3

Using Proportional Relationships
Reteach

Indirect measurement can be used to find unknown heights and distances using similar triangles and proportional side lengths.

In the figure, the observer is looking up at a building. Both the observer and the building are casting shadows that can be measured. The observer's height can also be measured.

If the figure is labeled with just heights and lengths, notice the similar triangles.

$\triangle ACD \sim \triangle ABE$

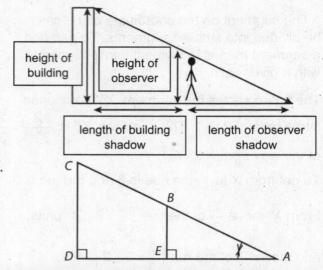

A 6-foot tall man, casting a 2-foot long shadow, is looking up at a building that casts a 22-foot long shadow. Use the figure below to help calculate the height of the building.

1. Which segment represents the height of the building? _____

2. On the figure below, label the segments that represent the height of the man and the shadows with their lengths.

3. What triangles are similar in the figure? _____

   and _____

4. Write a proportion that shows the relation between the corresponding segments in the triangles.

5. How tall is the building? _____

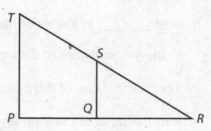

LESSON 12-4 — Similarity in Right Triangles
Reteach

In the proportion $\dfrac{a}{b} = \dfrac{b}{c}$, b is called the *geometric mean* of a and c.

The geometric mean of 16 and 4 can be found by setting up the proportion $\dfrac{16}{b} = \dfrac{b}{4}$ and solving for b by cross-multiplying.

$$16 \times 4 = b^2 \qquad b = \sqrt{64} = 8$$

Find the geometric mean of the given numbers.

1. 4 and 25

2. 9 and 100

3. 8 and 12

The altitude of a right triangle is the geometric mean of the lengths of the segments of the hypotenuse.

In the figure, $\dfrac{9}{x} = \dfrac{x}{4}$ $9 \cdot 4 = x^2$ $x = \sqrt{36} = 6$.

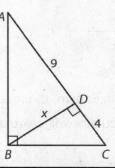

Find the missing length in the right triangle.

4. $EH = 6$, $GH = 3$, $FH = $ _____

5. $EH = 12$, $FH = 6$, $HG = $ _____

6. $EG = 19$, $EH = 15$, $FH = $ _____

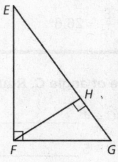

LESSON
13-1
Tangent Ratio
Reteach

In a right triangle, the longest side, the side opposite
the right angle, is called the *hypotenuse*.
In the figure, the side opposite of $\angle X$ is $\overline{YZ}$.
$\overline{XY}$ is the side *adjacent* to $\angle X$.

The *tangent* (tan) ratio for $\angle X$ is $\dfrac{\text{opposite}}{\text{adjacent}}$.

If $YZ = 3$ and $XY = 4$, then $\tan X = \dfrac{3}{4} = 0.75$.

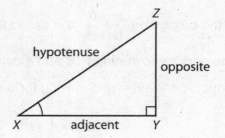

Find the tangent of $\angle R$ and $\angle T$.

1. $\tan R =$ _____

2. $\tan T =$ _____

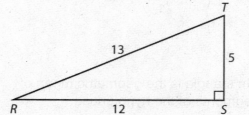

If a tangent ratio is known, the *inverse tangent* $\left(\tan^{-1}\right)$
function on a calculator will calculate the angle
measurement.

In the figure, $\tan X = \dfrac{8}{16}$.

So, $m\angle X = \tan^{-1}\dfrac{8}{16} = 26.6°$.

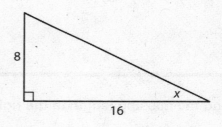

Find the measure of angle C. Round to the nearest tenth if necessary.

3. $AB = 3$ and $BC = 4$ _____

4. $BC = 9$ and $AB = 5$ _____

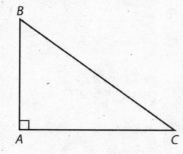

LESSON 13-2

Sine and Cosine Ratios
Reteach

In a right triangle, the sine of an angle is the ratio of the length of the side opposite side to the hypotenuse.

The cosine of an angle is the ratio of the length of the side adjacent to the hypotenuse.

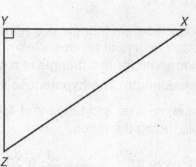

In the figure:

$$\sin \angle X = \frac{YZ}{XZ} \text{ and } \cos \angle X = \frac{XY}{XZ} \qquad \sin \angle Z = \frac{XY}{XZ} \text{ and } \cos \angle Z = \frac{YZ}{XZ}.$$

Find the sine and cosine of angles *A* and *B* in the figure.

1. sin *A* = _____   cos *A* = _____

2. sin *B* = _____   cos *B* = _____

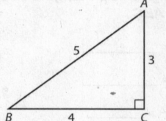

When the sine or cosine ratio of an angle is known, the angle measure can be determined using inverse operations.

The sine of an angle is equal to the cosine of that angle's complement.

In the figure, the sin of $\angle A = \frac{12}{13}$, so $m\angle A = \sin^{-1}\left(\frac{12}{13}\right) \approx 67.4°$.

So, sin 67.4° is equal to cos 22.6° because 90° − 67.4° = 22.6°.

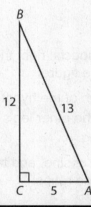

Calculate the following values from triangle *RST*. Round to the nearest tenth, if necessary.

3. cos ∠*R* = _____

4. m∠*R* = _____

5. sin ∠*S* = _____

6. m∠*S* = _____

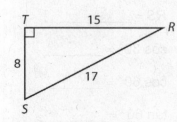

LESSON 13-3

Special Right Triangles
Reteach

An isosceles-right triangle is a right triangle with two congruent legs. The base angles of an isosceles-right triangle both measure 45°, so another name for this triangle is a 45-45-90 triangle. Both legs are the same length. The hypotenuse length is the leg length times $\sqrt{2}$.

The sine, cosine, and tangent of 45° can be calculated from the triangle, using the ratios.

$$\sin 45° = \cos 45° = \frac{x}{x\sqrt{2}} = \frac{1}{\sqrt{2}} = \frac{\sqrt{2}}{2} \qquad \tan 45° = \frac{x}{x} = 1$$

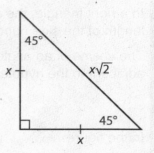

Find the given side lengths and angle measurements for triangle *ABC*.

1. BC = _____

2. AC = _____

3. m∠A = _____

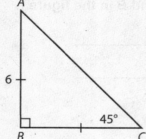

Another special right triangle is the 30-60-90 triangle like triangle *XYZ* in the figure.

The length of the hypotenuse is double the length of the shorter leg, and the other leg's length is $\sqrt{3}$ times the length of the shorter leg.

The sine, cosine, and tangent of 30° and 60° can be calculated using these ratios.

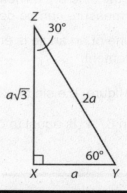

Find the indicated values from the figure.

4. RT = _____   5. RS = _____

6. sin 30° = _____   7. cos 30° = _____

8. sin 60° = _____   9. cos 60° = _____

10. tan 30° = _____   11. tan 60° = _____

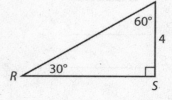

LESSON 13-4

Solving Right Triangles
Reteach

A triangle is *solved* when the measures of all three angles and all three sides are known. We can solve a right triangle using trigonometry ratios and the Pythagorean theorem.

Using the given information in the figure, we can

solve the triangle by finding *DF* and the measures

of all three angles.

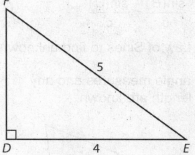

$\cos \angle E = \dfrac{4}{5}$, so $m\angle E = \cos^{-1}\left(\dfrac{4}{5}\right) \approx 36.9°$

$m\angle F = 90° - m\angle E \approx 53.1°$

$FE^2 = FD^2 + DE^2$

$FD = \sqrt{FE^2 - DE^2}$

$FD = \sqrt{5^2 - 4^2} = \sqrt{9} = 3$

Solve the triangle by finding the missing information. Round to the nearest tenth, if necessary.

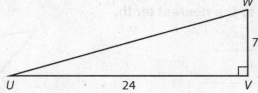

1. $m\angle U = $ _____

2. $m\angle W = $ _____

3. $UW = $ _____

The area of a triangle can be found if the measures of one of its angles and the length of the sides adjacent to that angle are known.

The area of triangle *ABC* can be found using the formula:

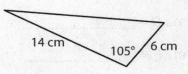

$\dfrac{1}{2}ab\sin C$ or $\dfrac{1}{2}bc\sin A$ or $\dfrac{1}{2}ac\sin B$, depending on the information given. In the figure, the triangle has an area of

$\dfrac{1}{2}(14)(6)\sin(105°) \approx 40.6$ cm².

What is the area of triangle *XYZ* in the figure?
Round to the nearest tenth, if necessary.

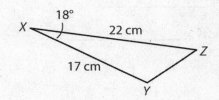

4. Area of *XYZ* is about _____.

LESSON 14-1

Law of Sines
Reteach

The Law of Sines

For $\triangle ABC$,

$$\frac{\sin(A)}{a} = \frac{\sin(B)}{b} = \frac{\sin(C)}{c}$$

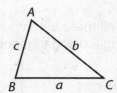

Use the Law of Sines to find unknown measures of a triangle when:

Two angle measures and any side length are known.	Two side lengths and the measure of a non-included angle are known.

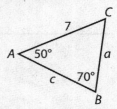

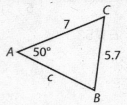

In the figure, the Law of Sines could be used to find c, $m\angle B$, and $m\angle C$.

In the figure, the Law of Sines could be used to find c, a, and $m\angle C$.

Use the Law of Sines to find the unknown measures for the given triangle. Round to the nearest tenth.

1. $n =$ _____

   $p =$ _____

   $m\angle P =$ _____

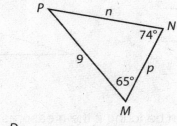

2. $d =$ _____

   $m\angle D =$ _____

   $m\angle F =$ _____

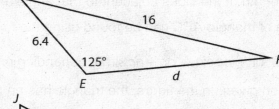

3. $g =$ _____

   $k =$ _____

   $m\angle K =$ _____

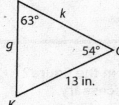

LESSON 14-2

Law of Cosines

Reteach

The Law of Cosines

For $\triangle ABC$,

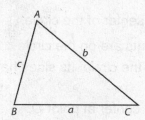

$a^2 = b^2 + c^2 - 2bc \cos A$

$b^2 = a^2 + c^2 - 2ac \cos B$

$c^2 = a^2 + b^2 - 2ab \cos C$

Use the Law of Cosines to find unknown measures of a triangle when:

Two side lengths and the measure of the included angle are known.

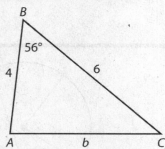

In the figure, the Law of Cosines could be used to find b, m$\angle A$, and m$\angle C$.

Three side lengths are known.

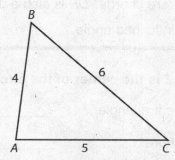

In the figure, the Law of Cosines could be used to find m$\angle A$, m$\angle B$, and m$\angle C$.

Use the Law of Cosines to find the unknown measures for the given triangle. Round to the nearest tenth.

1. $y =$ _____

   m$\angle X =$ _____

   m$\angle Z =$ _____

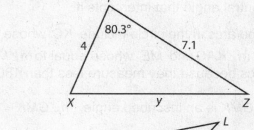

2. m$\angle J =$ _____

   m$\angle K =$ _____

   m$\angle L =$ _____

3. $d =$ _____

   m$\angle E =$ _____

   m$\angle F =$ _____

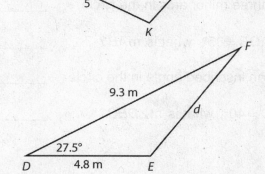

LESSON 15-1

Central Angles and Inscribed Angles
Reteach

A central angle has its vertex at the center of the circle.

A chord is a segment whose endpoints are on the circle.

An inscribed angle has its vertex on the circle. Its sides have points on the circle.

In the figure, there is a circle with its center at point *O*.

There are several central angles in the figure.

∠*EOB*, ∠*BOA*, ∠*AOD*, and ∠*BOD* are the four central angles in the figure.

$\overline{CD}$ and $\overline{DE}$ are chords. $\overline{DE}$ is also a diameter.

∠*CDE* is an inscribed angle.

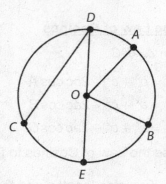

In the figure, *Z* is the center of the circle.

1. Name a central angle. _____

2. Name a chord. _____

3. Name an inscribed angle. _____

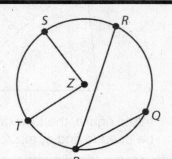

An arc is part of a circle. A semicircle is an arc that is half the circle. The measure of an arc is equal to the measure of the central angle that intercepts it.

Two of the arcs in the circle include $\overset{\frown}{KC}$ whose measure is equal to m∠*KAC* and $\overset{\frown}{ME}$ whose equal to m∠*MAE*. These are *minor* arcs because they measure less than 180 degrees.

Since ∠*GMK* is an inscribed angle, $m∠GMK = \frac{1}{2}m\overset{\frown}{GK}$.

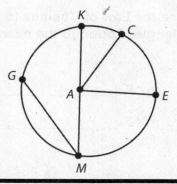

In the figure, *O* is the center of the circle.

4. Name three minor arcs in the circle. _____

5. If m∠*AOB* = 85°, what is m$\overset{\frown}{AB}$? _____

6. Name an inscribed angle in the circle. _____

7. If m$\overset{\frown}{DC}$ = 40°, what is m∠*DEC*? _____

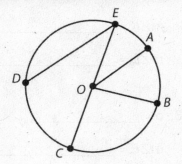

LESSON 15-2

Angles in Inscribed Quadrilaterals

Reteach

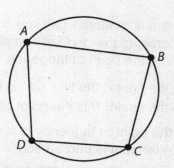

In the figure, quadrilateral *ABCD* is *inscribed* in the circle. Its four vertices are points on the circle.

In an inscribed quadrilateral, the opposite angles are supplementary to each other. Their measures add up to 180°. This is based on the inscribed quadrilateral theorem which is proved in questions 1–5 below.

In the figure, $m\angle A + m\angle C = 180°$ and $m\angle B + m\angle D = 180°$.

Answer the following questions to prove the theorem about inscribed quadrilaterals.

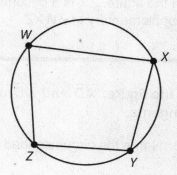

1. $m\angle$ _____ is $\frac{1}{2} m\widehat{SPQ}$.

2. $m\angle$ _____ is $\frac{1}{2} m\widehat{SRQ}$.

3. Complete the equation: $m\widehat{SPQ} + m\widehat{SRQ} =$ _____

4. Complete the equation: $\frac{1}{2} m\widehat{SPQ} + \frac{1}{2} m\widehat{SRQ} =$ _____

5. Substitute angle measure expressions from 1 and 2 that state the theorem:

$$m\angle \text{\_\_\_\_} + m\angle \text{\_\_\_\_} = \text{\_\_\_\_}°$$

In the figure, quadrilateral *WXYZ* is inscribed in the circle.

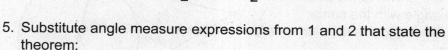

6. If $m\angle W = 85°$, what is $m\angle Y$? _____

7. If $m\angle Z = 95°$, what is $m\angle X$? _____

LESSON 15-3

Tangents and Circumscribed Angles
Reteach

A line is tangent to a circle if it
intercepts the circle at exactly one
point, the point of tangency.

In the figure, the line $\overleftrightarrow{QP}$ is tangent
to the circle. *P* is the point of tangency.

If the point of tangency is the endpoint of a radius,
the tangent is perpendicular to that radius.

In the figure, since $\overline{OP}$ is a radius, $\overleftrightarrow{QP} \perp \overline{OP}$.

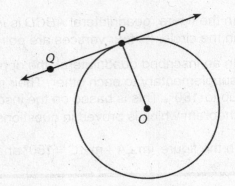

In the figure, $\overline{XY}$ is a radius of circle *X*, and $\overline{ZY}$ is a tangent.

1. Name the point of tangency. _____

2. What is the measure of ∠ZYX? _____

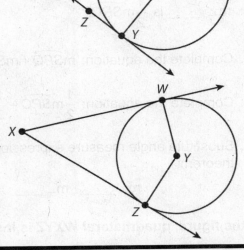

A circumscribed angle is an angle whose rays are
tangent to a circle. If radii are drawn to the point
of tangency, they form an angle with the center
of the circle as the vertex. That angle is supplementary
to the circumscribed angle.

In the figure, ∠X is a circumscribed angle. ∠ZYW is
supplementary to ∠WXZ.

**In the figure, $\overline{AD}$ and $\overline{DC}$ are radii of circle *D*. $\overline{BA}$ and $\overline{BC}$ are
tangents.**

3. Name the circumscribed angle in the figure. _____

4. What is the measure of ∠DAB? _____

5. If m∠B = 45°, what is m∠CDA? _____

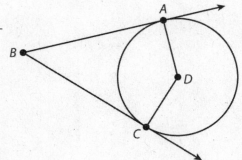

LESSON 15-4
Segment Relationships in Circles
Reteach

When two chords intersect in the interior of a circle, the products of the lengths of the segments of the chords are equal.

In the figure, $\overline{AB}$ and $\overline{CD}$ are chords that intersect at point E.

$$AE \cdot BE = CE \cdot DE$$

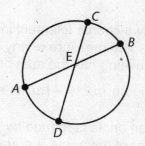

$\overline{WY}$ and $\overline{XZ}$ are chords that intersect at point V.

1. If $WV = 8$, $VY = 3$, $ZV = 6$, then $XV =$ _____

2. If $XZ = 9$, $ZV = 6$, $VY = 2$, then $WV =$ _____

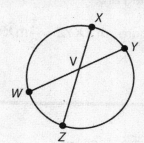

Segments that intersect a circle at two points are called *secants*. In the first figure $\overline{RT}$ and $\overline{RU}$ are secants with the common exterior point R.

When two secants share a common exterior point, the product of the lengths of the secants and their exterior segments are equal. In the figure, $RT \cdot RS = RU \cdot RV$.

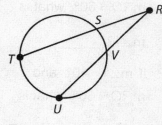

In the second figure, $\overline{MJ}$ is a tangent, and $\overline{MK}$ is a secant. Here the product of the length of the secant and its exterior segment is equal to the square of the length of the tangent segment.

$$KM \cdot LM = JM^2$$

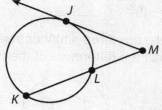

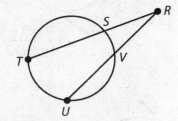

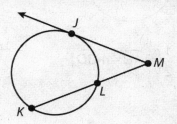

3. If $RT = 8$, $SR = 4$, $VR = 2$, then $UR =$ _____   4. If $JM = 4$, $ML = 2$, then $MK =$ _____

Angle Relationships in Circles
Reteach

When two chords intersect inside a circle, four angles are formed. The measure of any of these angles can be found by calculating half the sum of the arcs intercepted by the chords.

In the figure, $m\angle 1 = \frac{1}{2}\left(m\widehat{AB} + m\widehat{CD}\right)$.

When an angle is formed by a secant and a tangent, the measure of the angle is equal to half the measure of the intercepted arc.

In the figure, $m\angle XYZ = \frac{1}{2}m\widehat{XY}$.

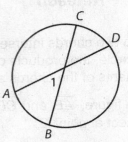

1. If $m\widehat{PS} = 30°$, and $m\widehat{RQ} = 60°$, what is

   $m\angle 1$? _____

2. If $m\angle 1 = 40°$, and $m\widehat{RQ} = 60°$, what is

   $m\widehat{PS}$? _____

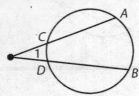

3. If $m\widehat{LN} = 160°$, what is $m\angle MLN$? _____

4. If $m\angle MLN = 92°$, what is $m\widehat{LN}$?

   _____

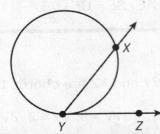

There are three situations where the measure of an exterior angle is equal to half the difference of the two intercepted arcs.

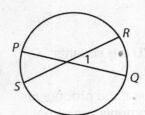

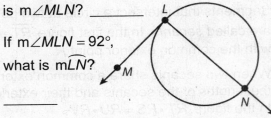

$m\angle 1 = \frac{1}{2}\left(m\widehat{AB} - m\widehat{CD}\right)$ $m\angle 1 = \frac{1}{2}\left(m\widehat{AC} - m\widehat{BC}\right)$ $m\angle 1 = \frac{1}{2}\left(m\widehat{BDC} - m\widehat{BC}\right)$

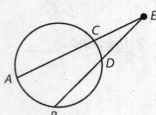

5. If $m\widehat{AB} = 60°$, and $m\widehat{CD} = 20°$, what is $m\angle E$?

   _____

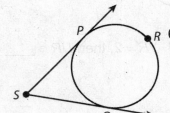

6. If $m\widehat{PRQ} = 260°$, and $m\widehat{PQ} = 100°$, what is $m\angle S$?

   _____

LESSON 16-1 Justifying Circumference and Area of a Circle
Reteach

The *circumference* of a circle is the distance around the circle. So, it is the same as the perimeter of a circle.

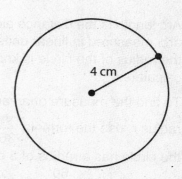

If the radius of a circle is known, the circumference is calculated by using the formula $C = 2\pi r$, where r is the radius of the circle.

If the diameter is known, the formula $C = \pi d$, where d is the diameter of the circle, is used to find the circumference. The length of the diameter is twice the length of the radius.

In the figure, the circumference of the circle is $2 \cdot \pi \cdot 4 = 8\pi \approx 25.13$ cm.

Find the circumference of each of the circles shown. Use 3.14 for pi and round your answer to the nearest hundredth.

1. radius = 6 in. C = _____

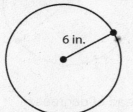

2. diameter = 12 cm C = _____

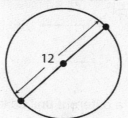

3. radius = 5 ft C = _____

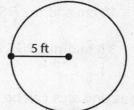

The area of a circle is calculated using the formula $A = \pi r^2$.

To find the area of the circle in the figure, first we take half of 10, since 10 is the length of the diameter, then use the formula.

$A = \pi \cdot 5^2 = 25\pi \approx 78.54$ cm^2

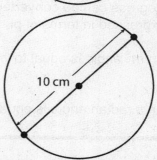

Find the area of each of the circles shown. Use 3.14 for pi and round to the nearest hundredth.

4. radius = 4 ft   Area = _____

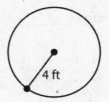

5. diameter = 12 cm   Area = _____

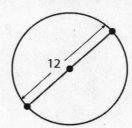

LESSON 16-2

Arc Length and Radian Measure
Reteach

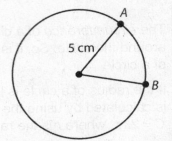

Arc length is the distance along a circular arc, measured in linear units. If the measure of the arc and the radius of the circle is known, the arc length can be calculated.

To find the measure of an arc of $m°$ in a circle of radius r, use the formula $\dfrac{m}{360} \cdot 2\pi r$. In the figure, $m\overset{\frown}{AB} = 60°$ and the circle has a radius of 5 centimeters. Therefore, the length of $\overset{\frown}{AB}$ is $\dfrac{60}{360} \cdot 2\pi(5) = \dfrac{1}{6} \cdot 10\pi \approx 5.24$ centimeters.

In the figure, $\angle RST$ intercepts $\overset{\frown}{RT}$. Find the measure of $\overset{\frown}{RT}$.

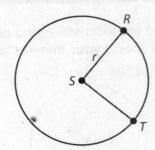

1. $r = 9$ m and $m\angle RST = 100°$ $m\overset{\frown}{RT} =$ _____

2. $r = 10$ cm and $m\angle RST = 90°$ $m\overset{\frown}{RT} =$ _____

3. $r = 3$ ft and $m\angle RST = 75°$ $m\overset{\frown}{RT} =$ _____

Angles and arcs can be measured in a different unit called *radians* instead of degrees. Degrees can be converted to radians (and vice versa) using a formula. Radians are usually expressed in terms of pi.

An $m°$ angle is equal to $m \cdot \dfrac{\pi}{180}$ radians. So, a 30° angle = $30 \cdot \dfrac{\pi}{180} = \dfrac{\pi}{6}$ radians

An n radian angle is equal to $n \cdot \dfrac{180°}{\pi}$. So, a $\dfrac{\pi}{4}$ radian angle = $\dfrac{\pi}{4} \cdot \dfrac{180}{\pi} = 45°$

Convert the following angles from degrees to radians.

4. 90° _____   5. 120° _____   6. 65° _____

Convert the following angles from radians to degrees.

7. $\dfrac{\pi}{3}$ rad _____   8. $\dfrac{3\pi}{4}$ rad _____   9. π rad _____

LESSON 16-3

Sector Area
Reteach

A *sector* is a portion of the area of a circle.

In the figure, central angle *AOB* intercepts the arc *AB*. The shaded region is a sector of the circle, which would be a fractional part of the entire area, which is πr^2.

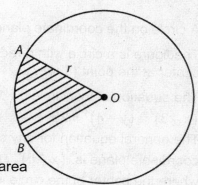

The area of a sector can be found using a formula that we can derive.
Remember that an entire circle is 360°. So, the fraction of the area for the sector is going to be the measure of the central angle divided by 360.

Calculate the missing information for the circles described.

1. A central angle of 30° would intercept what fraction (in lowest terms) of

   an entire circle? _____

2. If the circle had a radius of 5 cm, what would be the area of the circle?

   _____

3. The area of the sector would be found by the formula $-\times \pi \_\_^2$ which

   is about _____ cm².

$A = \dfrac{m}{360} \cdot \pi r^2$ where *m* is the measure of the central angle, and *r* is the radius of the circle, is the formula for the area of a sector.

If the radius of a circle is 2 feet and the central angle measures 60°, the area of the sector

measures $A = \dfrac{60}{360} \cdot \pi \cdot 2^2 = \dfrac{2\pi}{3} \approx 2.09 \text{ ft}^2$.

In the figure, $\angle XYZ$ is a central angle of a circle with radius *r*. Find the area of the sector.

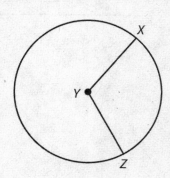

4. $r = 8$ cm and $m\angle XYZ = 90°$ _____

5. $r = 12$ in. and $m\angle XYZ = 45°$ _____

6. $r = 10$ ft and $m\angle XYZ = 180°$ _____

LESSON 17-1

Equation of a Circle

Reteach

A circle on the coordinate plane is represented by an equation.

The figure is a circle with a radius of 5 and center at the point (3, 4).

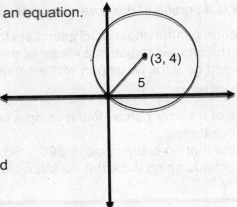

The equation of this circle is

$(x-3)^2 + (y-4)^2 = 25$

The general equation for any circle on the coordinate plane is. $(x-h)^2 + (y-k)^2 = r^2$

where the center of the circle is the point (h, k) and r is the radius.

Write the equation of the circle whose center and radius are given.

1. center (2, –2), r = 6

2. center (0, 0), r = 10

3. center (–4, –2), r = $\sqrt{5}$

_____   _____   _____

Sometimes a circle is given in the general form $x^2 + y^2 + Ax + By + C = 0$, where A, B, and C are constants. These equations can be changed into the form $(x-h)^2 + (y-k)^2 = r^2$ by completing the square as shown below.

$x^2 + y^2 - 2x - 4y - 4 = 0$	Original equation
$x^2 - 2x + y^2 - 4y = 4$	Group the variables.
$x^2 - 2x + 1 + y^2 - 4y + 4 = 4 + 1 + 4$	Complete the square.
$(x-1)^2 + (y-2)^2 = 9$	Factor and simplify.

The circle's center is (1, 2) and its radius is 3.

Write the equation in standard form for these circles written in general form.

4. $x^2 + y^2 - 4x - 6y + 8 = 0$

5. $x^2 + y^2 + 6x - 8y + 9 = 0$

_____   _____

LESSON 17-2

Equation of a Parabola
Reteach

A **parabola** is the set of all points P in a plane that are equidistant from a given point, called the **focus**, and a given line, called the **directrix**.

The general equation for a parabola on the coordinate plane is $(x - h)^2 = 4p(y - k)$

where the vertex of the parabola is the point (h, k) and p is the distance from the vertex to the focus.

A parabola with the vertex at the origin has a vertex of $(0, 0)$. When the vertex is at the origin, you replace (h, k) with $(0, 0)$ and the equation is $(x)^2 = 4p(y)$.

This can be rewritten as $y = \dfrac{1}{4p}x^2$.

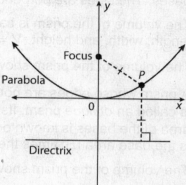

Given the focus and directrix, write the equation for the parabolas with the vertex at the origin. Write the equations in the $(x)^2 = 4p(y)$ and $y = \dfrac{1}{4p}x^2$ forms.

1. focus: $(0, 4)$, directrix: $y = -4$

_____

_____

2. focus: $(0, -1)$, directrix: $y = 1$

_____

_____

Now, imagine the first parabola is shifted 3 units to the right 3 and 1 unit up.

$(0, 4)$	Original focus.	$(3, 5)$	Shifted focus.
$y = -4$	Original directrix.	$y = -3$	Shifted directrix.
4	Original p.	4	Shifted p.
$(0, 0)$	Original vertex.	$(3, 1)$	Shifted vertex.

The equation for the original parabola is $(x - 0)^2 = 4(4)(y - 0)$.

The equation for the shifted parabola is $(x - 3)^2 = 4(4)(y - 1)$.

3. Write the equation for the second parabola after it is shifted 3 units to the right and 1 unit up.

_____

Name _____ Date _____ Class _____

Volume of Prisms and Cylinders
Reteach

A right prism is shown. The top and bottom quadrilaterals are the bases. The sides are perpendicular to the bases.

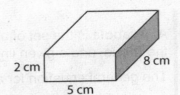

The volume of the prism is calculated by finding the product of its length, width, and height. $V = l \cdot w \cdot h$.

The volume of the prism shown is $2 \cdot 5 \cdot 8 = 80 \text{ cm}^3$.

A prism whose edges are not perpendicular to the bases is called an *oblique* prism. Its volume can be found if the area of the bases is known or can be calculated. The volume is the base area (B) times the height. $V = B \cdot h$

The volume of the prism shown is $15 \cdot 25 = 375 \text{ cm}^3$.

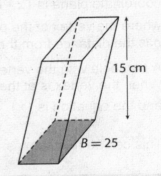

Calculate the volume of the following prisms.

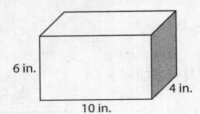

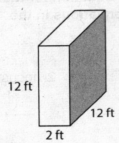

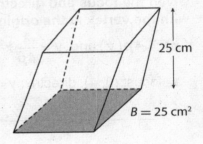

1. $V =$ _____

2. $V =$ _____

3. $V =$ _____

A right cylinder is shown. The volume is calculated using the formula $V = \pi r^2 \cdot h$, where h is the height of the cylinder, and r is the radius of the bases.

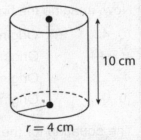

The volume of the cylinder is $V = \pi \cdot 4^2 \cdot 10 = 160\pi \approx 502.65 \text{ cm}^3$.

Calculate the volume of the following cylinders. Round to the nearest hundredth.

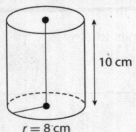

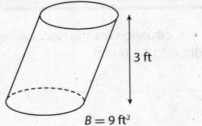

4. $V =$ _____

5. $V =$ _____

LESSON 18-2

Volume of Pyramids
Reteach

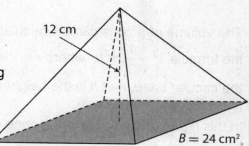

The height (*h*) of a pyramid is the distance from the top of the pyramid perpendicular to the base.

The volume of a pyramid can be found by first calculating the area of the base (*B*). Then, use the formula

$V = \dfrac{1}{3}Bh$ to find the volume.

In the figure, the volume of the pyramid is $\dfrac{1}{3}(24)(12) = 96 \text{ cm}^3$.

12 cm

$B = 24 \text{ cm}^2$

Calculate the volume of the following prisms.

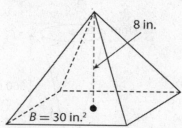

8 in.

$B = 30 \text{ in.}^2$

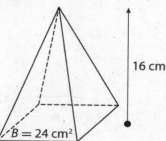

16 cm

$B = 24 \text{ cm}^2$

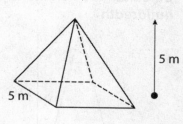

5 m

5 m

1. $V =$ _____

2. $V =$ _____

3. $V =$ _____

A *composite* solid is a combination of cubes, pyramids, and/or cylinders. The volume can be found by calculating the volumes of the individual parts and adding them together.

The solid is composed of a cube and a pyramid.

The volume of the cube is $2 \cdot 6 \cdot 4 = 48 \text{ cm}^3$ and the volume of the pyramid

is $\dfrac{1}{3} \cdot 8 \cdot 10 \approx 26.67 \text{ cm}^3$. The total volume is $48 + 26.67 = 74.67 \text{ cm}^3$.

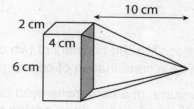

10 cm

2 cm

4 cm

6 cm

Answer the questions and find the missing values.

4. The composite figure consists of what three parts?

_____

5. Calculate the volumes of the parts.

_____

6. What is the total volume of the figure?

_____

10 m — 8 m — 10 m

1 m

1 m

LESSON
18-3

Volume of Cones
Reteach

The volume of a cone can be calculated using

the formula $V = \frac{1}{3}\pi r^2 h$, where r is the radius of

the circular base, and h is the height of the cone, perpendicular to the base.

In this figure, the volume of the cone is

$V = \frac{1}{3} \cdot \pi \cdot 6^2 \cdot 15 = 180\pi \approx 565.49 \text{ cm}^3$.

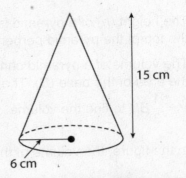

15 cm

6 cm

Calculate the volume of the following cones. Round to the nearest hundredth.

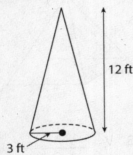

12 ft

3 ft

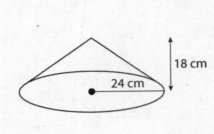

18 cm

24 cm

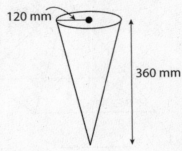

120 mm

360 mm

1. $V = $ _____

2. $V = $ _____

3. $V = $ _____

A *composite* solid consists of two or more solids joined together into a single shape. It can be a combination of cones, pyramids, cylinders, and/or rectangular prisms.

The volume of a composite solid can be calculated by finding the volumes of the individual pieces, then adding their volumes together.

Answer the questions about the figure.

4. The composite figure consists

of a _____ and a _____.

5. The volume of *a* is _____.

6. The volume of *b* is _____.

7. The total volume of the composite figure is

_____

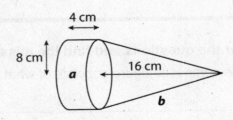

4 cm

8 cm

a

16 cm

b

_____ _____

LESSON 18-4

Volume of Spheres
Reteach

The volume of a sphere can be calculated using a formula when the radius of the sphere is known. The radius is measured from the center of the sphere to any point on the surface of the sphere.

The formula for the volume of a sphere is $V = \dfrac{4}{3}\pi r^3$.

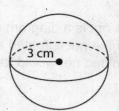

3 cm

In the figure, the volume of the sphere is $\dfrac{4}{3} \cdot \pi \cdot 3^3 = 36\pi \approx 113.10 \text{ cm}^3$.

Calculate the volume of the following spheres. Round to the nearest hundredth.

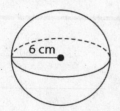

6 cm

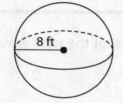

8 ft

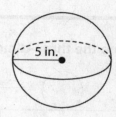

5 in.

1. $V =$ _____

2. $V =$ _____

3. $V =$ _____

A *composite* solid is a figure that consists of two or more solids. A composite solid can be made of spheres, cones, pyramids, cylinders, and/or rectangular prisms.

The volume of a composite solid is found by calculating the volumes of the individual parts and adding the volumes together.

Answer the questions about the composite figure.

4. What two solids make up the composite figure?

_____ and _____

5. The volume of **a** is _____.

6. The volume of **b** is _____. (Hint: how much of the part is seen in the figure?)

7. What is the total volume of the figure? _____

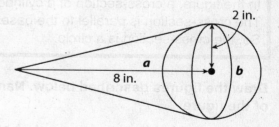

2 in.

a

8 in.

b

LESSON 19-1

Cross-Sections and Solids of Rotation
Reteach

A *net* is a diagram of the surfaces of a three-dimensional figure.
If the net is folded along the lines in the figure in the same direction, the
folded net would form a rectangular prism.

The figure…   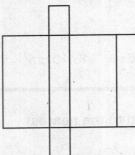   can fold to form:

Name the three-dimensional figures that the nets would form.

1. 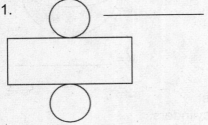 _____

2. 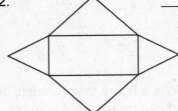 _____

A *cross-section* is a region of a plane that intersects a solid figure.
A cross-section is often a two-dimensional figure such as
a circle, parallelogram, or triangle.

In the figure, a cross-section of a cylinder is shown.
The cross-section is parallel to the bases of the cylinder.
So, the cross-section is a circle.

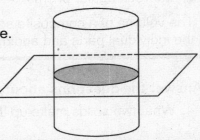

**Draw the figures described below. Name the cross-section
of the figure.**

3. A cylinder with a cross-section perpendicular to the bases.

4. A cone with a cross-section perpendicular to the bases.

5. A cone with a cross-section parallel to the bases.

LESSON 19-2
Surface Area of Prisms and Cylinders
Reteach

The surface area of a figure is the total area of the faces of the figure. For example, the figure is a rectangular prism with six faces. The surface area is the sum of the areas of the six faces.

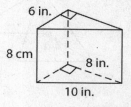

12 cm

2 cm

The top and bottom faces each have an area of 24 cm², the front and back each have an area of 60 cm², and the left and right each have an area of 10 cm². The total surface area would be $(2 \cdot 24) + (2 \cdot 60) + (2 \cdot 10) = 48 + 120 + 20 = 188$ cm².

The best strategy for calculating the surface area of a figure is to identify the parts that make up the figure (triangles, parallelograms, etc.), calculate their surface areas, and add the areas of the parts together.

Calculate the surface area of the figures shown below.

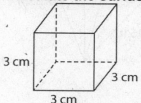

3 cm
3 cm
3 cm

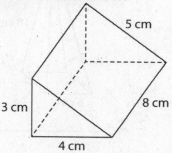

5 cm
3 cm
8 cm
4 cm

6 in.
8 cm
8 in.
10 in.

1. S = _____   2. S = _____   3. S = _____

The surface area of a cylinder can be found by adding the areas of the two bases and the area of the curved surface that wraps around the cylinder.

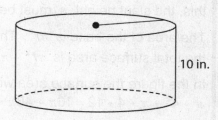

10 in.

The area of the two bases in the figure is $2 \cdot \pi \cdot 6^2 = 72\pi$

The curved area is the circumference of the base times the height, which is $10 \cdot 12 \cdot \pi = 120\pi$. The total surface area is $192\pi \approx 603.19$ in².

Calculate the surface area of the cylinders shown below.

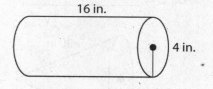

16 in.
4 in.

10 cm
5 cm

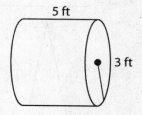

5 ft
3 ft

4. S = _____   5. S = _____   6. S = _____

LESSON 19-3

Surface Area of Pyramids and Cones
Reteach

A regular pyramid consists of a square base and four sides that are isosceles triangles. The surface area of the pyramid is calculated by adding the areas of those parts. To calculate the area of the triangles, the slant height (ℓ) of the pyramid must be known.

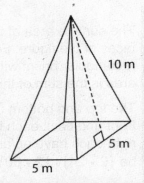

In the figure, the base area is 25 m², and each triangle has an area of $\frac{1}{2} \cdot 5 \cdot 10 = 25$ m². There are 4 triangles, so the triangles have a total area of 100 m². The total area of the pyramid is 125 m².

Calculate the surface area of the following regular pyramids.

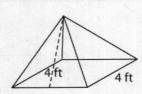

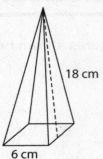

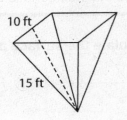

1. S = _____

2. S = _____

3. S = _____

The surface area of a cone can be found by adding the area of the base, which is a circle, to the area of the curved surface around the cone. For this, the slant height, *s*, must be known.

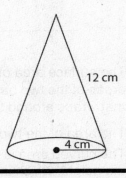

The area of the base is πr^2. The area of the curved surface is πrs, so the total surface area is $\pi r^2 + \pi rs$.

In the figure the surface area would be
$\pi \cdot 4^2 + \pi \cdot 4 \cdot 12 = 16\pi + 48\pi = 64\pi \approx 201.06$ cm².

Calculate the surface area of the following regular cones. Round to the nearest hundredth.

4. S = _____

5. S = _____

6. S = _____

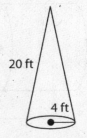

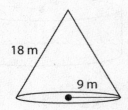

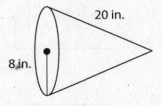

LESSON 19-4 Surface Area of Spheres
Reteach

The surface area of a sphere is calculated using the formula $S = 4\pi r^2$.

The radius (*r*) of a sphere is the distance from the center of the sphere to any point on the surface of the sphere.

In the figure, the surface area of the sphere is
$S = 4 \cdot \pi \cdot 6^2 = 144\pi \approx 452.39 \text{ cm}^2$.

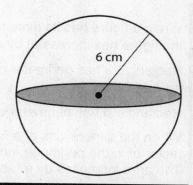

6 cm

Calculate the surface area of the following spheres. Round to the nearest hundredth.

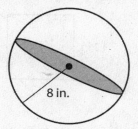

8 in.

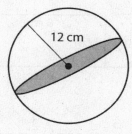

12 cm

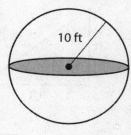

10 ft

1. $S =$ _____

2. $S =$ _____

3. $S =$ _____

The total surface area of this composite figure is found by calculating the surface areas of the parts and adding them together. The parts are a hemisphere and a cone.

The surface area of the hemisphere is $2\pi r^2 = 18\pi$.

The surface area of the cone is $\pi r^2 + \pi rs = 36\pi$.
The total surface area is 54π.

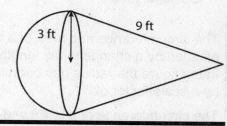

3 ft   9 ft

4. What are the shapes that make this composite figure?

_____

5. The surface area of **a** is _____.

6. The surface area of the curved part of **b** is _____.

7. The surface area of **c** is _____.

8. The surface area of the composite figure is _____.

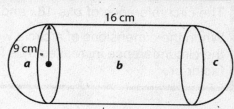

9 cm
a   16 cm
b   c

LESSON 20-1

Scale Factor
Reteach

When a figure has its dimensions doubled, it means the figure has increased by a *scale* factor of 2.

Rectangle **a** has perimeter of 16 cm and area of 12 cm^2.

Rectangle **b** has perimeter of 32 cm and area of 48 cm^2.

When the dimensions of a figure were increased by a scale factor of x, the perimeter increases by a factor of x. The area increases by a factor of x^2.

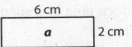
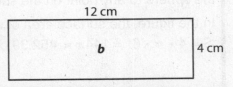

Find the perimeter and area of the figures when increased by scale factor.

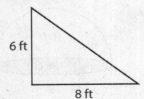
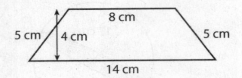
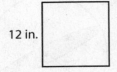

1. $P =$ _____ $A =$ _____

Scale factor 3

2. $P =$ _____ $A =$ _____

Scale factor 2

3. $P =$ _____ $A =$ _____

Scale factor 4

The circumference and area of a circle are affected by a change in the length of the radius. In the figure the radius has been increased by a scale factor of 3.

The circumference of **a** is 6π and its area is 9π.

The circumference of **b** is 18π and its area is 81π.

When the dimensions of a circle were increased by a scale factor of x, the circumference increases by a factor of x. The area increases by a factor of x^2.

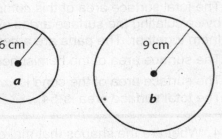

To the nearest hundredth, find the circumference and area when the circles are increased by the given scale factor.

By 2; $C =$ ____ $A =$ ____

By 10; $C =$ ____ $A =$ ____

By 25; $C =$ ____ $A =$ ____

LESSON 20-2

Modeling and Density

Reteach

There is a party with 45 people. The model shows where people are standing during the majority of the party.

To find the density of the population of the party, calculate the number of people per square foot.

First, find the area of the room.

$50 \times 30 = 1500$ square feet

Then, divide the population by the area. Since there were 45 people at the party:

$\dfrac{45}{1500} = 0.03$

The population density of the party room is 0.03 people per square foot.

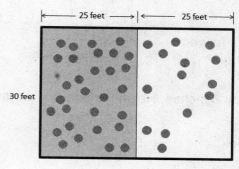

50 feet

30 feet

During the party, people were dancing. The area of the dance floor is shaded in the model.

To find the population density of the dance floor, calculate the number of people per square foot.

First, find the area of the dance floor.

$25 \times 30 = 750$ square feet

Then, divide the population by the area.

There were 30 people on the dance floor.

$\dfrac{30}{750} = 0.04$

The population density of the dance floor is 0.04 people per square foot.

25 feet ──── 25 feet

30 feet

Use the models above to answer the questions.

1. What is the area of the room that did not contain the dance floor?

   _____

2. What is the population of the part of the room that did not contain the dance floor? _____

3. What is the population density of the part of the room that does not contain the dance floor? _____

Problem Solving with Constraints
Reteach

An aquarium's height is equal to the measure of its width. The length of the aquarium is equal to $\frac{3}{2}$ of the width. The volume of the aquarium is 768 in³.

What are the aquarium's dimensions?

Known Dimensions: *height = width* *length = $\frac{3}{2}$ width* *volume = 768 in³*	Missing Dimensions: *width = ?* inches

Substitute the known dimensions into the formula for volume of a prism.

Volume = $l \times w \times h$

$768 = \frac{3}{2}w \times w \times w = \frac{3}{2}w^3$

Solve for width. $w^3 = \frac{2}{3}(768)$

$w = \sqrt[3]{512} = 8$

Width: 8 inches. Height: 8 inches. Length: $\frac{3}{2} \times 8 = 12$ inches

Check:

Volume = $l \times w \times h$

$V = 12 \times 8 \times 8 = 768$

The volume of the aquarium is 768 in³.

The cylinder's height is equal to twice the measure of the cylinder's radius. The volume of the cylinder is 50.24 ft³. Use 3.14 for π. Find the missing dimension.

1. What is the cylinder's height? _____

2. What is the cylinder's radius? _____

3. What is the cylinder's diameter? _____

LESSON 21-1 Probability and Set Theory
Reteach

Basic Set Vocabulary:

- **element** an object in a set (often a number or event)
- **empty set** a set with no elements; symbol is $\varnothing$
- **set** a collection of distinct objects called elements
- **subset** a smaller set of elements within a universal set
- **universal set** a complete collection of elements

The **theoretical probability** of an event is the likelihood that an event will happen, where all possible outcomes are equally likely.

Theoretical Probability of A: $P(A) = \dfrac{\text{number of outcomes for event } A}{\text{total possible outcomes in universal set}} = \dfrac{n(A)}{n(U)}$

1. Consider the universal set of all odd numbers between 1 and 15: $U = \{1, 3, 5, 7, 9, 11, 15\}$.
   Complete the chart for each subset of the universal set.

Description of Subset	Set Notation	Number of Elements in Subset	Number of Elements in Universal Set
Multiples of 3	$A = \{$ _____ $\}$	$n(A) =$ _____	$n(U) = 7$
Multiples of 5	$B = \{$ _____ $\}$	$n(B) =$ _____	$n(U) = 7$

Suppose each element in *U* is written on a card. Calculate the theoretical probability of randomly choosing a number of each type from the set of cards.

2. $P(A) = \dfrac{n(A)}{n(U)} =$ _____

3. $P(B) = \dfrac{n(B)}{n(U)} =$ _____

The **intersection** of sets A and B, $A \cap B$, is the set of all elements in **both A and B.**

The **union** of sets A and B, $A \cup B$, is the set of all elements in A **and/or** in B.

The **complement** of set A is the set of all elements in the universal set that are **not** in A.

4. Use the Venn diagram at right to organize the elements in
   $U = \{0, 4, 6, 9, 12, 16, 20\}$,
   when $C = \{0, 6, 12\}$ and
   $D = \{0, 4, 16\}$.

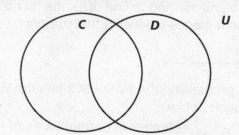

LESSON 21-2

Permutations and Probability

Reteach

To find the number of permutations of 3 objects chosen out of 10 total objects, use the "blank method."

A Draw the number of blanks in which the objects will be placed: ☐ ☐ ☐ .

B Record the number of options you have for the first blank: 10 ☐ ☐ .

C Record the number of options you have for the second blank, after the first object has been placed: 10 9 ☐

D Record the number of options you have for the third blank, after the first two objects have been placed: 10 9 8

E Continue until all blanks are filled with a number. Multiply the numbers in the blanks to find the total permutations of 3 objects chosen out of 7 objects: $10 \cdot 9 \cdot 8 = 720$

You can use this method to find the total number of permutations in the sample space, $n(S)$, as well as the total number of permutations of a specific type, $n(A)$. Calculate the probability of A as $\dfrac{n(A)}{n(S)}$.

1. A jewelry store clerk will choose 4 pieces of jewelry to display on a shelf. The clerk will choose the 4 pieces randomly from a group of 8 pieces. Solve for $n(S)$, the total number of different possible ways to choose the jewelry to display on the shelf.

   a. Use the space above to draw the appropriate number of blanks.

   b. How many options are there for the first blank, given that the clerk is choosing from 8 pieces? Record that number in the first blank.

   c. After the first piece is placed, how many options are there for the second blank? Record that number in the second blank.

   d. Fill in each remaining blank with the number of options that are left for each one.

   e. Write and solve a multiplication sentence to find how many possible ways there are to choose the jewelry to display on the shelf.

   $n(S) = $ _____

2. Suppose that, 5 of the pieces of jewelry the clerk can select from are made of gold. Let event A be "All 4 pieces on display are gold." What is the probability of A?

   a. Use the blank method to find $n(A)$, the number of different possible ways there are to choose 4 pieces of jewelry that are gold.

   $n(A) = $ _____

   b. Find the probability of A by substituting the values you found into the equation below.

   $P(\text{all gold}) = P(A) = \dfrac{\text{number of permutations of 4 gold pieces}}{\text{total possible permutations of 4 pieces}} = \dfrac{n(A)}{n(S)} = $ _____

<table>
<tr><td>LESSON
21-3</td><td># Combinations and Probability
Reteach</td></tr>
</table>

Permutations vs. Combinations

- Remember to use a **permutation** when **order matters,** and a **combination** when **order does not matter**.

- There are fewer combinations of a group of objects than there are permutations. You must divide the number of permutations by the number of permutations of the "blanks" in order to find the smaller number of combinations.

To find the number of combinations of 4 objects chosen out of 9 total objects, use the following steps.

A Draw the number of blanks in which the objects will be placed: ☐ ☐ ☐ ☐

B Use the "blank method" to find the number of permutations: $9 \cdot 8 \cdot 7 \cdot 6 = 3024$.

C Find the factorial of the number of blanks: $4! = 4 \cdot 3 \cdot 2 \cdot 1 = 24$

D Divide the number from **B** by the number from **C**: $\dfrac{3024}{24} = 126$

You can use this method to find the total number of combinations in the sample space, $n(S)$, as well as the total number of combinations of a specific type, $n(A)$. Calculate the probability of A as $\dfrac{n(A)}{n(S)}$.

For 1–2, say whether each is an example of a combination or a permutation.

1. Picking a group of 3 winners to come in first place, second place, and third place. _____

2. Picking a group of 3 winners from a group of 8 finalists. _____

3. Mike is choosing 3 books to borrow from a friend. He selects the books from the shelf at random. The shelf contains 11 books.

　a. Use the blank method to find how many permutations there are of 3 books chosen from the 11 on the shelf.

　　_____

　b. Find the factorial of the number of blanks.

　　_____

　c. Write and solve a division sentence to find the total number of combinations, $n(S)$, of 3 books.

　　$n(S) =$ _____

4. Suppose that the shelf contains 5 fiction books. Let event A be "All books that Mike chooses are fiction." What is the probability of A?

　a. Write and solve a division sentence to find the total number of combinations, $n(A)$ of 3 fiction books.

　　$n(A) =$ _____

　b. Find the probability of A by substituting the values you found into the equation below.

$$P(\text{all fiction}) = P(A) = \frac{\text{number of combinations of 3 fiction books}}{\text{total possible combinations of 3 books}} = \frac{n(A)}{n(S)} = \underline{\hspace{2cm}}$$

LESSON 21-4 Mutually Exclusive and Overlapping Events
Reteach

If two events are **mutually exclusive**, then they cannot occur at the same time.
If two events are **overlapping**, then they can occur at the same time.

A and B are
mutually exclusive

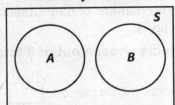

A and B are
overlapping

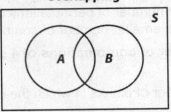

The **Addition Rule** tells you how to find the probability that *A* **or** *B* occurs.

- Addition Rule for mutually exclusive *A* and *B*: $P(A \text{ or } B) = P(A) + P(B)$

- Addition Rule for overlapping *A* and *B*: $P(A \text{ or } B) = P(A) + P(B) - P(A \text{ and } B)$

Examples of the Addition Rule:

- Find the probability that a multiple of 5 or an even number is rolled on a number cube.
  The events are mutually exclusive because they cannot both occur at once:

$$P(A \text{ or } B) = P(A) + P(B) = \frac{1}{6} + \frac{1}{6} = \frac{2}{6} = \frac{1}{3}$$

- Find the probability that a multiple of 3 or an even number is rolled on a number cube.
  The events are overlapping because both occur when 6 is rolled:

$$P(A \text{ or } B) = P(A) + P(B) - P(A \text{ and } B) = \frac{2}{6} + \frac{3}{6} - \frac{1}{6} = \frac{4}{6} = \frac{2}{3}$$

For 1–4, determine whether the two events are mutually exclusive or overlapping.

1. rolling an even number on a die; rolling a 6 on a die _____

2. rolling an odd number on a die; rolling a 2 on a die _____

3. drawing a face card from a deck of cards; drawing a 5 from a deck of cards _____

4. drawing a spade from a deck of cards; drawing a 7 from a deck of cards _____

Use the appropriate version of the Addition Rule to find each probability.

5. P(rolling an even number on a die or rolling a 6 on a die) = _____

6. P(rolling an odd number on a die or rolling a 2 on a die) = _____

7. P(drawing a spade from a deck of cards or drawing a 7 from a deck of cards) = _____

LESSON 22-1

Conditional Probability
Reteach

The **two-way frequency table** shows the genders and grade levels of students who attended a school district meeting.

	Boys	Girls	TOTAL
Middle School	20	25	45
High School	35	20	55
TOTAL	55	45	100

Let *A* be that a student is a boy and let *B* be that a student is a middle-schooler. To find the **conditional probability** that a student who is a boy is also a middle-schooler,

use $P(A|B) = \dfrac{P(\text{both middle-schooler and boy})}{P(\text{boy})} = \dfrac{n(A \cap B)}{n(B)}$.

- Look at the column that shows event *B*: This is the **Boys** column. Now look at the cell in this column that shows **both *A* and *B***, the number of middle school boys: 20.

- $n(B)$ is the total in the column: $n(B) = 55$.

- $n(A \cap B)$ is the number in the cell: $n(A \cap B) = 20$.

So, $P(A|B) = \dfrac{n(A \cap B)}{n(B)} = \dfrac{20}{55} \approx 36\%$. The probability that a student is

middle-schooler, given that he is a boy, is about 36%.

Use the table above to identify the totals, and then calculate the conditional probabilities.

1. Let *A* be that a student is a high-schooler. Let *B* be that a student is a boy. Find $P(A|B)$, the probability that a student who is a boy is also a high-schooler.

   a. What is the total in the *B* column? $n(B) =$ _____

   b. What is the total in the cell for *A* and *B*? $n(A \cap B) =$ _____

   c. $P(A|B) = \dfrac{n(A \cap B)}{n(B)} =$ _____

2. Let *A* be that a student is a girl. Let *B* be that a student is a middle-schooler. Find $P(A|B)$, the probability that a student who is a middle-schooler is also a girl.

   a. What is the total in the *B* row? $n(B) =$ _____

   b. What is the total in the cell for *A* and *B*? $n(A \cap B) =$ _____

   c. $P(A|B) = \dfrac{n(A \cap B)}{n(B)} =$ _____

LESSON
22-2

Independent Events
Reteach

If $P(A) = P(A|B)$ and $P(A \text{ and } B) = P(A) \cdot P(B)$, then A and B are independent.

	Prefers Rock	Prefers Classical	TOTAL
Male	12	3	15
Female	24	6	30
TOTAL	36	9	45

The table shows the genders and music preference in a group of people. Let A be that a person prefers rock and let B be that a person is male. Are A and B independent?

Method 1: Test whether $P(A) = P(A|B)$.

- $P(A) = \dfrac{36}{45} = \dfrac{4}{5}$ and $P(A|B) = \dfrac{12}{15} = \dfrac{4}{5}$. Therefore, $P(A) = P(A|B) = \dfrac{4}{5}$ and whether a person likes rock is independent of whether the person is male.

Method 2: Test whether $P(A \text{ and } B) = P(A) \cdot P(B)$.

- $P(A) = \dfrac{36}{45} = \dfrac{4}{5}$, $P(B) = \dfrac{15}{45} = \dfrac{1}{3}$, and $P(A \text{ and } B) = \dfrac{4}{15}$. Therefore,

  $P(A \text{ and } B) = P(A) \cdot P(B) = \dfrac{4}{5} \cdot \dfrac{1}{3} = \dfrac{4}{15}$ and whether a person likes

  rock is independent of whether the person is male.

If events A and B are independent, then $P(A \text{ and } B) = P(A) \cdot P(B)$.

Let C be that a person is female. Let D be that a person prefers rock. Use the table above to answer the questions.

1. Use **Method 1** to determine whether C is independent of D.

   a. $P(C) =$ _____   b. $P(C|D) =$ _____

   c. Is C independent of D? _____

2. Use **Method 2** to determine whether C is independent of D.

   a. $P(C) =$ _____   b. $P(D) =$ _____   c. $P(C \text{ and } D) =$ _____

   d. Is C independent of D? _____

3. Events E and F are independent. $P(E) = \dfrac{1}{2}$ and $P(F) = \dfrac{2}{5}$. What is

   the probability that both E and F will occur?

   $P(E \text{ and } F) =$ _____

LESSON 22-3

Dependent Events
Reteach

If *A* and *B* are **independent events**, then whether *A* happens or not has no effect on whether *B* happens. In cases of **selection with replacement**, the events are independent.

If *A* and *B* are **dependent events**, then the outcome of *A* has an effect on whether *B* happens. In cases of **selection without replacement**, the events are dependent.

Suppose a card is randomly selected from a deck, the deck is shuffled, and then a second card is drawn from the deck. Let *A* be selecting a spade on the first draw. Let *B* be selecting a spade on the second draw.

- If the first card is replaced, you start with the same set of cards for each draw. In this case, *A* and *B* are **independent** events.

- If the first card is **not** replaced before the second draw, the deck on the second draw is not exactly the same as the deck on the first draw. In this case, *A* and *B* are **dependent** events.

For each pair of events, determine whether *A* and *B* are independent or dependent.

1. Event *A* is rolling a 3 on the first roll of a number cube.
   Event *B* is rolling a 2 on the second roll of the number cube.

   _____

2. Event *A* is pulling a blue marble from a bag of colored marbles.
   Event *B* is pulling a blue marble on the second draw, given that the first marble pulled is **not** put back in the bag.

   _____

If events A and B are dependent, then $P(A \text{ and } B) = P(A) \cdot P(B|A)$.

A card is randomly selected from a deck and not replaced, the deck is shuffled, and then a second card is selected from the deck. Let *A* be selecting a spade on the first draw. Let *B* be selecting a spade on the second draw. What is the probability of getting a spade on both draws?

- There are 13 spades in a complete deck of 52 cards: $P(A) = \dfrac{13}{52}$

- If a spade is drawn first, there are 12 spades and 51 cards at the start of the second draw: $P(B|A) = \dfrac{12}{51}$

- $P(A \text{ and } B) = P(A) \cdot P(B|A) = \dfrac{13}{52} \cdot \dfrac{12}{51} = \dfrac{1}{17}$

3. A card is randomly selected from a deck and not replaced. The deck is shuffled, and then a second card is drawn. Let *A* be selecting a 2 on the first draw. Let *B* be selecting a 2 on the second draw. What is the probability that a 2 will be drawn both times?

   a. $P(A) =$ _____   b. $P(B|A) =$ _____   c. $P(A \text{ and } B) =$ _____

LESSON 23-1

Using Probability to Make Fair Decisions
Reteach

Using Probabilities and a Spinner

Suppose 4 people are playing a game. Each player is assigned one of the equally sized number sections on the spinner. When the spinner lands on your number, you get to go first in the game.

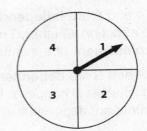

Two more people want to join the game; now there are 6 players. Since the spinner only has 4 sections, 2 more sections were created by drawing on the current spinner. Now there are 6 sections.

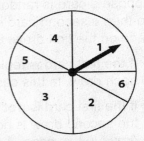

Use the original spinner and the altered spinner to determine whether the statements are true or false. For each statement, explain your reasoning.

1. The original spinner gave each of the 4 players a fair chance at going first.

   _____

2. Why?

   _____

3. The adjusted spinner gave each of the 6 players a fair chance at receiving a point.

   _____

4. Why?

   _____

5. Players 2, 4, 5, and 6 did not want to use the adjusted spinner because their sections on the spinner were smaller than the sections for players 1 and 3. The players decide to create a new spinner containing 6 equally sized sections. Draw a new spinner that all 6 players will be happy using to determine who will go first in the game.

Analyzing Decisions

LESSON 23-2

Reteach

Some professional sports teams test for illegal substances in players. The *Play Clean* test claims to detect an illegal substance, called *Perform X*.

Play Clean's developer tested their product on a large number of people. Of the people tested, only 2% had *Perform X* in their system. Of those people that had *Perform X* in their system, 87% of them tested positive using the *Play Clean* test. For those that did not have *Perform X* in their system, the Play Clean test accurately tested negative 90.2% of the time.

Play Clean Testing Data

	Perform X Users (2%)	Never Used Perform X (98%)
Tested Positive	87%	9.8%
Tested Negative	13%	90.2%

Analyzing the Testing Data

	Perform X Users (2%)	Never Used Perform X (98%)
Tested Positive	True Positive: 2% × 87%	False Positive: 98% × 9.8%
Tested Negative	False Negative: 2% × 13%	True Negative: 98% × 90.2%

To determine the accuracy of the *Play Clean* test, determine what the chances are that a person with *Perform X* in his or her system would test positive on the *Play Clean* test. Find the probability of having *Perform X* in the system and testing positive on the *Play Clean* test.

To do this, use **Bayes' Theorem**.

$$P(B \mid A) = \frac{P(A \mid B)P(B)}{P(A)}$$

Bayes' theorem finds the actual probability of an event from the results of the tests and lets you relate the actual probability to the measured test probability.

$$P(Perform\ X \mid Positive) = \frac{P(Perform\ X) \times P(Positive \mid Perform\ X)}{P(Positive)} = \frac{2\% \times 87\%}{2\% \times 87\% + 98\% \times 9.8\%}$$

$$= \frac{0.0174}{0.0174 + 0.09604} = \frac{0.0174}{0.11344} = 15.3\%$$

So, if the *Play Clean* test shows positive for *Perform X*, then the chance that the person actually has *Perform X* in his or her system is about 15%.

1. Use the information above. If 1000 people took the *Play Clean* test, about how many people would test positive for *Perform X*?

   _____

2. Of those that tested positive for *Perform X*, about how many would actually have that substance in their system?

   _____

Algebraic Representations of Transformations

KEY TEACHING POINTS

Example 1

Be sure students understand how the direction of movement in a translation relates to the change in coordinates between the preimage and the image.

Say: A translation describes movement on the coordinate plane. A translation rule tells you the direction of movement and how many units to move in that direction.

Ask: In triangle *ABC*, how can you move from point *A* to point *A'* on the coordinate plane? **[Move right 2 units, and then move down 4 units.]**

Ask: Which coordinate is changed by a horizontal translation? **[*x*-coordinate]**

Ask: Which coordinate is changed by a vertical translation? **[*y*-coordinate]**

Ask: How do you represent a translation 2 units right and 4 units down algebraically? **[Add 2 to the *x*-coordinate and subtract 4 from the *y*-coordinate.]**

Ask: Did the translation change the shape or size of a figure? **[No.]** Did the translation change the orientation of a figure? **[No.]**

Check

Check that students understand that the prime symbol (') is used to name the vertices of the image and that a double prime (") represents a second image (Problem 8 in the next Check).

Problem 3

Ask: What number can you add to the *x*-coordinate of each vertex in the preimage that results in the *x*-coordinate of each vertex in the image? **[Add 5.]**

Example 2

Ask: When a point is reflected over the *x*-axis, which coordinate stays the same? **[*x*-coordinate]** When a point is reflected over the *y*-axis, which coordinate stays the same? **[*y*-coordinate]**

Ask: Which points in the preimage are 4 units from the *x*-axis? **[points *W* and *X*]** Which points in the image are 4 units from the *x*-axis? **[points *W'* and *X'*]**

Ask: Did the reflection change the shape or size of a figure? **[No.]** Did the reflection change orientation of a figure? **[Yes.]**

Check
Problem 5

Ask: Will the *x*-coordinates of the vertices change? **[Yes; the *x*-coordinates will be multiplied by −1]** Will the *y*-coordinates of the vertices change? **[No.]**

Problem 6

Ask: Which coordinate remains unchanged? **[*y*-coordinate]**

Problem 8

Be sure students understand that they are performing two reflections.

Example 3

Ask: How can you describe the change in coordinates for a 90° clockwise rotation about the origin? **[Sample answer: Reverse the order of the *x*- and *y*-coordinates; then multiply the *x*-coordinate by −1]**

Ask: What are the coordinates of point *T*? **[(−4, 0)]** point *T'*? **[(0, 4)]**

Ask: What would be the coordinates of point *T'* after a 180° rotation? **[(4, 0)]** 270° rotation? **[(0, −4)]**

Ask: Did the rotation change the shape or size of a figure? **[No.]** Did the rotation change orientation of a figure? **[Yes.]**

Have students verify with a ruler that each vertex in the preimage is the same distance from the origin as the corresponding vertex in the image.

Check
Problem 12

Ask: Within what quadrant does the image lie? **[Quadrant I]**

Ask: If the image has been rotated 270° clockwise about the origin, within what quadrant does the preimage lie? **[Quadrant IV]**

Problem 13

Bring students' attention to the horizontal side of the triangle with endpoints (−1, 2) and (−4, 2).

Ask: Will this side of the triangle be a horizontal line segment or a vertical line segment after a 90° rotation? **[vertical]** 180° rotation? **[horizontal]** 270° rotation? **[vertical]**

Example 4

Ask: The scale factor is 2. Will this dilation result in an enlargement or a reduction? **[enlargement]**

Ask: How can you find the coordinates of the image after a dilation about the origin? **[Multiply each coordinate by 2.]**

Ask: What is the length of segment *JM*? **[4 units]**

Ask: What is the length of segment *J'M'*? **[8 units]**

Ask: What is the ratio of the length of *JM* to the length of *J'M'*? **[2:1]**

Ask: Did the dilation change the shape or size of a figure? **[Yes; the size changed]** Did the dilation change orientation of a figure? **[No]**

Check
Problem 15

Encourage students to sketch a graph before solving the problem.

Ask: Is the dilation an enlargement or a reduction? **[reduction]** Will the scale factor be less than 1 or greater than 1? **[less than 1]**

ALTERNATE STRATEGY

Strategy: Draw lines through the origin to verify a dilation.

1. Have students copy the graph from Example 4.

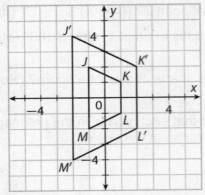

2. Have students start at the origin and draw a line from the origin through each vertex of the preimage and the image.

3. **Ask:** What do you notice about the lines? **[The vertices of the preimage lie on the same line as the corresponding vertices of the image.]**

4. Have students measure each of the lines they drew. For example, students will measure the line from (0, 0) to point *J* and measure the line from (0, 0) to point *J'*.

5. **Ask:** What do you notice about the distance from the origin of the vertices of the image compared to the distance from the origin of the vertices of the preimage? **[The distance from the origin of the vertices of the image are 2 times the distance from the origin of the vertices of the preimage.]**

After students have worked through Problem 15, have them copy the graph and draw a line from the origin through each vertex of the preimage and image. Since the vertices of the preimage and the corresponding vertices of the image do not lie on the same line, this is not a dilation about the origin. Challenge students to use a ruler to redraw the preimage or the image so that the dilation is correct.

COMMON MISCONCEPTION

Example 1

Students may be in the habit of finding the vertical change and then finding the horizontal change between two points, based on their experience of finding slope, $\frac{\text{rise}}{\text{run}}$. Emphasize that the *x*-coordinate changes by the value of the horizontal translation and the *y*-coordinate changes by the value of the vertical translation.

Problem 14

Students may recognize that the side lengths of $\triangle X'Y'Z'$ are $\frac{1}{2}$ the measures of the side lengths of $\triangle XYZ$. However, since you cannot map $\triangle XYZ$ onto $\triangle X'Y'Z'$ using $(x,y) \rightarrow \left(\frac{1}{2}x, \frac{1}{2}y \right)$, this is not a dilation about the origin.

Error: The coordinates of the image are not multiplied by the scale factor $\frac{1}{2}$.

Solution: $\triangle X'Y'Z'$ is the image of $\triangle XYZ$ with vertices $X(2, 6)$, $Y(6, 6)$, $Z(6, 2)$ after a dilation of $\frac{1}{2}$ about the origin.

ADDITIONAL ONLINE INTERVENTION RESOURCES

 Use the following for students who have not mastered the concepts in Skill 1.

- Math on the Spot videos

- Personal Math Trainer with customized intervention

- Building Block worksheets (Skill 46: Graph Ordered Pairs (First Quadrant); Skill 51: Integer Operations; Skill 55: Logical Reasoning)

SKILL 1 — Algebraic Representations of Transformations

A transformation maps a figure, called the preimage, onto a new figure called the image. Types of transformations include translations, reflections, rotations, and dilations.

Example 1

Vocabulary
Transformation
Preimage
Image
Translation
Reflection
Line of reflection
Rotation
Dilation

A translation moves a figure to a new position without turning it.

To translate a figure, add the horizontal translation to the x-coordinate and add the vertical translation to the y-coordinate of each vertex.

$(x, y) \rightarrow (x + a, y + b)$

- If a is positive, the figure is translated to the right.

- If a is negative, the figure is translated to the left.

- If b is positive, the figure is translated up.

- If b is negative, the figure is translated down.

Triangle ABC with vertices $A(-2, 3)$, $B(2, 5)$, and $C(2, 2)$ is translated 2 units right and 4 units down.
$(x, y) \rightarrow (x + 2, y - 4)$

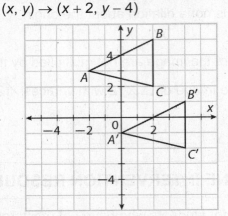

The coordinates of the image are $A'(0, -1)$, $B'(4, 1)$, and $C'(4, -2)$.

Check

1. $\triangle DEF$ has vertices $D(1, 1)$, $E(2, 4)$, and $F(5, 2)$. What are the coordinates of the vertices of the image after a translation 3 units right and 2 units up?

   _____

2. Graph $\triangle JKL$ with vertices $J(3, -1)$, $K(4, -4)$, and $L(2, -4)$. Then graph the image of $\triangle JKL$ after a translation 4 units left and 1 unit up.

3. Parallelogram $GHIJ$ has vertices $G(-4, -3)$, $H(-1, -2)$, $I(-2, -5)$, and $J(-5, -6)$. The coordinates of its image after a translation are $G'(1, 0)$, $H'(4, 1)$, $I'(3, -2)$, and $J'(0, -3)$. Describe the translation.

   _____

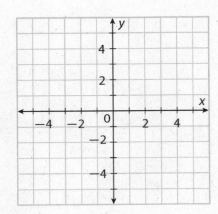

Example 2

A reflection is a mirror image of the original figure over a line of reflection.

Reflection over the x-axis

To reflect a figure over the x-axis, multiply the y-coordinate by –1.

$(x, y) \rightarrow (x, -y)$

Reflection over the y-axis

To reflect a figure over the y-axis, multiply the x-coordinate by –1.

$(x, y) \rightarrow (-x, y)$

In a reflection, each point of the preimage and its image is the same distance from the line of reflection.

Trapezoid *WXYZ* with vertices $W(-2, 4)$, $X(2, 4)$, $Y(3, 2)$, and $Z(-3, 2)$ is reflected over the x-axis.

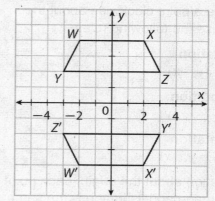

The coordinates of the image are $W'(-2, -4)$, $X'(2, -4)$, $Y'(3, -2)$, and $Z'(-3, -2)$.

Check

Find the coordinates of the image after each reflection.

4. Triangle *LMN* with vertices $L(-1, 3)$, $M(2, 5)$, and $N(2, 2)$ over the

   x-axis _____

5. Quadrilateral *EFGH* with vertices $E(-4, 2)$, $F(-1, 1)$, $G(-1, -2)$, and

   $H(-3, -3)$ over the y-axis _____

The coordinates of a point and its image are given. Determine whether the reflection is over the x-axis or the y-axis.

6. $(3, 0) \rightarrow (-3, 0)$ _____

7. $(-2, -6) \rightarrow (-2, 6)$ _____

8. Graph the reflection of rectangle *QRST* over the y-axis. Then graph the image of rectangle *QRST* after a reflection over the x-axis. What are the coordinates of rectangles *Q'R'S'T'* and *Q"R"S"T"*?

   _____

Example 3

A rotation turns a figure about a fixed point.

To rotate a point clockwise about the origin, use the following rules:

90° Rotation
$(x, y) \rightarrow (y, -x)$

180° Rotation
$(x, y) \rightarrow (-x, -y)$

270° Rotation
$(x, y) \rightarrow (-y, -x)$

In a rotation about the origin, each point of the preimage and its image is the same distance from the origin.

Triangle TUV with vertices $T(-4, 0)$, $U(-3, 4)$, and $V(-1, 2)$ is rotated 90° clockwise about the origin.

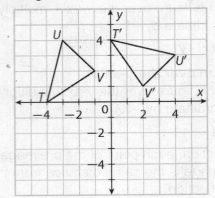

The coordinates of the image are $T'(0, 4)$, $U'(4, 3)$, and $V'(2, 1)$.

Check

Pentagon $ABCDE$ has vertices $A(-3, 1)$, $B(-1, -2)$, $C(-1, -4)$, $D(-5, -4)$, and $E(-5, -2)$. Find the coordinates of the image after each clockwise rotation about the origin.

9. 90° rotation _____

10. 180° rotation _____

11. 270° rotation _____

12. Triangle XYZ is rotated 270° clockwise about the origin. The coordinates of the image are $X'(1, 4)$, $Y'(5, 6)$, $Z'(2, 1)$. What are the coordinates of triangle XYZ?

13. Graph the image of the figure after a 90°, 180°, and 270° clockwise rotation about the origin on the same coordinate plane.

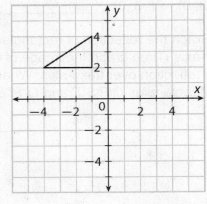

Example 4

A dilation uses a scale factor to enlarge or reduce the size of a figure.

To dilate a figure about the origin, multiply each coordinate by the scale factor k.

$$(x, y) \rightarrow (kx, ky)$$

The scale factor determines the size of the image

- If $k > 1$, the dilation is an enlargement.

- If $k < 1$, the dilation is a reduction.

- If $k = 1$, the size of the original figure does not change.

In a dilation for $k \neq 1$, the preimage and its image are the same shape, but not the same size.

Trapezoid *JKLM* with vertices $J(-1, 2)$, $K(1, 1)$, $L(1, -1)$, and $M(-1, -2)$ is dilated by a factor of 2.

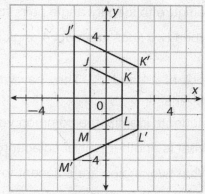

The coordinates of the image are $J'(-2, 4)$, $K'(2, 2)$, $L'(2, -2)$, and $M'(-2, -4)$.

Check

14. Explain the Error. Use the graph to the right. Find the correct solution. Triangle *XYZ* is dilated about the origin by a scale factor of $\frac{1}{2}$.

_____

_____

15. A triangle has vertices $C(-3, 3)$, $D(3, 3)$, and $E(0, 6)$. The coordinates of the image after a dilation is $C'(-2, 2)$, $D'(2, 2)$, and $E'(0, 4)$. What is the scale factor of the dilation?

_____

SKILL 1 ALGEBRAIC REPRESENTATIONS OF TRANSFORMATIONS

Angle Relationships

KEY TEACHING POINTS

Example 1
Use the figure to identify angle pairs formed by intersecting lines.

Say: When two lines intersect 4 angles are formed. Some of these angles form special angle pairs.

Say: Look at ∠1 and ∠2. They have a common vertex and share a common side. These are adjacent angles.

Have students identify the common vertex and the common side for angles 1 and 2.

Ask: What is another pair of adjacent angles that includes ∠1? **[∠1 and ∠4]**

Ask: What two angles are adjacent to ∠4? **[∠1 and ∠3]**

Say: Look at ∠1 and ∠3. These are vertical angles. Vertical angles are opposite angles and they are congruent.

Ask: Which angle has the same measure as ∠2? Why? **[∠4; ∠2 and ∠4 are vertical angles, so they are congruent.]**

Check
Problem 3
Remind students that the symbol m∠4 means the measure of angle 4.

Example 2
Make sure students can identify a right angle and a straight angle.

Say: Look at the first figure.

Ask: What type of angle is formed by ∠5 and ∠6? **[a right angle]**

Ask: What is the measure of a right angle? **[90°]** What is the sum of the measures of ∠5 and ∠6? **[90°]**

Say: The sum of the measures of complementary angles is 90°. So, ∠5 and ∠6 are complementary angles.

Say: Look at the second figure.

Ask: What type of angle is formed by ∠7 and ∠8? **[a straight angle]**

Ask: What is the measure of a straight angle? **[180°]** What is the sum of the measures of ∠7 and ∠8? **[180°]**

Say: The sum of the measures of supplementary angles is 180°. So, ∠7 and ∠8 are supplementary angles.

Check
Problems 5–7
Check that students correctly identify the angles that combine to form right angles and straight angles.

Ask: What two angles form a straight angle? **[∠1 and ∠2]** What is the sum of these angle measures? **[180°]**

Ask: What two angles form a right angle? **[∠4 and ∠5]** What is the sum of these angle measures? **[90°]**

Problem 8
Ask: What equation can you use to find the value of x? **[x + 50 = 180]**

Example 3
Say: In this example, you will use what you know about angle relationships to find missing angle measures.

Ask: What angle measure is known? **[m∠3 = 23°]** What angle measure do you need to find? **[m∠1]**

Ask: Does ∠3 form a special angle relationship with ∠1? **[No.]**

Say: Look for other angle relationships in the figure.

Ask: Does ∠3 form a special angle relationship with another angle? **[Yes; ∠3 and ∠5 are vertical angles.]**

Ask: Does ∠1 form a special angle relationship with another angle? **[Yes; ∠1 and ∠5 are complementary angles.]**

Say: You can use the known measure of ∠3 to find the measure of ∠5. Then you can use the measure of ∠5 to find the measure of ∠1.

Ask: What is the measure of ∠5? How do you know? **[23°; ∠3 and ∠5 are congruent.]**

Ask: What equation can you use to find the measure of ∠1? **[m∠1 + 23 = 90]**

Check
Problems 11–15
Have students analyze the figure before completing the problems.

Ask: What are all of the vertical angle pairs in the figure? **[∠1 and ∠4, ∠2 and ∠5, ∠3 and ∠6]** Which angles are complementary angles? **[∠1 and ∠6]**

Problem 16
Ask: What is the sum of ∠ACB, ∠ECD, and ∠BCD? **[180°]** How do you know? **[They form a straight angle.]**

Problem 17
Ask: What equation can you use to find the value of x? **[3x + 45 = 90]**

Problem 18
Ask: Since the angles are vertical angles, what do you know about their angle measures? **[The angle measures are equal.]** Since the angles are supplementary angles, what do you know about the sum of their angle measures? **[The sum of the angle measures is 180°.]**

ALTERNATE STRATEGY

Strategy: Reposition angles to form right angles and straight angles.

1. Tell students that angles do not need to be adjacent to be complementary or supplementary angles.

2. Have students use a protractor to draw the following angles.

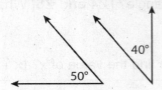

3. **Ask:** Are these angles complementary, supplementary, or neither? Why?
   [complementary; The sum of the angle measures is 90°]

4. Have students check their answer by repositioning the angles to form a right angle as shown.

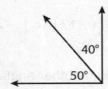

5. Have students use a protractor to draw the following angles.

6. **Ask:** Are these angles complementary, supplementary, or neither? Why?
   [supplementary; The sum of the angle measures is 180°.]

7. Have students check their answer by repositioning the angles to form a straight angle as shown.

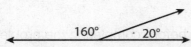

COMMON MISCONCEPTIONS

Check
Problem 10

Ask: What is the measure of each angle? **[90°]** What is the sum of the angle measures? **[180°]**

Error: Students may associate 90° angles with complementary angles, instead of finding the sum of the angles.

Solution: The sum of the angle measures is 180°, so the angles are supplementary.

KEY TEACHING POINTS

Example 3
Students may incorrectly classify angle pairs when working with multiple intersecting lines. Watch for students who incorrectly identify ∠2 and ∠4 as vertical angles. Encourage students to identify the lines that intersect to create each angle. If the same two lines are used to create both angles, then the angles are vertical.

Other students may incorrectly identify ∠2 and ∠3 as complementary angles. Remind students that they can only use what is given in the figure. The figure shows that ∠1 and ∠5 form a right angle. Since ∠5, ∠1, and ∠2 form a straight line, ∠2 is a right angle.

ADDITIONAL ONLINE INTERVENTION RESOURCES

 Use the following for students who have not mastered the concepts in Skill 2.

- Math on the Spot videos

- Personal Math Trainer with customized intervention

- Building Block worksheets (Skill 7: Angle Relationships; Skill 15: Classify Angles; Skill 16: Classify Lines; Skill 53: Line Symmetry; Skill 56: Measure Angles; Skill 66: Name and Classify Angles; Skill 95: Solve Proportions; Skill 98: Solve Two-Step Equations; Skill 102: Symmetry)

SKILL 2 — Angle Relationships

Example 1

Adjacent angles are pairs of angles that share a common vertex and a common side. Adjacent angles: ∠1 and ∠2, ∠2 and ∠3, ∠3 and ∠4, ∠4 and ∠1	Vertical angles are opposite angles formed by the intersection of two lines. Vertical angles are congruent. 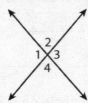 Vertical angles: ∠1 and ∠3, ∠2 and ∠4 Also, ∠1 ≅ ∠3 and ∠2 ≅ ∠4.

Vocabulary
Adjacent angles
Vertical angles
Congruent
Complementary angles
Supplementary angles

Check

Classify each pair of figures as *adjacent* or *vertical* angles.

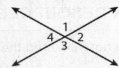

1. ∠1 and ∠2 _____

2. ∠1 and ∠3 _____

3. ∠3 and ∠4 _____

4. ∠2 and ∠4 _____

5. ∠2 and ∠3 _____

6. ∠1 and ∠4 _____

7. If m∠4 = 80°, find m∠2. _____

8. If m∠3 = 100°, find m∠1. _____

Example 2

The sum of the measures of complementary angles is 90°.

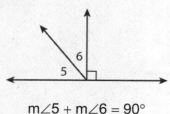

$$m\angle 5 + m\angle 6 = 90°$$

The sum of the measures of supplementary angles is 180°.

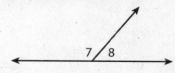

$$m\angle 7 + m\angle 8 = 180°$$

Check

Use the figure. Describe each pair of angles as *complementary*, *supplementary*, or *neither*.

9. $\angle 1$ and $\angle 5$ _____

10. $\angle 1$ and $\angle 2$ _____

11. $\angle 4$ and $\angle 5$ _____

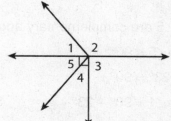

Find the measure of *x* in each figure.

12.

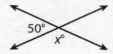

13.

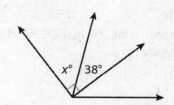

_____

14. Explain the Error. Find the correct solution.

Each angle has a measure of 90°, so the angles are complementary.

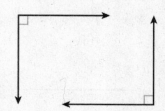

Example 3

The measure of ∠3 is 23°. Find the measure of ∠1.

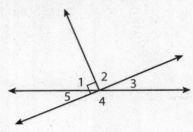

∠5 and ∠3 are vertical angles, so ∠5 ≅ ∠3.

∠5 ≅ ∠3

m∠5 = 23°   m∠3 = 23°

∠1 and ∠5 are complementary angles, so m∠1 + m∠5 = 90°.

m∠1 + m∠5 = 90°

m∠1 + 23° = 90°   m∠5 = 23°

m∠1 = 90° − 23°   Subtract 23° from each side.

m∠1 = 67°   Simplify.

Check

The measure of ∠6 is 72°. Find the measure of each angle. Explain your answer.

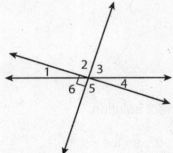

15. m∠1 _____

16. m∠2 _____

17. m∠3 _____

18. m∠4 _____

19. m∠5 _____

20. ∠P and ∠Q are adjacent angles. ∠P and ∠R are vertical angles. The measure of ∠Q is 36° and the measure of ∠R is 121°. What is the measure of ∠P?

_____

21. Write an equation to represent the sum of the measures of ∠ACB, ∠BCD, and ∠ECD. Then find m∠BCD.

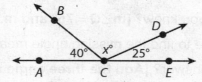

_____

22. ∠A and ∠B are complementary angles. The measure of ∠A is (3x)° and the measure of ∠B is 45°. What is the value of x?

_____

23. Two vertical angles are supplementary. What is the measure of each angle?

_____

24. Angles S and T are complementary angles. If m∠S is x° and m∠T is (x + 10)°, find the measure of each angle.

_____

SKILL 2 ANGLE RELATIONSHIPS

Angle Theorems for Triangles

KEY TEACHING POINTS

Example 1

Ask: What is the sum of the measures of the interior angles of a triangle? **[180°]**

Ask: What angle measures do you know? **[m∠Q = 75° and m∠R = 45°]**

Ask: What equation can you use to find the missing angle measure? **[x + 45 + 75 = 180]**

Ask: How can you check your answer? **[Add the three angle measures to make sure the sum is 180: 60 + 45 + 75 = 180.]**

Check
Problem 4

Make sure students include the right angle in their equations.

Ask: What two angle measures are given in the figure? **[25° and 90°]**

Problem 5

Ask: What information are you given in the problem? **[The sum of two angles is 118°.]**

Ask: How can you solve this problem without knowing the measures of the two angles? **[You can use the sum of two of the angles to find the measure of the third angle.]**

Ask: What equation can you use to solve the problem? **[x + 118 = 180]**

Problem 7

Ask: What equation can you use to solve the problem? **[x + x + 80 = 180 or 2x + 80 = 180]**

Example 2

Make sure students understand how to solve multi-step equations.

Ask: What are the three angle measures shown in the figure? **[2x, x, and 120]**

Ask: What is the sum of these angles? **[180]**

Ask: What equation can you write to solve for x? **[x + 2x + 120 = 180]**

Say: Once we find the value of x are we finished with the problem? **[No.]** What do we need to find? **[the measures of the three angles]**

Ask: What are the angle measures of the triangle? **[m∠J = 40°, m∠K = 20°, and m∠L = 120]**

Remind students that the question asks for all of the angle measures, so they should include the given angle measure of 120°. Encourage students to add the measures of the angles to check their answers.

Check

Problems 8–11

Check that students correctly set up the equations for each triangle.

Problem 12

Ask: What do you know about the angle measures in an equilateral triangle? **[The angles are equal.]**

Ask: What equation can you write to solve for x? **[$4x + 4x + 4x = 180$]**

Some students may determine that each angle in an equilateral triangle measures 60° and solve the equation $4x = 60$.

Example 3

Say: An exterior angle is formed by one side of the triangle and the extension of the adjacent side. An exterior angle always forms a linear pair with one of the interior angles. Each exterior angle has two remote interior angles that are not adjacent to the exterior angle.

Ask: What are the interior angles of the triangle? **[∠1, ∠2, ∠3]**

Ask: Which angle is an exterior angle? **[∠4]**

Ask: Which angle is adjacent to ∠4? **[∠3]**

Ask: What two angles are the remote interior angles for ∠4? **[∠1 and ∠2]**

Say: The measure of an exterior angle of a triangle is equal to the sum of the measures of its two remote interior angles. In this example, you need to find the measure of ∠2.

Ask: What angle measures do you know? **[m∠4 = 150° and m∠1 = 58°]**

Ask: What equation can you use to find m∠2? **[$x + 58 = 150$]**

Check

Problems 14–16

Suggest to students that for each exterior angle, they cover the adjacent angle so they can more easily identify the two remote interior angles.

Problem 23

Ask: What two relationships do you know about angle measures in a triangle? **[The sum of the interior angles is 180° and the exterior angle of a triangle is equal to the sum of its two remote interior angles.]**

Ask: Do you have enough information to solve for x using the relationship that the sum of the interior angles is 180°? **[No.]** Do you have enough information to solve for x using the relationship between exterior angles and remote interior angles. **[Yes.]**

Problem 25

Ask: Why do the two angles with a measure of $x°$ have equal measures? **[They are vertical angles, so they are congruent.]**

Ask: What relationship will you use to solve this problem? **[The sum of the interior angles of a triangle is 180°.]**

ALTERNATE STRATEGY

Strategy: Use models to show angle relationships in triangles.

1. Have students draw a triangle on a piece of paper. They should label the corners 1, 2, and 3 as shown below.

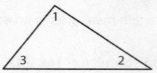

2. Have students cut or tear off the corners of the triangle. Rearrange the corners so that they meet in one point with no gaps or overlaps.

3. **Ask:** What do the torn corners represent? **[the angles of a triangle]** What is the sum of the measures of the angles? **[180°]** How do you know? **[They form a straight angle and the measure of a straight angle is 180°.]**

4. Have students repeat the activity using different-sized triangles.

5. **Ask:** Can you always arrange the three angles of a triangle so that they form a straight angle? **[Yes.]** What does that tell you about the sum of the angles in a triangle? **[The sum is 180°.]**

6. Have students draw another triangle with an exterior angle. Have students tear off the two remote interior angles and rearrange the pieces to show that the sum of the measures of the two interior angles is equal to the measure of the exterior angle.

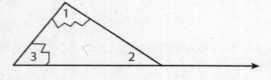 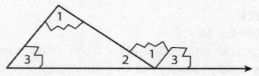

COMMON MISCONCEPTION

Problem 19
Some students may not correctly identify the exterior angle as an interior angle and find the sum of the interior angles. Remind students to check the reasonableness of their answers. Since the exterior angle is acute, the value for x should be less than 90°.

Problem 21
Ask: What is the sum of the interior angles that are given in the problem.
[20 + 90 + 110 = 220]

Ask: Why is this answer incorrect? **[The sum of the measures of a triangle is 180°.]**

Error: These are the measures of an exterior angle and its two remote interior angles.

Solution: The measures of the interior angles of the triangle are 20°, 70°, and 90°.

If students need additional help with this problem, have them draw a picture to represent the triangle with the given measurements. This will help them see that the right angle has to be a remote interior angle.

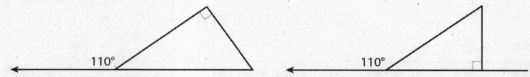

ADDITIONAL ONLINE INTERVENTION RESOURCES

Use the following for students who have not mastered the concepts in Skill 3.

- Math on the Spot videos

- Personal Math Trainer with customized intervention

- Building Block worksheets (Skill 8: Angles in Polygons; Skill 48: Identify Congruent Figures; Skill 74: Polygon Angle Measures; Skill 98: Solve Two-Step Equations; Skill 102: Triangle Sum Theorem)

SKILL 3

Angle Theorems for Triangles

Example 1

The sum of the measures of the interior angles of a triangle is 180°.
Find the value for x in △PQR.

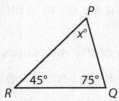

Vocabulary
Interior angle
Exterior angle

m∠P + m∠Q + m∠R = 180   Write an equation.

    x + 75 + 45 = 180   m∠P = x, m∠Q = 75, and m∠R = 45

       x + 120 = 180   Simplify.

           x = 60   Subtract 120 from each side.

The value of x is 60.

Check

Find the value of x in each triangle.

1.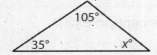

_____

2.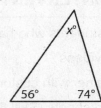

_____

3.

_____

4.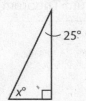

_____

5. The sum of two angles in a triangle is 118°. What is the measure of the
   third angle? _____

6. Two angles in a triangle measure 24° and 92°. What is the measure of
   the third angle? _____

7. A picture has a triangular frame. The measures of the two base angles
   are equal. The third angle measures 80°. What are the measures of
   the base angles? _____

Example 2

Find the measures of the angles.

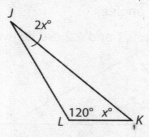

$m\angle J + m\angle K + m\angle L = 180$ Write an equation.

$x + 2x + 120 = 180$ $m\angle J = 2x$, $m\angle K = x$, and $m\angle L = 120$

$3x + 120 = 180$ Combine like terms.

$3x = 60$ Subtract 120 from each side.

$x = 20$ Divide each side by 20.

Replace x with 20 to find the missing angle measures.

$m\angle K = 20$ and $m\angle J = 2(20)$ or 40

The measures of the angle are 20°, 40°, and 120°.

Check

Find the measures of the unknown angles in each triangle.

8.

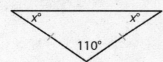

_____

9.

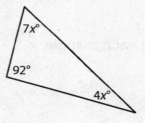

_____

10.

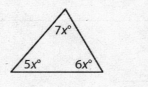

_____

11.

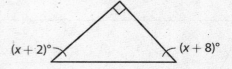

_____

12. The measure of an angle in an equilateral triangle is $4x$? What is the

    value of x? _____

13. The two acute angles in a right triangle measure $2x$ and $3x$. What are

    the measures of the angles in the triangle? _____

Example 3

The measure of an exterior angle of a triangle is equal to the sum of the measures of its two remote interior angles.

In the figure ∠4 is an exterior angle. ∠1 and ∠2 are its two remote interior angles.

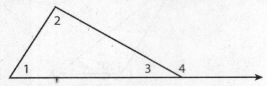

Suppose m∠4 = 150° and m∠1 = 58°. Find m∠2.

m∠1 + m∠2 = m∠4	Write an equation.
58 + m∠2 = 150	m∠1 = 58 and m∠4 = 150
m∠2 = 92	Subtract 58 from each side.

Check

Name the two remote interior angles for each exterior angle.

14. ∠4 _____

15. ∠5 _____

16. ∠6 _____

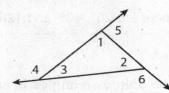

Find the value of x in each triangle.

17.

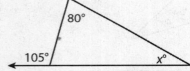

18.

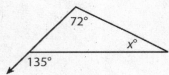

_____ _____

19.

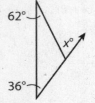

20.

_____ _____

21. Explain the Error. Find the correct solution.

    The exterior angle of a right triangle measures 110°. The measures of the interior angles in the right triangle are 20°, 90°, and 110°.

22. The measure of an exterior angle is 60°. The measures of its two remote interior angles are 2x and 3x. What are the angle measures of the triangle?

23. What is the value of x in the figure? Explain how you solved the problem.

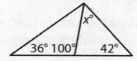

36° 100° 42°

_____

_____

24. The measures of two remote interior angles are $x + 5$ and $x - 2$. If $x = 20$, what is the measure of the exterior angle?

_____

25. Find the value of x and y in the figure. Show your work.

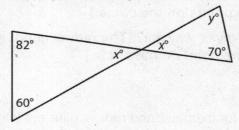

82°   x°   x°   70°   y°
60°

_____

_____

SKILL 3 ANGLE THEOREMS FOR TRIANGLES

Area of a Circle

KEY TEACHING POINTS

Example 1

Begin by reviewing the definition of a circle. Point out that a circle is a set of points that are all an equal distance from the center. Hence, every circle must have a center. Point out that this is important for knowing how to measure a circle.

The measure of a circle is determined by the longest segment that can be drawn between two points on the circle. This longest segment must go through the center of the circle and is called the diameter.

Review Example 1 with students. Be sure to focus on how a diameter, chord, and radius are alike and how they are different.

Ask: How are the radius and diameter the same? **[Both must contain the center of the circle.]**

Ask: How are the radius and diameter different? **[The endpoints of the radius are the center and a point on the circle. The endpoints of the diameter are points on the circle such that the diameter goes through the center.]**

Ask: Is the diameter a chord? Why or why not? **[The diameter is a chord because it is a segment that connects two points on the circle.]**

Ask: Is the radius a chord? Why or why not? **[The radius is not a chord because it connects the center with one point on the circle.]**

Check
Problem 1–3

Although each problem asks for diameter and radius, different information is given. Prompt students to take their time determining the measure given, and the associated radius and diameter.

Problem 3

If students mistake the chord for the diameter, review the definitions in the example.
Point out that the diameter is the longest chord on the circle and must go through the center of the circle.
If students assume the diameter is 11 ft and the radius is 9 ft, review definition of a radius. Remind students that a radius must contain the center and it is equal to half the diameter.

Example 2

Introduce the formula for area of a circle to students. If desired, show the derivation of the formula as shown in the Alternate Strategy.

Say: Let's review the terms in the formula for area of a circle.

Ask: What is the meaning of r? **[The variable r stands for radius.]**

Ask: What is the meaning of r^2? **[It means that r must be multiplied by itself. So $r^2 = r \times r$.]**

Ask: What are some examples of numbers and their squares? **[Sample response: $5^2 = 25$; $7^2 = 49$; $4^2 = 16$, etc.]**

Next, draw students' attention to π. If desired, have a brief discussion about where they may have used π in the past. Students may recall using it when determining the circumference of a circle in $C = 2\pi r$.

Ask: What is the value of π? **[$\pi \approx 3.14$]**

Point out that although π has a value, it can also be used in its exact form. For example, it is possible to add $2\pi + 3\pi$ to get 5π.

Explain to students that while they are beginning to practice using the formula for area, they may keep their answers in terms of π. This keeps calculations much simpler and also provides an exact value for the circle area.

Check
Problem 6
Because the area of a circle with diameter 4 is 4π, students might assume the area formula is simply the diameter multiplied by π. Be sure students understand that the radius of the circle is $\frac{4}{2} = 2$ so the area is $A = \pi(2)^2 = 4\pi$.

Example 3
Explain to students that they will continue to calculate area in the same way. However, they can take the solution a step further by using an approximation of π to yield an answer appropriate for a real-life situation.

Ask: Why do you think it is more useful to give an approximation for the window rather than leaving the answer in terms of π? **[Sample answer: The answer 9π ft^2 is much harder to visualize than 28.26 ft^2.]**

Ask: If the window was positioned as shown, would the answer be the same?

Check
Problem 12
Some students may have difficulty using the ordered pairs to calculate the diameter.

Ask: How would you determine the diameter measure if the grid were also shown? **[I would count the units.]**

Say: Try to visualize the grid. Start from one side and begin to count. Think about how to use the coordinates to determine the number of units.

Ask: How could you use only the coordinates to determine the diameter? **[Because this is a horizontal line, I could find the difference between the *x*-coordinates.]**

ALTERNATE STRATEGY

Strategy: Understanding the Circle Area Formula

Some students have difficulty relating the area of a circle to what they know about area of a polygon.

1. Help students recall the area of a triangle as $A = \frac{1}{2}bh$.

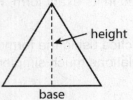

height

base

2. Show students a circle with a hexagon inscribed.

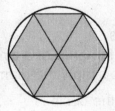

Ask: How many triangles are in this hexagon? **[6]**

Ask: What is the area of the hexagon? $\left[A = 6\left(\frac{1}{2}bh\right) \right]$

3. Show students an increasing number of polygon sides inscribed in a circle.

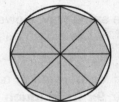 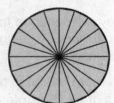 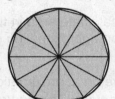

4. Point out that as the number of sides, n, increases, the figure approaches a circle.

Ask: What is the area of a polygon with n sides? $\left[A = n\left(\frac{1}{2}bh\right) \right]$

5. Rearrange the formula so that $A = n\left(\frac{1}{2}bh\right) = h\frac{1}{2}bn$.

6. Guide students to see that bn is base $\times n$ or the perimeter of the polygon. The perimeter or circumference of a circle is $2\pi r$ The height or h is in fact the radius. Thus,

$$A = h\frac{1}{2}bn = r\frac{1}{2}(2\pi r).$$

7. Finally, simplify the formula to see that $A = r\frac{1}{2}(2\pi r) = \pi r^2$.

COMMON MISCONCEPTION

Check
Problem 7

Ask: What is the diameter of the circle? **[5 inches]**

Ask: What is the radius of the circle? Explain. **[The radius is half the diameter so the radius is $\frac{1}{2} \times 5 = 2.5$.]**

Error: Students may use the diameter measure as the radius measure, especially when the diameter is not easily divisible by 2.

Solution: The radius of the circle is 2.5 in. so $A = \pi (2.5)^2 = 6.25\pi$.

If students continue to confuse radius, diameter, and chord, supply students with pictures of circles, a straightedge, and colored pencils. Direct students to draw diameters in one color, radii in another, and chords in a third color.

Error: Students may evaluate the exponent in $A = \pi r^2$ incorrectly.

Problems 4–6

Students may evaluate the exponent incorrectly by multiplying a base by 2 rather than raising it to the second power. Help students evaluate correctly by writing the area formula as $A = \pi \times r \times r$. Then have students substitute and simplify.

ADDITIONAL ONLINE INTERVENTION RESOURCES

 Use the following for students who have not mastered the concepts in Skill 4.

- Math on the Spot videos

- Personal Math Trainer with customized intervention

- Building Block worksheets (Skill 9: Area of Circles; Skill 14: Circumference and Area of Circles; Skill 38: Find the Square of a Number; Skill 100: Squares and Square Roots)

SKILL 4 — Area of a Circle

Example 1

		Vocabulary
		Area
		Chord
		Diameter
		Radius

The area of a circle measures the space inside the circle.

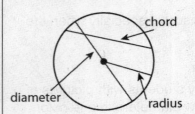

Circle area can be calculated using the radius or the diameter of the circle.

The radius is the segment from the center of the circle to a point on the circle.

The diameter is the segment that connects two points on the circle and goes through the center of the circle.

The radius is equal to $\frac{1}{2}$ the diameter.

A segment that connects two points on the circle is called a chord.

Check

State the diameter and radius of each circle.

1.

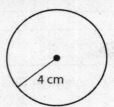

The diameter is _____.

The radius is _____.

2.

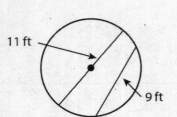

The diameter is _____.

The radius is _____.

3.

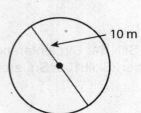

The diameter is _____.

The radius is _____.

4. If the diameter of a circle is x, what is the radius? _____

Example 2

The formula for area of a circle is $A = \pi r^2$ where r is the radius of the circle.

Sample 1

What is the area of the circle?

Because $r = 11$ meters, then

$A = \pi r^2$

$A = \pi(11)^2$

$A = 144\pi$ m²

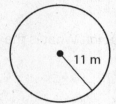

11 m

If you know the diameter of the circle, divide the diameter by 2 to determine the radius. Then, use $A = \pi r^2$ to calculate the area.

Sample 2

What is the area of the circle?

The diameter is 20 m, so the radius is $\frac{20}{2} = 10$ meters. Therefore,

$A = \pi r^2$

$A = \pi(10)^2$

$A = 100\pi$ m²

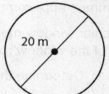

20 m

Check

Calculate the area of each circle.

5. 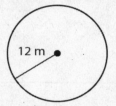 12 m	_____ _____
6. 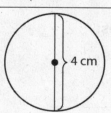 4 cm	_____ _____
7. A circle has a diameter of 7 feet.	_____ _____

8. Parts of a circle's area can also be determined using the area formula. Explain your strategy to calculate the area of the half-circle.

_____

_____

9. Explain the Error. Find the correct solution.

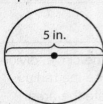

5 in.

The area of this circle is $A = \pi(5)^2 = 25\pi$.

_____

_____

Example 3

Any area given in terms of π is an exact measure. In real-life situations, it makes sense to estimate the circle area to the nearest decimal. A common approximation of π is 3.14.

A circular window measures 6 feet across at its widest point. What is the area of the window rounded to the nearest hundredth?

Step 1) Determine the radius.

If the window measures 6 feet across at its widest point, the diameter is 6 feet. This means the radius is $\dfrac{6}{2} = 3$ feet.

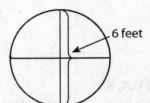

6 feet

Step 2) Substitute using $A = \pi r^2$. Simplify.

If $r = 3$, then $A = \pi(3)^2 = 9\pi$

Step 3) Approximate.

Because $\pi \approx 3.14$, then $9\pi \approx 9(3.14) = 28.26$ ft^2.

Check

Calculate the area of each circle. Round each area to the nearest hundredth.

10.

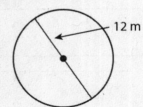

12 m

_____

_____

11.

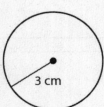

3 cm

_____

_____

12. A circle is graphed on a coordinate plane. The endpoints of the diameter are shown. Determine the area of the circle to the nearest hundredth.

A   Explain how to determine the diameter of the circle.

_____

_____

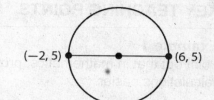

$(-2, 5)$ ● $(6, 5)$

B   The radius of the circle is _____ units.

C   The area of the circle in terms of π is _____.

D   The area of the circle to the nearest hundredth is _____.

| Leaving the area in terms of π can make operations easier. |

13. One garden has a radius of 8 feet. Another has a radius of 6 feet. How much larger is the first garden area than the second?

A   What is area of garden 1 in terms of π? _____

B   What is area of garden 2 in terms of π? _____

C   What is difference between areas in terms of π? _____

D   What is the approximate difference between areas? _____

14. A student claims the difference in garden areas could be calculated using the difference between the radius measures. The student stated that the difference radius measures is 2 feet so the difference in garden areas is $A = \pi(2)^2 = 4\pi$. Why is this student's strategy incorrect?

_____

_____

_____

SKILL 4 AREA OF A CIRCLE

Area of Composite Figures

KEY TEACHING POINTS

Example 1

Point out that in mathematics, problems are often broken into simpler tasks to make calculations easier.

Ask: What are some different strategies for multiplying 3×18? **[Multiply 3×9 and double the answer. Determine 3×10 and 3×8, then add the products.]**

Remind students about the meaning of area. It may be necessary to discuss how it differs from perimeter.

Direct students' attention to the figure.

Ask: What is the name of this figure? How do you know? **[It is a pentagon because it has 5 sides.]**

Have students read the measurements and trace the corresponding lengths with a finger.

Ask: Does the picture tell you how long the slanted sides are? **[No.]**

Ask: Do you think you will need to know the measures of the slanted sides to determine the area? **[Answers will vary.]**

Say: We will find the answer to that question in the next example.

Say: Instead of trying to find the area of a pentagon, let's divide the figure into two simpler figures.

Direct students to view figure with dashed line drawn. Have students trace this dashed line with their pencil.

Ask: What two figures has this pentagon been divided into? **[rectangle and triangle]**

Prompt students to recall the area of a rectangle and triangle and write these on the board.

Area of a rectangle = length $\times$ width ($A = l \times w$). Area of a triangle = $\frac{1}{2} \times$ base $\times$ height $\left(A = \frac{1}{2}bh \right)$.

Check
Problem 2

Some students may draw two vertical lines to divide the figure into three parts. First, confirm that this is acceptable. Next, point out that the students will have to calculate three individual areas and add them to find the total area. Suggest that the students think about how to use only one line to divide the figure into two figures. Remind the students that the purpose of dividing a composite figure is to make calculating the total area simpler.

Problem 3

Help students visualize the half circle and rectangle by sketching a whole circle on the figure. Invite students who see this visualization to explain to others who might be having difficulty.

Example 2

Using given measures to determine other measures can be challenging for many students. You may wish to recreate the figure on the board, then draw in measures as they are determined.

Ask: In the previous example, we divided this pentagon into a rectangle and triangle. Why? **[We divided it into simpler figures to make calculating the area simpler.]**

Draw the figure from Example 1 with dashed line on the board.

Ask: How can you find area of a rectangle? **[Multiply the length by the width.]**

Point out that the orientation of the rectangle often determines which side is called "length" and which side is called "width".

Ask: What is the width of this rectangle? **[5 cm]**

Ask: What is the length of this rectangle? **[8 cm]**

Ask: If someone thinks the length of the rectangle is 12 cm, how could you explain their error? **[Sample response: I'd tell them to shade in the part that is only the rectangle, then think about how long each side is.]**

Ask: What is the area of the rectangle? **[40 cm^2]**

Point out that the units of the area are squared because centimeters are multiplied by centimeters.

Say: Now take a look at the triangle.

Ask: How can you find the area of a triangle? **[Multiply $\frac{1}{2}$ by base by height.]**

Have students think about which part of the figure is the base. Ask if they see the base drawn or is it something they must imagine. Guide students to see that the dashed line they used to divide the figure is the base of the triangle.

Say: I see that the dashed line is the base of the triangle.

Ask: Does the figure give you enough information to determine the length of the base? Explain your reasoning. **[Yes. I see that the base of the triangle is also the width of the rectangle. That means the base of the triangle is 5 cm.]**

Ask: What is meant by the height of the triangle? **[The height is the shortest distance (also called the perpendicular distance) from the base of the triangle to the vertex or highest point.]**

Encourage students to reorient the figure if it helps them to visualize base and height of the triangle. Some students may not be familiar with "perpendicular distance". If desired, draw a separate triangle on the board and draw several non-perpendicular lines from the vertex to the base. Use a ruler to show that these non-perpendicular lines are longer than the perpendicular line.

Ask: What is the height of this triangle? Explain how you got your answer. **[I know from the figure that the distance from the side of the rectangle to the top of the triangle is 12 cm. I see that the length of the rectangle is 8 cm. So, the height of the triangle must be the difference between these two measures or 12–8. The height of the triangle is 4 cm.]**

Say: Now you know the base of the triangle is 5 cm and the height is 4 cm.

Ask: What is the area of the triangle? **[10 cm²]**

Say: Now it is time to add both areas together.

Ask: What is the total area of the figure? **[40 cm² + 10 cm² = 50 cm²]**

Check
Problem 6

Guide students, if needed, to see that the area of a half-circle is $A = \dfrac{1}{2}\pi r^2$. Because the area of the circle is being added to the area of the triangle, students can round the area of the circle to the nearest square centimeter.

Example 3

Say: Now you are going to find the area using all of the steps you've learned.

Guide students through Steps 1 through 4 and refer to the diagram as needed. If students have difficulty determining the missing measure, draw the original figure. Then, use one color (e.g. red) to trace the side length measuring 11 inches. Next, use a different color (e.g. blue) to trace the side measuring 3 inches as well as the unknown side. Point out that the length of the red segment will be equal to the sum of the lengths of the blue segments.

Say: Now, let's think about other ways this shape could have been divided.

Draw or show students the original figure and ask students to suggest other division lines. Samples might include the following:

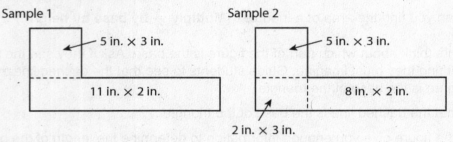

Then encourage students to find the area of each figure and sum the figures to verify that the total area is the same. Have students discuss which sample they prefer and why. Be sure students notice that Sample 2 requires finding the area of three figures.

Check
Problem 8

Point out that sometimes, the simplest method to find total area requires dividing into three parts. Encourage students to fill in all missing measures before dividing the figure.

Alternatively, students can complete the rectangle, then subtract the missing part.
For example,

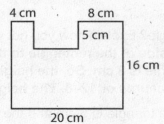

Ask: How could you find the area of the larger rectangle? **[The large rectangle has an area of 20 cm × 16 cm = 320 cm^2.]**

Ask: What are the dimensions of the small portion that must be subtracted? Explain how you know. **[The small portion has a height of 5 cm. The length of the large rectangle is 20 cm so the missing portion is 20 cm − 8 cm − 4 cm = 8 cm.]**

Ask: What is the area of the small portion? **[5 cm × 8 cm = 40 cm^2]**

Direct students to subtract areas to see that 320 cm^2 − 40 cm^2 = 280 cm^2.

Example 4

If possible, demonstrate finding area through subtraction by drawing a large rectangle on a piece of paper. Mark side lengths of 8 units and 12 units.

Ask: What is the area of this rectangle? Explain how you know. **[The area is 96 units squared because 8 units times 12 units is 96 units squared.]**

Next, take a pair of scissors and cut out a rectangle from the middle of the larger rectangle.

Ask: This rectangle has side measurements of 8 units and 4 units. What is the area of the smaller rectangle? **[32 units squared]**

Say: So, I had a large rectangle with an area of 96 units squared. I cut out a smaller rectangle with an area of 32 units squared.

Ask: How can you find the area of the remaining large rectangle? What is the area? **[I can find the remaining area by subtracting the smaller area from the larger area. The area of the remaining rectangle is 96 − 32 = 64 units^2.]**

Check
Problem 10
Have students discuss their strategy for finding the shaded area before they begin writing.

Ask: What shapes do you see in problem 10? **[a circle and a square]**

Ask: How will you calculate the area of the shaded area? **[Subtract the area of the square from the area of the total circle.]**

Problem 11
Students may have difficulty determining the diameter of the circle from the measures given. If desired, suggest to students that they use a ruler to draw several horizontal lines across the square.

Ask: What is the measure of each of the horizontal lines? Explain. **[The measure is always 6 feet because the sides of the square measure 6 feet.]**

Have students continue drawing lines until they reach the widest part of the circle.

Ask: Which line represents the diameter of the circle? **[The longest line connecting two points on the circle.]**
Ask: What is the diameter of this circle? **[6 feet]**

ALTERNATE STRATEGY

Strategy: Visualizing Composite Figures

1. Have students work backwards by using shapes such as tangrams or other pattern blocks to create composite figures.
2. Direct students to choose two shapes and use a ruler to measure the sides to the nearest centimeter.
3. Then have students calculate the area of each shape.
4. Next, have students place the shapes together and add the areas to determine the total area of the composite figure.
5. Direct students to sketch the composite figure and write in the relevant measures.
6. Have students exchange composite figures with a partner, then calculate total area.
7. Finally, have partners check their answers and clear up any misunderstanding.

COMMON MISCONCEPTION

Ask: What two figures has the composite shape been divided into? **[a rectangle and a half-circle]**

Ask: How is the area of a half-circle calculated? **[$\frac{1}{2}\pi r^2$]**

Error: Students may skip steps and forget to think carefully about the shapes being created with the dividing line.

Solution: The circular part shown is only a half circle. So, the diameter of the circle is 8 m and the radius is 4 m. Therefore, the area of the half-circle is $\frac{1}{2}\pi(4)^2 = 8\pi \approx 25.1 \text{ m}^2$.
The total area is $40 \text{ m}^2 + 25.1 \text{ m}^2 = 65.1 \text{ m}^2$.

Problem 7
When dividing the figure into a rectangle and a triangle, students may have difficulty determining the length of the triangle base. Direct students to shade in the entire rectangle area. Then mark the bottom length at 6 m as shown.

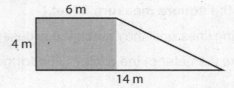

Say: The whole length of the bottom of the figure is 14 m. The length of just the rectangle part is 6 m.

Ask: How long is the triangle base? Explain. **[The triangle base is 8 m because 14 m – 8 m = 6 m.]**

Problem 14

Students often believe it is not possible to calculate the area because the radius or diameter of the circles is not given. Encourage students to draw a horizontal line through the middle of the figures to represent the diameters of all three circles.

Ask: How long is the horizontal line you drew through the three circles? **[15 meters]**

Say: Separate this line so that you see three diameters.

Ask: If all the diameters are equal, what must the diameter of one circle be? Explain.
[5 meters because 15 divided by 3 is 5.]

Problem 16

Students are often confused on where to draw a line to create simpler figures. Allow students to cut out figures, then cut along the "dividing" line to see the resulting shapes.

For example, students cutting the figure under Method 1 will note the area of the smaller figures are not easily calculated without additional cuts. Cutting the figure under Method 2 results in a triangle and a rectangle.

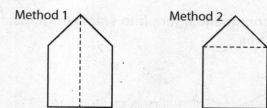

ADDITIONAL ONLINE INTERVENTION RESOURCES

 Use the following for students who have not mastered the concepts in Skill 5.

- Math on the Spot videos

- Personal Math Trainer with customized intervention

- Building Block worksheets (Skill 9: Area of Circles; Skill 10: Area of Polygons; Skill 11: Area of Squares, Rectangles, and Triangles; Skill 35: Find Area in a Coordinate Plane; Skill 73: Perimeter; Skill 112: Write Ratios)

Area of Composite Figures

SKILL 5

Example 1

		Vocabulary
		Area
		Composite

The area of a figure measures the space inside the figure.

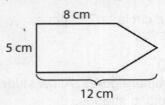

8 cm

5 cm

12 cm

To find area, some composite figures can first be divided into circles, rectangles, and/or triangles.

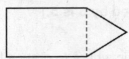

This figure is divided into a rectangle and a triangle.

Check

Draw a line to divide each composite figure into smaller figures.
Then, name the smaller figures.

1.

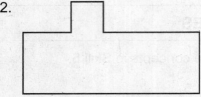

This figure is divided into _____.

2.

This figure is divided into _____.

3.

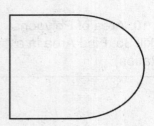

This figure is divided into _____.

4.

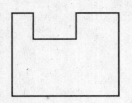

This figure is divided into _____.

Example 2

Use all the parts of the figure to determine the lengths needed to calculate the area.

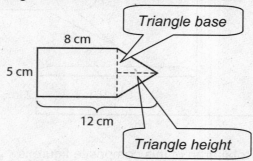

Some measures might need to be added or subtracted.

Rectangle Area

length = 8 cm and width = 5 cm

$$A = l \times w = 8 \times 5 = 40 \text{ cm}$$

Think:

The triangle base is the same as the rectangle width. So the triangle base is 5 cm.

The total length of the figure is 12 cm. The length of the rectangle is 8 cm. So, the height of the triangle is 12 − 8 = 4 cm.

Triangle Area

base = 5 cm and height = 4 cm

$$A = \frac{1}{2} \times b \times h \text{ or } \frac{1}{2} \times 5 \times 4 = 10 \text{ cm}$$

Check

Determine the total area of each figure.

5.	6.
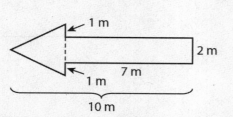	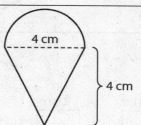
The length of the rectangle is _____ m.	The base of the triangle is _____ cm.
The width of the rectangle is _____ m.	The height of the triangle is _____ cm.
The area of the rectangle is _____ m².	The area of the triangle is _____ cm².
The base of the triangle is _____ m.	The radius of the circle is _____ cm.
The height of the triangle is _____ m.	_Think: The radius of a full circle is $A = \pi r^2$. How could you calculate the radius of a half circle?_
The area of the triangle is _____ m².	
	The area of the half circle is _____ cm².
The total area of this figure is	The total area of this figure is
_____ m² + _____ m² = _____ m².	_____ cm² + _____ cm² = _____ cm².

Example 3

To find area of a composite figure:

Step 1) Divide the figure into smaller figures.

Step 2) Determine the measures of the smaller figures.

Step 3) Calculate the area of each smaller figure.

Step 4) Add the areas of the smaller figures to determine the total area of the composite figure.

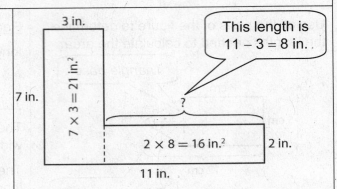

The total area of this composite figure is
21 in.^{2} + 16 in.^{2} = 37 in.^{2}

Check

**Use the measures shown to fill in the unknown sides if needed.
Then divide the figure and calculate the total area.**

7.

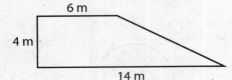

6 m

4 m

14 m

_____

_____

8.

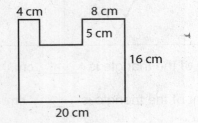

4 cm   8 cm

5 cm

16 cm

20 cm

_____

_____

9. Explain the Error. Find the correct solution.

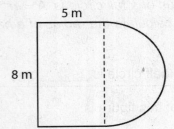

5 m

8 m

The area of the rectangle is 8 m × 5 m = 40 m^2.
The area of the circular part is $\pi(4)^2 = 16\pi \approx 50.3\,\text{m}^2$.
The total area is 40 + 50.3 = 90.3 m^2.

_____

_____

Example 4

Sometimes you can subtract to find the area of a composite figure.

Calculate the shaded area of the rectangle. The unshaded area is also in the shape of a rectangle.

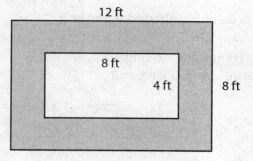

12 ft

8 ft

4 ft

8 ft

Plan: Find the total area of the large rectangle. Find the area of the small rectangle. Subtract the area of the small rectangle from the area of the large rectangle.

Step 1) Calculate the area of the entire rectangle.

$$A = 12 \times 8 = 96 \text{ ft}^2$$

Step 2) Calculate the area of the small unshaded rectangle.

$$A = 8 \times 4 = 32 \text{ ft}^2$$

Step 3) Subtract the areas to find the shaded area.

$$96 \text{ ft}^2 - 32 \text{ ft}^2 = 64 \text{ ft}^2$$

Check

State the plan to find the area of the shaded region. Then, calculate the area.

10.

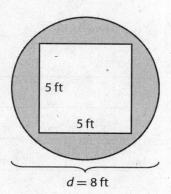

5 ft

5 ft

$d = 8$ ft

My plan

_____

_____

_____

_____

The area of the shaded figure is _____.

11.

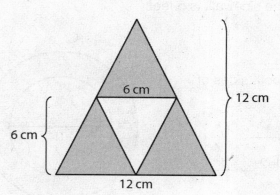

6 cm

12 cm

6 cm

12 cm

My plan

_____

_____

_____

_____

The area of the shaded figure is _____.

12.

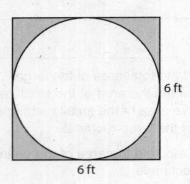

6 ft

6 ft

My plan

_____

_____

_____

_____

The area of the shaded figure is _____.

13. Explain how to find the shaded area algebraically. (Hint: Use the grid to determine the measures.) Then, check your answer by counting and estimated the shaded square units.

_____

_____

_____

_____

The area of the shaded figure is _____.

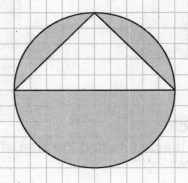

14. Is it possible to calculate the area of the shaded part with the information given? Explain your reasoning.

15 m

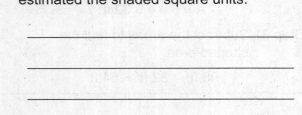

_____

_____

_____

_____

15. A park has a fountain in the shape of a circle. A sidewalk is being built around the fountain. The width of the sidewalk is 5 feet. The diameter of the fountain is 20 feet.

A What is the diameter of the whole circle? _____

(Hint: Be sure to include the fountain and both sides of the sidewalk.)

B What is the area of the whole circle? _____

C What is the diameter of the unshaded circle? _____

D What is the area of the unshaded circle? _____

E What is the area of the sidewalk? _____

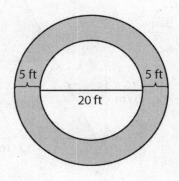

5 ft   5 ft

20 ft

16. Two students divided their composite figures in different ways. Which
method would you chose to calculate area. Why?

Method 1 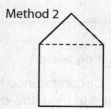   Method 2

_____

_____

_____

_____

SKILL 5 AREA OF COMPOSITE FIGURES

Circumference

KEY TEACHING POINTS

Example 1

Review the parts of a circle and rounding decimals, if necessary.

Say: Circumference is the distance around a circle. Circumference is similar to perimeter for polygons. Both circumference and perimeter are used to measure distance around a figure. For circles, circumference can be calculated using either the length of the radius or the length of the diameter.

Ask: What is the relationship between the radius and the diameter of a circle? **[The radius is twice the length of the diameter.]**

Demonstrate that both formulas for circumference are really the same formula. Using the relationship $d = 2r$, one formula is written in terms of d and one formula is written in terms of r.

$C = \pi d$

$C = \pi(2r)$ Substitute $2r$ for d.

$C = 2\pi r$ Commutative Property

Ask: In this example, you are given the length of the diameter. Which formula for circumference should you use? **[$C = \pi d$]**

Ask: What is the length of the diameter? **[18 in.]** What value will you use for π? **[3.14]**

Say: Notice that π is a numerical value and does not have a measurement unit. So, the circumference will have the same unit as the radius or diameter.

Ask: What measurement unit will you use for the circumference? **[inches]**

Say: The exact circumference of the circle is 18π inches. Since an approximation for π is used, the circumference is also an approximation. So, the circumference of the circle is *about* 56.5 inches.

Say: Another approximation for π is 3. You can use this value to quickly check the reasonableness of your answer.

Ask: Use $\pi = 3$ to estimate the circumference. What is $18 \bullet 3$? **[54]** Is this estimate close to answer, 56.5 inches? **[Yes.]**

Check

Make sure students use the appropriate formula for circumference. Encourage students to evaluate the reasonableness of their answers using $\pi = 3$.

Ask: If you are given the diameter of a circle, what formula will you use for circumference? **[$C = \pi d$]** If you are given the radius of a circle, what formula will you use? **[$C = 2\pi r$]**

Ask: What value will you use for π? **[3.14]**

Remind students that their answers should be rounded to the nearest tenth and include a measurement unit.

Example 2

Make sure students understand how to simplify fractions before multiplying.

Say: The fraction $\frac{22}{7}$ is equivalent to 3.14285714…, so it is a good approximation for π. You can use this value when the radius or diameter is a multiple of 7.

Ask: Do you know the measure of the radius or the diameter? **[radius]** Which formula for circumference should you use? **[$C = 2\pi r$]**

Ask: What is the length of the radius? **[63 cm]** Is 63 a multiple of 7? **[Yes]**

Ask: What value will you use for π? $\left[\dfrac{22}{7}\right]$

Ask: What is the greatest common factor of 7 and 21? **[7]**

Ask: After you divide by the greatest common factor, what is the simplified equation?
[$C = 2 \bullet 22 \bullet 9$]

Ask: How can you check the reasonableness of your answer? **[Use $\pi = 3$ and evaluate the equation 2(3)(63) = 378.]**

Check
Problem 9

What equation will you use to find the circumference? $\left[C = 2\left(\dfrac{22}{7}\right)(48)\right]$

Problem 10

What equation will you use to find the circumference? $\left[C = \left(\dfrac{22}{7}\right)(42)\right]$

Problem 13

Ask: What is the exact circumference of the circle? **[49π]** See Example 3.

Say: If you know the circumference of a circle you can find the diameter or the radius.

Ask: What information is given in the problem? **[The circumference is 60 ft.]**

Ask: What do you need to find? **[the radius]** Which formula for circumference should you use? **[$C = 2\pi r$]**

Ask: How can you solve for r? **[Divide the circumference by 2π.]**

Ask: What value will you use for π? **[3.14]**

Ask: What is the radius of the circle? **[about 9.6 ft]**

Ask: How can you check the reasonableness of your answer? **[Substitute $\pi = 3$ and $r = 10$ in the equation $C = 2\pi r$.]** Is the estimate close to the actual answer? **[Yes, 2(3)(10) = 60.]**

Check
Problems 14–19
Remind students to read the problems carefully to determine what information is missing.

Problem 21
Ask: How can you estimate the answer? **[Round 9.45 to 9 for the circumference and use** $\pi = 3$ **in the equation** $d = \dfrac{C}{\pi}$. **The diameter is** $\dfrac{9}{3} = 3$, **so the radius is** $\dfrac{1}{2}(3) = 1.5$.]

Problem 25
Ask: What is the radius of the tire rim? [13 − 2 = 11 in.]

ALTERNATE STRATEGIES

Strategy: Investigate the relationship between the circumference of a circle and its diameter.

1. Have students use a centimeter ruler to measure the circumference of several circular objects by wrapping a string around the object and then measuring the length of the string. Students should then measure the diameter of the object. Measurements should be to the nearest tenth of a centimeter.

2. Have students calculate the ratio of the circumference to the diameter, $\dfrac{C}{d}$, for each object to the nearest hundredth.

3. **Ask:** Is the ratio close to the same value for all of the circular objects? **[Answers will vary, but students should find that all of the ratios are close to 3.14.]**

4. Discuss with students that ratio $\pi = \dfrac{C}{d}$ is a constant value. So, the ratio of the circumference of a circle to its diameter is the same for all circles, regardless of the size of the circles.

Strategy: Solve a problem in a different way.

1. Remind students that sometimes there is more than one way to solve a problem. Have students look at Problem 26.

2. **Ask:** What is the equation for the circumference of the rim of the basketball hoop in terms of π? [$C = 18\pi$]

3. **Ask:** What is the equation for the circumference of the basketball in terms of π? [$C = 9.55\pi$]

4. **Ask:** What expression represents the difference of the circumferences? [$18\pi − 9.55\pi$] How can you rewrite this expression using the Distributive Property? [$(18 − 9.55)\pi$]

5. The second expression represents subtracting the diameters first, then multiplying by π. Have students verify that $18\pi − 9.55\pi$ and $(18 − 9.55)\pi$ are equivalent expressions and result in the same answer.

6. Present this problem. A small plate has a diameter of 4 inches. A large plate has a diameter of 8 inches. **Ask:** Does the expression $(8 − 4)\pi$ represent the difference in the circumferences of the two plates? **[Yes, $(8 − 4)\pi$ is equivalent to $8\pi − 4\pi$.]**

COMMON MISCONCEPTIONS

Problem 22

Some students may not analyze the problem correctly and use 100 in their calculations instead of 100π. Remind students to write the original formula before they substitute known values to help avoid errors.

Ask: What is the circumference of the circle? **[100π]**

Ask: Which formula for circumference should you use to find the radius? **[$C = 2\pi r$]**

Ask: How can you solve for r? **[Divide the circumference by 2π.]**

Ask: After you substitute 100π for C, what is the expression for r? $\left[r = \dfrac{100\pi}{2\pi} \right]$

Ask: Why is this answer in the problem incorrect? **[In the equation for r, the value for the circumference is not correct; π is missing from the numerator.]**

Error: The value for circumference is 100π, not 100.

Solution: The radius is $r = \dfrac{100\pi}{2\pi}$ or 50 cm.

Present the problem another way. Have students find the diameter of the circle first, then find the radius. Students should be able to quickly identify the diameter as 100 since $C = d\pi$. So, $r = \dfrac{1}{2}(100)$ or 50 cm.

Problem 24

Since the figure is a semicircle, some students may only find the value of $\dfrac{1}{2}C$ and neglect to add the distance of the diameter.

Ask: How can you find the distance around the curved part of the figure? **[Find the circumference of the entire circle and then divide by 2 to find the circumference of half of the circle.]**

Ask: Does the circumference of the semicircle include the straight part of the figure? **[No.]**

ADDITIONAL ONLINE INTERVENTION RESOURCES

 Use the following for students who have not mastered the concepts in Skill 6.

- Math on the Spot videos
- Personal Math Trainer with customized intervention
- Building Block worksheets (Skill 14: Circumference and Area of Circles; Skill 38: Find the Square of a Number; Skill 65: Multiply with Fractions and Decimals; Skill 100: Squares and Square Roots)

SKILL 6 — Circumference

Example 1

Circumference is the distance around a circle. The circumference of a circle can be calculated using its radius or its diameter.

$$C = \pi d \text{ or } C = 2\pi r$$

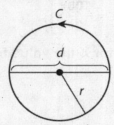

The value of pi (π) is a constant number with a value of 3.141592654…. However, 3.14 is often used as an approximation for π in calculations.

To find the circumference of a circle with a diameter of 18 inches, use the formula $C = \pi d$.

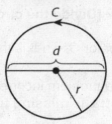

$C = \pi d$
$C \approx 3.14(18)$ $\pi \approx 3.14, d = 18$
$C \approx 56.52$ Simplify.
Round the circumference to the nearest tenth. The circumference of the circle is about 56.5 inches.

Vocabulary
Circumference
Radius
Diameter
Pi (π)

Check

Find the circumference of each circle. Use 3.14 for π.
Round to the nearest tenth.

1.

15 cm

2.
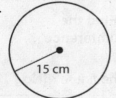
20 in.

3.
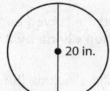
8 ft

4.
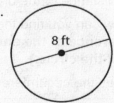
9 yd

5.
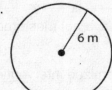
6 m

6.
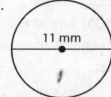
11 mm

Solve. Use 3.14 for π. Round to the nearest tenth.

7. What is the circumference of a circle with a radius of 6.5 feet?

_____

8. Find the circumference of a circular mirror with a diameter of 16 inches.

_____

Example 2

Another approximation for π is $\frac{22}{7}$. Use this value when the radius or the

diameter is a multiple of 7.

Find the circumference of the circle with a radius of
63 centimeters.

$C = 2\pi r$	Circumference formula
$C \approx 2\left(\dfrac{22}{7}\right)(63)$	$\pi \approx \dfrac{22}{7},\ r = 63$
$C \approx 2\left(\dfrac{22}{\underset{1}{7}}\right)\left(\dfrac{\overset{9}{63}}{1}\right)$	Divide by the GCF, 7.
$C \approx 396$	Simplify.

The circumference of the circle is about 396 centimeters.

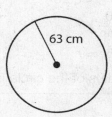

63 cm

Check

Find the circumference of each circle. Use $\frac{22}{7}$ for π. Round to the

nearest tenth.

9.

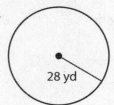

28 yd

10.

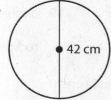

42 cm

11.

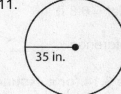

35 in.

12. The diameter of a tree trunk is 14 inches. What is the approximate circumference of the tree trunk?

_____

13. Calculate the circumference of a circle that has a diameter of 49 inches using each of the following approximations for π. Round to the nearest tenth.

$\pi = \dfrac{22}{7}$ _____ $\pi = 3.14$ _____ $\pi = 3.14159$ _____

Example 3

A circle has a circumference of 60 feet. Find the radius of the circle.

$C = 2\pi r$

$60 \approx 2(3.14)r$ $C = 60, \pi \approx 3.14$

$60 \approx 6.28r$ Multiply.

$\dfrac{60}{6.28} \approx r$ Divide each side by 6.28.

$9.6 \approx r$ Simplify.

The radius of the circle is about 9.6 feet.

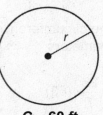

$C = 60$ ft

Check
Finding the missing measure. Use 3.14 for π. Round to the nearest tenth.

14. circumference = 30 yd

    radius = _____

15. circumference = 4 ft

    diameter = _____

16. circumference = 18 in.

    diameter = _____

17. radius = 42 mm

    circumference = _____

18. diameter = 6.8 ft

    circumference = _____

19. circumference = 82.4 cm

    radius = _____

Solve. Use 3.14 for π. Round to the nearest tenth.

20. Find the diameter of a circular rug with a circumference of 8 feet.

_____

21. What is the radius of a circular magnifying glass that has a circumference of 9.45 inches?

_____

22. Explain the Error. Find the correct solution.

The circumference of the circle is 100π centimeters. The radius of the circle is

$r = \dfrac{100}{2\pi}$ or about 15.9 centimeters.

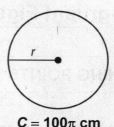

$C = 100\pi$ cm

23. A circular pathway around a lake has a diameter of 200 yards. If you walk around the lake two times, what is the total distance you will walk?

_____

24. The diameter of the semicircle is 80 meters. Find the total distance around the figure.

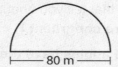

├─── 80 m ───┤

_____

25. The radius of an inflated bicycle tire is 13 inches. The radius of the tire rim is 2 inches shorter than the radius of the inflated tire. What is the circumference of the tire rim?

_____

26. The diameter of the rim of a basketball hoop is 18 inches. The diameter of a basketball is about 9.55 inches. How much greater is the circumference of a basketball hoop than the circumference of a basketball?

_____

SKILL 6 CIRCUMFERENCE

Congruent Figures

KEY TEACHING POINTS

Example 1

Say: The figure shows two congruent triangles. Since congruent figures have the same size and the same shape, the parts (angles and sides) of the congruent figures are also congruent. The congruent parts of congruent figures that "match" are called *corresponding parts*.

Ask: What symbols are used to indicate congruent angles? **[arcs]** What symbols are used to indicate congruent sides? **[tick marks]**

Ask: In triangle *ABC*, how many tick marks are drawn on side *BC*? **[two]**

Ask: Which side in triangle *DEF* has two tick marks? **[side *EF*]**

Ask: Since there are two tick marks on both $\overline{BC}$ and $\overline{EF}$, what does that tell you about the sides? **[Side *BC* and side *EF* are corresponding sides and they are congruent.]**

Ask: What angle is congruent to $\angle B$? **[$\angle E$]** How do you know? **[The angles have the same number of arcs.]**

Ask: What side is congruent to $\overline{CA}$? **[$\overline{FD}$]** How do you know? **[The sides have the same number of tick marks.]**

Say: The congruence statement $\triangle ABC \cong \triangle DEF$ is read as "triangle *ABC* is congruent to triangle *DEF*." It is important to write the vertices of each triangle in order of their corresponding parts.

Demonstrate that there is more than one way to write a congruence statement for the following triangles:

$\triangle ACB \cong \triangle DFE$, $\triangle BCA \cong \triangle EFD$, $\triangle BAC \cong \triangle EDF$, $\triangle CAB \cong \triangle FDE$, and $\triangle CBA \cong \triangle FED$

Point out that the vertices in each congruence statement are still listed in order of their corresponding parts.

Check

An easy way to write a congruence statement is to use the list of corresponding angles to easily identify the corresponding vertices of the triangle.

Problem 1

Students still need to follow the order of the corresponding vertices when writing corresponding sides.

Ask: Look at the side between the vertices *G* and *H*. What two ways can you name this side? **[$\overline{GH}$ and $\overline{HG}$]**

Ask: Is $\overline{GH}$ congruent to $\overline{KL}$? **[Yes.]** Is $\overline{HG}$ congruent to $\overline{LK}$? **[Yes.]**

Ask: Does $\overline{GH}$ correspond to $\overline{KL}$? **[Yes.]** Does $\overline{HG}$ correspond to $\overline{KL}$? **[No.]**

Explain that $\overline{GH} \cong \overline{KL}$ means that $\angle G$ corresponds to $\angle K$ and $\angle H$ corresponds to $\angle L$, and $\overline{HG} \cong \overline{KL}$ means that $\angle H$ corresponds to $\angle K$ and $\angle G$ corresponds to $\angle L$.

Example 2

Use congruence statements without figures to identify corresponding parts.

Ask: Why is the order of the vertices important when you write a congruence statement? **[The congruence statement tells you which angles correspond and which sides correspond.]**

Ask: What does the congruence statement $\triangle JKL \cong \triangle XYZ$ tell you about the angles in both triangles? **[$\angle J \cong \angle X$, $\angle K \cong \angle Y$, $\angle L \cong \angle Z$]**

Ask: How do you know that $\angle J \cong \angle X$? **[Vertex *J* is listed in the first position on the left side of the congruence statement and vertex *X* is listed in the first position on the right side of the congruence statement, so they are corresponding vertices.]**

Ask: What side corresponds to side *LK*? **[side *ZY*]**

Make sure students understand how to find corresponding parts in various orders. To find the corresponding side to *LK*, look at the position of the vertices in the congruence statement. *L* is in the third position and *K* is in the second position on the left side of the congruence statement, and *Z* is in the third position and *Y* is in the second position on the right side of the congruence statement. So, $\overline{LK}$ corresponds to $\overline{ZY}$.

Check

If students need additional help, have them make a sketch of the two triangles in the same position and label the corresponding parts.

Example 3

Say: You can determine if two figures are congruent by verifying that all of the corresponding angles are congruent and all of the corresponding sides are congruent.

Ask: How can you determine which angles are congruent? **[The arcs indicate which angles are congruent.]**

Ask: Are all of the corresponding angles congruent? **[Yes.]**

Ask: What are the corresponding angles? **[$\angle Q \cong \angle H$, $\angle R \cong \angle E$, $\angle S \cong \angle F$, and $\angle T \cong \angle G$]**

Ask: How can we determine which sides are congruent? **[Compare the side lengths of corresponding sides.]**

Ask: Which side corresponds to $\overline{QR}$? **[$\overline{HE}$]** Is $\overline{QR} \cong \overline{HE}$? **[Yes; *QR* = *HE* = 8 cm]**

Ask: Which side corresponds to $\overline{RS}$? **[$\overline{EF}$]** Is $\overline{RS} \cong \overline{EF}$? **[Yes; *RS* = *EF* = 9 cm]**

Ask: Which side corresponds to $\overline{ST}$? **[$\overline{FG}$]** Is $\overline{ST} \cong \overline{FG}$? **[Yes; *ST* = *FG* = 11 cm]**

Ask: Which side corresponds to $\overline{TQ}$? **[$\overline{GH}$]** Is $\overline{TQ} \cong \overline{GH}$? **[Yes; *TQ* = *GH* = 10.5 cm]**

Check
Problem 11

Ask: What is the unknown measure in right triangle *PQR*? **[30°]**

Ask: What is the unknown measure in right triangle *STU*? **[60°]**

Example 4

Ask: Which angle in triangle *ABC* corresponds to ∠*L*? [**∠*A***] How do you know? [**The order of the vertices in the congruence statement tells you which angles are corresponding angles.**]

Ask: What is the measure of ∠*A*? [**53°**]

Ask: What is true about corresponding angles of congruent figures? [**Corresponding angles are congruent.**]

Ask: Which side in triangle *ABC* corresponds to $\overline{MN}$? [$\overline{BC}$]

Ask: What is the length of $\overline{BC}$? [**8 ft**]

Ask: What is true about corresponding sides of congruent figures? [**Corresponding sides are congruent.**]

Find the values of the remaining parts of triangle *LMN*.

Ask: What is the measure of ∠*M*? [**37°**] How do you know? [**∠*M* ≅ ∠*B* and m∠*B* = 37°**]

Ask: What is the length of $\overline{LM}$? [**10 ft**] How do you know? [$\overline{LM} \cong \overline{AB}$ **and *AB* = 10 ft**]

Ask: What is the length of $\overline{NL}$? [**6 ft**] How do you know? [$\overline{NL} \cong \overline{CA}$ **and *CA* = 6 ft**]

Check
Problem 12

Ask: Which side in triangle *LNM* corresponds to $\overline{AB}$? [$\overline{LN}$]

Ask: Which angle in triangle *ABC* corresponds to ∠*M*? [**∠*C***]

Problem 14
Point out that m∠*WXY* is equal to m∠*WXZ* + m∠*ZXY*.

Ask: What congruence statement can you write for triangles? [**△*WXZ* ≅ △*YZX***]

ALTERNATE STRATEGY

Strategy: Use models to identify congruent triangles.

1. Have students draw a pair of congruent triangles. Students should use arcs and tick marks to label the corresponding parts.

2. Have students cut out the triangles and position the triangles side-by-side so that both triangles have the same orientation. This is the starting position.

3. Tell students to reflect one of the triangles horizontally and draw a picture of the results. Students should note the orientation of the triangles and the position of the corresponding parts.

4. Students return the triangles to the starting position. Next, have students reflect one triangle vertically and record the results.

5. Return the triangles to the starting position. Have students rotate one triangle 90° and record the results. Repeat the process for 180° and 270° rotations.

COMMON MISCONCEPTIONS

Problems 1–2

Watch for students who write the order of the vertices in alphabetical order rather than in the order of the vertices. Other students may correctly find the first pair of corresponding vertices, but then write the order of the other vertices in a clockwise direction without checking all of the corresponding parts. Remind students to make sure the number of arcs and tick marks match for all of the corresponding parts.

Problem 3

Point out that point L is used as a vertex in both triangles. Students should not refer to $\angle L$ or state that $\angle L \cong \angle L$ by the Reflexive Property. Remind students that they must specify $\angle KLJ$ or $\angle NLM$ and $\angle KLJ \cong \angle NLM$ because they are vertical angles.

Ask: According to the congruence statement, what angle corresponds to $\angle J$? **[$\angle N$]** Is $\angle J$ congruent to $\angle N$? **[No.]**

Ask: Which angle is congruent to $\angle J$? **[$\angle M$]**

Ask: Why is this answer incorrect? **[The vertices are not listed in order by their corresponding parts.]**

Error: The corresponding parts are not listed in the correct order.
Solution: The congruence statement should be $\triangle JKL \cong \triangle MNL$.

ADDITIONAL ONLINE INTERVENTION RESOURCES

Use the following for students who have not mastered the concepts in Skill 7.

- Math on the Spot videos

- Personal Math Trainer with customized intervention

- Building Block worksheets (Skill 8: Angles in Polygons; Skill 16: Classify Lines; Skill 48: Identify Congruent Figures; Skill 74: Polygon Angle Measures; Skill 98: Solve Two-Step Equations; Skill 103: Transformations)

Name _____ Date _____ Class_____

Congruent Figures

Example 1

Congruent figures have the same size and the same shape.
Corresponding parts are the parts of congruent figures that
have the same measurements.

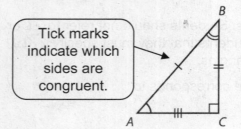

Tick marks indicate which sides are congruent.

Arcs indicate which angles are congruent.

Corresponding angles: $\angle A \cong \angle D$, $\angle B \cong \angle E$, $\angle C \cong \angle F$

Corresponding sides: $\overline{AB} \cong \overline{DE}$, $\overline{BC} \cong \overline{EF}$, $\overline{CA} \cong \overline{FD}$

In a congruence statement, congruent figures are named by
listing their vertices in order of their corresponding parts.

Congruence statement: $\triangle ABC \cong \triangle DEF$

Vocabulary

Congruent

Corresponding parts

Check

**List the corresponding angles and the corresponding sides for each
pair of congruent triangles. Then write a congruence statement.**

1.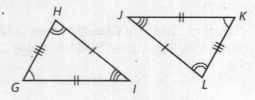

Corresponding angles: _____

Corresponding sides: _____

Congruence statement: _____

2.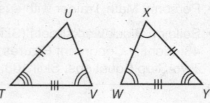

Corresponding angles: _____

Corresponding sides: _____

Congruence statement: _____

3. Explain the Error. Find the correct solution.
   One congruence statement for the two triangles is
   $\triangle JKL \cong \triangle NML$.

   _____

   _____

Example 2

If two figures are congruent, then their corresponding angles are congruent and their corresponding sides are congruent.

Use the congruence statement $\triangle JKL \cong \triangle XYZ$ to complete the statement

$\triangle KLJ \cong \triangle$ _____ .

Since the triangles are congruent, their corresponding angles are congruent and their corresponding sides are congruent. Use the order of the vertices to identify the corresponding parts.

Corresponding Angles: $\angle J \cong \angle X$, $\angle K \cong \angle Y$, $\angle L \cong \angle Z$.

Corresponding Sides: $\overline{JK} \cong \overline{XY}$, $\overline{KL} \cong \overline{YZ}$, $\overline{LJ} \cong \overline{ZX}$

Complete the congruence statement.

$\triangle KLJ \cong \triangle YZX$

Check

List the corresponding parts. Then complete the congruence statement.

4. $\triangle CDE \cong \triangle QRS$

   $\triangle EDC \cong$ _____

5. $\triangle BAC \cong \triangle MNP$

   $\triangle ABC \cong$ _____

6. $\triangle UVT \cong \triangle FGH$

   $\triangle UTV \cong$ _____

7. $\triangle KIJ \cong \triangle WZX$

   $\triangle IJK \cong$ _____

Example 3

If two figures have congruent corresponding angles and congruent corresponding sides, then the figures are congruent.

Determine whether the figures are congruent. If so, write a congruence statement.

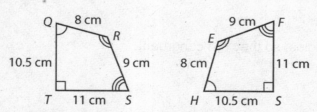

The matching arcs show that $\angle Q \cong \angle H$, $\angle R \cong \angle E$, $\angle S \cong \angle F$, and $\angle T \cong \angle G$.

The sides with equal measures show that $\overline{QR} \cong \overline{HE}$, $\overline{RS} \cong \overline{EF}$, $\overline{ST} \cong \overline{FG}$, and $\overline{TQ} \cong \overline{GH}$.

Since all pairs of corresponding angles are congruent and all pairs of corresponding sides are congruent, the figures are congruent.

Therefore, quadrilateral $QRST \cong$ quadrilateral $HEFG$.

Check

Determine whether the figures are congruent. If so, write a congruence statement.

8.

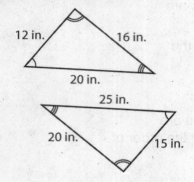

10.

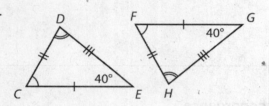

9.

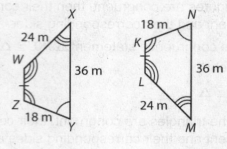

11.

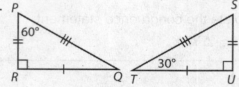

Example 4

You can use corresponding parts of congruent figures to find unknown measures of angles and sides.

In the figures below, $\triangle ABC \cong \triangle LMN$.

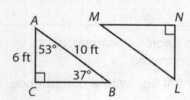

What is the measure of $\angle L$?

$\angle A$ and $\angle L$ are corresponding angles, so they are congruent.
$m\angle L = 52°$.

What is the length of $\overline{MN}$?

$\overline{BC}$ and $\overline{MN}$ are corresponding sides, so they are congruent.
$MN = 8$ feet.

Name _____ Date _____ Class_____

Check

12. In the figures below, $\triangle ABC \cong \triangle LNM$. Find the values for x and y.

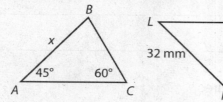
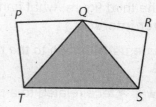

_____

13. In the design at the right, $\triangle QPT \cong \triangle QRS$.

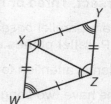

   a. If $m\angle PTQ = 48°$ and $m\angle R = 92°$. What is $m\angle RSQ$?

   _____

   b. The length of $\overline{QT}$ is 15 inches and the length of $\overline{QR}$ is 20 inches. What is the length of $\overline{QP}$?

14. Use the figure at the right.

   a. The $m\angle WXZ = 65°$ and the $m\angle XZW = 45°$. What is $m\angle WXY$?

   _____

   b. The length of $\overline{WX}$ is 24 centimeters and the length of $\overline{XY}$ is 30 centimeters. What is the perimeter of the figure?

   _____

15. Draw arcs and tick marks on the figures to show that $\triangle MNP \cong \triangle SRQ$.

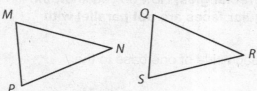

SKILL 7 CONGRUENT FIGURES

Cross Sections

KEY TEACHING POINTS

Example 1

Review the properties of planes and three-dimensional figures.

Ask: In the first figure, where do plane *A* and plane *B* intersect? **[line ℓ]**

Ask: In the second figure, where do plane *A*, plane *B*, and plane *C* intersect? **[point *P*]**

Ask: In the third figure, what can you say about planes *A*, *B*, and *C*? **[They are parallel, so they never intersect.]**

Direct students' attention to the rectangular prism. Relate the parts of the prism to properties of planes.

Ask: How is a *face* related to a plane? **[A face is a flat surface. A face is part of a plane.]**

Ask: How is an *edge* related to how planes intersect? **[An edge is a line segment where two faces intersect. Two planes intersect in a line.]**

Ask: How is a *vertex* related to how planes intersect? **[A vertex is where three or more faces intersect. Three or more planes may intersect at a point.]**

Ask: How are parallel *bases* related to how planes intersect? **[Parallel bases do not intersect. Parallel planes never intersect.]**

Direct students' attention to the triangular prism.

Say: Prisms have two congruent parallel bases. Prisms are categorized by the shape of their bases.

Ask: What shape are the bases? **[triangles]** What type is the figure? **[triangular prism]** Name the bases. **[triangle *ADE* and triangle *BCF*]**

Say: Because bases are flat surfaces, they are also faces.

Ask: What shape are the other faces of the prism? **[rectangles]** How do you know the rectangular faces are not also bases? **[The rectangular faces are not parallel with another face.]**

Say: Notice that the rectangular faces extend from each side of one base to the corresponding side of the other base.

Ask: How many sides touch each base? **[3]** How many rectangular faces are there? **[3]** Name the rectangular faces. **[*ABCD, EFCD, ABFE*]**

Say: The edges are both the sides of each base and the line segments that extend from one base to the other base.

Ask: How many edges are in the prism? **[9]** Name the edges. **[$\overline{AD}$, $\overline{DE}$, $\overline{EA}$, $\overline{BC}$, $\overline{CF}$, $\overline{FB}$, $\overline{AB}$, $\overline{DC}$, $\overline{EF}$]**

Ask: How many vertices are in the prism? **[6]** Name the vertices. **[*A, B, C, D, E, F*]**

Check

Remind students that prisms and pyramids are categorized by the shape of their bases.

Problem 1

Note that any pair of parallel faces can be the bases in a rectangular prism. They do not need to be on the top and bottom of the figure.

Ask: Does the figure have parallel bases? **[Yes.]**

Ask: What shape are the bases? **[rectangles]**

Problem 2

Note that pyramids and cones only have one base.

Ask: Does the figure have parallel bases? **[No.]**

Ask: What shape is the base? **[square]**

Ask: At what point do the triangular faces meet? **[point *J*]**

Problem 3

Ask: Does the figure have parallel bases? **[No.]**

Ask: What shape is the base? **[circle]**

Ask: Does the figure have any edges? **[No.]**

Problem 4

Ask: Does the figure have parallel bases? **[Yes.]**

Ask: What shape are the bases? **[circles]**

Ask: Does the figure have any edges? **[No.]**

Problem 6

Ask: How many bases does the prism have? **[2]**

Ask: How many bases does each pyramid have? **[1]**

Example 2

Say: When a plane intersects a three-dimensional figure, the result is called a cross section. Imagine slicing a figure into two pieces and pulling the pieces apart. The resulting shape at the location of the slice on the figure is the shape of the cross section.

Say: Look at the vertical slice of the square pyramid.

Ask: Is the slice parallel or perpendicular to the base? **[perpendicular]**

Ask: If you pulled the two pieces of the pyramid apart at the cross section, what shape would you see? **[triangle]**

Say: Look at the horizontal slice of the square pyramid.

Ask: Is the slice parallel or perpendicular to the base? **[parallel]**

Ask: What shape is the cross section? **[square]**

Say: Notice that when a slice is parallel to the base, the cross section will be the same shape as the base.

Say: Look at the angled slice of the square pyramid.

Ask: Is the slice parallel or perpendicular to the base? **[neither]**

Ask: Does the plane intersect the base? **[No.]**

Say: Look at the shape of the intersection. The top and bottom sides of the shape are parallel. The top side is shorter than the bottom side. The sides of the shape are angled.

Ask: What shape is formed by the cross section? **[trapezoid]**

If students have trouble visualizing the shape of the cross section, display a triangular face of the pyramid. Make parallel cuts along the top and bottom of the face to represent the slice.

Check
Problem 7
Ask: What is the type of the figure? **[triangular prism]**

Ask: What are the shapes of the faces that make up a triangular prism? **[triangles and rectangles]**

Ask: What is the shape of the face that is parallel to the cross section? **[rectangle]**

Problem 8
Ask: What are the shapes of the bases of the figure? **[circles]**

Ask: Is the slice parallel or perpendicular to the bases? **[parallel]**

ALTERNATE STRATEGY

Strategy: Use models to show cross sections of three-dimensional figures.

Cross sections can be very complicated and are difficult for some students to visualize. Students will gain a better understanding of cross sections through concrete models.

1. Have students work in small groups or prepare a demonstration for the class. Use modeling clay to build a cube, rectangular prism, triangular prism, square pyramid, triangular pyramid, cone, cylinder, and sphere.

2. Use fishing line or dental floss to make horizontal, vertical, and angled slices in the figures.

3. Tell students to make a table like the one shown. Students should write the name and draw a picture of the three-dimensional figure and the shape of each cross section.

Figure	Horizontal Cross Section	Vertical Cross Section	Angled Cross Section

COMMON MISCONCEPTION

Problem 13

Some students incorrectly determine that since a cube has six congruent faces that are squares, every cross section will result in a square.

Error: The angled cross section of a cube usually results in a rectangle, not a square. In fact, it may result in a triangle if the slice just cuts off a corner of the cube.

Solution: The horizontal and vertical cross sections of a cube always result in a square.

If students need additional help with this problem, have them draw a square to represent one of the faces of a cube. Tell them that the width of the cross section will be the same length as the side length of the square face. In order for an angled cross section to be a square, the length of the cross section needs to be the same length as the side length.

Have students draw several diagonal lines from one side of the square to the other side. Point out that all of the diagonal lines are longer than the side length. Explain that the diagonal can represent the hypotenuse of a right triangle. Since the hypotenuse is always the longest side in a right triangle, the diagonal will always be longer than the side length.

ADDITIONAL ONLINE INTERVENTION RESOURCES

 Use the following for students who have not mastered the concepts in Skill 8.

- Math on the Spot videos

- Personal Math Trainer with customized intervention

- Building Block worksheets (Skill 31: Faces of Prisms and Pyramids; Skill 32: Faces, Edges, and Vertices)

SKILL 8

Cross Sections

Example 1

A plane is a two-dimensional flat surface that extends forever in all directions. Planes can intersect in a line, at a point, or they may be parallel.

Vocabulary
- Plane
- Base
- Face
- Edge
- Vertex
- Cross section

Intersect in a Line   **Intersect at a Point**   **No Intersection**

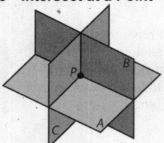

Intersecting planes can form three-dimensional figures.

In prisms, parallel congruent faces are called bases.

A face is a flat surface.

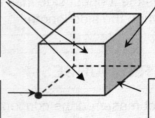

A vertex is where three or more faces intersect.

An edge is the line segment where two faces intersect.

The figure below is a triangular prism. Name the bases, faces, edges, and vertices.

bases: *ADE, BCF*

faces: *ADE, BCF, ABCD, EFCD, ABFE*

edges: $\overline{AD}, \overline{DE}, \overline{EA}, \overline{BC}, \overline{CF}, \overline{FB},$
$\overline{AB}, \overline{DC}, \overline{EF}$

vertices: *A, B, C, D, E, F*

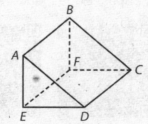

Check

Identify the type of figure. Name the bases, faces, edges, and vertices.

1. type: _____

   bases: _____

   faces: _____

   edges: _____

   vertices: _____

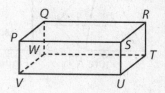

2. type: _____

   base: _____

   faces: _____

   edges: _____

   vertices: _____

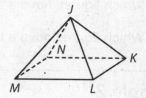

3. type: _____

   base: _____

   faces: _____

   edges: _____

   vertices: _____

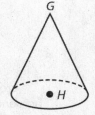

4. type: _____

   bases: _____

   faces: _____

   edges: _____

   vertices: _____

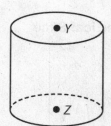

5. The gift box shown is in the shape of a pentagonal prism. Identify the number and shape of the faces.

   _____

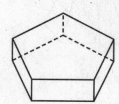

6. Use the figures to answer the following questions.

Figure A   Figure B   Figure C

a. Which figures are prisms? _____

b. Which figures are pyramids? _____

c. Which figures have a square base? _____

d. Which figures have a triangular base? _____

Example 2

The intersection of a plane and a three-dimensional figure is called a cross section.

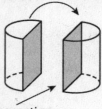 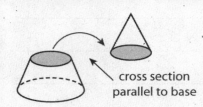

cross section
perpendicular to base

cross section
parallel to base

Describe the shape that results from a vertical, horizontal, and angled slice of a square pyramid.

Vertical Slice	**Horizontal Slice**	**Angled Slice**
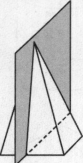	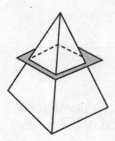	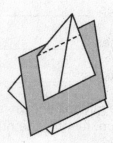
The cross section is a triangle.	The cross section is a square.	The cross section is a trapezoid.

Check

Describe the shape of the cross section that results from each slice.

7.

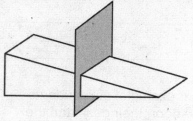

_____

8.

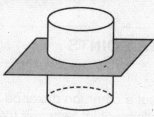

_____

9.

_____

10.

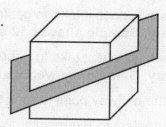

_____

Describe the shape of the cross section that results from the slice for each figure.

11. horizontal slice

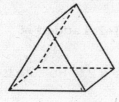

_____

12. horizontal slice

_____

13. Explain the Error. Find the correct solution.
The horizontal, vertical, and angled cross sections of a cube always result in a square.

_____

_____

SKILL 8 CROSS SECTIONS

Distance and Midpoint Formula

KEY TEACHING POINTS

Example 1

Start by pointing out a common distance in the classroom. For example, ask students to estimate the halfway point between their own desk and the door, their desk and the trashcan, etc.

Ask: How many steps does it take to get from your desk to the classroom door? **[Answers will vary: Sample answer 12 steps]**

Ask: How many steps does it take to get halfway from your desk to the classroom door? **[Answers will vary: Sample answer: 6 steps]**

Say: Notice that the halfway point means that the distance is divided equally in two.

Direct students' attention to Example 1. Point out the segment on the grid and ask students to approximate the halfway distance on the segment and plot a point. This will be their guess.

Say: Now let's learn how to find the midpoint exactly.

Ask: Look at just the x-axis. Where does the segment start on the left? **[at the –6]**

Ask: At which x-value does the segment stop on the right? **[at the 2]**

Remind students that the average of two numbers is found by adding the numbers and dividing by 2.

Ask: What is the average of –6 and 2? Explain how you got your answer. **[–2; I added –6 and 2 to get –4. Then I divided –4 by 2 to get –2.]**

Repeat for the y-coordinates to show that the average of the y-coordinates is 2.5. Be sure to point out that the midpoint is not necessarily an integer.

Check

Problems 1–2

Encourage students to write the ordered pairs at each endpoint on the graph. For example, problem 1 is from (1, 3) to (3, –3). Allow students to draw vertical and horizontal lines if desired to help them see the distance between the x-values and the distance between the y-values.

Problem 5

Students may be confused when averaging the x-values and see that $2 + -2 = 0$. Point out that the segment is 2 units to the left of 0 and 2 units to the right of 0 so the average is 0.

Ask: What is 0 divided by any number (other than 0)? **[0]**

Example 2

Connect students' prior knowledge by having them create right triangles using the segment as the hypotenuse. It may be necessary to review the parts of a right triangle.

Work through Example 2 with students. Have them practice tracing the dashed line to create the right triangle. Point out that the legs of the right triangle will always be vertical and horizontal lines.

Ask: The legs of the right triangle in the example were drawn above the segment. Will the triangle be the same if we draw the legs below the segment? **[Yes.]**

Encourage students to draw another triangle below the segment in the example to verify that it does not matter where the triangle is drawn. Some students may remember this method for finding slope. If time permits, allow students to explore the difference in using the right triangles this way. Help students recall that slope is determined by dividing the vertical distance by the horizontal distance.

Ask: What does 4^2 mean? **[It means 4 × 4 or 16.]**

Ask: What does 6^2 mean? **[It means 6 × 6 or 36.]**

Take a few minutes to review square roots with students. List common square roots on the board and a draw number line to help students estimate. Next, have students estimate where $\sqrt{52}$ will be located on the number line.

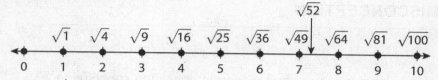

Check
Problems 6–7
Remind students to start at the endpoint, then trace only on the horizontal or vertical line to get to the other endpoint.

Ask: Does the length of the segment depend on whether the segment is sloping up or down? Why or why not? **[No, because direction does not matter when finding distance.]**

Example 3
The distance formula can be difficult to memorize so help students see the connection to the Pythagorean theorem.

Ask: How might you describe the distance formula in words? **[Sample answer: Take the difference of the *x*-values and the difference of the *y*-values, square both, then add them together and take the square root.]**

Direct students attention to the Sample in Example 3. Point out that keeping track of labeling each coordinate pair can help when using the formula.

Refer to the number line to help students estimate $\sqrt{117}$.

Check
Problem 10
Use this problem to encourage students to think about the distance before applying the formula.

Ask: What are the *x*-coordinates? **[8 and 8]**

Ask: What do you know about the line segment if the *x*-coordinates are the same? **[This is a vertical line.]**

Ask: Can you think of a simpler way to calculate the length of a vertical line? What is it? **[Yes, find the difference of the *y*-coordinates.]**

Ask: Would the distance formula still give the correct solution? Explain. **[Yes. If the *x*-coordinates are the same, the difference of *x*-values will be 0 and $0^2 = 0$.]**

ALTERNATE STRATEGY

Strategy: Visual Representation of Midpoint

1. If students have difficulty with understanding midpoint of a segment, allow them to trace the segment on a piece of patty paper or other tracing paper.

2. Then, have them fold the paper so the endpoints are aligned. Direct them to place a point on the line segment at the crease.

3. Finally, have students lay the traced segment over the original segment to the midpoint found using the algebraic method.

4. Students can use this tracing method to help them estimate before finding the midpoint algebraically or after to check their answers.

COMMON MISCONCEPTION

Check
Problem 12
Error: Students may confuse the *x*- and *y*-coordinates when substituting into the distance formula.

Ask: What are the *x*-coordinates? **[3 and –5]**

Ask: What are the *y*-coordinates? **[–8 and 1]**

Encourage students to use colored pencils or other markings to remind themselves that the difference of the *x*-coordinates and the difference of the *y*-coordinates must be found.

Solution: Find the distance between (3, –8) and (–5, 1).

$$d = \sqrt{\left(3-(-5)\right)^2 + \left(-8-1\right)^2}$$
$$d = \sqrt{8^2 + (-9)^2}$$
$$d = \sqrt{64 + 81}$$
$$d = \sqrt{145}$$
$$d \approx 12.0$$

Error: Students often have difficulty simplifying the distance formula.

Encourage students to avoid algebraic mistakes by writing steps carefully. Most errors will occur when subtracting negatives as some students believe the exponent means they can ignore the negative sign. Point out that order of operations specifies they add/subtract in the parentheses before applying the exponent.

Problem 13
Students may make assumptions about lengths from graphs because of the orientation of the segment. Point out that precision is necessary and all segment lengths must be calculated before the triangle can be classified.

ADDITIONAL ONLINE INTERVENTION RESOURCES

 Use the following for students who have not mastered the concepts in Skill 4.

- Math on the Spot videos

- Personal Math Trainer with customized intervention

- Building Block worksheets (Skill 10 Area of Polygons; Skill 11 Area of Squares, Rectangles, Triangles; Skill 27 Evaluate Expressions; Skill 38 Find the Square of a Number; Skill 45 Graph Ordered Pairs (First Quadrant); Skill 69 Order of Operations; Skill 70 Ordered Pairs; Skill 98 Solve Two-Step Equations; Skill 100 Squares and Square Roots)

Distance and Midpoint Formula

Example 1

Vocabulary
Midpoint
Hypotenuse
Legs

A midpoint is a point that divides a segment into two congruent segments.

The midpoint of any segment is the "average" of the coordinates.

$$x = \frac{x_1 + x_2}{2} \qquad y = \frac{y_1 + y_2}{2}$$

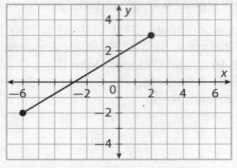

Endpoints: (−6, −2) and (2, 3)

$$x = \frac{x_1 + x_2}{2} = \frac{-6 + 2}{2} = \frac{-4}{2} = -2$$

$$y = \frac{y_1 + y_2}{2} = \frac{2 + 3}{2} = \frac{5}{2} = 2.5$$

The midpoint is (−2, 2.5).

Check

State the midpoint of each line segment.

1.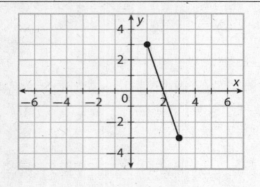

_____

2.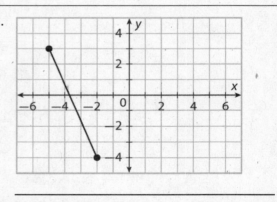

_____

3. Segment with endpoints at (−4, 10) and (−6, −2)   _____

4. Segment with endpoints at (−1, 15) and (3, 0)   _____

5. Segment with endpoints at (2, −3) and (−2, −5)   _____

Name _____ Date _____ Class_____

Example 2

The length of any segment, in a right triangle, can be found using the Pythagorean theorem.

The Pythagorean theorem states: In any right triangle where a and b are legs and c is the hypotenuse, then $a^2 + b^2 = c^2$. The hypotenuse is the side opposite the right angle in a right triangle. The legs are the sides adjacent to the right angle.

Calculate the length of $\overline{JK}$.	Step 1 Draw a triangle so that $\overline{JK}$ is the hypotenuse.	Step 2 Use the Pythagorean theorem.
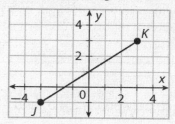	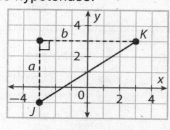 $a = 4$ and $b = 6$	$4^2 + 6^2 = c^2$ $16 + 36 = c^2$ $52 = c^2$ $\sqrt{52} = c$ $7.2 \approx c$

Check

Create a right triangle with the segment as the hypotenuse. Then calculate the length.

6.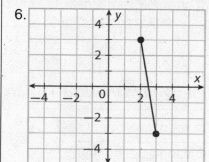

_____

_____

7.

_____

_____

Name _____ Date _____ Class _____

8.

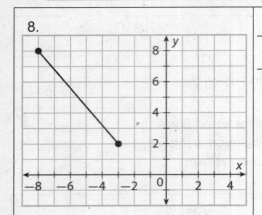

Example 3

The distance formula is based on the Pythagorean theorem.

$$c^2 = a^2 + b^2$$

$$c^2 = (x_2 - x_1)^2 + (y_2 - y_1)^2$$

$$c = \sqrt{(x_2 - x_1)^2 + (y_2 - y_1)^2}$$

The distance formula is:

$$d = \sqrt{(x_2 - x_1)^2 + (y_2 - y_1)^2}.$$

Sample
What is the distance between (−2, −5) and (7, 1)?

Let $(x_1, y_1) = (-2, -5)$ and $(x_2, y_2) = (7, 1)$

$$d = \sqrt{(7 - (-2))^2 + (1 - (-5))^2}$$

$$d = \sqrt{9^2 + 6^2}$$

$$d = \sqrt{81 + 36}$$

$$d = \sqrt{117}$$

$$d \approx 10.8$$

Check
Calculate the distance between each set of ordered pairs.

9. (13, −2) and (−5, 7)

_____

_____

10. (8, −6) and (8, 7)

_____

_____

11. (−11, 5) and (6, 0)

_____

_____

12. Explain the Error. Find the solution.

Find the distance between (3, –8)
and (–5, 1).

$d = \sqrt{(3-(-8))^2 + (-5-1)^2}$

$d = \sqrt{11^2 + (-6)^2}$

$d = \sqrt{121 + 36}$

$d = \sqrt{157}$

$d \approx 12.5$

_____

_____

_____

_____

13. Is $\triangle CDE$ a scalene, isosceles, or
equilateral triangle?
(Hint: First, find the measure of each side.)

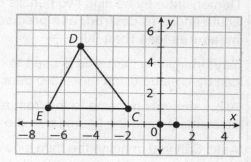

A What is CD? _____

B What is DE? _____

C What is CE? _____

D Classify $\triangle CDE$ by its sides. _____

14. A map is shown on a coordinate system as shown.
What is the distance on the map between Springfield
and Chester? Each unit is 1 cm.

_____

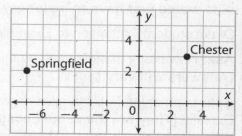

15. The map legend states that 1 cm = 5 miles. What is the
real distance between cities?

_____

SKILL 9 DISTANCE AND MIDPOINT FORMULA

Geometric Drawings

KEY TEACHING POINTS

Example 1

If students need practice with drawing segments with centimeter rulers, provide them with rulers and a blank piece of paper and instruct them to draw segments of a given length. For example, tell students to draw a segment of length 6 cm. Then have students compare. You may also have students practice drawing triangles of any length sides on a blank piece of paper.

Demonstrate by holding two pencils of different lengths and place them end to end at an acute angle. **(If desired, use precise vocabulary and explain that an acute angle measures less than 90°.)**

Say: Imagine a third side is used to create a triangle. Can you think of a different triangle that can be created using these two pencils?

Allow students to come to the front and adjust the angle of the two pencils. After each adjustment, hold the figure up to the class.

Ask: Can you imagine the third side? Does this form a triangle? **[Answers will vary.]**

If students continue demonstrating triangles with only acute angles, increase the angle of the pencils to form an obtuse angle.

Ask: Does this larger (or obtuse) angle form a different triangle? Explain. **[Yes, the third side would just have to be longer to create the triangle.]**

Direct students' attention to Example 1 and have a volunteer read Question 1 aloud.

Ask: How many triangles do you think can be drawn with side lengths of 3 cm and 5 cm? **[Answers will vary.]**

Ask: Look at the four triangles drawn. How are they the same? How are they different? Explain. **[They are the same because two of the sides measure 3 cm and 5 cm. They are different because the third side is a different length. Also, the interior angles appear to have different measures.]**

If desired, provide grid paper to students to assist with their drawings.

Check
Problem 1

Encourage students to use their rulers to determine the side length of the third side and label their drawing. Then have them share their drawing with a partner to see that many triangles can be created using two given side lengths. Point out that the triangles drawn will have different angle measures and different side lengths.

Problem 2

This problem might be more difficult for students as they attempt to use the given sides. Encourage students as they attempt this and provide scratch paper for additional attempts.

Say: When you are finished drawing a triangle for Problem 2, show your triangle to a partner. Then think about how the triangles are the same and how they are different.

For this problem, students should only get one triangle. To convince students the triangles are the same, have them place the triangles on top of each other to show congruency.

Example 2

Review drawing angles of a given angle measure. If desired, allow students to practice drawing angles on a blank piece of paper.

Direct students' attention to Example 2.

Ask: How many angles are in a triangle? **[3]**

Ask: What is the sum of the interior angles of any triangle? **[180°]**

Ask: What are some possible angle measures in a triangle? **[Answers will vary. Sample answers: 45°, 45°, 90°; 60°, 60°, 60°; 10°, 20°, 160°; 30°, 60°, 90°; etc.]**

Ask: What if one of the measures in a triangle is 100°? What are the other possible measures? **[Answers will vary. Sample answers: 40° and 40°; 50° and 30°; 65° and 15°; etc.]**

Ask: What if two of the measures are 60° and 80°? What are the other possible measures? **[40°]**

Ask: Why is there only one other possible measure for the third angle? **[Because the sum of the interior angles of the triangle is 180°. This means the third angle must be 180° − 60° − 80° = 40°.]**

Guide students through the Question in Example 2. Point out that although the angle measures are all the same, there is no restriction on the side measures. Therefore, many triangles can be created when two or three angle measures are given.

Check
Problem 3

Because side lengths are not specified, suggest to students that they draw line segments beyond the lengths they think they will need. Then construct the angle and triangle. A triangle may look like:

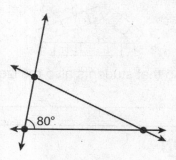

After students have answered the question, point out that they can create many different triangles with different angle measures and different side lengths.

Problem 4

Explain to students that they can create many different triangles with angle measures the same and different side lengths.

Example 3

Next, explain that students will explore triangles given side and angle measures. Emphasize that this is an exploration activity and students may not be able to reach conclusions about all combinations of given sides and angles. If preferred, a student volunteer can demonstrate a method for drawing to the whole class and students can follow along.

Remind students that their goal is only to determine if there exists no triangle, one triangle, or more than one triangle.

Check
Problem 6

You may provide a hint to students by providing grid paper and suggesting they draw the 10 cm segment first. Because the side measures are the same, the 8 cm sides will meet in the middle. Suggest that students find the midpoint of the segment, and then draw the 8 cm sides so they intersect above the midpoint.

ALTERNATE STRATEGY

Strategy: Creating Triangle Lengths

Some students may have difficulty using the ruler to draw the appropriate side lengths and determine if a triangle can be formed.

1. Provide students with strips of 1 cm grid paper and have them cut each strip to the appropriate length. For example, a triangle being formed with sides 3 cm, 5 cm, and 7 cm will use strips that look like the following:

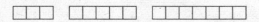

2. Next, have students use the strips to try and form the triangle. Instruct students to use the "inside" part of the strips to form the triangle. The triangle will then be the figure formed in the interior of the lengths.

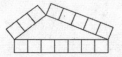

3. Repeat with various lengths so that students also realize not all sets of three lengths will form a triangle.

COMMON MISCONCEPTION

Problem 7

Ask: What is the sum of the interior angles of a triangle? **[180°]**

Error: Students may assume that because three angle measures are given, a triangle exists. Remind students to always keep in mind that the sum of the interior angles of a triangle must equal 180°.

Solution: There is no way to draw a triangle with angle measures of 20°, 40°, 60° because they do not sum to 180°. Therefore, no triangle exists.

Problem 9

Encourage students to explore sufficiently and share answers in order to determine that some triangles are not possible. If appropriate, lead students to at least discover that the length of the third side must be greater than the sum of two sides. For example, a triangle of side lengths 4 cm, 5 cm, and 12 cm cannot exist because the 4 cm and 5 cm would not join the 12 cm side.

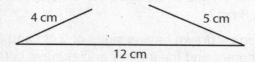

4 cm 5 cm

12 cm

ADDITIONAL ONLINE INTERVENTION RESOURCES

 Use the following for students who have not mastered the concepts in Skill 5.

- Math on the Spot videos

- Personal Math Trainer with customized intervention

- Building Block worksheets (Skill 99: Special Right Triangles, Skill 104: Triangle Sum Theorem)

SKILL 10

Geometric Drawings

Example 1

Vocabulary
Interior angle

Question 1: How many different types of triangles can be drawn if two of the sides measure 5 cm and 3 cm?

Answer 1: Many triangles can be drawn having sides of 5 cm and 3 cm. The third side lengths are different and the interior angles have different measures.

An interior angle of a triangle is the angle formed by the sides and is in the interior of the triangle.

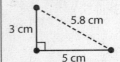 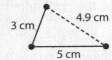 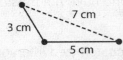 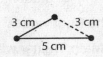

Question 2: How many different types of triangles can be drawn if the three sides measure 5 cm, 3 cm and 7 cm?

Answer 2: Only one triangle can be drawn with side lengths 5, 3, and 7 cm.

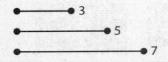 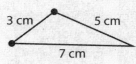

Check

Use a ruler to draw the triangles as described if they exist. Then note whether no triangle, one triangle, or more than one triangle exists for the given measures.

1. Triangles with side lengths 4 cm and 2 cm

_____

2. Triangles with side lengths 5 cm, 5 cm, and 8 cm

_____

Example 2

To Draw an Angle

Use a ruler to draw a segment.	Place the protractor so an endpoint of the segment is at the bottom center. Mark a dot for the desired angle.	Use a ruler to connect the new point and endpoint.
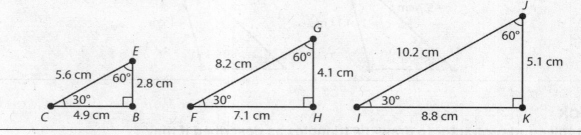		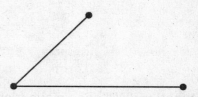

Question: How many different types of triangles can be drawn if two of the angle measures are 30° and 60°?

Answer: The sum of the interior angles of a triangle must be 180°. If two of the angles are 30° and 60°, then the remaining angle must be 180° − 30° − 60° = 90°. Because the side lengths can be different measures, many triangles can be drawn when given two angles.

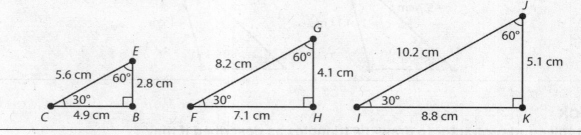

Check

Use a ruler and protractor to draw the triangles as described if they exist. Then note whether no triangle, one triangle, or more than one triangle exists for the given measures.

3. Triangle with one angle measuring 80°.

_____

4. Triangle with one angle measure of 100° and one angle measure of 30°.

_____

Example 3

Question: How many different types of triangles can be drawn if two of the sides measure 3 cm and 5 cm and the angle between the sides is 40°?

Answer: Because two side lengths and an angle measure is specified, there is only one unique way to draw this triangle.

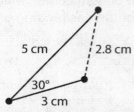

Question: Will one unique triangle always exist when two side and an angle are known?

Answer: When two side lengths are known and an angle that is not between the sides is known, there are exactly two different triangles that can be drawn.

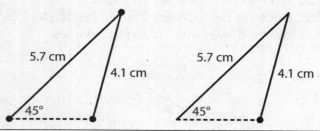

Check

Use a ruler and protractor to draw the triangles as described if they exist. Then note whether no triangle, one triangle, or more than one triangle exists for the given measures.

5. Triangle with side of 4 cm, angle of 30°, then a side of 8 cm

_____

6. Triangle with sides 8 cm, 8 cm, and 10 cm.

_____

7. Explain the Error. Find the solution.

Question: How many ways are there to draw a triangle with angle measures 20°, 40°, 60°?

_____

_____

Solution: Because three angles are given, there are many different triangles that can be drawn. They will have the same angle measures but different side lengths.

_____

_____

8. The Triangle Toy Company makes plastic sticks with magnets on each end that can be formed into a triangle. The company makes sticks of length 4 cm, 5 cm, 8 cm, 10 cm, 12 cm, and 15 cm. There are at least three sticks of each length.

   A Draw a triangle having two sides the same length.

   B Draw a triangle having all sides of different lengths.

9. The director of marketing for the Triangle Toy Company would like to advertise that triangles can be made with any of the sticks. Is this statement true? Explain. (Hint: Start with two sides lengths. Then see if any of the remaining lengths can be the third side.)

_____

_____

SKILL 10 GEOMETRIC DRAWINGS

Making Predictions with Probability

KEY TEACHING POINTS

Example 1
Make sure students understand how to solve proportions.

Say: When you make a prediction based on a sample, you make an assumption that the ratio of the preferences in the sample will be the same as the ratio of the preferences of a larger group.

Ask: How can you write a ratio for the number of students who ride the bus using the survey results? **[Compare the number of students who ride the bus to the total number of students in the survey.]**

Ask: How many of the students surveyed ride a bus to school? **[22]**

Ask: How can you find the total number of students surveyed? **[Add the number of responses in the table.]** How many students were surveyed? **[40]**

Ask: What ratio of the students surveyed ride a bus? **[22 out of 40, or $\frac{22}{40}$, or $\frac{11}{20}$]**

Say: Remember that a proportion states that two ratios are equivalent. If you want to find an equivalent ratio for a larger group, you can solve a proportion.

Ask: How can you represent the ratio for the number of students who ride a bus in the entire school? $\left[\frac{n}{300}\right]$

Work through the steps to solve the proportion. Have students check their answers by showing that the ratios are equivalent since $\frac{11}{20} = 0.55$ and $\frac{165}{300} = 0.55$.

Ask: Do you know for certain that 165 students in the school ride the bus? **[No; it is only a prediction.]**

Check
Make sure students can set up proportions correctly.

Problem 1
Ask: What proportion can you write to represent the problem? $\left[\frac{3}{8} = \frac{n}{1200}\right]$

Problem 3
Ask: How many students were surveyed? **[80]**

Ask: What is the ratio of students who want to learn German to the total number of students surveyed? $\left[\frac{12}{80}\right]$

Example 2

Make sure students can convert between fractions, decimals, and percents.

Say: Probability is a ratio. It compares the number of favorable outcomes to the number of possible outcomes.

Ask: What is the favorable outcome? **[blocking a shot]**

Ask: What are the possible outcomes? **[blocking a shot and not blocking a shot]**

Ask: What are you trying to predict? **[the number of shots that were scored]**

Say: If a team scores a point that means that the shot was not blocked.

Ask: Do you want to find the number of shots that were blocked or the number of shots that were not blocked? **[not blocked]**

Say: You are given the probability that a goalie will block a shot. If the goalie blocks 12 out of 15 attempts, then the goalie does not block 3 out of 15 attempts. So, the probability of not blocking a shot is $\frac{3}{15} = \frac{1}{5}$ or 20%.

After students work through the example, show them that they can also solve the problem using a proportion.

$$\frac{1}{5} = \frac{n}{25}$$ Write a proportion.

$25 = 5n$ Find the cross products.

$5 = n$ Divide each side by 5.

Check
Problem 4

Ask: What is the ratio of 25% coupons to the total number of coupons? **[5 out of 75 or 1 out of 15]**

Problem 5

Ask: What is $\frac{3}{5}$ written as a decimal and a percent? **[0.6; 60%]** Point out that the answer is not an integer so it is given as an approximation.

Problem 6

Students can approach the problem in two ways. They can determine the probability of not winning a prize and then make a prediction, or they can make a prediction for the people who will win a prize and subtract that number from 120 to find the number of people who will not win a prize.

Ask: What are the possible outcomes of spinning the wheel? **[winning a prize and not winning a prize]**

Ask: What is the probability of winning a prize? $\left[\frac{1}{15}\right]$

Ask: What is the probability of not winning a prize? $\left[\frac{14}{15}\right]$

Example 3

Ask: If you want to know the probability of rolling a 4, what is the favorable outcome? **[rolling a 4]** How many favorable outcomes are there? **[1]**

Ask: What are the possible outcomes for rolling the number cube? **[1, 2, 3, 4, 5, 6]** How many possible outcomes are there? **[6]**

Say: The probability of rolling a 4 is $\frac{1}{6}$ since 1 out of the 6 numbers on the cube is a 4. This means that you expect to roll a 4 one time out of every six rolls. To find how many times you expect to roll a 4 out of 100 tosses, use a proportion.

Ask: In the proportion why is the denominator 100 in the second ratio? **[The number cube is rolled 100 times.]**

Ask: Is it possible to roll a number cube 100 times, and land on 4 more than 17 times or less than 17 times? **[Yes; 17 is only a prediction.]**

Check
Problem 10

Ask: How many different kinds of fruit are in the dried fruit mix? **[6]**

Ask: What is the probability of randomly choosing a raisin? $\left[\frac{1}{6}\right]$

Problem 12

Ask: How many cards were purchased altogether as shown in the table? **[60]**

Ask: What is the ratio of birthday cards purchased to the total number of cards? $\left[\frac{30}{60} \text{ or } \frac{1}{2}\right]$

Ask: What is the ratio of thank you cards purchased to the total number of cards? $\left[\frac{12}{60} \text{ or } \frac{1}{5}\right]$

ALTERNATE STRATEGY

Strategy: Use a different approach.

Example 2

Show students that you can also solve the problem by using the given probability to find the number of blocked shots. Then subtract the number of blocked shots from the total number of attempts to find the number of scores.

Say: There were 25 attempts to score a goal. The probability of blocking a shot is $\frac{4}{5}$. Use this probability to find the number of shots blocked.

$$\frac{4}{5} \cdot 25 = 20$$

Ask: If 20 out of 25 shots were blocked, how many shots were not blocked? Explain.
[5 shots; 25 − 20 = 5]

COMMON MISCONCEPTIONS

Problem 6

The question asks for the number of people who will NOT win a prize. Students may have misread the question or forgotten to find the complement. Remind students to read problem statements carefully and look for key words.

Problem 11

The question asks for the number of monkeys left in the box. The solution given, 16 monkeys, is the result of finding the number of monkeys that have been given out so far, instead of finding the number of monkeys left in the box. Students do not need to recognize that 16 is the number of monkeys given away, but they should know that the correct equation is $\frac{1}{4} \cdot 36 = 9$.

Ask: How many stuffed animals have been given away? **[64]**

Ask: How many stuffed animals are left in the box? **[36]**

Ask: What is the probability of randomly choosing a monkey? **[1 out of 4 or $\frac{1}{4}$]**

Ask: Is it reasonable to predict that 16 out of 36 stuffed animals left in the box are monkeys? **[No; only about $\frac{1}{4}$ of the stuffed animals should be monkeys.]**

Error: There were 16 monkeys that were given away, not left in the box. There are 36 stuffed animals left in the box. The probability of randomly choosing a monkey is $\frac{1}{4}$ and $\frac{1}{4} \cdot 36 \neq 16$.

Solution: The number of monkeys left in the box should be $\frac{1}{4} \cdot 36 = 9$ monkeys.

ADDITIONAL ONLINE INTERVENTION RESOURCES

 Use the following for students who have not mastered the concepts in Skill 11.

- Math on the Spot videos
- Personal Math Trainer with customized intervention
- Building Block worksheets (Skill 6: Analyze Data; Skill 95: Solve Proportions)

SKILL 11 Making Predictions with Probability

Example 1

Surveys are used to collect information about a group.
Sometimes the group is too large to survey every individual.
A sample can be used to predict the actions of a larger group.

Suppose you randomly surveyed a group of students in your
school about the transportation they use to get to school.
The table shows the results of a survey.

Transportation to School	
Bus	22
Walk	6
Bicycle	5
Car	7

If there are 300 students at the school, predict how
many students ride a bus to school.

Write a ratio for the number of students who ride a
bus to the total number of students surveyed.

Students who ride bus: 22

Total number of students surveyed: $22 + 6 + 5 + 7 = 40$

Ratio: $\frac{22}{40}$ or $\frac{11}{20}$

The survey shows that 11 out of every 20 students
surveyed ride a bus to school. Set up a proportion to
find the number of n students out of 300 who ride a
bus.

$\frac{11}{20} = \frac{n}{300}$ Write a proportion.

$11 \cdot 300 = 20 \cdot n$ Find the cross products.

$3300 = 20n$ Multiply.

$165 = n$ Divide each side by 20.

So, the survey predicts that about 165 students in
the school ride the bus.

Check

1. The manager of a movie theater kept track of the number of tickets sold for each type of movie for one week. The manager found that every 3 out of 8 people bought tickets for action films. If the movie theater sold 1200 tickets during a weekend, predict how many people watched an action film.

   _____

2. The results of a survey show that 42 out of 100 people take a vitamin every day. How many people would you expect to take a vitamin every day out of 2000 people?

   _____

3. The table shows the results of a survey that asked incoming students what foreign language they were interested in learning. If 240 students signed up for a foreign language class, predict how many students chose German.

   _____

Language	Number of Students
French	24
Spanish	36
German	12
Latin	8

Example 2

The probability of an event is a ratio that compares the number of favorable outcomes to the total number of possible outcomes. In soccer, a shot is an attempt to score a goal. When a goal is attempted, there are two possible outcomes: the shot is blocked or the shot is scored.

During soccer practice, a goalie blocks 12 out of 15 attempts to score a goal. Find the probability that the goalie will block a shot on the goal.

The number of favorable outcomes is 12 blocked shots and the total number of outcomes is 15 attempts. So, the probability that the goalie will block a shot is $\frac{12}{15}$ or $\frac{4}{5}$.

You can write probability as a fraction, a decimal, or a percent: $\frac{4}{5} = 0.8 = 80\%$.

Suppose that in a game there were 25 attempts to score a goal by the other team. Predict how many shots were scored.

If the goalie blocks 80% of the shots, then 20% of the shots are scored. Multiply the probability by the number of attempts.

$n = 0.2 \cdot 25$ $20\% = 0.20$

$n = 5$

A good prediction is that 5 shots were scored.

Check

4. A clothing store is giving coupons to its customers worth 10%, 15%, 20%, or 25% off every purchase. The company prints five 25% off coupons out of every 75 coupons. What is the probability that you will choose a 25% off coupon out of a box with 300 coupons?

_____

5. The probability that a basketball player makes a basket during a game is $\frac{3}{5}$.

   During a recent game the player attempted 24 shots. Predict how many shots she made.

_____

6. In a carnival game, participants spin a wheel to win a prize. The probability of winning a prize is 1 out of every 15 spins. If 120 people play the game, predict how many people will not win a prize.

_____

Use the following information 7–8.
A toothbrush manufacturer determines that 3 out of 150 toothbrushes have a defect.

7. What is the probability that a randomly chosen toothbrush has a defect?

_____

_____

8. Predict how many toothbrushes will have a defect out of a box of 1000 toothbrushes.

_____

_____

Example 3

Some outcomes have an equal probability of occurring.

If you roll a number cube with numbers 1–6 on the faces, the probability of rolling each number is equally likely. Since there are 6 possible outcomes, the probability of rolling each number is $\frac{1}{6}$.

Predict how many times you will roll a 4 if you roll a number cube 100 times.

$\frac{1}{6} = \frac{n}{100}$	Write a proportion.
$1 \cdot 100 = 6 \cdot n$	Find the cross products.
$100 = 6n$	Multiply.
$16.7 \approx 6n$	Divide each side by 6.

You should expect to roll a 4 about 17 times.

Check

9. A spinner has 8 equal sections numbered 1–8. How many times would you expect to land on an even number out of 20 spins?

   _____

10. A package of dried fruit mix contains apricots, bananas, raisins, pineapple cubes, dates, and cranberries in equal amounts. If you take a random handful of 20 pieces, predict how many apricots you will get.

    _____

11. Explain the Error. Find the correct solution.

    A zoo is having a customer appreciation day and is giving away stuffed animals to every visitor. In the first hour, the zoo gives away 64 stuffed animals that are randomly chosen from a box with 100 stuffed animals.

    If the box contains an equal number of elephants, tigers, monkeys, and bears, there should be about 16 monkeys left in the box.

    _____

    _____

12. The table shows the number of cards that were purchased last week at a gift shop. The store manager is placing an order for 500 cards. How many more birthday cards should the manager order than thank you cards? Show your work.

Type of Card	Number of Cards
Birthday	30
Get Well	13
Thank You	12
Sympathy	5

_____

_____

SKILL 11 MAKING PREDICTIONS WITH PROBABILITY

Parallel Lines Cut by a Transversal

KEY TEACHING POINTS

Example 1

Say: A transversal is a line that intersects two or more lines in a plane. The figure shows three lines, line *t*, line *m*, and line *n*.

Ask: Which line is the transversal? **[line *t*]** How do you know? **[Line *t* intersects two lines, line *m* and line *n*].**

Ask: Is line *m* a transversal? **[No, it only intersects one line in the diagram, line *t*.]**

Ask: How many angles are formed when a transversal intersects two lines? **[8]**

Say: The angle pairs that are formed when a transversal intersects two lines have special names.

Review the definitions for same-side interior angles, same-side exterior angles, alternate exterior angles, alternate interior angles, and corresponding angles.

Say: Notice that each angle pair includes one angle that is formed by line *t* and line *m* and one angle that is formed by line *t* and line *n*.

Make sure students understand what is meant by angles that lie inside or outside the intersected lines and what angles are in the same position in relation to the intersected lines.

Ask: Which angles lie outside the intersected lines? **[∠1, ∠2, ∠7, ∠8]**

Say: Notice that the angles are above line *m* or below line *n*.

Ask: Which angles lie inside the intersected lines? **[∠3, ∠4, ∠5, ∠6]**

Say: Notice that the angles are below line *m* or above line *n*. These angles lie between line *m* and line *n*.

Ask: Look at ∠1 and ∠8. Are the angles on the same side of the transversal or on opposite sides? **[same side]** Are the angles on the inside or the outside of lines *m* and *n*? **[outside]** How would you classify the angles? **[same-side exterior angles]**

Ask: Look at ∠4 and ∠6. Are the angles on the same side of the transversal or on opposite sides? **[opposite sides]** Are the angles on the inside or the outside of lines *m* and *n*? **[inside]** How would you classify the angles? **[alternate interior angles]**

Say: Look at ∠1 and ∠5. ∠1 is to the left of the transversal and above line *m*. ∠5 is to the left of the transversal and above line *n*. The angles are in the same position in relation to line *t* and the intersected line that forms each angle, so they are corresponding angles.

Ask: Which angle corresponds to ∠3? **[∠7]** Why? **[The angles are in the same position, to the right of the transversal and below the intersected lines.]**

Check

Check students' understanding before beginning the problems.

Ask: What special angle pairs can you form with ∠5? **[∠5 and ∠1 are alternate exterior angles, ∠5 and ∠2 are same-side exterior angles, and ∠5 and ∠3 are corresponding angles.]**

Example 2

Ask: In the figure, which lines are parallel? **[lines *p* and *q*]** How can you tell which lines are parallel from the figure? **[Parallel lines are marked with arrows going in the same direction.]**

Ask: What line is the transversal? **[line *t*]**

Ask: When a transversal intersects parallel lines, which type of angle pairs are congruent? **[alternate interior angles, alternate exterior angles, and corresponding angles]**

Ask: How are ∠3 and ∠5 related? **[They are alternate interior angles.]** Are they congruent? **[Yes]**

Ask: How are ∠3 and ∠6 related? **[They are same-side interior angles.]** Are they congruent? **[No]**

Ask: How are ∠2 and ∠7 related? **[They are same-side exterior angles.]** Are they congruent? **[No]**

Ask: How are ∠2 and ∠8 related? **[They are alternate exterior angles.]** Are they congruent? **[Yes]**

As you work through the example, have students highlight congruent angle pairs. Use one color for all angles that measure 110° and another color for angles that measure 70°.

Say: Notice that all of the angle measures are either 70° or 110°.

Check
Problems 6–9

The orientation of the transversal and the parallel lines are different in the figure for these problems. Make sure students can still identify the angle pairs. Refer students to the definitions for each type of angle pair, if necessary.

Ask: In the figure, which lines are parallel? **[lines *a* and *b*]**

Ask: What line is the transversal? **[line *t*]**

Ask: How are ∠8 and ∠6 related? **[They are corresponding angles.]**

Ask: How are ∠8 and ∠4 related? **[They are alternate exterior angles.]**

Ask: How are ∠7 and ∠3 related? **[They are alternate interior angles.]**

Example 3

Ask: What do you know about supplementary angles? **[The sum of the measures of supplementary angles is 180°.]**

Ask: How do you know from the figure that ∠1 and ∠2 are supplementary? **[The angles form a linear pair.]**

Ask: How are ∠1 and ∠3 related? **[They are vertical angles.]** What is true about vertical angles? **[Vertical angles are congruent, so the angles have equal measures.]**

Ask: How are ∠1 and ∠4 related? **[They form a linear pair, so they are supplementary.]**

Hold a discussion about how to find the measures of ∠5, ∠6, ∠7, and ∠8. There are different approaches students can use to find the missing measures. One way is to use corresponding angles for each of the unknown angles.

Check
Problems 11–22

Have students analyze the figure before they begin work on the problems.

Ask: In the figure, which lines are parallel? **[lines *r* and *s*]**

Ask: Which line is the transversal that intersects the parallel lines? **[Line *f* and line *g* are both transversals that intersect the parallel lines.]**

Ask: Is line *r* a transversal? **[Yes]** What lines does line *r* intersect? **[line *f* and line *g*]** Is line *f* parallel to line *g*? **[No]**

Ask: What is the measure of ∠1? **[112°]** What kind of angle pairs can be formed with ∠1? **[∠1 and ∠2 are supplementary angles, ∠1 and ∠4 are vertical angles, ∠1 and ∠3 are supplementary angles, ∠1 and ∠5 are congruent corresponding angles, and ∠1 and ∠8 are congruent alternate exterior angles.]**

Ask: How are ∠1 and ∠9 related? **[They are corresponding angles.]** Are they congruent? **[No]** Why? **[They are not congruent because line *f* is not parallel to line *g*.]**

Problem 28

Point out that the single arrows on lines *m* and *n* indicate line *m* is parallel to line *n* and the double arrows on lines *r* and *t* indicate that line *r* is parallel to line *t*.

ALTERNATE STRATEGY

Strategy: Investigate corresponding angles when parallel lines are cut by a transversal.

1. Have students draw two intersecting lines and label the four angles that are formed as shown. Have students draw a duplicate copy of the figure using tracing paper or a ruler and a protractor.

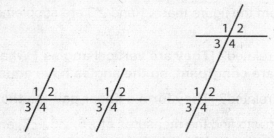

2. Have students align the two figures using one of the lines. Tell students to draw the figure they created and complete the figure by labeling all lines and marking lines that are parallel. Then have students align the two figures using the other line. Students should complete the drawing and label all parts of the figure.

3. Have students compare and contrast the two figures. Students should identify the transversal, parallel lines, and corresponding angles.

COMMON MISCONCEPTIONS

Example 1
Some students may classify ∠3 and ∠4 as alternate interior angles because they are on the opposite side of the transversal and inside the intersected lines. Remind students that each angle pair includes one angle that is formed by line *t* and line *m* and one angle that is formed by line *t* and line *n*.

Problem 10
Some students may not consider the condition that the lines cut by a transversal must be parallel in order for corresponding angles to be congruent.

Ask: Which line is the transversal? **[line *t*]**

Ask: Are ∠4 and ∠8 corresponding angles? **[Yes]**

Ask: Is line *v* parallel to line *w*? **[No]**

Error: The lines intersected by the transversal are not parallel, so corresponding angles are not congruent.

Solution: ∠4 and ∠8 are corresponding angles. Since the transversal does not intersect parallel lines, corresponding angles are not congruent. Therefore, you cannot determine the measure of ∠8.

Problem 27
Some students may conclude that ∠ACD and ∠ABD are congruent because they are alternate interior angles. They may come to this conclusion based on the figure containing parallel lines and the angles appear to opposite of each other. Point out that the angles do not share a transversal. ∠ACD is formed by line *s* and line segment *CD*. ∠ABD is formed by line *t* and line segment *AB*.

Have students identify that ∠ACD forms an alternate interior angle pair with ∠CDF using $\overline{CD}$ as the transversal. However, the angles are not congruent because the intersected lines, lines *s* and *t*, are not parallel.

ADDITIONAL ONLINE INTERVENTION RESOURCES

 Use the following for students who have not mastered the concepts in Skill 12.

- Math on the Spot videos
- Personal Math Trainer with customized intervention
- Building Block worksheets (Skill 71: Parallel Lines and Transversals)

SKILL 12 — Parallel Lines Cut by a Transversal

Example 1

A **transversal** is a line that intersects two or more lines in a plane. In the figure, line *t* is a transversal that intersects line *m* and line *n*.

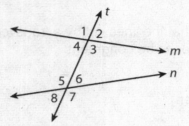

Certain types of angle pairs are formed when a transversal intersects two lines.

Same-side interior angles lie on the same side of the transversal and inside the intersected lines. Examples: ∠3 and ∠6, ∠4 and ∠5

Same-side exterior angles lie on the same side of the transversal and outside the intersected lines. Examples: ∠1 and ∠8, ∠2 and ∠7

Alternate interior angles lie on opposite sides of the transversal and inside the intersected lines. Examples: ∠4 and ∠6, ∠3 and ∠5

Alternate exterior angles lie on opposite sides of the transversal and outside the intersected lines. Examples: ∠1 and ∠7, ∠2 and ∠8

Corresponding angles lie on the same side of the transversal and are in the same position in relation to the two intersected lines. Examples: ∠1 and ∠5, ∠2 and ∠6, ∠3 and ∠7, ∠4 and ∠8

Vocabulary

Transversal

Same-side interior angles

Same-side exterior angles

Alternate interior angles

Alternate exterior angles

Corresponding angles

Parallel lines

Check

Use the figure. Classify each pair of angles as *same-side interior*, *same-side exterior*, *alternate interior*, *alternate exterior*, or *corresponding* angles.

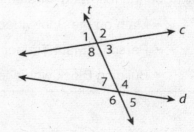

1. ∠1 and ∠7 _____

2. ∠2 and ∠6 _____

3. ∠4 and ∠8 _____

4. ∠3 and ∠4 _____

5. ∠6 and ∠8 _____

Example 2

Parallel lines lie in the same plane and never intersect. In the figure, line *p* is parallel to line *q*.

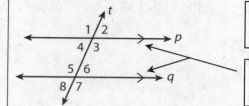

Line *p* is parallel to line *q* is written as *p* ∥ *q*.

The arrows on the line are used to indicate parallel ...

When parallel lines are cut by a transversal, the following angle pairs are congruent.

Alternate interior angles: ∠4 ≅ ∠6, ∠3 ≅ ∠5

Alternate exterior angles: ∠1 ≅ ∠7, ∠2 ≅ ∠8

Corresponding angles: ∠1 ≅ ∠5, ∠2 ≅ ∠6, ∠3 ≅ ∠7, ∠4 ≅ ∠8

In the figure above, m∠1 = 110°. What other angles have a measure of 110°?
Since ∠1 and ∠5 are corresponding angles, m∠5 = 110°.
Since ∠1 and ∠7 are alternate exterior angles, m∠7 = 110°.
Since ∠7 and ∠3 are corresponding angles, m∠3 = 110°.

In the figure, m∠2 = 70°. What other angles have a measure of 70°?
Since ∠2 and ∠6 are corresponding angles, m∠6 = 70°.
Since ∠2 and ∠8 are alternate exterior angles, m∠8 = 70°.
Since ∠8 and ∠4 are corresponding angles, m∠4 = 70°.

Check

In the figure, *a* ∥ *b*, m∠1 = 82° and m∠2 = 98°. Find each angle measure. Explain your reasoning.

6. m∠3 _____

7. m∠4 _____

8. m∠5 _____

9. m∠6 _____

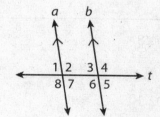

10. Explain the Error. Find the correct solution.

In the figure, line *t* is a transversal and m∠4 = 65°.
Since ∠4 and ∠8 are corresponding angles, ∠4 ≅ ∠8,
so m∠8 = 65°.

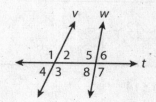

_____

Example 3

When parallel lines are cut by a transversal, the angles formed are either congruent or supplementary. If you know the measure of one of the angles, you can find the measures of all of the angles.

In the figure, m∠1 = 96°.

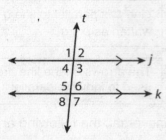

∠1 and ∠2 are supplementary. So, m∠2 = 84°.

∠1 and ∠3 are vertical angles. So, m∠3 = 96°.

∠1 and ∠4 are supplementary. So, m∠4 = 84°.

You can find the measures of ∠5, ∠6, ∠7, and ∠8 by identifying corresponding, alternate interior, alternate exterior, or supplementary angles.

Check

In the figure, f ∥ g, m∠1 = 112° and m∠16 = 78°. Find each angle measure.

11. m∠2

_____

12. m∠3

_____

13. m∠4

_____

14. m∠5

_____

15. m∠6

_____

16. m∠7

_____

17. m∠8

_____

18. m∠9

_____

19. m∠10

_____

20. m∠11

_____

21. m∠12

_____

22. m∠13

_____

23. m∠14

_____

24. m∠15

_____

25. Find the values for *x* and *y*. Explain your reasoning.

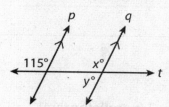

_____

Use the following information for 26–27. The figure below shows the rungs of a ladder. In the figure, $\overline{AB} \parallel \overline{CD} \parallel \overline{EF}$.

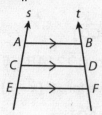

26. Is ∠*ACD* ≅ ∠*AEF*? Explain your reasoning.

_____

27. Is ∠*ACD* ≅ ∠*ABD*? Explain your reasoning.

_____

28. In the figure *m* ∥ *n* and *r* ∥ *t*. The lines intersect to form a parallelogram. What are the angle measures of the interior angles of the parallelogram?

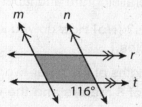

_____

SKILL 12 PARALLEL LINES CUT BY A TRANSVERSAL

Parallelograms

KEY TEACHING POINTS

Example 1

Say: What is the name of this figure? **[parallelogram]**

Ask: What properties of parallelograms do you know? **[A parallelogram has four sides with opposite sides congruent and parallel.]**

Ask: Which sides are opposites? **[$\overline{AB}$ and $\overline{CD}$ are opposite sides, and $\overline{AD}$ and $\overline{BC}$ are opposite sides.]**

Ask: Which side is congruent to $\overline{AB}$? **[$\overline{CD}$]**

Ask: What are the measures of $\overline{AB}$ and $\overline{CD}$? **[$AB = 6$ centimeter and $CD = x$ centimeter]**

Ask: What equation can you use to solve for x? **[$x = 6$]**

Ask: Which side is congruent to $\overline{BC}$? **[$\overline{AD}$]**

Ask: What are the measures of $\overline{AD}$ and $\overline{BC}$? **[$AD = 2y$ centimeter and $BC = 5$ centimeter]**

Ask: What equation can you use to solve for y? **[$2y = 5$]**

Check
Problem 1

Ask: What equation can you write to solve for x? **[$4x = 12$]**

Problem 2

Ask: What equation can you write to solve for x? **[$x + 7 = 18$]**

Problem 3

Encourage students to sketch the parallelogram and label the vertices in order.

Ask: Are $\overline{KL}$ and $\overline{LM}$ opposite sides? **[No]** How do you know? **[The side measures are not equal, so the sides are not opposites.]**

Ask: How can you determine the lengths of the other two sides of the parallelogram? **[The opposite side of $\overline{KL}$ has a length of 8 meters and the opposite side of $\overline{LM}$ is 6 meters.]**

Problem 4

Ask: Which sides are opposite sides in the parallelogram? **[$\overline{DE}$ is opposite $\overline{FG}$ and $\overline{EF}$ is opposite $\overline{DG}$.]** How do you know? **[The sides are parallel, and opposite sides are parallel in a parallelogram.**

Ask: Which sides are congruent? **[$\overline{DE} \cong \overline{FG}$ and $\overline{EF} \cong \overline{DG}$]**

Problem 5

Ask: What do you know about $\overline{PQ}$ and $\overline{RS}$? **[They are opposite sides of a parallelogram, so they are parallel and congruent.]**

Example 2

Ask: In parallelogram *ABCD*, which angle is opposite ∠*A*? **[∠*C*]**

Ask: Which angle is opposite ∠*B*? **[∠*D*]**

Ask: Which angles are congruent? **[∠*A* ≅ ∠*C* and ∠*B* ≅ ∠*D*]**

Check
Problem 10

Ask: What equation can you write to solve for *x*? **[4*x* + 2 = 106]**

Problem 11

Ask: What equation can you write to solve for *x*? **[3*x* − 8 = 82]**

Problem 12

Ask: Which angles are congruent in the parallelogram? **[∠*D* ≅ ∠*F* and ∠*E* ≅ ∠*G*]**

Problems 13–14

In problems 13 and 14, extra information is given. Students need to decide which angle measure or side measure is needed to solve the problems.

Ask: Which angle is congruent to ∠*P*? **[∠*R*]**

Ask: Which side is congruent to $\overline{PQ}$? **[$\overline{RS}$]**

Example 3

Say: Two interior angles of a parallelogram are called the consecutive angles if some side of the parallelogram is the common side of these two angles.

Say: ∠*A* and ∠*B* are consecutive angles.

Ask: Which common side do both angles share? **[$\overline{AB}$]**

Ask: Is there another angle that has a common side with ∠*A*? **[Yes; ∠*D*]**

Ask: Are ∠*A* and ∠*D* consecutive angles? **[Yes]**

Say: Consecutive angles of a parallelogram are supplementary.

Ask: What do you know about supplementary angles? **[The sum of supplementary angles is 180°.]**

Ask: What is the sum of m∠*A* and m∠*B*? **[180°]**

Ask: If you know the measure of ∠*A*, how can you find the measure of ∠*B*? **[Subtract the measure of ∠*A* from 180.]**

Ask: If m∠*A* is 98°, what is the m∠*C*? **[98°]** Why? **[∠*A* and ∠*C* are opposite angles, so they are congruent.]**

Ask: If m∠*A* is 98°, what is the m∠*D*? **[82°]** Why? **[∠*A* and ∠*D* are consecutive angles, so the sum of their measures is 180; 180 − 98 = 82]**

Ask: If you only know the measure of one angle of a parallelogram, how can you determine the measures of the other three angles? **[Find the measure of a consecutive angle by subtracting the known measure from 180. Then find the measures of the congruent angles that are opposite each of the two known angles.]**

Check that students understand the relationship between the angles in a parallelogram with the following questions.

Say: Suppose you know two angles in a parallelogram each measure 80°.

Ask: Are these angles opposite angles or consecutive angles? **[Opposite angles]** How do you know? **[The angles have equal measures so they are congruent. Opposite angles are congruent.]**

Ask: How can you find the unknown angle measures? **[Subtract 80 from 180.]**

Ask: What are the measures of the two unknown angles? **[Both angles measure 100°.]**

Say: Suppose one angle in a parallelogram measures 55° and another angle measures 125°.

Ask: Are these angles opposite angles or consecutive angles? **[consecutive angles]** How do you know? **[The sum of the angle measures is 180°, so the angles are supplementary. Consecutive angles are supplementary.]**

Ask: How can you find the unknown angle measures? **[Each of the unknown angles will be congruent to the given angles.]**

Ask: What are the measures of the two unknown angles? **[55° and 125°]**

Ask: Can a parallelogram have two angles that measure 60° and 100°? **[No; the angles are not congruent and they are not supplementary.]**

Check
Problem 19
Ask: Will the unknown angles have the same measure or different measures? **[the same measure]**

Problem 20
Ask: What is the relationship between $\angle R$ and $\angle Q$? **[They are consecutive angles, so they are supplementary.]**

Ask: What is the relationship between $\angle R$ and $\angle S$? **[They are consecutive angles, so they are supplementary.]**

Ask: What is the relationship between $\angle R$ and $\angle P$? **[They are opposite angles, so they are congruent.]**

Problem 22
Ask: What is the relationship between $\angle M$ and $\angle N$? **[They are consecutive angles so they are supplementary.]**

Ask: What is the sum of m$\angle M$ and m$\angle N$? **[180°]**

Ask: What equation can you use to find the value of x? **[$x + (2x + 18) = 180$]**

Ask: Once you know the value of x, what is the next step? **[Replace x with its numeric value in the expressions for $\angle M$ and $\angle N$.]**

Ask: How can you check that your value for x is correct? **[The measures for $\angle M$ and $\angle N$ should have a sum of 180.]**

Example 4

Ask: What line segments are the diagonals of parallelogram *ABCD*? [$\overline{AC}$ and $\overline{BD}$]

Ask: What does bisect mean? [**to divide into two equal parts**]

Ask: What is a midpoint of a line segment? [**the point on the line that is exactly halfway between the endpoints of the line segment**]

Say: Since the diagonals of a parallelogram bisect each other, the point of intersection is the midpoint of both diagonals. *E* is the midpoint of $\overline{AC}$ and *E* is the midpoint of $\overline{BD}$.

Ask: Which line segment is congruent to $\overline{AE}$? [$\overline{EC}$]

Ask: Which line segment is congruent to $\overline{BE}$? [$\overline{ED}$]

Ask: What is the relationship between the measures of $\overline{AE}$ and $\overline{AC}$. [**The length of $\overline{AE}$ is half the length of $\overline{AC}$.**]

Review linear measures and midpoints, if necessary. Make sure students understand that since *E* is the midpoint of $\overline{AC}$, the following relationships are true.

- $AE + EC = AC$
- $AE = \dfrac{1}{2}AC$
- $EC = \dfrac{1}{2}AC$
- $AC = 2AE$
- $AC = 2EC$

Have students write similar equations for diagonal $\overline{BD}$.

Check
Problem 23

Ask: What is midpoint of both diagonals? [**point *K***]

Ask: What equation can you use to find *x*? [$8x + 9 = x + 16$]

Ask: What equation can you use to find *y*? [$3y - 4 = 2y + 4$]

Remind students that after they find the values of *x* and *y*, they should use the values to check that congruent segments have the same measure.

Problem 24

Ask: How can you find the length of $\overline{GI}$? [**Add the measures of $\overline{GK}$ and $\overline{KI}$; $GK + KI = GI$**]

Problems 25–27

Remind students that $CG + GE = CE$ and $FG + GD = FD$.

Ask: Which line segment is congruent to $\overline{CG}$? [$\overline{GE}$]

Ask: Which line segment is congruent to $\overline{FG}$? [$\overline{GD}$]

Ask: Is $\overline{CE} \cong \overline{FD}$? [**No**]

ALTERNATE STRATEGY

Strategy: Use models to show angle and side relationships in parallelograms.

1. Have students carefully draw two copies of a parallelogram on a piece of paper. They should label the vertices as shown below. Then draw a diagonal from *A* to *C*.

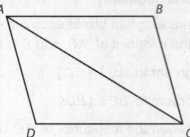

2. Students should mark the congruent parts of the parallelograms as shown below.

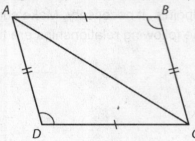

3. Tell students to cut along the diagonal of the parallelogram to form two triangles. Students should manipulate the triangles so that one triangle fits on top of the other. Have students list the congruent sides and the congruent angles.

4. Have students repeat the activity drawing the same size parallelogram. This time students should draw the diagonal from *B* to *D* and mark the congruent parts. Have students list the congruent sides and the congruent angles.

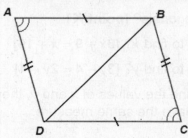

5. Finally, have students compare the diagonals of the two different triangles.

6. **Ask:** Are the opposite sides of the parallelogram congruent? **[Yes]** Are the opposite angles of the parallelogram congruent? **[Yes]** Are the diagonals of the parallelogram congruent? **[No]**

COMMON MISCONCEPTIONS

Problem 4
Opposite sides should be congruent. Students should use the given information about which sides are parallel to identify which sides are opposites. Since $\overline{DE} \parallel \overline{FG}$ and $\overline{EF} \parallel \overline{DG}$, $\overline{DE}$ and $\overline{FG}$ are opposite sides, and $\overline{EF}$ and $\overline{DG}$ are opposite sides.

Error: Opposite sides are not identified correctly.

Solution: $DE = FG = 11$ feet and $DG = EF = 14$ feet

Problems 13 and 14
These problems have additional information. Students need to identify opposite angles and use the correct angle measure or side measure in their calculations.

Encourage students to label figures with the information given in the question.

Problem 22
Watch for students who write an incorrect equation $x = 2x + 18$ to solve for x. Students didn't recognize that the angles are supplementary, not congruent.

Example 4
Some students may assume that the diagonals are congruent or that the diagonals bisect the angles of the parallelogram. Use examples to show that this is not true, unless the parallelogram is a rectangle.

Problems 25–27
Some students may not read the given information carefully and use $GD = 20$ instead of $FD = 20$ in their calculations. Encourage students to label figures with the information given in the question.

ADDITIONAL ONLINE INTERVENTION RESOURCES

 Use the following for students who have not mastered the concepts in Skill 13.

- Math on the Spot videos
- Personal Math Trainer with customized intervention
- Building Block worksheets (Skill 8: Angles in Polygons; Skill 49: Identify Polygons; Skill 74: Polygon Angle Measures)

SKILL 13 Parallelograms

Example 1

A parallelogram is a special type of quadrilateral. One property of parallelograms is that its opposite sides are congruent and parallel.

In parallelogram $ABCD$, $\overline{AB} \parallel \overline{CD}$, $\overline{BC} \parallel \overline{AD}$, $\overline{AB} \cong \overline{CD}$ and $\overline{AD} \cong \overline{BC}$.

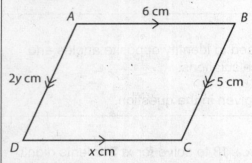

Find the values for x and y.

$\overline{AB}$ and $\overline{CD}$ are opposite sides, so $\overline{AB} \cong \overline{CD}$.

$AB = CD$	Write an equation.
$6 = x$	$AB = 6$, $CD = x$

$\overline{AD}$ and $\overline{BC}$ are opposite sides, so $\overline{AB} \cong \overline{CD}$.

$AD = BC$	Write an equation.
$2y = 5$	$AD = 2y$, $BC = 5$
$y = 2.5$	Divide each side by 2.

So, $x = 6$ and $y = 2.5$.

Check
Find the value of x for each parallelogram.

1.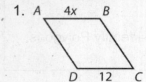

_____

2.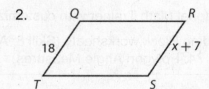

_____

3. Find the perimeter of parallelogram $JKLM$, if $KL = 8$ meters and $LM = 6$ meters.

_____

4. Explain the Error. Find the correct solution.

In parallelogram DEFG, $\overline{DE} \parallel \overline{FG}$ and $\overline{EF} \parallel \overline{DG}$.

If DE = 11 feet and DG = 14 feet, then EF = 11 feet and FG = 14 feet.

_____

5. $\overline{PQ}$ and $\overline{RS}$ are opposite sides of a parallelogram. If PQ = 84 inches and RS = 6x, what is the value of x?

_____

Example 2

Another property of parallelograms is that their opposite angles are congruent.

In parallelogram ABCD, $\angle A \cong \angle C$ and $\angle B \cong \angle D$.

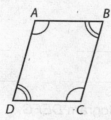

If m∠A = 105°, find m∠C.

∠A and ∠C are opposite angles, so $\angle A \cong \angle C$.

m∠A = m∠C	Write an equation.
105° = m∠C	m∠A = 105°

If m∠B = (5x + 35)° and m∠D = 75, find the value of x.

∠B and ∠D are opposite angles, so $\angle B \cong \angle D$.

m∠B = m∠D	Write an equation.
5x + 35 = 75	m∠B = 5x + 35 and m∠D = 75
5x = 40	Subtract 35 from each side.
x = 8	Divide each side by 5.

Use x = 8 to check that m∠B = 75°.

m∠B = 5x + 35

m∠B = 5(8) + 35

m∠B = 75

So, m∠A = m∠C = 105° and m∠B = m∠D = 75°.

Check

For 6–9, use parallelogram *ABCD*. Find each measure.

6. m∠C _____

7. m∠D _____

8. *AB* _____

9. *DA* _____

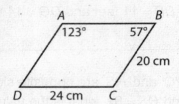

Find the value of *x* in each parallelogram.

10.

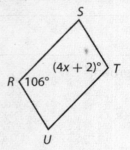

_____

_____

11.

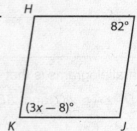

_____

_____

12. Find the values of *x* and *y* in parallelogram *DEFG*.

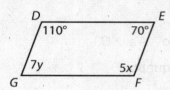

_____

For 13 and 14, use parallelogram *PQRS*.

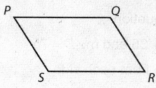

13. If m∠P = (2x + 15)°, m∠Q = 117°, and m∠R = 63°, find the value for *x*.

_____

14. If *PQ* = (5y − 6) feet, *RS* = 19 feet, and *SP* = 24 feet, find the value for *y*.

_____

Example 3

Consecutive angles of a parallelogram are supplementary. Two interior angles of a parallelogram are consecutive if they have a common side.

In the parallelogram *ABCD,* the following pairs of angles are supplementary.

∠A and ∠B, ∠B and ∠C, ∠C and ∠D, ∠D and ∠A

So, m∠A + m∠B = 180, m∠B + m∠C = 180, m∠C + m∠D = 180, and m∠D + m∠A = 180.

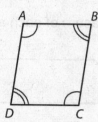

If m∠A = 98°, find the measures of the remaining angles.

∠A and ∠C are opposite angles, so ∠A ≅ ∠C.

m∠A = m∠C = 98°

∠A and ∠B are consecutive angles. The sum of consecutive angles is 180°.

m∠A + m∠B = 180	Write an equation.
98 + m∠B = 180	m∠A = 82
m∠B = 82	Subtract 82 from each side.

∠B and ∠D are opposite angles, so ∠B ≅ ∠D.

m∠B = m∠D = 82°

So, m∠A = 98°, m∠B = 82°, m∠C = 98° and m∠D = 82°.

Check
Use the given angle to name two pairs of consecutive angles.

15. ∠S _____

16. ∠T _____

17. ∠U _____

18. ∠V _____

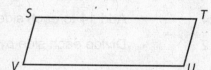

19. Two angles of a parallelogram measure 57°. What is the measure of the other two angles?

_____

Name _____ Date _____ Class_____

Find the unknown angle measures in each parallelogram.

20.

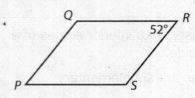

21.

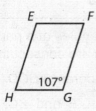

_____   _____

22. Find the value of x. Then find the measure of each angle in the parallelogram.

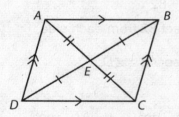

_____

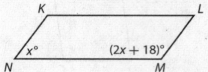

Example 4

Diagonals of a parallelogram bisect each other. In the parallelogram $ABCD$ below, E is the midpoint of $\overline{AC}$ and $\overline{BD}$. So, $\overline{AE} \cong \overline{EC}$ and $\overline{BE} \cong \overline{ED}$.

Suppose $AE = 5x - 14$ and $EC = 3x + 10$. Solve for x.

$AE = EC$	Write an equation.
$5x - 14 = 3x + 10$	$AE = 5x - 14$ and $EC = 3x + 10$
$2x - 14 = 10$	Subtract $3x$ from each side.
$2x = 24$	Add 14 to each side.
$x = 12$	Divide each side by 2.

Find the length of $\overline{AE}$ and $\overline{EC}$.

Replace x with 12 in the equations $AE = 5x - 14$ and $EC = 3x + 10$.

$AE = 5(12) - 14$ or 46 $EC = 3(12) + 10$ or 46

Check
For 23 and 24, use parallelogram *GHIJ*.

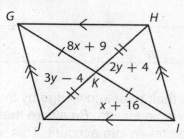

23. Find the values for *x* and *y*.

_____

24. What is the length of each diagonal?

_____

For 25–27, use the following information.
In parallelogram *CDEF*,
$FG = 2x - 4$, $FD = 20$, $CG = 3y + 2$, and $GE = 5y - 6$.

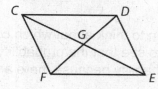

25. Find the values for *x* and *y*.

_____

26. What is the length of $\overline{GD}$?

_____

27. What is the length of $\overline{CE}$?

_____

SKILL 13 PARALLELOGRAMS

Probability of Compound Events

KEY TEACHING POINTS

Example 1

Encourage students to build upon their prior knowledge by thinking of the probability of compound events as the sum of simple events. Be aware that students might ask questions in which mutual exclusivity must be taken into account. This will be addressed in Example 2.

Work through the example with students.

Ask: What would be the probability of rolling a number less than 6? $\left[\dfrac{5}{6}\right]$

Ask: What is the probability of rolling a number less than 7? Explain. **[The probability of rolling a number less than 7 is 100%. This is because all of the numbers are less than 7 and it is certain to happen.]**

Ask: How can you show this using the addition method? **[P(less than 7) = P(1) + P(2) + P(3) + P(4) + P(5) + P(6) = $\dfrac{1}{6} + \dfrac{1}{6} + \dfrac{1}{6} + \dfrac{1}{6} + \dfrac{1}{6} + \dfrac{1}{6} = \dfrac{6}{6} = 1$]**

Check
Problem 2

Explore with students by asking them to think about which compound event would have the highest probability. Guide students to see that the probability of selecting a green or red marble would result in a greater probability because there are a greater number of green and red marbles.

Example 2

The concept of mutual exclusivity can be a confusing one to students. Point out that the word mutual means that it is the same for both events. The word exclusive usually means that something is excluded. In this case, mutually exclusive is the idea that the events are excluded from each other.

With the students, read through the situation in the example. Spend time discussing the data given in the table. Ask several questions so that students focus on reading the correct information in the rows and columns.

Ask: How many boys are in choir? **[3]**

Ask: How many students are in choir? **[7]**

Ask: How many students are there in total? **[20]**

Continue as time permits so that students feel comfortable with the data.

Direct students' attention to the solution method.

Ask: How many students are girls? **[12]**

Ask: How many students are in choir? **[7]**

Ask: How many students are girls and in choir? **[4]**

Ask: What answer would you get if you forgot to subtract the girls in choir? What would that mean? [I would get $\frac{19}{20}$ which means that if a student were randomly selected, it is almost certain the student would be a girl or in the choir.]

Point out that students should check that their answers make sense each time.

Check
Problem 5

If students forget to subtract the number of patients with a fever and an earache, they will get an answer of 110%.

Ask: Can the probability of an event be 110%? Explain. [No, if the probability of an event is 100% is certain to happen. So, a probability of 110% makes no sense.]

Remind students that probability must be between 0% and 100% inclusive. Students can use this information to see if their answers make sense.

Example 3

Explain to students that often a difficult part of probability is finding the total number in the sample space. A tree diagram or list can help a student visualize the possible outcomes.

Because the tree diagram or list provides every possible outcome, the probability of this compound event can be determined by simply counting the appropriate events.

Check
Problem 10

Students are often confused about when to use the totals in a table.

Ask: What is the total number of students in the 10th grade? [17]

Ask: What is the total number of females? [45]

Ask: Are these events mutually exclusive? Explain. [No, because a student can be female and in the 10th grade.]

Ask: How many students are females and in the 10th grade? [6]

Say: Now, determine the probability by adding the individual probabilities and subtracting the number counted twice.

Problem 11

Continue questioning in the same manner as Problem 10 so that students understand how the calculation is different for events that are mutually exclusive.

Ask: What is the total number of students in the 11th grade? [39]

Ask: What is the total number of students in the 12th grade? [21]

Ask: Are these events mutually exclusive? Explain. [Yes, because a student cannot be in the 11th and 12th grade at the same time.]

Ask: How many students are in the 11th and 12th grade? [0]

Say: Notice you can think still think about subtracting the number of students who are double counted. But because these events are mutually exclusive, the amount is 0.

ALTERNATE STRATEGY

Strategy: Manipulatives and Prediction

Use colored discs or other manipulatives and guide students through the following activity.

1. Place 10 yellow discs, 10 green discs, 1 blue, and 1 red disc in a box.

   Ask: How likely is it to get a yellow or green disc? **[very likely]**

2. Conduct several trials by randomly selecting a disc to verify the student's prediction. Then, continue asking and conducting trials to verify the predictions.

   Ask: How likely is it to get a yellow or red disc? **[likely]**

   Ask: How likely is it to get a red or blue disc? **[unlikely]**

3. Point out to students that a compound event using *or* means that there are more ways for the compound event to occur. Thus, it makes sense to add the probabilities together to yield a higher probability.

4. Continue by marking 5 yellow discs and 5 green discs with a large X.

   Ask: How likely is it to get a yellow disc or a disc with an X? **[likely]**

5. Point out that now there are some yellow discs with an X. So adding the yellow discs to the discs with an X would mean some of the discs are double counted. Encourage students to see that by subtracting the double counted items, the correct probability can be determined.

COMMON MISCONCEPTION

Problem 6

Ask: What are the even numbers? **[2, 4, 6, 8, 10]**

Ask: What are the numbers less than 6? **[1, 2, 3, 4, 5]**

Ask: What numbers are even and less than 6? **[2, 4]**

Error: Students may forget to consider whether the events are mutually exclusive. If events are mutually exclusive, they cannot happen at the same time. An even number and number less than 6 are not mutually exclusive. Therefore, some of the numbers were double counted.

Show students a Venn diagram to help them visualize the double counted numbers.

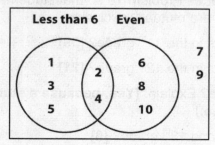

Solution: $P(\text{even or less than 6}) = \dfrac{5}{10} + \dfrac{5}{10} - \dfrac{2}{10} = \dfrac{8}{10} = 80\%$

ADDITIONAL ONLINE INTERVENTION RESOURCES

Use the following for students who have not mastered the concepts in Skill 14.

- Math on the Spot videos

- Personal Math Trainer with customized intervention

- Building Block worksheets (Skill 37 Find the Percent of a Number; Skill 39 Fractions, Decimals, and Percents; Skill 65 Multiply with Fractions and Decimals; Skill 72 Percents and Decimals; Skill 82 Simplify Fractions; Skill 86 Simplify Ratios; Skill 95 Solve Proportions; Skill 112 Write Ratios)

SKILL 14

Probability of Compound Events

<table>
<tr><td>

Example 1

A <mark>compound event</mark> is more than one outcome.

What is the probability of rolling a number less than 5?

Sample Space Method

P(rolling a number less than 5) = ?

      Outcome of "less than 5": 4, 3, 2, 1

      Sample Space: 1, 2, 3, 4, 5, 6

      P(rolling a 4) = $\dfrac{4}{6}$

Addition Method

P(less than 5) = $P(1) + P(2) + P(3) + P(4)$

      $\dfrac{1}{6} + \dfrac{1}{6} + \dfrac{1}{6} + \dfrac{1}{6} = \dfrac{4}{6}$

</td><td>

Vocabulary

Compound event

Mutually exclusive

</td></tr>
</table>

Check

Determine the probability.

1. A drawer holds 8 black socks and 6 brown socks and 4 blue socks. What is the probability of randomly selecting a brown or black sock?

          _____

2. A box contains 12 chocolate chip cookies, 10 sugar cookies, and 5 oatmeal cookies. What is the probability of randomly selecting a sugar or oatmeal cookie?

          _____

3. A bag of marbles contains 8 green, 8 red, and 4 yellow. What is the probability of randomly selecting a green or yellow marble?

          _____

Example 2

Some events cannot happen at the same time. For example, a coin can't land heads and tails. Events that cannot happen at the same time are mutually exclusive.

Some events can happen at the same time. For example, a number can be both less than 4 and odd. These events are not mutually exclusive.

When compound events are not mutually exclusive, the probability of the event happening at the same time must be subtracted.

The table shows boys and girls in drama and choir. What is the probability of randomly selecting a student who is a girl or in choir?

	Girls	Boys	Total
Drama	8	5	13
Choir	4	3	7
Total	12	8	20

Addition Method

$P(\text{girl or choir}) = P(\text{girl}) + P(\text{choir}) - P(\text{girl and choir})$

$$\frac{12}{20} + \frac{7}{20} - \frac{4}{20} = \frac{15}{20}$$

Check

Calculate each probability.

4. A number cube is rolled. What is the probability of rolling a number that is less than 5 or odd?

_____

5. At a hospital, 70% of patients have a fever and 40% have an earache. 25% of patients have a fever and an earache. What is the probability that a patient randomly selected will have a fever or an earache?

_____

6. Explain the Error. Find the solution.

Question: The numbers 1–10 are in a box and will be drawn randomly. What is the probability of selecting an even number or a number less than 6?

_____

_____

_____

Solution: The probability of selecting an even number is $\frac{5}{10}$. The probability

of selecting a number less than 6 is $\frac{5}{10}$.

Therefore, $P(\text{even or less than 6}) =$

$$\frac{5}{10} + \frac{5}{10} = \frac{10}{10} = 1$$

Example 3

You can use a tree diagram or list to help organize and count events in a sample space. A family has 3 children. What is probability the family has at least 2 girls?

Tree Diagram	List	
Girl — Girl — Girl Girl — Girl — Boy Girl — Boy — Girl Girl — Boy — Boy Boy — Girl — Girl Boy — Girl — Boy Boy — Boy — Girl Boy — Boy — Boy	GGG GGB GBG GBB BGG BGB BBG BBB	$P(\text{2 girls or 3 girls}) = \frac{4}{8} = \frac{1}{2}$

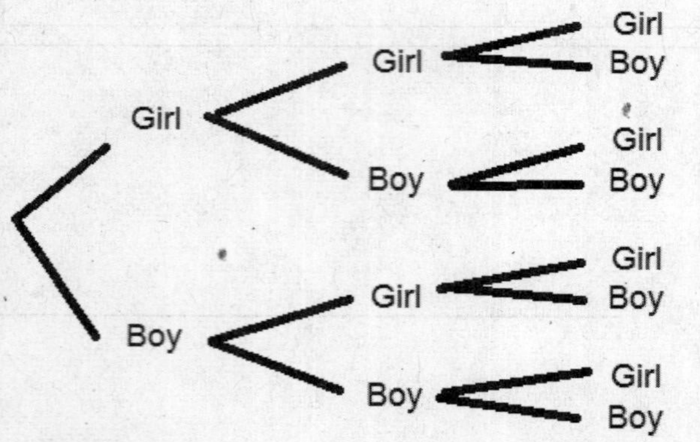

Check
Draw a tree diagram.

7. A coin is tossed and a number cube is rolled.

Use the tree diagram to calculate the probabilities.

8. What is the probability of tossing a head or a 3? _____

9. What is the probability of tossing a tails or an even number? _____

Use this information for 10–13.

A school is looking for a student representative to the city council. One hundred students applied. The data is shown. The representative will be chosen randomly.

	Female	Male	Total
9th	14	8	22
10th	6	11	17
11th	17	23	39
12th	8	13	21
Total	45	55	100

10. What is the probability the student representative is in 10th grade or female? _____

11. What is the probability the student representative is in 11th or 12th grade? _____

12. What is the probability the student representative is male or in 9th grade? _____

13. Which event or events described above are mutually exclusive? Explain.

_____

_____

SKILL 14 PROBABILITY OF COMPOUND EVENTS

Probability of Simple Events

KEY TEACHING POINTS

Example 1

Some students have a difficult time visualizing the sample space of experiments. Refer to the alternate strategy for ideas on how to use experimental probability to help students understand.

Start the class by flipping a coin in the air. Ask students to choose which side will come up. Repeat several times.

Say: When you called out heads or tails, you were predicting the event you thought would occur. So "heads" and "tails" are events.

Ask: How come you only called "heads" or "tails" when I flipped the coin? **[Because there are no other sides to the coin.]**

Say: The sample space is all the types of events that could occur. Because only heads and tails are possible, there are only two possible events in the sample space.

Direct students' attention to Example 1. Have students read through the vocabulary descriptions and examples.

Ask: How come no one would predict the number 27 when rolling a number cube? **[Because 27 is not a number on the cube.]**

Remind students that the sample space includes only those events that are possible.

Check
Problem 2

Allow students to experiment with two coins to determine the total sample space. Some students might argue that HT and TH are one single event. To help students understand these are two separate events, make a mark on one coin to distinguish it from another. You may also use a coin that is a different color or a different value to help explain. For example, students might see that a dime landing heads and a penny landing tails is different from a dime landing tails and a penny landing heads.

Problem 4

Although not addressed specifically, point out that the areas on the spinner are equal which means each number has an equal chance of being selected.

Example 2

Direct students' attention to the Probability ratio and guide them through the samples. If students are confused by the probability notation, help them understand by writing P (rolling a 4) rather than $P(4)$. Continue until students understand the shortened meaning.

In sample 2, point out that students can list the sample space if preferred. However, the probability ratio only requires the number of events in the sample space.

Ask: How can you determine the sample space without listing all the marble colors? **[Just add 5 green marbles plus 7 blue marbles to get 12 marbles.]**

To help students understand the meaning of the fractional probability, encourage them to state the probability in the following way:

Sample 1

Say: A probability of $\frac{1}{6}$ means there is 1 way to get the number out of 6 possible numbers.

Sample 2

Say: A probability of $\frac{5}{12}$ means there are 5 ways to get the marble out of 12 possible marbles.

Check
Problem 6

Have the students write each letter in the word DEFINITION vertically to help them see the individual letters composing the word. If necessary, review that the vowels are A, E, I, O, U. All other letters are consonants.

Problem 7

Remind students that the apple pies are also included in the sample space. If desired, prompt students to think about the probability of selecting a different pie.

Example 3

Review the meaning of probability with students to help them understand that probability will always be between 0% and 100% inclusive. The greater the probability of an event, the more likely it is to happen.

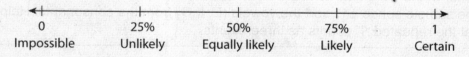

Encourage students to think of ways in which probability is used every day. Examples include: chance of rain or snow, probability of car breaking down, probability of traffic congestion, probability of an A on a test, etc.

Direct students' attention to Example 3. Ask a volunteer to read the sample aloud.

Guide students through the probability calculation.

Ask: Which company's phone has a higher probability of being defective? **[Company A]**

Ask: Which company would you prefer to buy a phone from? Why? **[Company B because I am less likely to get a defective phone.]**

Say: One student said that Company B makes more defective phones because they had 6 defective phones in the sample and Company A only had 2.

Ask: What might you say to the student to explain the error? **[Possible answer: You have to compare how large the sample is to see which has the greater percent or probability.]**

Check
Problem 10
Remind students to count the number of possible events in the sample space to determine the denominator of the probability fraction.

ALTERNATE STRATEGY

Strategy: Experimental Probability
Have students conduct experiments using number cubes, coins, and cards to help them become comfortable with the vocabulary and its meaning.

1. Provide each student with a number cube or any manipulative that can be used to generate random numbers. Tell students they will conduct an experiment by rolling the manipulative and writing down the event that occurs. Continue to use the vocabulary with students and encourage them to use it while discussing.

2. Have students conduct their experiments 10–20 times, time permitting. Direct students to take a look at the results of their experiment. Answers to the following questions will depend on the number generator used.

   Ask: What numbers did you roll? **[Answers will vary. Sample answer: 2, 5, 6, 4, 1]**

   Say: These are called events.

   Ask: What numbers were possible to roll? **[Answers will vary. Sample answer: 1, 2, 3, 4, 5, 6]**

   Say: This is called the sample space.

3. Throughout the lesson, encourage students to create a hands-on method to understand what is happening in each experiment. For example, in problem 6, have students write each letter of the word DEFINITION on an index card. Then have them mix the cards up, write the sample space and sort the vowels (E, I, O) from the consonants. Help students see that the repeated "I" counts as three events.

COMMON MISCONCEPTION

Problem 6
Ask: How many yellow marbles? **[20]**

Ask: How many red marbles? **[30]**

Ask: How many marbles are in the sample space? Explain. **[50 because 20 + 30 = 50]**

Error: Students may forget to include the desired event in the sample space. Encourage students to visualize the experiment to determine the actual number of items in the sample space.

Solution: $P(\text{yellow}) = \dfrac{20}{50} = \dfrac{2}{5}$

Problem 11

When the events involve numbers, students often confuse the number of the event with the number of times the event can happen. If students mistakenly believe that $P(5) = \dfrac{5}{6}$, restate the question and emphasize how many times.

Say: How many times will the 5 occur?

Problem 12

If students make an error, point out that they can check their answers by adding all the probabilities. If the sum is not equal to 1, then one or more of the probabilities is incorrect.

ADDITIONAL ONLINE INTERVENTION RESOURCES

 Use the following for students who have not mastered the concepts in Skill 15.

- Math on the Spot videos

- Personal Math Trainer with customized intervention

- Building Block worksheets (Skill 6: Analyze Data, Skill 12: Certain, Impossible, Likely, Unlikely, Skill 39: Fractions, Decimals, Percents)

SKILL 15 — Probability of Simple Events

Example 1

An **experiment** is anything where an observer can obtain data.

> Experiment: Rolling a six-sided number cube

An **event** is the result of one experiment.

> Event: the number cube shows "4"

The **sample space** is the set of all possible events of an experiment.

> Sample space: 1, 2, 3, 4, 5, 6

Vocabulary
Event
Experiment
Probability of event
Sample Space

Check

List a possible event and the sample space for each experiment.

1. Flipping one coin

    Possible event: _____

    Sample space: _____

2. Flipping two coins

    Possible event: _____

    Sample space: _____

3. Answering a multiple choice question with choices A, B, C, D, E

    Possible event: _____

    Sample space: _____

4. Spinning a spinner shown

    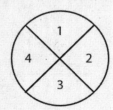

    Possible event: _____

    Sample space: _____

Example 2

The probability of an event is the likelihood that a certain thing or event will occur.
To calculate the probability of an event:

$$P(\text{event}) = \frac{\text{number of ways event can happen}}{\text{total number of events in the sample space}}$$

Sample 1	Sample 2
A number cube is rolled. What is the probability of rolling a 4?	A box has 5 green marbles and 7 blue marbles. What is the probability of selecting a marble at random and getting a green marble?
$P(4) = ?$	$P(\text{green}) = ?$

Step 1   Event: rolling a 4
          Sample Space:
          1, 2, 3, 4, 5, 6
	Step 1 Event: green
	          Sample Space: 5 green and 7 blue OR
	          G, G, G, G, G, B, B, B, B, B, B, B,

Step 2 $P(4) = \dfrac{1}{6}$	Step 2 $P(\text{green}) = \dfrac{5}{12}$

Check
Determine the probability of each event.

5. There are 15 boys and 20 girls in a class. What is the probability of selecting a student at random and selecting a boy?

                    _____

6. The word DEFINITION has vowels and consonants. What is the probability of selecting a letter at random and selecting a vowel?

                    _____

7. A bakery has 3 apple pies, 4 lemon pies, and 5 blueberry pies. What is the probability of selecting a pie at random and selecting apple?

                    _____

8. Find the Error. Explain the solution.

   A bag has 20 yellow marbles and 30 red marbles. What is the probability that a marble selected at random will be yellow?

                    _____

   $P(\text{yellow}) = \dfrac{20}{30} = \dfrac{2}{3}$

                    _____

                    _____

Example 3

Probability is often shown as a percentage so comparisons can be made. The higher the probability, the more likely the event is to occur.

Sample:

Two companies manufacture phones. Company A found 2 defective phones in a sample of 50. Company B found 6 defective phones in a sample of 250.

What is the probability of buying a phone at random from each company and getting a defective phone?

$$P(\text{defective phone}) = \frac{\text{number of defective phones}}{\text{total number of phones}}$$

Company A	Company B
$P(\text{defective phone}) = \frac{2}{50} = 0.04 = 4\%$	$P(\text{defective phone}) = \frac{6}{250} = 0.04 = 0.024 = 2.4\%$

Check

9. A manufacturer of car parts for air conditioners found 5 defective hoses out of 200. What is the probability that a hose selected at random will be defective?

_____

10. A multiple choice test question has choices A, B, C, D. If a student guesses the answer randomly, what is the probability the student will guess correctly?

_____

Determine the probability for each event. Write your answer as a fraction.

11. A six-sided number cube is rolled. What is the probability of rolling a 5?

_____

12. A vase holds 9 roses, 5 tulips, 3 carnations, and 3 lilies. A flower is selected at random. Find each probability.

P(rose) _____

P(tulip) _____

P(carnation) _____

P(lily) _____

Use probability as percent for 13–15.

13. A software company finds that one of its programs is not working. It was reported that the program crashes 3 times out of 30 times being opened. What is P(crash)?

_____

_____

_____

14. The company is trying to sell more of its programs. Instead of mentioning how many times it crashes, it would like to mention how many times the program is successful. What is P(not crashing)?

_____

_____

_____

15. How are P(crash) and P(not crash) related? What do you notice? Explain.

_____

_____

_____

16. A manufacturer of computer chips checks batches of chips. The manufacturer found that 5 items in a batch of 200 were defective. Find the probability of a defective chip.

_____

Find the probability of a chip that is not defective.

_____

SKILL 15 PROBABILITY OF SIMPLE EVENTS

Properties of Dilations

KEY TEACHING POINTS

Example 1
Review the meaning of similar figures and congruent figures.

Ask: Does a dilation affect the size of a figure? **[Yes.]**

Say: Since the size of the figure changes, the image and the preimage are not congruent. A dilation is the only transformation that changes the size of a figure.

Ask: Does a dilation affect the shape of a figure? **[No.]**

Say: Since the size of the figure is enlarged or reduced by a scale factor, the image is similar to the preimage, so the figures have the same shape.

Ask: How can you determine whether the triangles represent a dilation? **[Check to see if the ratios of the side lengths are equal.]**

Ask: Which side lengths are written in the numerator of the ratio? **[the side lengths of the image]** Which side lengths are written in the denominator of the ratio? **[the side lengths of the preimage]**

Ask: Are the ratios of the corresponding side lengths equal? **[Yes.]**

Ask: What is the scale factor? **[2]**

Check
Check that students understand that the preimage is the original figure and the image is the figure that results from the dilation. A prime symbol is used to name the vertices of the image.

Problems 1–2
Ask: Which figure is the preimage? $[\triangle DEF]$

Ask: Is the image larger or smaller than the preimage? **[smaller]** Will the scale factor be greater than 1 or less than 1? **[less than 1]**

Problems 3–4
Tell students that they need to check that all sides of the image and the preimage have equal ratios to determine that it is a dilation. However, if they find just one pair of ratios that is not equal to another, that is enough information to determine that it is not a dilation, and they do not need to check the rest of the sides.

Problem 6
Ask: What is the side length of the enlarged logo that corresponds to the side length of 2 centimeters on the original logo? **[5 centimeters]**

Example 2

Remind students that improper fractions are greater than 1.

Ask: What is the scale factor? $\left[\dfrac{3}{2}\right]$ How can you write $\dfrac{3}{2}$ as a mixed number? $\left[1\dfrac{1}{2}\right]$

Ask: Is $\dfrac{3}{2}$ greater than 1? **[Yes]** Will this dilation result in an enlargement or a reduction?

[enlargement]

Ask: How can you find the coordinates of the image after a dilation about the origin?

[Multiply each coordinate by $\dfrac{3}{2}$.]

Remind students that when a figure is dilated about the origin, they can check their work by drawing a line from the origin through each of the corresponding vertices.

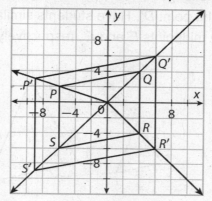

Check
Problem 12

Show students how to write an equation to find the scale factor. Use $T(-2, 4) \rightarrow T'\left(-\dfrac{1}{2}, 1\right)$

and solve for k: $-2 \cdot k = -\dfrac{1}{2}$ and $4 \cdot k = 1$.

Provide a hint for students to look for corresponding coordinates with whole numbers, such as the y-coordinates in T and T', to solve for k. Once they determine the scale factor, they should check the remaining coordinates.

Problem 13

Encourage students to write the rule for the dilation and the coordinates of the image to help them see how to approach the problem.

Problem 14

Be sure students understand that they are performing two dilations. Have students reverse the order of the dilations to see that the order in which the dilations are performed does not matter; the final figure will be the same. Challenge students to find a single dilation that has

the same result as both dilations. $\left[4 \cdot \dfrac{1}{3} = \dfrac{4}{3}\right]$

ALTERNATE STRATEGY

Strategy: Draw a dilation.

1. Have students draw a triangle and point C. Point C is the center of dilation. Have students draw a line from point C to each vertex of the triangle.

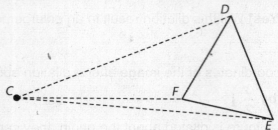

2. Tell students to measure the length of $\overline{CD}$ with a ruler. Students should draw the midpoint of $\overline{CD}$ and label the point D'. Have students similarly draw the midpoints for $\overline{CE}$ and $\overline{CF}$, and label the midpoints E' and F', respectively. The students should then draw triangle $D'E'F'$.

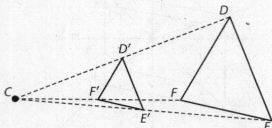

3. **Ask:** How is the length of $\overline{CD'}$ related to the length of $\overline{CD}$? $\left[CD' = \dfrac{1}{2}CD\right]$ How is the length of $\overline{CE'}$ related to the length of $\overline{CE}$? $\left[CE' = \dfrac{1}{2}CE\right]$ How is the length of $\overline{CF'}$ related to the length of $\overline{CF}$? $\left[CF' = \dfrac{1}{2}CF\right]$

4. Have students measure the corresponding angles of both triangles with a protractor.

5. **Ask:** How is the measure of $\angle D'$ related to the measure of $\angle D$? **[m$\angle$D′ = m$\angle$D]** How is the measure of $\angle E'$ related to the measure of $\angle E$? **[m$\angle$E′ = m$\angle$E]** How is the measure of $\angle F'$ related to the measure of $\angle F$? **[m$\angle$F′ = m$\angle$F]**

6. **Ask:** Are the corresponding sides congruent? **[No.]** Are the corresponding angles congruent? **[Yes.]**

7. Point out that the triangles have the same shape because the corresponding angles are congruent. The triangles do not have the same size because the corresponding sides are not congruent. The sides of triangle $D'E'F'$ are reduced by a scale factor of $\dfrac{1}{2}$.

COMMON MISCONCEPTIONS

Problem 3

Some students may assume that since the smaller figure is on the left, the dilation is an enlargement. Remind students that prime symbols are used to indicate which figure is the image.

Students may also reverse the order of the side lengths of the image and the preimage when writing ratios. This will result in the multiplicative inverse of the scale factor. Students should check the reasonableness of their answers to make sure that a scale factor greater than 1 results in an enlarged image and a scale factor less than 1 results in a reduced image.

Problem 5

Remind students that a dilation does not change the orientation of a figure. Students should use the prime symbols to match corresponding vertices.

Ask: What side corresponds to $Q'R'$? **[QR]**

Ask: What is the length of $\overline{Q'R'}$? **[12 units]**

Ask: What is the length of $\overline{QR}$? **[4 units]**

Ask: Does a dilation change the orientation of a figure? **[No, the orientation stays the same.]**

Error: The ratios of corresponding sides are not equal since $\dfrac{Q'R'}{QR} = \dfrac{12}{4} = 3$ and

$\dfrac{R'S'}{RS} = \dfrac{8}{6} = \dfrac{4}{3}$.

Solution: $Q'R'S'T'$ is not a dilation of rectangle $QRST$.

ADDITIONAL ONLINE INTERVENTION RESOURCES

Use the following for students who have not mastered the concepts in Skill 16.

- Math on the Spot videos

- Personal Math Trainer with customized intervention

- Building Block worksheets (Skill 86: Simplify Ratios; Skill 95: Solve Proportions; Skill 103: Transformations; Skill 112: Write Ratios)

SKILL 16 — Properties of Dilations

Example 1

A **dilation** uses a **scale factor** to enlarge or reduce the size of a figure, but it does not change its shape. The sides of the image are proportional to the corresponding sides of the preimage, so the image is **similar** to the preimage.

To determine whether an image is a dilation, write a ratio that compares the side lengths of the image to the corresponding sides of the preimage.

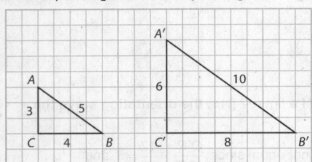

$$\frac{A'B'}{AB} = \frac{10}{5} = 2 \qquad \frac{B'C'}{BC} = \frac{8}{4} = 2 \qquad \frac{C'A'}{CA} = \frac{6}{3} = 2$$

Since the ratios are equal, the triangles are similar.
The scale factor is 2.
So, triangle $A'B'C'$ is a dilation of triangle ABC by a scale factor of 2.

Vocabulary
Dilation
Scale factor
Similar
Center of
 dilation

Check

Use the following information for 1–2. Triangle $D'E'F'$ is a dilation of triangle DEF. Each division on the graph is one unit.

1. Find the ratio of the corresponding side lengths.

$$\frac{D'E'}{DE} \; \underline{\hspace{3cm}}$$

$$\frac{E'F'}{EF} \; \underline{\hspace{3cm}}$$

$$\frac{F'D'}{FD} \; \underline{\hspace{3cm}}$$

2. What is the scale factor of the dilation?

_____

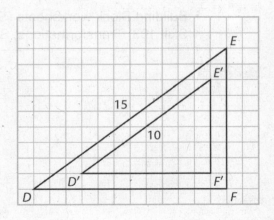

Determine if the image is a dilation of the preimage.
If so, find the scale factor.

3.

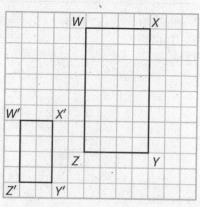

_____

4.

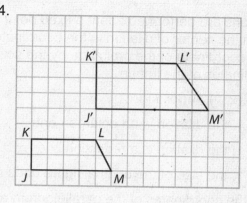

_____

5. Explain the Error. Find the correct solution.
Rectangle *Q′R′S′T′* is a dilation of rectangle
QRST with a scale factor of 2.

_____

_____

_____

_____

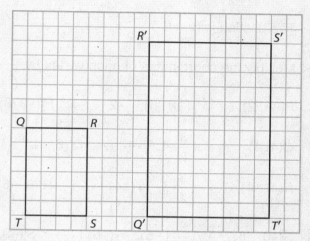

6. A graphic designer needs to enlarge the size of a company logo that is
2 centimeters by 4 centimeters for a new packaging design. The
enlarged logo needs to be 5 centimeters by 8 centimeters. Can the
graphic designer use a dilation? Explain.

_____

7. Jason is drawing a design on grid paper before he paints the design on
a larger canvas. He draws a square with a side length of 4 centimeters
on the grid paper. He wants to dilate the square to have a side length
of 15 centimeters on the painting. Will the square on the painting be a
dilation of the square on the grid paper? Explain.

_____

Example 2

Dilations are performed about a fixed point called the center of dilation.
When the center of dilation in the coordinate plane is the origin, multiply
each coordinate of the preimage by the scale factor k to find the
coordinates of the image.

Rule: $(x, y) \rightarrow (kx, ky)$

If $k > 1$, the dilation is an enlargement.

If $k < 1$, the dilation is a reduction.

If $k = 1$, the size of the original figure does not change.

Find the coordinates of the parallelogram after a dilation with a scale
factor of $\frac{3}{2}$.

The dilation is $(x, y) \rightarrow \left(\frac{3}{2}x, \frac{3}{2}y\right)$.

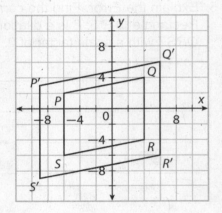

Multiply the coordinates of each vertex by $\frac{3}{2}$.

$P(-6, 2) \quad \rightarrow \quad \left(\frac{3}{2} \cdot (-6), \frac{3}{2} \cdot 2\right) \quad \rightarrow \quad P'(-9, 3)$

$Q(4, 4) \quad \rightarrow \quad \left(\frac{3}{2} \cdot 4, \frac{3}{2} \cdot 4\right) \rightarrow \quad Q'(6, 6)$

$R(4, -4) \quad \rightarrow \quad \left(\frac{3}{2} \cdot 4, \frac{3}{2} \cdot (-4)\right) \quad \rightarrow \quad R'(6, -6)$

$S(-6, -6) \quad \rightarrow \quad \left(\frac{3}{2} \cdot (-6), \frac{3}{2} \cdot (-6)\right) \quad \rightarrow \quad S'(-9, -9)$

The coordinates of the image are $P'(-9, 3)$, $Q'(6, 6)$, $R'(6, -6)$, and
$S'(-9, -9)$.

Check

8. Write the coordinates of the image after the
   dilation $(x, y) \rightarrow (2.5x, 2.5y)$.

   $A(0, 2) \quad \rightarrow$ _____

   $B(4, 0) \quad \rightarrow$ _____

   $C(4, -4) \quad \rightarrow$ _____

   $D(-4, -4) \rightarrow$ _____

   $E(-4, 0) \quad \rightarrow$ _____

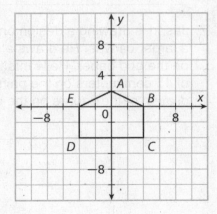

Name _____ Date _____ Class_____

Graph the image of the figure after each dilation.

9. scale factor: 2

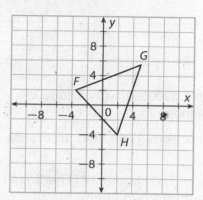

10. scale factor: $\dfrac{1}{3}$

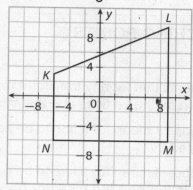

11. A triangle with vertices $P(9, 3)$, $Q(0, -6)$, and $R(-6, 12)$ is dilated by a scale factor of $\dfrac{4}{3}$.

   A   Find the coordinates of the image.

_____

   B   Is the dilation an enlargement or a reduction?

_____

12. A triangle has vertices $T(-2, 4)$, $U(-2, 6)$, and $V(8, 6)$. The coordinates of the image after a dilation are $T'\left(-\dfrac{1}{2}, 1\right)$, $U'\left(-\dfrac{1}{2}, \dfrac{3}{2}\right)$, and $V'\left(2, \dfrac{3}{2}\right)$. What is the scale factor of the dilation?

_____

13. The coordinates of the image after a dilation of $\dfrac{1}{5}$ are $W'(-3, 2)$, $X'(1, 2)$, $Y'(1, -5)$, and $Z'(-2, -3)$. What are the coordinates of the preimage?

_____

14. A figure has vertex $A(3, 6)$. The figure is dilated by a scale factor of 4. The resulting image is dilated by a scale factor of $\dfrac{1}{3}$. What are the coordinates of vertex A'' of the final image?

_____

SKILL 16 PROPERTIES OF DILATIONS

Properties of Reflections

KEY TEACHING POINTS

Example 1

Remind students that for any transformation of a figure, it is only necessary to perform the transformation on the vertices and that this will be the focus of these ideas.

Ask: What does it mean for a line to be perpendicular to another line? **[The lines intersect at a 90° angle.]**

Ask: What does it mean for a line to be perpendicular bisector of line segment? **[The lines are perpendicular and the bisector divides the line segment into two segments of equal length.]**

Go through the rule of a reflection in regards to when a point is on the line and when a point is not on the line and use this to work through example 1 with students.

Ask: How can we use the graph to verify that the line segment from B to its image is perpendicular to ℓ? **[The line segment forms a diagonal with the grid squares that is in the opposite direction of the diagonal formed by line ℓ.]**

Ask: Why is the image of C in the same location as C? **[This point lies on the line of reflection.]**

Ask: Will the angles of the triangle be preserved? Why? **[Yes; A reflection is a rigid motion.]**

Ask: Will the lengths of the sides of the triangle be preserved? **[Yes; A reflection is a rigid motion.]**

Check
Problem 1

Help students by pointing out that line ℓ passes through the diagonals of the grid and that this can be used to draw the line segment needed to find the image of P.

Problem 2

Students may be confused since this is a single point on the line of reflection. Remind students of the rule given for reflections.

Problem 4

This is the first problem that students will encounter where the figure and its reflection overlaps. Encourage them to use either a dashed line or a different color pen or pencil to make it easier to keep track of the two figures.

Problem 5

Encourage students to draw a picture to understand this problem. Their point and line can be anywhere as long as the given length holds true. It may be easiest to see if line m is drawn vertically or horizontally.

Problem 6

Problem 6 is similar to problem 5. A sketch will greatly help students understand how to approach the question.

Example 2

Remind students of the rules for reflecting any point across a given line. Using this and a point P in the coordinate plane, explain the different rules for reflection across each type of line.

For reflection across the y-axis: Use the point $P(2, 2)$.

Ask: If the y-axis is like line ℓ in the other examples, then how do we find P'? **[By drawing a line segment perpendicular to the y-axis that is 4 units long]**

Point out to students that the resulting point follows the given rule and that in general, since the y-axis will be a bisector, the length of the line segment will have to be the same on either side. This results in the rule $(x, y) \rightarrow (-x, y)$.

For reflection across the y-axis: Again, use the point $P(2, 2)$.

Ask: If the x-axis is like line ℓ in the other examples, then how do we find P'? **[By drawing a line segment perpendicular to the x-axis that is 4 units long]**

Once again, show students that to make sure the x-axis is a bisector, you will always need to follow the rule $(x, y) \rightarrow (x, -y)$ because the line between its point and its image will need to have the same length on either side.

Ask: Why would point P have the same coordinates as its image if we reflected it across the line $y = x$? **[Because it lies on the line $y = x$]**

Some students may point out the rule here, but make sure everyone sees that it is based on the original rules for a reflection as well. Anytime a point lies on the line of reflection, its image will have the same coordinates.

Now use the point $P(-1, 1)$ and sketch the line $y = x$ in the coordinate plane.

Ask: How can we use the diagonals of the grid to draw the image of the point? **[Since $y = x$ passes through the diagonals in one direction, the diagonal in the opposite direction can be used.]**

Explain to students that this same idea can be applied to deriving a rule for reflection across the line $y = -x$ and that these rules can be used to find the reflections without having to draw the perpendicular bisectors. Show them the process to get the image of each point in the figure shown for example 2 using the rules only.

Check
Problem 9

Students may be confused since this figure crosses the x-axis. Have them use the rule for reflection across this axis on each point individually and only then try to connect the points. Also, make sure they are correctly labeling the points as they go.

Problem 10

There are many points in this figure. Again, encourage students to work point by point and label each as they go.

Problem 11

Point out to students that they do not need the figure to apply the rules. However, if they get stuck, encourage them to draw the figure and its image.

Example 3

Remind students what the midpoint of any line segment represents.

Ask: How do we find the midpoint of a line defined in the coordinate plane? **[The *x*-coordinate of the midpoint is found by taking the sum of the two *x*-coordinates and dividing by 2. The *y*-coordinate of the midpoint is found by taking the sum of the two *y*-coordinates and dividing by 2.]**

Ask: What is the midpoint of the line segment connecting the points (1, 4) and (3, 2)? **[(2, 3)]** Once students correctly find the midpoint for the line segment asked about, sketch it and the midpoint to reinforce the idea and review.

Ask: How might a midpoint relate to a line of reflection if you had a figure and its image? **[Since the line of reflection is a bisector, the midpoint between a point and its image would be on the line of reflection.]**

Work through finding the midpoints needed for example 3, pointing out how this relates to the rules used in example 1.

Check
Problem 18

Students may be able to see the line of reflection here without calculation. Encourage them to try to make an educated attempt or guess at this but to also verify using the midpoints.

Problem 20

Working with this figure may be difficult for students since it reflected on itself very heavily. Encourage students to simply apply the rule at first and find the midpoints. Once they have found the midpoints, point out the line between *C* and its image and how it is contained within the line connecting *A* and its image. The line of reflection must bisect these lines based on the orientation of the points. This will help solidify their intuition in working with these types of questions.

Problem 22

Encourage students to sketch a square in the coordinate plane to better understand this problem. Sketching the square so that one set of sides is parallel to an axis would be most helpful.

ALTERNATE STRATEGY

Strategy: Tracing Paper

1. Have students trace the original figure and line in example 1 onto tracing paper.
2. Have the students fold the paper along the line of reflection.

Ask: What happens to points that were on the line? **[They remain in the same position.]**

3. Have the students use their folded paper to find the image.

Once students have gone through this process, have them verify that the lines connecting points not on the line with their images are perpendicular to the original line. Once they are comfortable with this, have them work through example 2 in a similar fashion with tracing paper. Make sure they include the *x-y* axes in their sketches.

COMMON MISCONCEPTION

Problem 14

Students may tend to not remember to reflect all points across the line of reflection and that is the case in this problem. Have the students graph the figure defined and the incorrect reflection so that they have a visual representation of what such a mistake may look like. Have them note that the incorrect figure does not maintain the same shape.

ADDITIONAL ONLINE INTERVENTION RESOURCES

 Use the following for students who have not mastered the concepts in Skill 5.

- Math on the Spot videos

- Personal Math Trainer with customized intervention

- Building Block worksheets (Skill 46: Graph Ordered Pairs (First Quadrant), Skill 103: Transformations)

SKILL 17

Properties of Reflections

Example 1

A reflection across a line ℓ maps a point P to its image P' using the rules:

    If P is on line ℓ, then $P = P'$.

    If P is not on line ℓ, then ℓ is the perpendicular bisector of $\overline{PP'}$.

Draw the image of $\triangle ABC$ after a reflection across line ℓ.

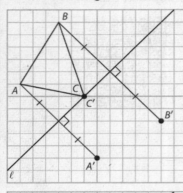

Draw a line segment from A to A' so that it is perpendicular to line ℓ and bisected by line ℓ.

Repeat this for each point. If a point is on the line, its image is itself.

Connect the points A', B', and C'. The resulting triangle is the image of $\triangle ABC$.

> ### Vocabulary
> Reflection
> Perpendicular
> Perpendicular
>   Bisector

Check

Find the image of each point or figure after a reflection across line ℓ.

1.

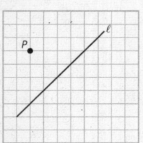

2.

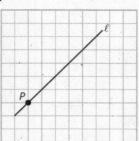

3.

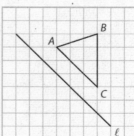

4.

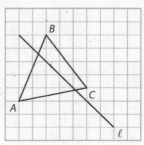

5. The straight line distance from a point *P* to a line *m* is 4 units. If *P* is reflected across the line, what is the straight line distance between its image and line *m*?

_____

6. The length of a line segment is 2.5 units. If this line segment is reflected across a line *m*, then what is the length of its image?

_____

Example 2

In the coordinate plane, reflections can be found using the following rules.

Reflection across the *y*-axis: $(x, y) \rightarrow (-x, y)$

Reflection across the *x*-axis: $(x, y) \rightarrow (x, -y)$

Reflection across the line $y = x$: $(x, y) \rightarrow (y, x)$

Reflection across the line $y = -x$: $(x, y) \rightarrow (-y, -x)$

Find the image of *ABCD* after it is reflected across the *x*-axis.

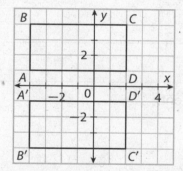

Find the image of each point using the rule and connect the new points.

$A(-4, 1) \rightarrow A'(-4, -1)$
$B(-4, 4) \rightarrow B'(-4, -4)$
$C(2, 4) \rightarrow C'(2, -4)$
$D(2, 1) \rightarrow D'(2, -1)$

Check

Find the image of each figure if it is reflected across the given axis or line.

7. *x*-axis

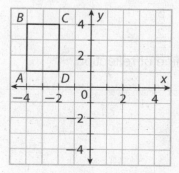

8. *y*-axis

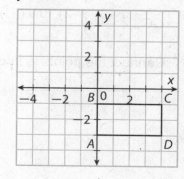

9. *x*-axis

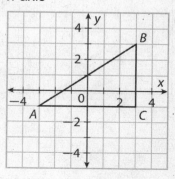

10. line $y = -x$

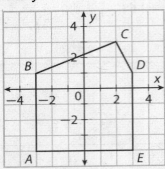

11. line $y = -x$

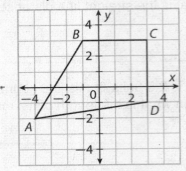

12. line $y = x$

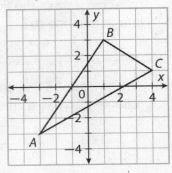

13. The triangle defined by the coordinates $A(1, -1)$, $B(0, -1)$, and $C(1, 4)$ is reflected across the y-axis. What are the coordinates of its image?

_____

14. Explain the Error. Find the correct solution.

A figure is defined by the three points $A(4, 0)$, $B(2, 3)$, and $C(-5, -1)$. When reflected across the line $y = x$, the resulting figure is defined by the points $A'(0, 4)$, $B'(2, 3)$, and $C'(-1, -5)$.

_____

_____

Example 3

The line of reflection passes through the midpoint of a line segment connecting a point and its image.

Find the line of reflection given $\triangle ABC$ and its image $\triangle A'B'C'$.

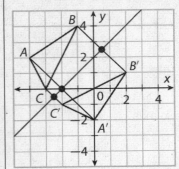

Find the midpoint of $\overline{AA'}$, $\overline{BB'}$, and $\overline{CC'}$.

$$\overline{AA'}: \left(\frac{-4+0}{2}, \frac{2+(-2)}{2}\right) = (-2, 0)$$

$$\overline{BB'}: \left(\frac{-1+2}{2}, \frac{4+1}{2}\right) = \left(\frac{1}{2}, \frac{5}{2}\right)$$

$$\overline{CC'}: \left(\frac{-3+(-2)}{2}, \frac{0+(-1)}{2}\right) = \left(-\frac{5}{2}, -\frac{1}{2}\right)$$

Connect the points to find the line of reflection.

Check

Find the midpoint of a line connecting the given pair of points.

15. (−1, 4) and (0, 9)

16. (8, 4) and (2, 1)

17. (0, 0) and (−4, 2)

Given the figure and its image, find the line of reflection.

18.

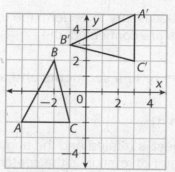

19.

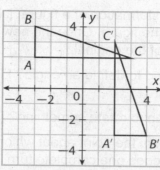

20.

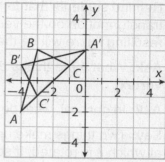

21. In the coordinate plane, $\triangle ABC$ is defined by the points $A(0, 0)$, $B(−3, 0)$, and $C(−1, 3)$. This triangle is reflected across a line m. If the images of A, B, and C are $A'(0, 0)$, $B'(0, −3)$, and $C'(3, −1)$, respectively, then give two points that lie along the line m.

_____

22. A square $ABCD$ is drawn in the coordinate plane and reflected across a line m such that the image of point A has the same coordinates as B and the image of point C has the same coordinates as point D. Describe the location of line m in relation to $\overline{AB}$ and $\overline{CD}$. Explain your reasoning.

_____

_____

_____

_____

SKILL 17 PROPERTIES OF REFLECTIONS

Properties of Rotations

KEY TEACHING POINTS

Example 1

Remind students that for any transformation of a figure, it is only necessary to perform the transformation on the vertices of the figure. Once the new vertices are connected, the resulting figure will be the image of the original.

Ask: What three things do we need to define an angle? **[Two rays or line segments and a vertex]**

Ask: In general, what does it mean to rotate something? **[To turn it]**

Say: Two things make up a rotation: the point about which an object is rotated and the angle at which it is rotated. If someone does one complete turn, the center of rotation is the center of where the person is standing and the angle is 360°. With rotation transformations in geometry, we apply this idea to shapes.

Review the rules for finding the image under a rotation transformation with the students and then direct the students' attention to the figure in example 1.

Ask: What point represents the image of point A? **[A']**

Walk through the steps used to find the image of point A as described in the example and explain that applying this to every vertex is how the image of triangle ABC is found.

Check
Problem 1

Students may have a tendency to incorrectly label the vertices of a rotation. In this and other problems, encourage them to label the images of each vertex as they go instead of after the entire triangle is drawn.

Problem 5

Encourage students to sketch the transformation of a point as described. Point out that to be equivalent, the counterclockwise rotation would have to take the point to the same image and that this together with the clockwise angle would form a complete rotation. Have them mark this angle as in the figure below.

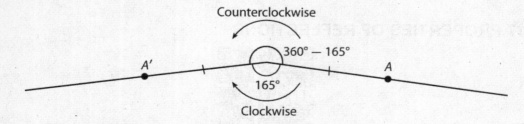

Point out that since the two angles together form a full rotation of 360°, the unknown equivalent counterclockwise rotation can be found by subtraction (specifically 360° − 165°).

Problem 6

Remind students of the steps that are used to rotate a figure around a point. Specifically, have them describe exactly how given point A, they would find the image (if they knew the angle).

Now explain to them that if they draw the line segments $\overline{AP}$ and $\overline{PA'}$, then they can measure the angle that was used in the rotation.

Ask: Is it necessary to do the same for each point? **[No; by definition, the angles formed by the drawn line segments will all be the same.]**

Ask: How can we verify that out first measurement was correct? **[By checking at least one other point since all the angles formed by the drawn line segments should be the same]**

Example 2

Review the rules for the different rotations listed and point out to students that in the coordinate plane, all rotations are assumed to be centered at the origin and be counterclockwise unless otherwise stated.

Direct the students' attention to the figure in the example.

Ask: What would be the steps to using a protractor to find the image of the point A? **[Draw a line segment from the origin to A and draw a ray to form an angle of 270°. The point A' will lie at a distance that makes $AP = A'P$.]**

Ask: How do we measure an angle larger than 180° with a protractor? **[Measure 180° and then measure the remaining portion (in this case 90°).]**

Say: Let's try the rotation with a protractor first and then see how to do it with the set of rules.

Explain that the rules given are based on the same strategies they used when working with a protractor. Have the students verify this on their papers by drawing a line segment from the origin to point A and then measuring an angle of 270° to find its image.

Once the students have done this, show them how to use the given rule to find the image. Point out that this is the same image as the one they found.

Now go through the step by step process of using the rule for the rotation to find the image of the given triangle by applying the rule to each of the remaining vertices.

Check
Problem 9

The image of this triangle will overlap with the original triangle somewhat. Explain to students that this may happen and it all depends on the angle of the rotation.

Problems 12–14

For students that are having trouble visualizing the rotations, an approach using the idea of coordinates may help. Have students write the general form of a point in each quadrant based on the sign. They should find the following to be true:

Quadrant I: Both x and y are positive.
Quadrant II: x is negative and y is positive.
Quadrant III: Both x and y are negative.
Quadrant IV: x is positive and y is negative.

Using this with problem 12: Based on the rule for rotation by 270°, any point in the first quadrant with two positive values will result in a point with a positive x-coordinate and a positive x-coordinate and a negative y-coordinate. This means the point is in the fourth quadrant.

For students who are more visual, sketching a general triangle in the indicated quadrant and then estimating the rotation on one of the vertices should be helpful. It is important that the triangle they draw is completely within the described quadrant.

ALTERNATE STRATEGY

Strategy: Tracing Paper

Tracing paper is a very effective method to allow students to see that they are actually already familiar with rotations.

When working with rotations around a point P, have students do the following:

1. Pick a vertex in the figure and draw a line segment from that vertex to P.
2. Draw a ray to form an angle equal to the angle of rotation (by using a protractor).
3. With tracing paper, trace the figure (with all vertices and labels) and point P.
4. Rotate the tracing paper using the angle they drew on the original figure as a guide and keeping point P aligned. The rotation is complete when the vertex they used to draw the angle is aligned with the ray.

After this, they will have rotated the figure and found its image. They can use this to draw the image in the correct location or to experiment and explore different angles of rotation.

COMMON MISCONCEPTION

Problem 15
Students may assume that the image of a figure rotated with a large angle will always end up in Quadrant IV. This problem illustrates the need to pay attention to multiples of 360°.

Ask: How many complete rotations are represented by 720°? **[2 complete rotations]**

Use this to point out that a complete rotation will result in the image being in the same position as the original figure. Therefore, any multiple of 360° will have the same effect.

Ask: What is 1440° ÷ 360°? **[4]**

Say: This means the image will be in the first quadrant.

Ask: What if the angle was 1460°? What quadrant would the image lie in? **[1st]**

Explain to students that the angle remaining after multiples of 360° are subtracted can be used to find the image and to predict the quadrant.

ADDITIONAL ONLINE INTERVENTION RESOURCES

Use the following for students who have not mastered the concepts in Skill 18.

- Math on the Spot videos

- Personal Math Trainer with customized intervention

- Building Block worksheets (Skill 46 Graph Ordered Pairs (First Quadrant),Skill 56 Measure Angles)

SKILL 18 Properties of Rotations

Example 1

Vocabulary
Rotation
Center of Rotation
Angle of Rotation

A rotation around the center of rotation P maps a figure to its image according to the following rules.

Every point and its image are the same distance from P.

All angles with vertex P formed by a point and its image have the same measure called the angle of rotation.

Draw the image of $\triangle ABC$ after it is rotated 170° counterclockwise around point P.

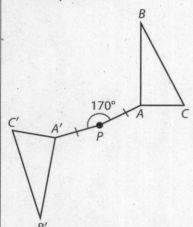

Use a straightedge to draw $\overline{PA}$.

Use a protractor to draw a ray that forms the given angle with $\overline{PA}$. Use a ruler to mark the image A' along the ray so that $PA = PA'$.

Repeat the process for each point.

Check

Find the image of each figure after it is rotated around the point P as indicated.

1. counterclockwise 40°

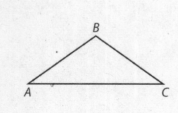

2. counterclockwise 120°

3. clockwise 75°

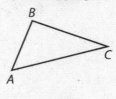

4. clockwise 160°

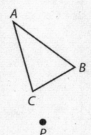

5. What counterclockwise angle of rotation around point P is equivalent to a clockwise rotation of 165° around point P?

_____

Problems 6 and 7 each show a triangle and its image after it was rotated in the given direction around a point P. Find the angle of rotation.

6. clockwise

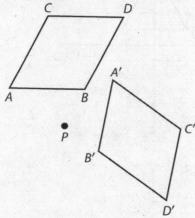

Angle of rotation: _____

7. counterclockwise

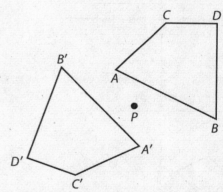

Angle of rotation: _____

Example 2

In the coordinate plane, rotations around the origin can be found using the following rules.

Rotation of 90°: $(x, y) \rightarrow (-y, x)$

Rotation of 180°: $(x, y) \rightarrow (-x, -y)$

Rotation of 270°: $(x, y) \rightarrow (y, -x)$

Rotation of 360°: $(x, y) \rightarrow (x, y)$

Find the image of $\triangle ABC$ after it is rotated 270° counterclockwise.

Name _____ Date _____ Class _____

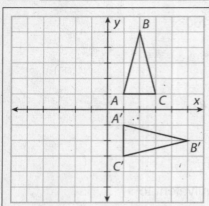

Find the image of each point using the rule and connect the new points.

$A(1, 1) \rightarrow A'(1, -1)$
$B(2, 5) \rightarrow B'(5, -2)$
$C(3, 1) \rightarrow C'(1, -3)$

Check

Find the image of each figure after the given rotation.

8. 90°

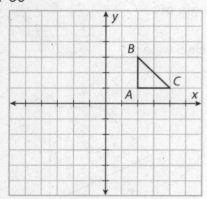

9. 270°

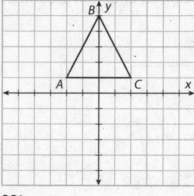

10. 180°

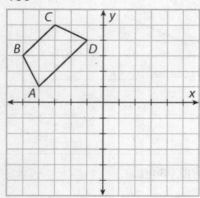

11. 90°

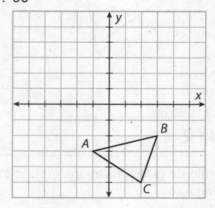

For questions 12–14, suppose that △ABC lies in the given quadrant. Determine which quadrant its image will lie in after the indicated rotation.

12. △ABC lies in Quadrant I and is rotated by 180°.

_____

13. △ABC lies in Quadrant IV and is rotated by 270°.

_____

14. △ABC lies in Quadrant I and is rotated by 90°.

   _____

   _____

15. Explain the Error. Find the correct solution.

   A student predicts that after a square in the first quadrant is rotated
   1440°, the image will lie in Quadrant IV.

   _____

   _____

SKILL 18 PROPERTIES OF ROTATIONS

Properties of Translations

KEY TEACHING POINTS

Example 1

Point out to students that when translating using paper and pencil, it is only necessary to translate the vertices. Then the entire figure can be drawn.

Have students come up with their own words to describe a translation. Some may call it a shift or a slide. Others might refer to it as a movement. Help students focus on the meaning of translation by asking questions.

Ask: Does the figure change when it is translated? Explain. **[Only the location changes. The size and shape do not change.]**

Guide students through Example 1. For the sample on the left, have them draw arrows from the original vertices to the new vertices to help them visualize the translation. Repeat with the sample on the right as shown below

Translate *ABC* 6 units to the right.   Translate *ABC* 5 units down.

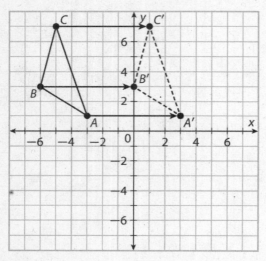   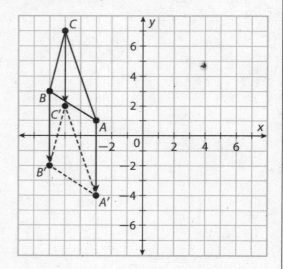

Check
Problem 1

Encourage students to begin by choosing one coordinate and counting up 7 units. Then have them mark the point and label it using the prime notation. Repeat with the remaining coordinates. Then instruct students to connect the vertices to recreate the triangle.

Problem 2

Point out to students that some of the translated figure can overlap. Encourage students to write the translated figure with a different color pencil if desired.

Example 2

Ask: Can a figure translate diagonally? If so, how? If not, why not? **[A figure can shift diagonally by using a combination of horizontal and vertical shifts.]**

Review the quadrant names and locations with students.

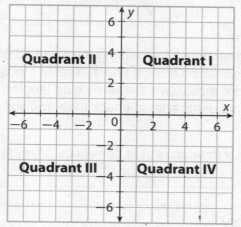

Ask: If a figure is in Quadrant III, what translation will move it to Quadrant II? **[a shift up]**

Ask: If a figure is in Quadrant II, what translation will move it to Quadrant I? **[a shift right]**

Ask: If a figure is in Quadrant II, what translation will move it to Quadrant IV? **[a shift right and a shift down or a shift down and a shift right]**

Guide students through Example 2. As in the previous example, have students use arrows to show the shift in each figure. Note that two arrows will be drawn for each vertex to indicate translations to the *x*- and *y*-coordinate.

Check
Problem 3

Have students anticipate the location of the translated figure.

Ask: Where will *A'B'C'D'* be located after the translation? Explain. **[Between Quadrant I and Quadrant II because the shift up is only 1 and the shift right is 6 units]**

Example 3

Have students practice using coordinates to represent a translation.

Ask: Which are the possible directions for a translation of the *x*-coordinate? **[left or right]**

Ask: Which are the possible directions for a translation of the *y*-coordinate? **[up or down]**

Ask: What is the coordinate rule if a figure is shifted 8 units to the right? Explain. **[$x + 8$, because the coordinate is moving right or in the positive direction]**

Ask: What is the coordinate rule if a figure is shifted 5 units to the down? Explain. **[$y - 5$, because the coordinate is moving down or in the negative direction]**

Write several descriptions of translations on the board and have students state the rule. Reverse the order of the description so students can practice relating up and down with the *y*-coordinate and left, right with the *x*-coordinate.

Ask: What is the rule for 3 units down and 5 units to the right? **[$(x + 5, y - 3)$]**

Ask: What is the rule for 8 units left and 7 units down? **[$(x - 8, y - 7)$]**

Guide students through Example 3. Have them underline or highlight the parts of the expression in the rule that describe the translation. This would be "+4" and "+2". Remind them that these operations must be performed on each original coordinate to arrive at the new translated coordinates.

Check
Problem 5
Encourage students to take their time when writing the rule and determining the new coordinates as errors can occur when adding and subtracting positive and negative numbers. Remind students that the figure must have the same side lengths and angle measures after the translation. If it does not, students should check their addition and subtraction.

Problem 7
Encourage students to check if their answer is correct by drawing the original figure and the translated figure.

ALTERNATE STRATEGY

Strategy: Tracing Paper

1. To help students understand the meaning of translation, provide them with patty paper or other tracing paper. Have them trace the figure in Example 1 and label the corresponding vertices A, B, and C. Slide it until it matches the translated image.

Ask: In what direction did you slide your triangle? **[to the right]**

Ask: What do you notice about the triangle you traced and the triangle you are covering? **[They are exactly the same size and shape.]**

2. Next, encourage students to trace the original figures in the graphs of problem 1 and 2. Encourage them to estimate where the translated image will be as they move 7 units up in #1 and 3 units right in #2.

3. After using the tracing paper to estimate, guide students through translating each vertex and drawing the translated figure.

COMMON MISCONCEPTION

Problem 6
Ask: What is meant by the rule $x - 4$? **[Subtract 4 from the x-coordinate to get the translated x-coordinate.]**

Ask: What is meant by the rule $y + 3$? **[Add 3 to the y-coordinate to get the translated y-coordinate.]**

Ask: What does $(x, y) \rightarrow (x - 4, y + 3)$ mean in words? **[It means the translated figure must be shifted 4 units to the left and 3 units up.]**

Error: Students may become confused when using mapping coordinates for translating figures. The error shows the student add 4 units to each of the coordinates, thereby shifting the figure to the right. In fact, the figure should be shifted to the left by 4 units and up by 3 units.

Solution:

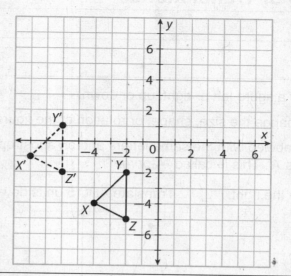

ADDITIONAL ONLINE INTERVENTION RESOURCES

Use the following for students who have not mastered the concepts in Skill 5.

- Math on the Spot videos
- Personal Math Trainer with customized intervention
- Building Block worksheets (Skill 46: Graph Ordered Pairs (First Quadrant), Skill 103: Transformations)

SKILL 19

Properties of Translations

Vocabulary
Translation

Example 1

A translation is a slide of a figure left or right, up or down.

A translation does not change the size, shape, or rotation of the figure.

The translated figure is labeled with the same letters and an apostrophe. For example, *A* becomes *A'*. This is called "*A*-prime."

Translate *ABC* 6 units to the right.   Translate *ABC* 5 units down.

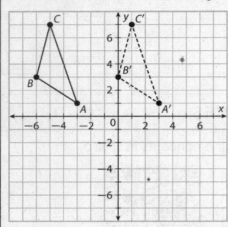
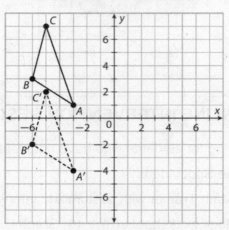

Check
Graph.

1. Translate the image 7 units up.

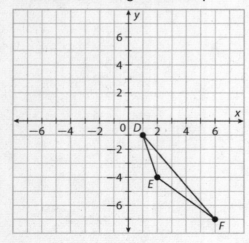

2. Translate the image 3 units right.

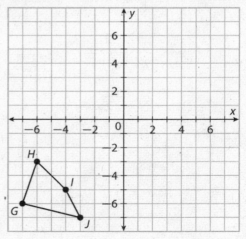

Example 2

A translation can be both vertical and horizontal. The translation can also be done in any order.

Translate *KLMN* 5 units left and 6 units up.

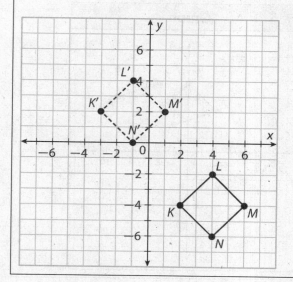

Translate *PQRS* 3 units right and 4 units down.

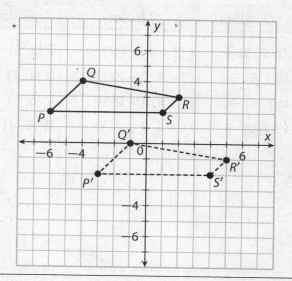

Check
Graph.

3. Translate the image 1 unit up and 6 units right.

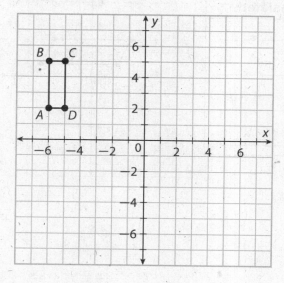

4. Translate the image 2 units up and 5 units right.

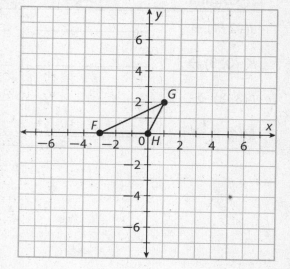

Example 3

Mapping can be used to indicate how the figure will be translated. Use the coordinates to determine the location of the translated figure.

$(x, y) \rightarrow (x + 4, y + 2)$ means translate the figure 4 units right and 2 units up.

Original	Rule	Translated	Graph
$T(-2, 3) \rightarrow$	$(-2 + 4, 3 + 2) \rightarrow$	$T'(2, 5)$	
$U(0, 5) \rightarrow$	$(0 + 4, 5 + 2) \rightarrow$	$U'(4, 7)$	
$V(1, 4) \rightarrow$	$(1 + 4, 4 + 2) \rightarrow$	$V'(5, 6)$	
$W(1, 2) \rightarrow$	$(1 + 4, 2 + 2) \rightarrow$	$W'(5, 4)$	

Check

Write the rule and the new coordinates for the transformation. Then graph.

5. $(x, y) \rightarrow (x + 2, y - 3)$

Original	Rule	Translated
$J(-2, 1) \rightarrow$	_____	_____
$K(-3, 3) \rightarrow$	_____	_____
$L(3, 3) \rightarrow$	_____	_____
$M(4, 1) \rightarrow$	_____	_____

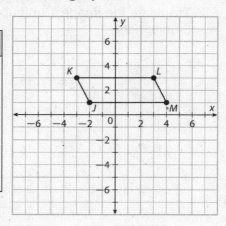

6. Find the Error. Explain the solution.

   Translate the figure using the rule
   $(x, y) \rightarrow (x - 4, y + 3)$.

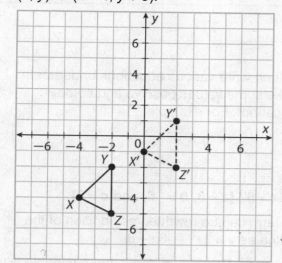

7. A park planner is planning on moving a shed from one location to
   another because of new sprinklers. The plans call for the original shed
   to be at a location given by the coordinates $A(-6, 2)$ $B(-6, 4)$ $C(-2, 4)$
   and $D(-2, 2)$. The shed must shift 5 units right and 8 units down.

   A Write a rule for the transformation.

   _____

   B What are the new translated points?

   _____

SKILL 19 PROPERTIES OF TRANSLATIONS

Quadratic Functions

KEY TEACHING POINTS

Example 1

Write the equation $y = ax^2 + bx + c$ on the board. Then write various equations underneath with different values for a, b, and c. Be sure to make some values positive and some negative. Point out that b and c can be zero but a cannot. For example:

Equation 1) $y = 3x^2 - 6x + 8$
Equation 2) $y = -5x^2 + x - 2$
Equation 3) $y = x^2 - 4x + 7$

Ask: What is the value of a, b, and c in $y = 3x^2 - 6x + 8$? **[a = 3, b = -6, and c = 8]**

Be sure students understand that subtraction of a term can be rewritten as addition of the opposite. Therefore, $y = 3x^2 - 6x + 8$ can be rewritten as $y = 3x^2 + -6x + 8$.

Repeat for the remaining equations written on the board. Remind students that a variable with no coefficient is understood to have a coefficient of 1.

Guide students through Example 1. Show them that an equation with x^2 will be the graph of a parabola. An equation with x to the first power will be linear.

If desired, use the tables in the Alternative Strategy to explain why this is true.

It might also be helpful to show students additional non-quadratic graphs and their equations. For example:

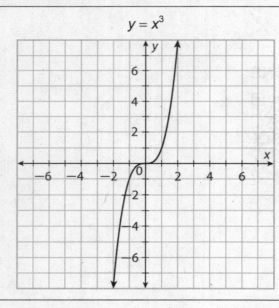

$y = x^3$

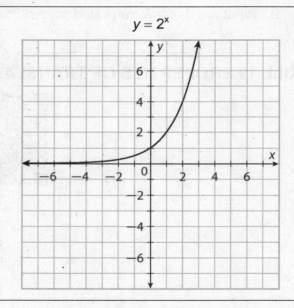

$y = 2^x$

Check

Problems 1–3

Point out that the values of b and c can be zero. It might help to write the equations with all terms. For example, problem 4 would become $y = -2x^2 + 4x + c$.

Example 2

Guide students through the definitions of maximum and minimum in Example 2.

Ask: How do you know what the value of a is? **[Look at the number in front of the x^2 term. That number is the value of a.]**

Ask: What do you think happens if $a = 0$? Explain. **[If $a = 0$, then there will be no x^2 term. That means the graph is no longer a quadratic function.]**

Point out both graphs in Example 2.

Say: The graph on the left opens up. The graph on the right opens down.

Have students reason as to why a graph is said to "open up" or "open down." For example, a student might say that a graph opening up looks like it could hold water. A graph opening down would not hold water. Allow students a chance to describe the difference between opening up and down in their own words.

Now direct students to look at the graph on the right in Example 2. Have students put their finger on the x^2 term and state the value of a.

Say: Notice that a is a positive 1. This means a is greater than zero. So, the graph is opening up.

Next, have students read aloud the vertex and the minimum.

Ask: How are the vertex and minimum the same? How are they different? **[Answers will vary. Sample answer: They are the same because they both have a −5. They are different because the vertex is a point and the minimum is a number.]**

Ask: How might you tell a friend to determine the minimum if only the vertex is known? **[The minimum is the y-coordinate of the vertex.]**

Ask: Can you determine if a quadratic function has a maximum or minimum by knowing only the vertex? Explain. **[No. You need to know whether the graph opens up or down before you can determine the maximum or minimum from the vertex.]**

Check

Problem 5

If students state that a graph opening up has a maximum, ask the student what that maximum would be. Allow the student to inspect the graph and explain.

Problem 9

Some students might argue that the equation $y = -7x^2 + 3$ is not a quadratic function because it does not have all three terms. Rewrite the equation on the board as $y = -7x^2 + 0x + 3$ to remind students that the values of b and/or c can be 0.

Example 3

Direct students' attention to Example 3. On the leftmost graph, have students trace along the x-axis. If desired, have students use colored pencils to trace the x-axis in one color and the parabola in another color.

Say: The zeros of a function occur where the parabola intersects the x-axis.

Have students draw points where the parabola intersects the x-axis.

Next, have students place each finger on the intersection parabola and x-axis.

Ask: What are the zeros of this function? **[3 and −3]**

Repeat for the remaining graphs.

Say: Now think about graphs opening down. How many zeros can those parabolas have?

Either sketch the following on the board or have students sketch on a piece of paper. Tell students to sketch downward opening parabolas that have 0, 1, or 2 zeros.

For example:

No zeros $-x^2 - 1$	Exactly 1 zero $y = -(x + 4)^2$	Exactly 2 zeros $y = (x - 2)(x - 3)$
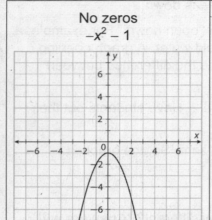	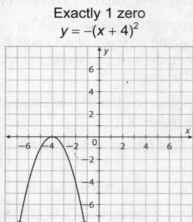	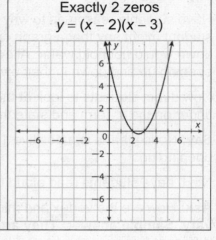

Check
Problems 10–11
If needed, review finding coordinate points with students. Have students draw a point at the minimum or maximum for each graph. Then have them find the x- and y-value that describes the point.

Example 4
If possible, cut out several pictures of graphs with parabolas. Some of the parabolas can open up and some can open down. Be sure to include some in which the axis of symmetry is something other than $x = 0$.

Tell students that they must show where to fold the parabola so that the sides match up exactly. Point out that this folded line is called the axis of symmetry.

Guide students through Example 4 and direct students' attention to the leftmost graph.

Ask: What is the vertex of this parabola? **[(0, −9)]**

Ask: What is the axis of symmetry? **[x = 0]**

Repeat questioning for the remaining graphs. For the middle graph, the vertex is (−2, 0) with an axis of symmetry of $x = -2$. **[For the rightmost graph, the vertex is (0, 4) with an axis of symmetry at $x = 0$.]**

Ask: How are the axis of symmetry and the vertex related? **[The axis of symmetry is the line defined by the x-coordinate of the vertex.]**

Check
Problem 14

If students are confused about the change in variables, point out that sometimes it makes sense to use a more descriptive variable. In this case, t is used for time in seconds on the horizontal axis and h is used for height in feet on the vertical axis.

The concepts shown here are most likely new to students. Acquaint students with the graph by asking the following:

Ask: What is the height of the ball one second after it is thrown? **[about 45 feet]**

Ask: What is the highest number of feet the ball will go? **[about 65 feet]**

Ask: What is this height known as? **[the maximum]**

Ask: What is the axis of symmetry? **[$t = 2$]**

Ask: What is the meaning of the axis of symmetry for this problem? **[At $t = 2$, the ball is at its maximum height.]**

If students struggle with part A, write $y = ax^2 + bx + c$ on the board.

Ask: Which variable is used to determine if the parabola opens up or down? **[a]**

Ask: Which term includes the a? **[the x^2 term]**

Direct students' attention to the equation $h(t) = -16t^2 + 64t$. Point out that the a would still occur in front of the squared term.

ALTERNATE STRATEGY

Strategy: Tables

1. Have students recall that an equation for a line will contain two variables, usually x and y. Students should be familiar with graphing a line using a table.

2. Have students graph the coordinates for $y = x$.

$y = x$

x	y
−2	−2
−1	−1
0	0
1	1
2	2

Ask: What do you notice about the pattern for x and y? **[As x increases, y increases.]**

3. Next, have students fill in the table for $y = x^2 - 4$.

$y = x^2 - 4$

x	y
-3	5
-2	0
-1	-3
0	-4
1	-3
2	0
3	5

Ask: What do you notice about the pattern for x and y? **[As x increases, y decreases and then increases again.]**

Ask: Why do the y-values decrease and increase? **[Because x is squared, any negative value for x will result in a positive y-value.]**

Point out that the increasing and decreasing indicates the graph will be curved. If desired, refer students to the graph of $y = x^2 - 4$ in Example 1.

Next, have students answer the following questions using a table:

Ask: Is the graph opening up or down? How can you tell? **[The graph opens up because as x gets larger, the y-values decrease and then increase. So, when moving left to right, the graph goes down and then up.]**

Ask: What is the vertex? Explain. **[The vertex is the point where the direction of the graph changes. For this graph, it happens at (0, -4).]**

Ask: Does it have a maximum or minimum? How do you know? What is the maximum or minimum? **[The graph opens up, which means it extends infinitely upward. This means it must have a minimum point. The vertex is at (0, -4), so the minimum is -4.]**

Ask: What are the zeros of the function? Explain. **[The zeros of the graph are the places where $y = 0$. This happens at -2 and 2.]**

COMMON MISCONCEPTION

Problem 15

Ask: Does the graph of the function open up or down? **[down]**

Explain that because the graph opens down, the parabola will extend to negative infinity in the y-direction.

Ask: If the graph opens down, will it have a minimum point? Why or why not? **[No, it just continues in the negative direction forever.]**

Error: Students are often confused because a parabola opening up has no maximum while a parabola opening down has no minimum. Remind students that the maximum or minimum value for a parabola opening up or down will be the y-coordinate. Encourage students to sketch an upward opening graph or a downward opening graph as determined by the equation before thinking about whether a maximum or minimum exists.

Solution: The variable a is 4, so $a > 0$. This means the graph opens up. Because the graph opens up, it extends infinitely upward. So, the graph will have a minimum.

ADDITIONAL ONLINE INTERVENTION RESOURCES

 Use the following for students who have not mastered the concepts in Skill 20.

- Math on the Spot videos

- Personal Math Trainer with customized intervention

- Building Block worksheets Skill 22 Connect Words and Algebra, Skill 23 Connect Words and Equations, Skill 53 Line Symmetry, Skill 100 Squares and Square Roots, Skill 102 Symmetry

SKILL 20

Quadratic Functions

Example 1

A quadratic function is a function of the form $y = ax^2 + bx + c$.
The value of a cannot be 0.

The graph of a quadratic function is in the shape of a parabola.

This is the graph of a quadratic function.	This is not a graph of a quadratic function. This is a linear function.
$y = x^2 - 4$	$y = 2x - 2$
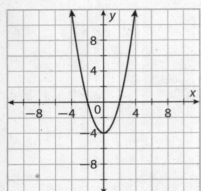	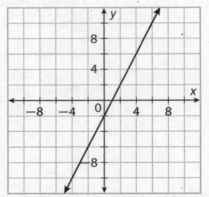

Vocabulary

Axis of symmetry

Maximum

Minimum

Vertex

Zeros

Check

State whether each function is a quadratic function. If it is, state the values of a, b, and c.

1. $y = 3x^2 + 5x - 8$ _____

2. $y = -4x + 2$ _____

3. $y = x^2 + 6x + 5$ _____

4. $y = -2x^2 + 4x$ _____

Example 2

In a quadratic function $y = ax^2 + bx + c$:

If $a > 0$, then the parabola opens up and the function has a minimum at the lowest point.

If $a < 0$, then the parabola opens down and the function has a maximum at the highest point.

The highest or lowest point of a parabola is called the vertex.

$y = x^2 + 2x - 4$

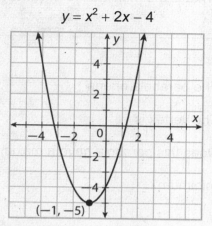

$a = 1$, so $a > 0$
The parabola opens up.
The vertex is $(-1, -5)$.
The minimum is -5.

$y = -x^2 + 2x + 2$

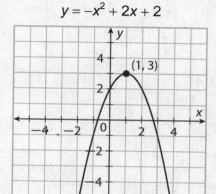

$a = -1$, so $a < 0$
The parabola opens down.
The vertex is $(1, 3)$.
The maximum is 3.

Check

Fill in the blank for each graph.

5. $-x(x + 6)$

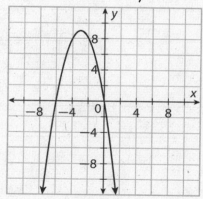

A The parabola opens _____.

B The vertex is _____.

C Does this parabola have a maximum or

  minimum? _____

D What is the maximum or minimum?

_____

Name _____ Date _____ Class_____

Fill in the blank for each graph.

6. $-(x + 1)(x - 3)$

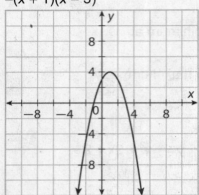

A The parabola opens _____.

B The vertex is _____.

C Does this parabola have a maximum or

minimum? _____

D What is the maximum or minimum?

_____

7. $x(x + 4)$

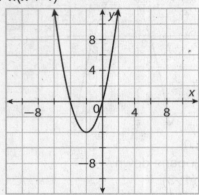

A The parabola opens _____.

B The vertex is _____.

C Does this parabola have a maximum or

minimum? _____

D What is the maximum or minimum?

_____

Determine whether the graph of each quadratic function opens up or down and how you know. Then, tell whether the graph has a maximum or minimum.

8. $y = -x^2 + 5x + 2$

_____

_____

9. $y = 7x^2 + 2$

_____

_____

Example 3

A quadratic function can intersect the x-axis twice, once, or not at all.

The x-coordinates at the points of intersection are called zeros of the function.

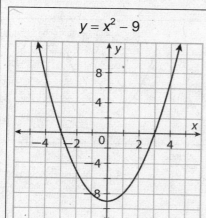

$y = x^2 - 9$

The zeros are at 3 and –3.

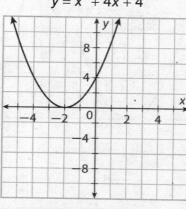

$y = x^2 + 4x + 4$

There is one zero at –2.

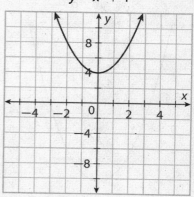

$y = x^2 + 4$

There are no zeros.

Check

Determine whether each quadratic function has 0, 1, or 2 zeros. If zeros exist, name them.

10. $-(x + 1)(x - 3)$

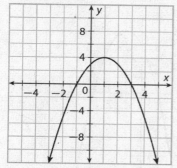

How many zeros are there? _____

If zeros exist, what are they?

_____

11. $1x^2 + 2x + 6$

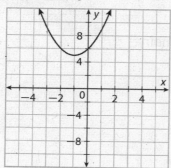

How many zeros are there? _____

If zeros exist, what are they?

_____

Example 4

Every quadratic function has symmetry. The axis of symmetry is the reflection line or line of symmetry for the parabola. For parabolas that open up or down, use the x-coordinate of the vertex to determine the equation for the axis of symmetry.

$y = x^2 - 9$

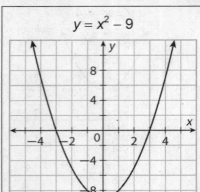

$y = x^2 + 4x + 4$

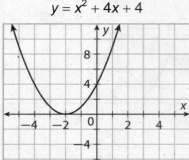

$y = x^2 + 4$

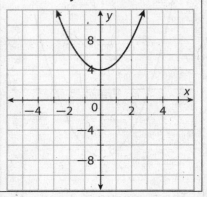

Check

Draw the axis of symmetry on each graph. Then write the equation for the axis of symmetry.

12. $x(x + 4)$

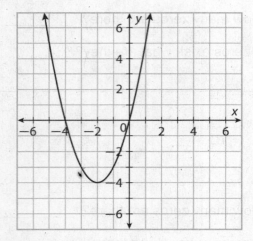

Axis of Symmetry: _____

13. $-(x + 1)(x - 3)$

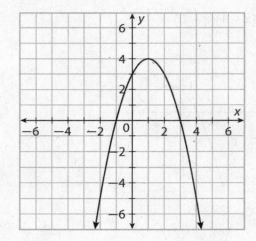

Axis of Symmetry: _____

14. A ball is thrown in the air. The height of the ball over time is represented by the quadratic function shown.

Use this graph to answer A through E.

$h(t) = -16t^2 + 64t$

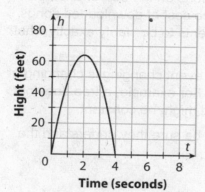

A Which part of the quadratic equation indicates if the parabola will open up or down? Explain.

_____

B What is the vertex?

_____

C Does the function have a maximum or minimum? What is it?

_____

D What is the axis of symmetry?

_____

E When does the ball hit the ground? How do you know?

_____

_____

_____

15. Find the Error. Explain your reasoning.

Question: Determine whether the graph of the quadratic function $y = 4x^2 - 3x + 10$ opens up or down. Then tell whether it has a maximum or minimum.

Solution: The variable a is 4, so $a > 0$. This means the graph opens up and it has a maximum.

_____

_____

_____

_____

SKILL 20 QUADRATIC FUNCTIONS

Rate of Change and Slope

KEY TEACHING POINTS

Example 1

Have students brainstorm things that change and write their ideas on the board. Examples might include: a tree grows in height, a puppy gains weight, the cost of downloaded songs increases with the number of songs. In each case, guide students to be clarify exactly what is changing.

For each suggestion, ask students to think about whether the event changing is changing at the same rate all the time. In most cases, this will not be true. For example, a tree does not grow at a constant rate. However, cost per songs downloaded might be constant.

Have students read through Example 1. Question students to be sure they understand the information in the table.

Ask: How much is 4 gallons of gas? **[$14.00]**

Ask: How much gas can you buy for $21.00? **[6 gallons]**

Ask: Do you think the total cost of gas will increase at a constant rate? Why or why not? **[Yes, because gas probably costs the same amount per gallon.]**

Next, tell students they are going to figure out the rate of change for the cost of gasoline.

Say: Look at the gallons of gas in the left column.

Ask: Are the gallons of gas increasing or decreasing? **[increasing]**

Ask: How much are the gallons increasing from one row to the next? **[by 2 gallons]**

Repeat the questioning so that students see the total cost is increasing also by $7.00 each row.

Explain that these changes in both the gallons of gasoline and the total cost are what determine the rate of change.

Next, have students think about the cost of a single gallon of gasoline. Some students may be able to deduce that gas is $3.50 per gallon. Formalize this by explaining that a rate of change that expresses the rate of change for one item is called the unit rate.

Point out that the unit rate can be helpful in determining cost per item, etc.

Check
Problem 2

Suggest to students that they think of a bathtub or pool draining to see how the water level would decrease. Point out that because the water level is decreasing, the change in water level is described as a negative number.

Ask: How is the time changing? **[increasing by 5 minutes]**

Ask: How is the water level changing? **[decreasing by 2 inches]**

Explain to students that the change in time is +5 while the change in water level is −2.

Example 2

Direct students' attention to Example 2 and work through the problem with them. Point out that the arrows comprising the right triangle began and ended at points on the line that intersect the grid.

Point out that slope can be determined from any points on the line. Have students start at point B and count up until they are level with point A. Then have them count across.

Ask: What is the distance from point B up until you are level with point A? **[6 units]**

Ask: What is the distance to the left until you reach point A? **[9]**

Ask: What is the slope using these changes? $\left[\dfrac{6}{-9}\right]$

Ask: Is this slope the same as the slope found in Example 2? Explain. **[Yes, it is the same because you can simplify $\dfrac{6}{-9}$ by $\dfrac{6 \div 3}{-9 \div 3} = \dfrac{2}{-3}$.]**

Allow students time to count the horizontal distance below the line. Remind students that the vertical change will always be in the numerator. You may need to remind students that moving left or down indicates a negative change.

Check
Problem 4

Additional points are marked on the line to aid students in determining points to use for calculating slope.

Example 3

Explain to students that they can also calculate slope knowing only the coordinates of two points on the line.

Direct students' attention to the slope ratio in Example 3. Point out that the change in y-coordinates is thought of algebraically as the difference between the coordinates. Likewise for the change in x-coordinates.

Explain to students that the smaller numbers to the right of each variable are simply a label that is used to keep track of the coordinates.

Check
Problems 9–10

Students explore slopes of horizontal and vertical lines by using the slope formula to calculate slope. Some students may need a reminder that a number cannot be divided by zero. This slope will be undefined.

Problem 12

Students are introduced to the real-life meaning of slope, and unit rate as well as the meaning of slope for horizontal and vertical lines. Encourage students to use the graph to determine slope of all three lines. Although some students may immediately realize that Plant D has the fastest growth, emphasize the importance of comparing unit rates to determine exactly how fast the growth is.

ALTERNATE STRATEGY

Strategy: Slope Triangles
Some students may benefit from the concept of slope triangles.

1. Draw the line through (2, 7) and (12, 2) several times on the board. Have students use the endpoints of a line to create a right triangle. Point out that triangles can be made above or below the line. The triangles can also be created using any points on the line. However, it is often simpler to begin by using the endpoints.

Graph 1	Graph 2	Graph 3
	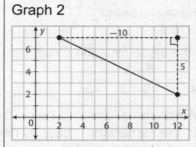	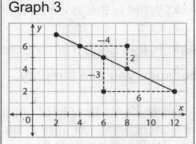
5 units down and 10 units right	5 units up and 10 units to the left	3 units down and 6 units to the left OR 2 units up and 4 units to the left

2. Help students by reading the vertical and horizontal changes aloud.

3. Direct students to write each slope as shown by the slope triangle.

   Graph 1: $\dfrac{-5}{10}$; Graph 2: $\dfrac{5}{-10}$; Graph 3: $\dfrac{-3}{6}$ or $\dfrac{2}{-4}$

4. Direct students to simplify each slope to see that the slope for each is $-\dfrac{1}{2}$.

5. Encourage students to continue drawing slope triangles, noting the difference in x- and y-coordinates, then writing and simplifying the slope.

COMMON MISCONCEPTION

Problem 15

Ask: Which coordinates would you like to use for (x_1, y_1)? **[(4, 7)]**

Ask: Which coordinates would you like to use for (x_2, y_2)? **[(2, 9)]**

Say: To find slope, divide the difference in the y's by the difference in the x's.

Ask: What is $(y_2 - y_1)$? Explain. **[$y_2 = 9$ and $y_1 = 7$, so the difference is $9 - 7 = 2$.]**

Ask: What is $(x_2 - x_1)$? Explain. **[$x_2 = 2$ and $x_1 = 4$, so the difference is $2 - 4 = -2$.]**

Ask: What is the slope? Explain how you got your answer. **[The difference in the y's is 2 and the difference in the x's is –2. So, the slope is $\dfrac{2}{-2}$ which is –1.]**

Point out to students that they can do a quick check of the slope by imagining the line and determining the sign of the slope. For example, the rightmost coordinate is (2, 9) and the leftmost coordinate is (4, 7). Note that as the x-coordinates increase from 2 to 4, the y-coordinates decrease from 9 to 7. Therefore, the slope must be negative.

Error: Students may confuse the order of the coordinates when calculating slope. Suggest that students label each point as (x_1, x_2) and (y_1, y_2) before making their calculations. Point out that it does not matter which ordered pair is labeled as (x_1, x_2) and (y_1, y_2). It only matters that after the labeling is completed and the calculations are made in the correct order.

Solution: The slope of the line through points (4, 7) and (2, 9) is $\frac{9-7}{2-4} = \frac{2}{-2} = -1$.

ADDITIONAL ONLINE INTERVENTION RESOURCES

 Use the following for students who have not mastered the concepts in Skill 21.

- Math on the Spot videos
- Personal Math Trainer with customized intervention
- Building Block worksheets Skill 87 Slopes of Parallel and Perpendicular Lines

Name ______________________ Date ______________ Class ______________

SKILL 21

Rate of Change and Slope

Example 1

Vocabulary

Rate of Change
Slope
Unit Rate

A rate of change is how one quantity changes in relation to another. Rate of change can be found from a table.

Gas (Gallons)	Total Cost ($)
0	0
2	7.00
4	14.00
6	21.00

Changes by +2

Changes by +7.00

The total cost increases by 7 and the number of gallons increases by 2.

So, the rate of change is $\frac{7}{2}$.

The unit rate is the rate of change for 1 item.

The unit rate for gasoline is $\frac{7}{2} = \frac{3.50}{1}$. So, gas costs $3.50 for 1 gallon.

Check

Determine the rate of change for each table. Then state the unit rate.

1.

Pretzels	Total Cost
0	0
3	6.75
6	13.50
9	20.25

A Rate of Change ______________

B Unit Rate ______________

2.

Time (min)	Water Level (inches)
0	10
5	8
10	6
15	4

A Rate of Change ______________

B Unit Rate ______________

Example 2

Rate of change can also be found using a graph. Rate of change on a graph is often called 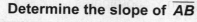 slope.

Slope is $\dfrac{\text{change in vertical distance}}{\text{change in horizontal distance}}$

Determine the slope of $\overline{AB}$	**To determine the slope:**

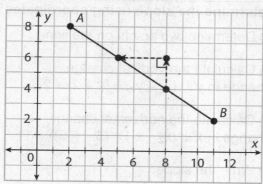	Step 1) Draw a right triangle using any two points on the line.
	
	 Step 2) Count the change in the vertical distance.
	      Vertical change = 2 units up
	
	 Step 3) Count the change in the horizontal distance.
	      Horizontal change = 3 units left (or −3)
	
	 Step 4) Write the slope.
	      Slope = $\dfrac{2}{-3}$

A positive slope goes up from left to right. A negative slope goes down from left to right.

Check

Use two points on each line to calculate the slope.

3. Slope: _____

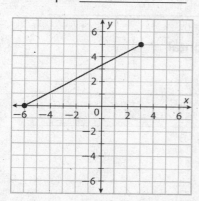

4. Slope: _____

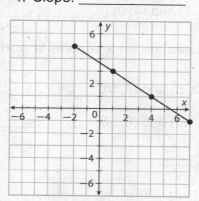

5. Slope: _____

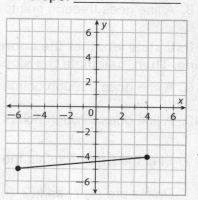

Example 3

Slope can be calculated using the coordinates of points on the line.
If a line has points (x_1, y_1) and (x_2, y_2), then:

$$\text{slope is } \frac{\text{change in vertical distance}}{\text{change in horizontal distance}} = \frac{\text{Change in } y\text{-coordinates}}{\text{Change in } x\text{-coordinates}} = \frac{y_2 - y_1}{x_2 - x_1}$$

Determine the slope of $\overline{AB}$

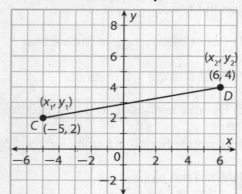

To determine the slope using coordinates:

Step 1) Determine two points on the line.

Step 2) Calculate the vertical change.
Change in y's: $(y_2 - y_1) = (4 - 2) = 2$

Step 3) Calculate the horizontal change.
Change in x's: $(x_2 - x_1) = (6 - (-5)) = 11$

Step 4) Write the slope.
$$\text{Slope} = \frac{2}{11}$$

Check
Calculate the slope of each line using the points.

6. A line goes through points (4, 2) and (6, –10). _____

7. A line goes through points (5, 1) and (–5, 7). _____

8. A line goes through points (9, 4) and (4, 0). _____

First, state whether the coordinates are on a vertical or horizontal line. Then, calculate the slope.

9. A line goes through points (13, 5) and (7, 5). _____

10. A line goes through points (2, –3) and (8, –3). _____

11. Find the Error. Explain the solution.

Points are (4, 7) and (2, 9).

Slope is $\dfrac{9-7}{4-2} = \dfrac{2}{2} = 1$.

_____

_____

_____

_____

12. A scientist is tracking the growth in inches of three different plants over 6 weeks.

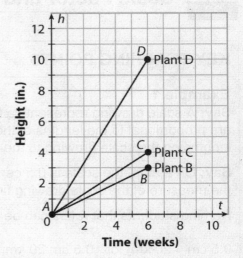

   A What is the slope of Plant B? _____

   B What is the slope of Plant C? _____

   C What is the slope of Plant D? _____

   D Compare unit rates to determine which plant had the fastest growth. How do you know your answer is correct?

      _____

      _____

   E Would it make sense for the growth of a plant to have a slope of zero? What about a slope that is undefined? Explain.

      _____

      _____

      _____

SKILL 21 RATE OF CHANGE AND SLOPE

Scale Factor and Scale Drawings

KEY TEACHING POINTS

Example 1

Say: A scale drawing represents a large or a small object. The lengths on a scale drawing are proportional to the lengths of the object it represents. The scale tells you the ratio of the lengths on the scale drawing to the actual lengths of the object.

Say: On a map, the scale is 0.5 centimeter = 20 kilometers. The scale is always written with the measure of the scale drawing first.

Remind students that ratios can be written in different ways, for example,

$$0.5 \text{ cm} = 20 \text{ km} \quad \text{or} \quad 0.5 \text{ cm}:20 \text{ km} \quad \text{or} \quad \frac{0.5 \text{ cm}}{20 \text{ km}}$$

Ask: What information is shown in the fraction on the left side of the proportion? **[the map scale]**

Ask: What distance is used in the numerator of each fraction in the proportion? **[the map distance]**

After students have solved the proportion, check to see if the answer is reasonable.

Ask: Should the actual distance between the cities be greater than or less than 20 kilometers? **[greater than]**

Ask: How many kilometers are represented by 1 centimeter on the map? **[40 kilometers]**

Say: If 1 centimeter = 40 kilometers, then 6.5 centimeters will represent 6.5 • 40 kilometers.

Ask: What is 6.5 • 40? **[260]**

Make sure students understand how to use given information to set up a proportion.

Ask: If the map on the scale was 1 centimeter = 20 kilometers, how would the proportion change? $\left[\dfrac{1}{20} = \dfrac{6.5}{d} \right]$

Ask: If the map on the scale was 0.5 centimeter = 30 kilometers, how would the proportion change? $\left[\dfrac{0.5}{30} = \dfrac{6.5}{d} \right]$

Ask: If the distance between the two cities on the map was 8 centimeters, how would the proportion change? $\left[\dfrac{0.5}{20} = \dfrac{8}{d} \right]$

Check
Problem 8
Ask: What proportion can you write with the given information if ℓ represents the actual length of the grasshopper on the scale drawing? $\left[\dfrac{1 \text{ cm}}{5 \text{ mm}} = \dfrac{\ell \text{ cm}}{40 \text{ mm}}\right]$

Problem 10
Tell students they can use equivalent ratios for the scale to make calculations easier. The scale $\dfrac{1}{4}$ inch = 3 feet is equivalent to 1 inch = 12 feet. Remind students that $\dfrac{1}{4}$ inch can also be rewritten as 0.25 inch.

Problem 11
Ask: What proportion can you write to find the length of the airplane on the scale drawing? $\left[\dfrac{1 \text{ in.}}{8 \text{ ft}} = \dfrac{\ell \text{ in.}}{100 \text{ ft}}\right]$

Example 2
Say: When the scale drawing or model has the same unit of measure, the scale can be written without units. This is called the scale factor.

Ask: How is the scale different than the scale factor? **[The scale is written with units and the scale factor is written without units]**

Say: First write the scale in simplest form so that the numerator or denominator is 1.

Ask: What is the scale 8 inches = 144 feet written in simplest form? $\left[\dfrac{8 \text{ in.}}{144 \text{ ft}} = \dfrac{1 \text{ in.}}{18 \text{ ft}}\right]$

Say: The scale is 1 inch = 18 feet. To find the scale factor, rewrite the scale so that both measurements are in inches.

Ask: What conversion factor can you use to convert feet to inches? **[1 foot = 12 inches]** How many inches are in 18 feet? **[216 inches]**

Say: Since the scale uses the same measurement unit, you can cancel the units to get the scale factor 1:216. So, the actual lighthouse is 216 times as tall as the scale model.

Say: The scale factor is always written so that the length of the model comes first. If the scale model represents a very small object, like a model of plant cell, then the first number of the scale will be larger than the second number.

Ask: If a scale model uses a scale of 15:1, is the scale model larger or smaller than the actual object? **[larger]**

Check
Problem 14
Ask: How can you rewrite the scale in simplest form? **[1 centimeter = 25 meters]**

Ask: What conversion factor can you use to convert meters to centimeters? **[1 meter = 100 centimeters]**

Problem 18

Ask: Is the scale model larger or smaller than the actual object? **[larger]** How do you know? **[The length of the scale model is written first in the scale factor]**

Ask: How many times larger is the scale model than the actual object? **[8 times larger]**

Problems 19–21

Tell students that a scale factor of 1:48 means that an object that is 48 feet long will be 1 foot long, or 12 inches, on a scale model.

ALTERNATE STRATEGY

Strategy: Make a scale drawing.

Say: You are going to make a scale drawing of the classroom using $\frac{1}{4}$-inch grid paper. Each square on the grid has sides of $\frac{1}{4}$ inch.

Ask: If you want to draw an object that is 2 inches long on the scale drawing, how many squares long will the object be? **[8 squares]**

Ask: If the scale is $\frac{1}{4}$ inch = 2 feet, what is the actual length of an object that is 2 inches on the scale drawing? **[16 feet]**

Have students follow these steps:

1. Measure the length and width of the classroom.
2. Choose an appropriate scale for the drawing. Use the scale to determine what the length and width of the classroom should be in the scale drawing.
3. Make the scale drawing. Include a key for the scale.

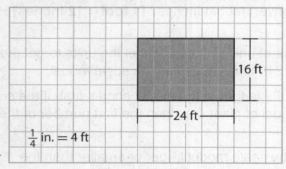

COMMON MISCONCEPTIONS

Problem 9

Students may not know how to write a proportion to find the scale. Since the scale can be written in the form 1 inch = d miles, always use 1 inch in the proportion.

$$\text{map distance} \rightarrow \quad \frac{1 \text{ in.}}{d \text{ mi}} = \frac{4 \text{ in.}}{3 \text{ mi}} \quad \leftarrow \text{map distance}$$
$$\text{actual distance} \rightarrow \qquad\qquad\qquad \leftarrow \text{actual distance}$$

Problem 16

Students need to convert the scale to a scale factor.
Since 1 inch = 60 inches, the scale factor is 1:60.

Ask: Is 1 inch = 60 inches a scale factor? Explain. **[No; A scale factor does not use units]**

Ask: How many inches are in 5 feet? **[60 in]**

Ask: What is the scale factor? **[1:60]**

Error: The scale is written with different measurement units. To compare the size of these two objects without units, you need to convert feet to inches and simplify to find the scale factor.

Solution: The actual objects are 60 times the length of the objects in the scale model.

Problem 22

Some students may find the area on the scale drawing and multiply by 3 to get an area of 3(20 • 18) = 1080 square ft. Have students find the actual width and length before determining the area so they can see their error.

ADDITIONAL ONLINE INTERVENTION RESOURCES

 Use the following for students who have not mastered the concepts in Skill 22.

- Math on the Spot videos
- Personal Math Trainer with customized intervention
- Building Block worksheets (Skill 48: Identify Congruent Figures ; Skill 50: Identify Similar Figures; Skill 80: Similar Figures; Skill 95: Solve Proportions)

SKILL 22 — Scale Factor and Scale Drawings

Example 1

A scale drawing is a diagram of an object that is too large or too small to be drawn at the actual size. The dimensions on a scale drawing are proportional to the dimensions of the actual object.

The scale shows how the dimensions in the scale drawing are related to the dimensions of the actual object.

Suppose a map has a scale 0.5 centimeter = 20 kilometers. The distance between two cities on a map is 6.5 centimeters. To find the actual distance between the cities, use a proportion.

Let d represent the actual distance.

$$\begin{array}{l}\text{map distance} \rightarrow \\ \text{actual distance} \rightarrow\end{array} \dfrac{0.5 \text{ cm}}{20 \text{ km}} = \dfrac{6.5 \text{ cm}}{d \text{ km}} \begin{array}{l}\leftarrow \text{ map distance} \\ \leftarrow \text{ actual distance}\end{array}$$

$\dfrac{0.5}{20} = \dfrac{6.5}{d}$ Write a proportion.

$0.5 \cdot d = 20 \cdot 6.5$ Find the cross products.

$0.5d = 130$ Multiply.

$\dfrac{0.5d}{0.5} = \dfrac{130}{0.5}$ Divide each side by 0.5.

$d = 260$ Simplify.

The actual distance between the cities is 260 kilometers.

Check
The scale on a blueprint is 0.5 inches = 8 feet. Find the actual length in feet for each given length on the blueprint.

1. 2 in.   _____

2. 5 in.   _____

3. 6.5 in.   _____

4. 8.25 in.   _____

5. 15.75 in.   _____

6. 24.6 in.   _____

7. An engineer makes a scale drawing of a bridge using a scale of 1 inch = 15 yards. The length of the bridge on the drawing is 24 inches. What is the length of the actual bridge?

_____

8. A science teacher is drawing a model of a grasshopper to use for a class. The teacher uses a scale of 1 centimeter = 5 millimeters. The length of the actual grasshopper is 40 millimeters. How long should the grasshopper be in the scale drawing?

_____

9. A park map shows that a specific trail is 4 inches long. The actual trail is 3 miles. What is the scale of the map? Write the scale in the form 1 inch = d miles.

_____

10. An artist made a sketch of a mural on $\frac{1}{4}$-inch grid paper using a scale $\frac{1}{4}$ inch = 3 feet.

The scale drawing of the mural is 8 inches long and 6 inches wide.

A   How many feet are represented by 1 inch on the scale drawing?

_____

B   What will be the dimensions of the actual mural when it is complete?

_____

11. The table shows the actual dimensions of an airplane.

Dimension	Actual Length
Length	100 feet
Height	36 feet
Wingspan	96 feet

Find the dimensions of the airplane on a scale drawing. Use a scale of 1 inch = 8 feet.

Length _____

Height _____

Wingspan _____

Example 2

A scale factor does not use units. To find the scale factor, convert the scale to a ratio with no units.

A scale model of a lighthouse has a height of 8 inches. The actual height of the lighthouse is 144 feet.

To find the *scale*, write a ratio of the height of the model to the actual height.

$$\frac{\text{height of model}}{\text{actual height}} = \frac{8 \text{ in.}}{144 \text{ ft}} \text{ or } \frac{1 \text{ in.}}{18 \text{ ft}}$$

The scale of the model is 1 in.:18 ft.

To find the *scale factor*, use a conversion factor that relates inches to feet and rewrite the scale so that the measurements are in the same units.

Since 1 foot = 12 inches, 18 feet = 12 • 18 or 216 inches.

$$\frac{1 \text{ in.}}{18 \text{ ft}} = \frac{1 \text{ in.}}{216 \text{ in.}} = \frac{1}{216}$$

The scale factor is $\frac{1}{216}$ or 1:216.

So, the model is $\frac{1}{216}$ as tall as the actual lighthouse. This also means that the actual lighthouse is 216 times as tall as the model.

Check

Find the scale factor for each scale.

12. 1 inch = 6 feet _____

13. 0.5 inch = 3 yards _____

14. 2 centimeters = 50 meters _____

15. 2.5 millimeters = 4 centimeters _____

16. Explain the Error. Find the correct solution.

   A miniature special effects model on a movie set uses a scale of 1 inch = 5 feet. This means that the actual objects are 5 times the length of the objects in the scale model.

_____

17. A model car is 5 inches long. The actual length of the car is 15 feet.

   A What is the scale of the model car?

   _____

   B How many times longer is the actual car than the model car?

   _____

18. A scale model uses a scale factor of 8:1. If the length of the actual object
    is 4 millimeters, what is the length of the object in the scale model?

_____

Use the following information for 19–21.
**The table shows some common scale factors used in model
train sets. The actual length of a typical box car is 40 feet.**

Scale Type	Scale Factor
N	1:160
HO	1:87
O	1:48
G	1:22.5

19. What is the length of a box car in inches for an N-scale model?

_____

20. What is the length of a box car in inches for an O-scale model?

_____

21. As the scale factor increases, does the size of the model train
    car increase or decrease?

_____

22. A playground area has a length of 20 inches and a width of 18 inches
    on a scale drawing. The drawing uses a scale of 1 inch = 3 feet.
    What is the actual area of the playground?

SKILL 22 SCALE FACTOR AND SCALE DRAWINGS

Similar Figures

KEY TEACHING POINTS

Example 1
Review how to identify corresponding parts.

Say: Similar figures have the same shape, but not the same size. Two figures are similar if their corresponding angles are congruent and their corresponding sides are proportional.

Ask: How do you know that $\triangle ABC$ and $\triangle DEF$ have corresponding angles that are congruent? **[The number of arcs indicates congruent angles]**

Ask: Which angle is congruent to $\angle C$? **[$\angle F$]**

Say: To determine whether the side lengths are proportional, write a ratio for each pair of corresponding sides. If the ratios are equal, then the side lengths are proportional.

Ask: Which side of $\triangle DEF$ corresponds to $\overline{AB}$? **[$\overline{DE}$]**

Ask: What fraction shows the ratio of the side length of $\overline{AB}$ to the side length of $\overline{DE}$? $\left[\dfrac{AB}{DE}\right]$

If students have difficulty identifying corresponding sides, remind them to use the corresponding angles to identify the corresponding vertices that name a side.

Check
Make sure students understand that just because the corresponding angles of two figures are congruent, that is not enough to determine that the figures are similar. The lengths of the corresponding sides must also be proportional.

Problems 1–3
Ask: What two properties are true about similar figures? **[Corresponding angles are congruent and the lengths of corresponding sides are proportional.]**

Ask: Which vertices correspond to each other? **[H and W, I and X, J and Y, K and Z]**

Ask: Are the corresponding angles congruent? **[Yes]**

Ask: Which side corresponds to $\overline{HI}$? **[$\overline{WX}$]**

Ask: What is the ratio of the side lengths of $\overline{WX}$ and $\overline{HI}$? $\left[\dfrac{WX}{HI} = \dfrac{9}{3} = 3\right]$

Ask: If the figures are similar, what will be true about the ratios of the other side lengths? **[The ratios will all be equal to 3]**

Problem 5
Remind students that the opposite sides of parallelograms are congruent. So, they only need to check the ratios of two adjacent sides.

Problem 10
Encourage students to draw a diagram to represent the situation and label the dimensions of each rectangle. This will help them identity the corresponding sides.

Example 2

Say: If it is stated that two figures are similar, you only need to find the ratio of one pair of corresponding sides to find the scale factor.

Ask: What are the corresponding sides? [$\overline{JK}$ and $\overline{PQ}$, $\overline{KL}$ and $\overline{QR}$, $\overline{LM}$ and $\overline{RS}$, $\overline{MJ}$ and $\overline{SP}$]

Ask: How do you find the scale factor? [**Find the ratio of the side lengths of two corresponding sides.**]

Ask: What is the ratio of the side lengths of $\overline{SP}$ and $\overline{MJ}$? $\left[\dfrac{2}{3}\right]$

Ask: What is the scale factor? $\left[\dfrac{2}{3}\right]$

After students have worked through the example, tell them that when writing a ratio, they can choose the side lengths of either figure for the numerator. They just need to be sure to write the rest of the lengths in the same order.

Ask: What is the ratio of the side lengths of $\overline{MJ}$ and $\overline{SP}$? $\left[\dfrac{15}{10} = \dfrac{3}{2}\right]$

Ask: What is the scale factor? $\left[\dfrac{3}{2}\right]$

Show students that the values of x and y are the same using the scale factor $\dfrac{3}{2}$.

$$\dfrac{15}{10} = \dfrac{9}{x} \qquad\qquad \dfrac{15}{10} = \dfrac{y}{8}$$

$$15x = 90 \qquad\qquad 120 = 10y$$

$$x = 6 \qquad\qquad\quad y = 12$$

Check

Problem 11

Ask: What ratio can you use to find the scale factor? $\left[\dfrac{25}{10} \text{ or } \dfrac{17.5}{7}\right]$

Ask: Will x be less than or greater than 20? [**Less than**]

Problem 12

Ask: What missing measure do you need to find first? [**DG**]

Ask: What proportion can you write from the given information? $\left[\dfrac{20}{5} = \dfrac{12}{DG}\right]$

ALTERNATE STRATEGY

Strategy: Investigate similar triangles.

1. Have students draw a triangle *ABC* and draw line segment *DE* parallel to line segment *CB* as shown bellow.

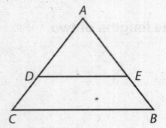

2. Have students investigate congruent angles.

   Ask: What two triangles are shown in the figure? **[△ABC and △AED]**

   Ask: What line segments are parallel? **[$\overline{DE}$ and $\overline{CB}$]** What line segments are transversals? **[$\overline{AC}$ and $\overline{AB}$]**

   Ask: Which angle is congruent to ∠ADE? **[∠ACB]** How do you know? **[The angles are corresponding angles of parallel lines cut by a transversal]**

   Ask: Which angle is congruent to ∠AED? **[∠ABC]**

   Ask: Are all of the angles congruent in △ABC and △AED? **[Yes]**

3. Have students measure the side lengths of each triangle and record the following measures: *AE, AB, ED, BC, CA,* and *DA.*

   Note: Students' measurements will vary based on the triangles they drew. However, the ratios of corresponding sides will be equal regardless of the size of the triangles.

   Ask: What are the corresponding sides of △ABC and △AED? **[$\overline{AE}$ and $\overline{AB}$, $\overline{ED}$ and $\overline{BC}$, $\overline{DA}$ and $\overline{CA}$]**

4. Have students use the measurements they found for each side length to write ratios for the corresponding sides of △ABC and △AED.

   Ask: Are the ratios of the corresponding side lengths equal? **[Yes]** Is △ABC similar to △AED? **[Yes]**

5. Have students draw a copy of △ABC and △AED as separate figures.

   Ask: Is △ABC still similar to △AED? **[Yes]**

COMMON MISCONCEPTIONS

Problem 7

In this problem, the ratios of two pairs of corresponding sides are equal: $\frac{6}{6} = \frac{5}{5} = 1$ and $\frac{5}{4} = \frac{10}{8}$. If students only check that two ratios are equal, they may incorrectly determine that the figures are similar. Remind students to check the ratios of all corresponding sides. Since $1 \neq \frac{5}{4}$, the figures are not similar.

Problem 8

Some students may assume that since all of the angles in a rectangle are congruent, all rectangles are similar. Remind students to check that the measures of the corresponding sides are proportional.

Some students may check the ratios of the corresponding sides and incorrectly determine that $\frac{3}{9} = \frac{4}{16}$, since $3^2 = 9$ and $4^2 = 16$. This could be the result of trying to do mental math instead of reducing the fractions.

Error: Since $\frac{3}{9} = \frac{1}{3}$ and $\frac{4}{16} = \frac{1}{4}$, $\frac{3}{9} \neq \frac{4}{16}$. So, the ratios of the corresponding sides are not equal.

Solution: Rectangle *ABCD* is not similar to rectangle *PQRS*.

Problem 12

In part B, students will find that the ratio of the perimeters is equal to the scale factor. Be sure students work through part C and do not assume that the ratio of the areas is also equal to the scale factor. After students have completed their work, point out that the ratio of the areas is equal to the square of the scale factor since $4^2 = 16$.

ADDITIONAL ONLINE INTERVENTION RESOURCES

 Use the following for students who have not mastered the concepts in Skill 23.

- Math on the Spot videos

- Personal Math Trainer with customized intervention

- Building Block worksheets (Skill 36: Find Missing Measures in Similar Figures; Skill 50: Identify Similar Figures; Skill 80: Similar Figures; Skill 86: Simplify Ratios; Skill 95: Solve Proportions)

SKILL 23

Similar Figures

Vocabulary
Similar figures
Scale factor

Example 1

Similar figures have the following properties:

- Corresponding angles are congruent.
- The measures of corresponding sides are proportional.

Since corresponding angles are congruent, similar figures have the same shape. Since corresponding sides are not congruent, similar figures do not have the same size.

Triangle *ABC* is similar to triangle *DEF*. The symbol ~ is used to indicate similar figures.

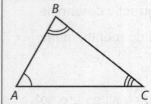
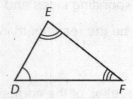

$$\triangle ABC \sim \triangle DEF$$

Corresponding angles: $\angle A \cong \angle D$, $\angle B \cong \angle E$, $\angle C \cong \angle F$,

Corresponding sides: $\dfrac{AB}{DE} = \dfrac{BC}{EF} = \dfrac{CA}{FD}$

Check

Use the figure for 1–3.

1. Write a congruence statement for the corresponding angles.

   $\angle H \cong$ _____

   $\angle I \cong$ _____

   $\angle J \cong$ _____

   $\angle K \cong$ _____

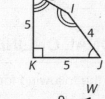

2. Find the ratio of the side lengths for the corresponding sides.

   $\dfrac{WX}{HI} =$ _____

   $\dfrac{XY}{IJ} =$ _____

   $\dfrac{YZ}{JK} =$ _____

   $\dfrac{ZW}{KH} =$ _____

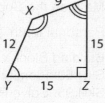

3. Is quadrilateral *HIJK* ~ quadrilateral *WXYZ*? Explain.

   _____

   _____

Determine whether each pair of figures is similar. Explain.

4.

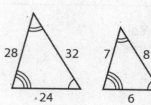

_____

_____

5.

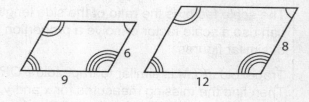

_____

_____

6.

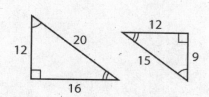

_____

_____

7.

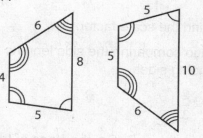

_____

_____

8. Explain the Error. Find the correct solution.

Rectangle *ABCD* is similar to rectangle *PQRS* because the corresponding angles are congruent.

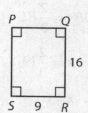

_____

_____

9. A baker has an 8-inch square baking dish and a 9-inch square baking dish. Is an 8-inch square similar to a 9-inch square? Explain.

_____

_____

10. A brand of computer tablets has two different sizes. Both tables have a rectangular shape. The smaller tablet measures 200 millimeters by 135 millimeters. The larger tablet measures 240 millimeters by 170 millimeters. Is the smaller tablet similar to the larger tablet? Explain.

_____

_____

Example 2

The scale factor is the ratio of the side lengths of two similar figures. You can use a scale factor or solve a proportion to find the missing measures of similar figures.

Trapezoid *JKLM* is similar to trapezoid *PQRS*. Find the scale factor. Then find the missing measures for *x* and *y*.

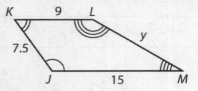 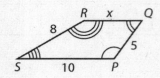

Step 1: Find the scale factor.

Write a ratio comparing the side lengths for one pair of corresponding sides.

$$\frac{SP}{MJ} = \frac{10}{15} = \frac{2}{3}$$

The scale factor is $\frac{2}{3}$. So, the sides of trapezoid *SRQP* are $\frac{2}{3}$ the size of the corresponding sides of trapezoid *JKLM*.

Step 2: Find *x*. Use the scale factor.

$$QR = \frac{2}{3}KL \quad \text{Write an equation.}$$

$$x = \frac{2}{3}(9) \quad QR = x, KL = 9$$

$$x = 6 \quad \text{Multiply.}$$

Step 3: Find *y*. Use a proportion.

$$\frac{SP}{MJ} = \frac{RS}{LM} \quad \text{Write an equation.}$$

$$\frac{10}{15} = \frac{8}{y} \quad SP = 10, MJ = 15, RS = 8, \text{ and } LM = y$$

$$10 \cdot y = 15 \cdot 8 \quad \text{Find the cross products.}$$

$$10y = 120 \quad \text{Multiply.}$$

$$y = 12 \quad \text{Divide each side by 10.}$$

Check

11. The figure below shows a pair of similar quadrilaterals.

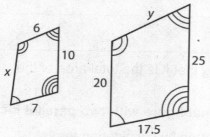

A   Find the value of x. Show your work.

_____

B   Find the value of y. Show your work.

_____

12. Rectangle *DEFG* is similar to rectangle *RSTU*.

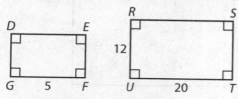

A   What is the scale factor?

_____

B   Find the perimeter of each rectangle. Then compare the scale
factor to the ratio of the perimeters.

_____

_____

C   Find the area of each rectangle. Then compare the scale factor to the ratio of the areas.

_____

_____

SKILL 23 SIMILAR FIGURES

Surface Area

KEY TEACHING POINTS

Introduce the idea of surface area to students by explaining that it is the total area of the faces of a three dimensional figure.

Ask: What is the definition of a prism? **[A three dimensional figure with two parallel faces]**

Explain to the students that the surface area can be calculated by considering the area of the base of the prism and the area of the remaining faces.

Example 1
To help students understand this example, draw the net of the figure as shown below.

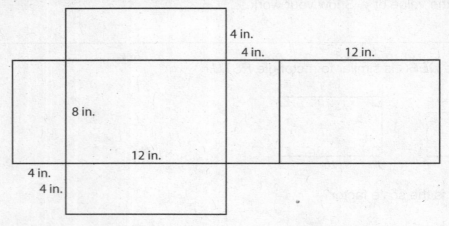

Say: The base is a rectangle, so the area is $8 \times 12 = 96$ square inches. However, there are two parallel faces with this measure. So, one component of the surface area will be $2B$ where B is the area of the base. Here that is $2(96) = 160$ square inches.

Say: The lateral area is the total area of the sides of the prism.

Ask: How many sides remain? **[4]**

Ask: How many shapes with different dimensions remain? What are their dimensions? **[2; one rectangle that is 4 inches by 8 inches and one rectangle that is 4 inches by 12 inches]**

Ask: What are their areas? **[32 square inches and 48 square inches]**

Explain that this means the lateral area is $2(32) + 2(48) = 160$ square inches. Point out to students that there is a shortcut to calculate the lateral area. This shortcut uses the formula Ph where P is the perimeter of the base and h is the height of the prism. Show them that this calculation results in the same lateral area.

Say: The surface area of any prism is found with the formula $2B + L$ where B is the area of the base and L is the lateral area.

Use this formula to find the surface area of the example figure. Point out to students that since it is an area, the units are square units.

Check
Problem 2
The base of this prism is triangular, but students are given enough information to find its area. You may have to remind students to use $\frac{1}{2}bh$ for the area of a triangular base.

Problem 3
Encourage students to draw a picture to represent the described figure. Make sure that they label each side correctly when doing so.

Problem 4
Remind students that an equilateral triangle has equal length sides and that they must find the height of the triangle before they can find the area of the base. Have them sketch the base as in the figure below.

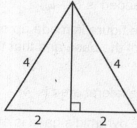

Students will have to use the Pythagorean Theorem to find the height of this triangle and then the area of the base. Make sure they understand the difference between this height and the height of the prism.

Example 2
Say: The idea of considering the lateral area and the area of the base allows us to find the surface area of any figure.

Ask: What shape is the base of any cylinder? **[A circle]**

Ask: What is the area of any circle? $\left[2\pi r^2\right]$

Explain that the curved surface of a cylinder is rolled out, the resulting shape is a rectangle. Since this rectangle connects the two parallel faces, its area is the lateral area of the cylinder.

Ask: What would be the length of the rectangle? **[The circumference of the circle that is the base]**

Ask: What would be the width of the rectangle? **[The height of the cylinder]**

Say: Since the area of any rectangle is the product of its length and width, the lateral area of a cylinder is the product of the circumference of the base and the height of the cylinder.

Ask: If the radius of the base is r, then what is its circumference? $[2\pi r]$

Say: This means the lateral area is $2\pi rh$.

Explain that as with the prism, the surface area will be $2B + L$.

Work through example 2 finding the area of the base and the lateral area separately. Explain to the students that an exact answer will be in terms of π.

Check
Problem 7
Students should draw a picture of the described storage container, making sure to label each known measurement. Point out to students that the question asks for an approximation, so they should use the pi button on their calculator or 3.14 in their calculations.

Example 3
Direct students' attention to the figure in the example as you describe the shape of a regular pyramid. Explain that the figure only has one side with the dimensions of the base (the base itself), so the surface area formula needed is $B + L$.

Point out that other than the base, the figure is made up of isosceles triangles each with a base length equal to the side length of the base and that the height of the triangle is called the slant height and denoted ℓ.

Since there are 4 triangular faces, the lateral area is $4\left(\dfrac{1}{2}bh\right) = 4\left(\dfrac{1}{2}s\ell\right)$ where s is a side

length of the pyramid's base. But, the pyramid's base is a square, so the perimeter P is $4s$.

Therefore, the formula for the lateral area can be simplified to $\dfrac{1}{2}P\ell$.

Work through the example step by step.

Check
Problem 11
Students will need to use the Pythagorean Theorem to find the slant length. Have them draw a picture of a right triangle within the pyramid, where the slant length is the hypotenuse as shown below as part of their approach to this problem.

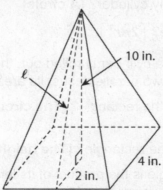

ALTERNATE STRATEGY

Strategy: Building Figures

1. Have students create each face of the prism from example 1 using a ruler and paperboard.

2. Have them measure and then calculate the area of each face of the prism.

3. Then ask them to use tape to build the prism and then use their calculations to verify the surface area found using the formula.

COMMON MISCONCEPTION

Problem 8

In this problem, the shown result comes from using the diameter instead of the radius. Commonly, students will simply use the numbers presented in the problem without checking that they are the needed values. Checking that they are using the correct values in every problem should be stressed. Here, the correct surface area is

$$S = 2(36\pi) + 2\pi(6)(14) = 240\pi \text{ cm}^2.$$

ADDITIONAL ONLINE INTERVENTION RESOURCES

 Use the following for students who have not mastered the concepts in Skill 24.

- Math on the Spot videos

- Personal Math Trainer with customized intervention

- Building Block worksheets (Skill 9 Area of Circles; Skill 10 Area of Polygons; Skill 11 Area of Squares, Rectangles, and Triangles; Skill 14 Circumference and Area of Circles; Skill 101 Surface Area)

Name _____ Date _____ Class_____

Example 1

	Vocabulary
	Surface Area
	Base
	Lateral Area

The surface area of a figure is the total area of its outside surface.

In general, this is found by calculating the area of the base and the lateral area (area of all other surfaces). In a prism, the lateral area is found by multiplying the perimeter of the base by the height of the prism.

Find the surface area of the given rectangular prism.

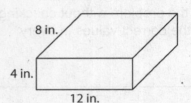

8 in.

4 in.

12 in.

Find the area of the base:
$B = 8 \times 12 = 96$ in^2

Find the perimeter of the base:
$P = 2(12) + 2(8) = 40$ in.

Find the lateral area:
$L = Ph = 40(4) = 160$ in^2

Find the surface area:
$S = L + 2B = 2(96) + 160 = 352$ in^2

Check
Find the surface area of each prism below.

1.

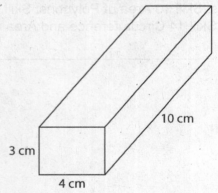

10 cm

3 cm

4 cm

2.

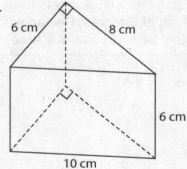

6 cm   8 cm

6 cm

10 cm

Area of the base: $B =$ _____

Perimeter of the base: $P =$ _____

Lateral area: $L =$ _____

Surface area $= 2B + L =$ _____

Area of the base: $B =$ _____

Perimeter of the base: $P =$ _____

Lateral area: $L =$ _____

Surface area $= 2B + L =$ _____

3. A prism has a rectangular base with a width of 5 inches and a length of 10 inches. If the height of the prism is 12 inches, find its surface area.

_____

_____

4. The base of a prism is an equilateral triangle with side lengths of 4 inches. If the height of the prism is 2 inches, find its surface area to the nearest tenth of a inch.

_____

_____

Example 2

The surface area of a cylinder can also be found by finding the area of the base and the lateral area. In this case, the base is a circle, so the area is πr^2 while the lateral area is found using the formula $2\pi rh$.

Find the surface area of the given cylinder.

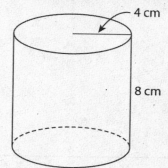

Find the area of the base:
$$B = \pi\left(4^2\right) = 16\pi \text{ cm}^2$$

Find the lateral area:
$$L = 2\pi(4)(8) = 64\pi \text{ cm}^2$$

Find the surface area:
$$S = 2B + L = 2(16\pi) + 64\pi = 96\pi \text{ cm}^2$$

Check

Find the surface area of the given cylinder.

5.

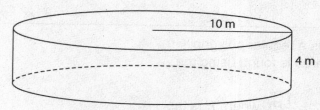

Area of the base: $B =$ _____

Lateral area: $L =$ _____

Surface area $= 2B + L =$ _____

6.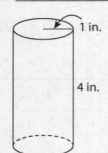

1 in.

4 in.

Area of the base: $B =$ _____

Lateral area: $L =$ _____

Surface area $= 2B + L =$ _____

7. A factory stores water for its manufacturing operation in a large cylindrical container. The container stands 30 feet tall and its base has a radius of 10 feet. The container will be painted with a new coat of paint in order to protect it from rust. To the nearest tenth of a foot, approximately how many square feet of paint will be required to paint the container?

_____

_____

8. Explain the Error. Find the correct solution.

The area of the given cylinder is found as follows.

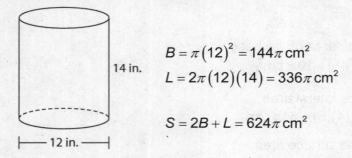

14 in.

12 in.

$B = \pi(12)^2 = 144\pi \text{ cm}^2$

$L = 2\pi(12)(14) = 336\pi \text{ cm}^2$

$S = 2B + L = 624\pi \text{ cm}^2$

_____

_____

_____

Example 3

A regular pyramid has a single base which is a regular polygon. Since it has only a single base, its surface area is found using the formula $S = B + L$.

The lateral area is found using the formula $L = \frac{1}{2}P\ell$ where P is the perimeter of the base and ℓ is the slant height.

Find the surface area of the given regular pyramid.

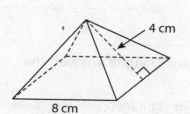

Find the area of the base:
$B = 8(8) = 64$ cm^2

Find the perimeter of the base:
$P = 8(4) = 32$ cm

Find the lateral area:
$L = \dfrac{1}{2}(32)(4) = 64$ cm^2

Find the surface area:
$S = L + B = 64 + 64 = 128$ cm^2

Check

Find the surface area of the given regular pyramid.

9.

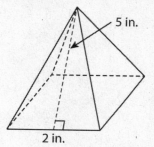

Area of the base: $B =$ _____

Perimeter of the base: $P =$ _____

Lateral area: $L =$ _____

Surface area $= B + L =$ _____

10.

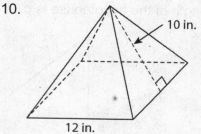

Area of the base: $B =$ _____

Perimeter of the base: $P =$ _____

Lateral area: $L =$ _____

Surface area $= 2B + L =$ _____

11. Find the surface area of a regular pyramid with a height of 10 inches
and a square base of 4 inches. (Hint: Find the slant length first.)
Round your answer to the nearest tenth of an inch.

_____

_____

SKILL 24 SURFACE AREA

The Pythagorean Theorem

KEY TEACHING POINTS

Ask: What are some properties of triangles? **[Answers may vary. Sample answer: the measures of the interior angles have a sum of 180°]**

Remind students that there are several types of triangles such as right triangles, isosceles triangles, and equilateral triangles. Explain that while some properties hold for all triangles, some are specific to one type of triangle.

Ask: What property defines a right triangle? **[The triangle has one interior angle of 90°]**

Ask: Which side is called the hypotenuse? **[The side opposite the right angle]**

On the board, draw a right triangle and label the hypotenuse and two legs as shown below. Explain that in the formula for the Pythagorean Theorem, the lengths of the legs are *a* and *b* and that the length of the hypotenuse is *c*.

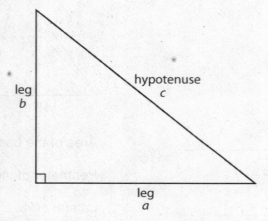

Write the Pythagorean Theorem on the board next to the right triangle so that students can see where the values come from.

Say: The Pythagorean Theorem is a property that applies only to right triangles so it can't be used to find side lengths for other types of triangles.

Explain to students that either leg can be thought of as the one with length *a* and the other as the one with length *b*. Encourage them to label which side they decide is *a* and which side they decide is *b* so that they will be consistent while working the problem. Reiterate that the lengths of the legs can't be interchanged with the length of the hypotenuse when working with the formula.

Example 1
Say: Let's let $a = 6$ and $b = 4$. Since *x* is the length of the hypotenuse, $c = x$.

Start with the Pythagorean Theorem and replace each value with the values from the problem.

Work through how to find the value of *x* and explain that only the positive square root is a solution since *x* represents a side length and side lengths are positive. It may be necessary to review how to simplify square roots.

Check
Problem 1
Students may assume every final answer must be simplified and therefore need verification that $\sqrt{13}$ is completely simplified. Remind them that 13 has factors of only 13 and 1 and that neither are perfect squares.

Problem 3
Once students have successfully worked this problem, point out that this triangle is both a right triangle and an isosceles triangle.

Ask: Is it possible for an equilateral triangle to also be a right triangle? **[No. The angles within an equilateral triangle all have a measure of 60°]**

Problem 5
Encourage students to sketch the right triangle formed by the height from the ground, horizontal extension of the loading platform, and the actual length of the loading platform.

Ask: Which of the three pieces of information represents the length of the hypotenuse? **[The length of the loading platform]**

Example 2
Say: Since the Pythagorean Theorem includes three variables, given the values of two of them, we can find the value of the third. We just saw this when we were given the lengths of each leg and then found the length of the hypotenuse. But, given the length of the hypotenuse and the length of one leg, it is also possible to find the length of the remaining leg.

Say: Since the leg lengths are 5 and x, let's let $a = 5$ and $b = x$. The length of the hypotenuse is 10, so $c = 10$.

Start with the basic form of the Pythagorean Theorem and then show students that by substituting in these values for a, b, and c you get the equation in the example.

Work through solving the equation step by step with the students.

Check
Problem 8
Students may have trouble squaring the length of the hypotenuse. To help them remember how to compute this value, remind them that exponents can be distributed across multiplication but not addition. Point out that since $3\sqrt{2} = 3 \times \sqrt{2}$, $\left(3\sqrt{2}\right)^2 = 3^2\left(\sqrt{2}\right)^2 = 9(2) = 18$. You may need to remind them that squaring $\sqrt{a}$ will always result in a.

Problem 9
Have students select whether a or b will represent the leg of length 5 and then use this to write an equation such as $3^2 + b^2 = 5^2$. For some, drawing the picture of the right triangle may assist them with understanding which values are missing. If this is done, be sure to check that the hypotenuse is correctly labeled with a length of 5 and that 5 was not used as a leg length.

Problem 10
Since each side length is the same, have the students give that side length a value such as x. When they then apply the Pythagorean Theorem, they will have the equation $2x^2 = 32$.

Example 3

Remind students what it means for a statement to be a converse of another statement and explain that the Pythagorean Theorem is an "if and only if" statement.

Explain to students that this means the Pythagorean Theorem can be used to check if a triangle is a right triangle.

Ask: In a right triangle, which side has the longest measure? **[The hypotenuse]**

Say: Since the hypotenuse has the longest measure, we can check if three numbers could be sides of a right triangle by seeing if the square of the longest side is the sum of the squares of the two shorter sides.

Work through example 3 step by step.

Check
Problem 15

In this problem, the given values do not represent lengths of the sides of a right triangle. Once students have verified this, ask them to find a length for the hypotenuse which could be used with leg lengths 5 and 12 to define the sides of a right triangle.

To do this correctly, they will need to calculate c when $5^2 + 12^2 = c^2$. The only correct answer is 13.

Problem 17

There are many correct answers to this question. If students have trouble finding one, encourage them to simply choose values for a and b and then find what value of c would be needed for the statement $a^2 + b^2 = c^2$ to hold.

ALTERNATE STRATEGY

Strategy: Verifying the Pythagorean Theorem

1. Have students create several different size right triangles from poster board or other easy to measure material. Ideally the triangles will have whole number side lengths measured in either inches or centimeters.

2. For each triangle, have students measure the lengths of the legs and the hypotenuse using a ruler and record them in a table.

3. Ask students to verify that the Pythagorean Theorem holds for these triangles by finding the sum of the squared leg lengths and comparing that sum to the square of the length of the hypotenuse.

COMMON MISCONCEPTION

Problem 12

Commonly, students will simply take the two known values and use these as leg lengths in the formula for the Pythagorean Theorem. Here, the leg lengths should be x and 4, but the hypotenuse was instead treated as though it has length x.

In order to avoid this mistake, have students mark the side opposite the right angle with the letter c and label the other sides as a and b. If they do this, they can rewrite the formula needed to find x as:

$$x^2 + 4^2 = 5^2$$

The correct answer will be $x = 3$.

ADDITIONAL ONLINE INTERVENTION RESOURCES

 Use the following for students who have not mastered the concepts in Skill 25.

- Math on the Spot videos
- Personal Math Trainer with customized intervention
- Building Block worksheets (Skill 38 Find the Square of a Number; Skill 46 Graph Ordered Pairs (First Quadrant); Skill 100 Squares and Square Roots)

SKILL 25 **The Pythagorean Theorem**

Example 1

The Pythagorean Theorem describes a relationship between the lengths of the legs of a right triangle and the length of its hypotenuse.

If the legs have lengths a and b and the hypotenuse has length c, then $a^2 + b^2 = c^2$.

Find the value of x in the triangle below.

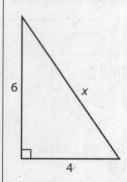

Calculate $a^2 + b^2$

$6^2 + 4^2 = x^2$

$36 + 16 = x^2$

$52 = x^2$

Find and simplify the positive square root.

$x = \sqrt{52} = \sqrt{4 \cdot 13} = 2\sqrt{13}$

Vocabulary
Leg
Hypotenuse

Check

Find the value of x for each of the triangles below.

1.

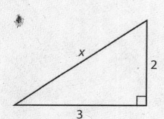

2.

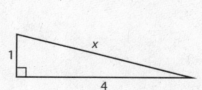

3.

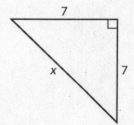

4. A right triangle has legs with lengths of 3 and 9 units. What is the length of the hypotenuse?

_____

5. As shown below, the loading platform extends out 6 feet from the back of a truck and is 3 feet above the ground at its highest point. To the nearest tenth of a foot, what is the length of the platform?

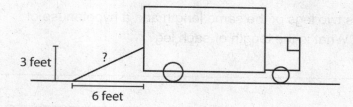

3 feet

?

6 feet

_____

_____

Example 2

The Pythagorean Theorem can be used to find the length of either leg in a right triangle.

Find the value of x in the triangle below.

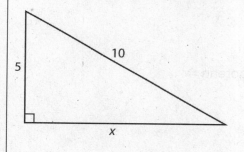

5

10

x

Write an equation using the Pythagorean Theorem.

$5^2 + x^2 = 10^2$

$25 + x^2 = 100$

Solve for x.

$x^2 = 75$

$x = \sqrt{75} = \sqrt{3 \cdot 25} = 5\sqrt{3}$

Check

Find the value of x in each of the triangles below.

6.

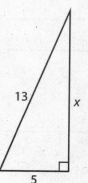

13

x

5

7.

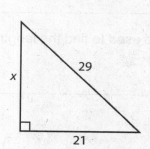

x

29

21

8.

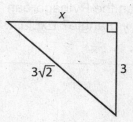

x

$3\sqrt{2}$

3

Name _____ Date _____ Class _____

9. A right triangle has a leg with a length of 3 units and a hypotenuse with a length of 5 units. What is the length of the other leg?

_____

10. A right triangle has two legs of the same length and a hypotenuse of length $4\sqrt{2}$ units. What is the length of each leg?

_____

_____

11. As shown below, a 10 foot ladder is placed against a tree. If the bottom of the ladder is 6 feet from the bottom of the tree, then how many feet above the ground does the ladder touch the tree?

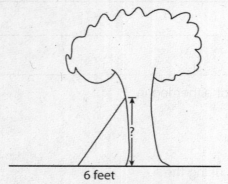

6 feet

_____

_____

_____

12. Explain the Error. Find the correct solution.

In the triangle below, the value of x is found using the Pythagorean Theorem as shown.

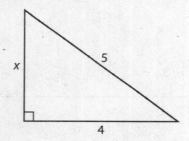

$$5^2 + 4^2 = x^2$$
$$25 + 16 = x^2$$
$$41 = x^2$$
$$\sqrt{41} = x$$

_____

_____

_____

13. Can the Pythagorean Theorem be used to find the length of a side of any triangle? Explain.

_____

_____

Example 3

The converse of the Pythagorean Theorem is also true.

If the square of one side of a triangle is equal to the sum of the squares of the other two sides, then the triangle is a right triangle.

Determine if a triangle with sides of length 10, 24, and 26 is a right triangle.

Let the longest side equal c and the other sides be a, and b:

$c = 26$, $a = 10$, and $b = 24$ and then check if $a^2 + b^2 = c^2$:

$c^2 = 26^2 = 676$

$a^2 + b^2 = 10^2 + 24^2 = 100 + 576 = 676$

Solution: Since $10^2 + 24^2 = 26^2$, the triangle with these side lengths is a right triangle.

Check

Determine if the given numbers could be the side lengths of a right triangle. If yes, explain why and if not, explain why not.

14. 9, 12, 15

_____

15. 5, 12, 14

_____

16. $8\sqrt{2}$, 8, 8

_____

17. Give an example of three numbers which could be side lengths of a right triangle. Justify your answer.

_____

SKILL 25 THE PYTHAGOREAN THEOREM

Using Slope and *y*-intercept

KEY TEACHING POINTS

Example 1
Review the meaning of slope.

Say: Slope is the rate of change of a graph. It is the ratio of the *rise over the run*. The rise is the vertical change between two points. The run is the horizontal change between two points.

Show students how to find the slope from the graph by counting the units on the coordinate plane to find the vertical change and the horizontal change.

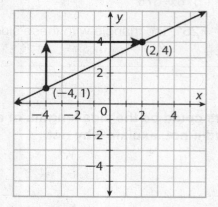

Ask: What is the vertical change between the two points? **[3 units]** What is the horizontal change? **[6 units]**

Say: So, the slope is $\dfrac{\text{rise}}{\text{run}} = \dfrac{3}{6}$ or $\dfrac{1}{2}$. Another way to find the vertical change is to find the difference of the *y*-coordinates. You can find the horizontal change by finding the difference of the *x*-coordinates.

Show students that it does not matter what point you use for (x_1, y_1) and (x_2, y_2), as long as you use the coordinates in the same order. The slope is the same.

$$m = \frac{y_2 - y_1}{x_2 - x_1} \qquad \text{Slope formula}$$

$$m = \frac{1 - 4}{-4 - 2} \qquad (x_1, y_1) = (2, 4) \text{ and } (x_2, y_2) = (-4, 1)$$

$$m = \frac{-3}{-6} \text{ or } \frac{1}{2} \qquad \text{Simplify.}$$

Say: The *y*-intercept is the point where the graph crosses the *y*-axis. The point $(0, y)$ is on the *y*-axis. Notice that the *x*-coordinate is 0. The *y*-coordinate is the *y*-intercept.

Ask: At what point does the graph cross the *y*-axis? **[(0, 3)]** What is the *y*-intercept? **[3]**

Check

Problem 1

Ask: Does the line slant up from left to right or slant down from left to right? **[The line slants up.]** Is the slope positive or negative? **[positive]**

Problem 3

Ask: Does the line slant up from left to right or slant down from left to right? **[The line slants down.]** Is the slope positive or negative? **[negative]**

Problem 5

Remind students that the slope represents the rate of change and the y-intercept represents the initial value, when $x = 0$.

Ask: What does x represent? **[the number of classes]**

Ask: What does y represent? **[the total cost of the classes]**

Ask: What point on the graph represents the cost of 0 classes? **[(0, 10)]**

Ask: As the number of classes x increases by 1, by how much does cost y increase? **[$5]**

Example 2

Ask: In the equation $y = mx + b$, which variable represents the slope? **[m]** Which variable represents the y-intercept? **[b]**

Ask: What do you have to do to rewrite the equation $-3x + 2y = 4$ in slope-intercept form? **[Solve the equation for y to isolate y on the left side of the equation.]**

Work through the example. Explain to students that when the slope is negative, they can assign the negative sign to either the numerator or denominator.

Ask: If the slope was $-\dfrac{3}{2}$, how would you graph the second point? **[Move down 3 units and right 2 units or move up 3 units and left 2 units.]**

Check

Make sure students understand how to write equations in slope-intercept form that have a negative y-intercept.

Ask: How can you rewrite $y = mx + (-b)$? **[$y = mx - b$]**

Ask: How can you write the equation $y = mx - b$ in the form $y = mx + b$? **[$y = mx + (-b)$]**

Problem 6

Ask: What value will you use for m in the equation $y = mx + b$? **[3]** What value will you use for b? **[−1]**

Problem 12

Ask: Will the graph of the equation have a positive slope or a negative slope? **[negative]**

Problem 13

Ask: Will the graph of the equation have a positive slope or a negative slope? **[positive]**

ALTERNATE STRATEGY

Strategy: Investigate the relationship between the equation of a line and its graph.

1. Have students graph the equations $y = x$, $y = x + 4$, and $y = x - 2$ on the same coordinate plane.

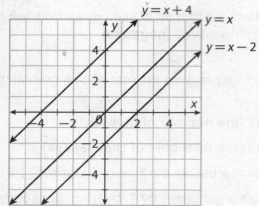

Ask: How are the equations similar? **[They have the same slope.]** How are the equations different? **[They have different y-intercepts.]**

Ask: How does changing the value of y-intercept affect the graph? **[Changing the y-intercept shifts the graph up or down along the y-axis.]**

2. Have students graph the equations $y = x$, $y = 2x$, and $y = \frac{1}{2}x$ on the same coordinate plane.

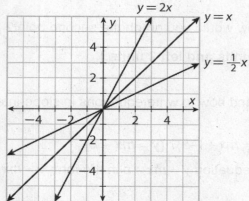

Ask: How are the equations similar? **[They have a y-intercept of 0.]** How are the equations different? **[They have different slopes.]**

Ask: How does changing the value of m affect the graph? **[Changing the slope affects the steepness of the graph.]**

COMMON MISCONCEPTIONS

Problem 3

Some students may incorrectly subtract integers. Watch for students who calculate the change in x-values as $3 - (-3) = 0$, resulting in an undefined slope. Remind them that only vertical lines have an undefined slope.

Problem 13

Some students may forget to divide the y-intercept by 4 resulting in the equation $y = \dfrac{3}{4}x + 8$.

Review how to divide each side of an equation by the same number. $\dfrac{4y}{4} = \dfrac{3x + 8}{4} \rightarrow y = \dfrac{3}{4}x + 2$

Problem 14

The error is a result of incorrectly writing the equation in slope-intercept form as $x = -2y + 4$.

Ask: How can you write $x + 2y = 4$ in slope-intercept form? $[\, y = -\dfrac{1}{2}x + 2\,]$

Error: The variables x and y were transposed. The given slope and y-intercept is for the equation $2x + y = 4$.

Solution: The slope is $-\dfrac{1}{2}$ and the y-intercept is 2.

ADDITIONAL ONLINE INTERVENTION RESOURCES

Use the following for students who have not mastered the concepts in Skill 26.
- Math on the Spot videos
- Personal Math Trainer with customized intervention
- Building Block worksheets (Skill 27: Evaluate Expressions; Skill 38: Find the Square of a Number; Skill 45: Graph Ordered Pairs (First Quadrant); Skill 69: Order of Operations; Skill 70: Ordered Pairs; Skill 98: Solve Two-Step Equations; Skill 100: Squares and Square Roots)

SKILL
26

Using Slope and *y*-intercept

Example 1

Slope is the rate of change on a graph. To find the slope *m* of a line passing through points (x_1, y_1) and (x_2, y_2), find the ratio of the difference of the *y*-coordinates to the difference of the *x*-coordinates.

$m = \dfrac{y_2 - y_1}{x_2 - x_1}$, where $x_2 \neq x_1$.

The *y*-intercept is the *y*-coordinate of the point at which a graph crosses the *y*-axis.

Find the slope and the *y*-intercept of the line that passes through (−4, 1) and (2, 4).

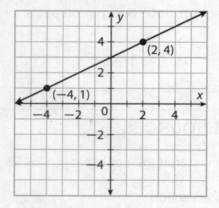

The graph crosses the *y*-axis at the point (0, 3). So, the *y*-intercept is 3.

Use the coordinates of two points on the line to find the slope.

$m = \dfrac{y_2 - y_1}{x_2 - x_1}$ Slope formula

$m = \dfrac{4 - 1}{2 - (-4)}$ $(x_1, y_1) = (-4, 1)$ and $(x_2, y_2) = (2, 4)$

$m = \dfrac{3}{6}$ or $\dfrac{1}{2}$ Simplify.

The slope is $\dfrac{1}{2}$.

Vocabulary
Slope
y-intercept
Slope-intercept form

Check
Find the slope and the *y*-intercept of each line.

1.

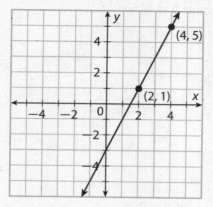

slope: _____

y-intercept: _____

2.

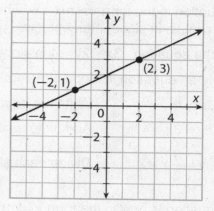

slope: _____

y-intercept: _____

3.

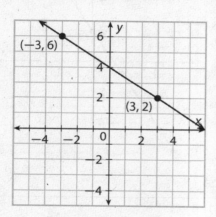

slope: _____

y-intercept: _____

4.

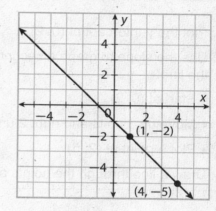

slope: _____

y-intercept: _____

5. A community center offers art classes for $5 per class plus a $10 registration fee. The graph represents the total cost *y* for *x* classes.

A What is the slope? Describe its meaning.

_____

_____

B What is the *y*-intercept? Describe its meaning.

_____

_____

Example 2

An equation in the form $y = mx + b$, where m is the slope and b is the y-intercept, is in slope-intercept form.

Write the equation $-3x + 2y = 4$ in slope-intercept form.

To write an equation in slope-intercept form, solve the equation for y.

$-3x + 2y = 4$	Write the equation.
$2y = 3x + 4$	Add $3x$ to each side.
$y = \dfrac{3}{2}x + 2$	Divide each side by 2.

The equation is now in the form $y = mx + b$, where $m = \dfrac{3}{2}$ and $b = 2$.

Graph the equation.

The slope is $\dfrac{3}{2}$ and the y-intercept is 2.

Step 1: Plot the y-intercept at (0, 2).

Step 2: Use the slope to graph a second point on the line.

- Start at (0, 2).
- Move up 3 units and right 2 units.
- Plot a point at (2, 5).

Step 3: Draw a line through the points and extend the line.

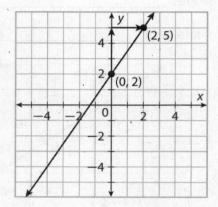

Check

Write an equation in slope-intercept form for the given slope and y-intercept.

6. slope: 3; y-intercept: −1

_____

7. slope: −4; y-intercept: 5

_____

8. slope: $\dfrac{3}{4}$; y-intercept: 2

_____

9. slope: $-\dfrac{4}{5}$; y-intercept: −3

_____

State the slope and y-intercept of the graph of each equation.

10. $y = -3x + 1$

slope: _____

y-intercept: _____

11. $y = \dfrac{1}{4}x - 5$

slope: _____

y-intercept: _____

Write each equation in slope-intercept form. Then graph the equation.

12. $2x + y = 3$ _____

13. $-3x + 4y = 8$ _____

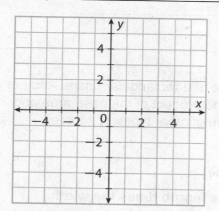

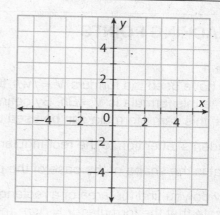

14. **Explain the Error. Find the correct solution.**

In the equation $x + 2y = 4$, the slope is -2 and the y-intercept is 4.

_____

_____

15. The cost to repair a bicycle is $20 per hour for labor plus $30 in parts. The equation $y = 20x + 30$ represents the total cost of the repair.

   A What is the slope and y-intercept of the graph of the equation? Describe their meanings.

   _____

   _____

   B Graph the equation.

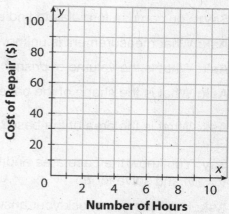

SKILL 26 USING SLOPE AND Y-INTERCEPT

KEY TEACHING POINTS

Example 1

Say: You have used the formula $V = \ell wh$ to find the volume of a rectangular prism. Another way to write this formula is $V = Bh$. By defining volume as the product of the base area and the height, this same formula can be used to find the volume of other types of figures.

Direct students' attention to the rectangular prism.

Ask: What is the shape of the base of the prism? **[rectangle]**

Ask: How do you find the area of a rectangle? **[Multiply the length times the width.]** Demonstrate that the formulas $V = \ell wh$ and $V = Bh$ are equivalent equations, since the area of a rectangular base is $B = \ell w$.

Ask: What is the area of the base of the rectangular prism? **[14 × 8 = 112 square meters]**

Ask: What is the height of the prism? **[5 meters]**

Ask: What is the volume of the prism? **[112 × 5 = 560 cubic meters]**

Direct students' attention to the triangular prism.

Say: You can use formulas to find any unknown measurement.

Ask: What measurement is unknown? **[the height]**

Ask: What is the volume of prism? **[252 cubic inches]**

Ask: What is the shape of the base of the prism? **[triangle]**

Ask: What is the area of the base? $[\frac{1}{2} \times 6 \times 7 = 21\,\text{square inches}]$

Say: You know the base area and the volume. Replace the known values in the formula $V = Bh$ and solve for h.

Ask: How can you check your answer? **[Multiply the base area by the height and check to see that the volume is 252 cubic inches.]**

Point out that the formula for the area of a triangle is $\frac{1}{2}bh$. The variable b represents the measurement of the base of the triangle. The variable B represents the area of a base of a three-dimensional figure.

Check
Problem 3
Ask: What measurement is unknown? **[the height of the prism]**

Problem 4
Ask: What measurement is unknown? **[the height of the triangular base]**

Example 2

Say: The formula for any pyramid is $V = \frac{1}{3}Bh$. However, the area of the base B depends on the shape of the base.

Ask: What is the shape of the base of the pyramid? **[rectangle]**

Ask: How do you find the area of a rectangle? **[Multiply the length times the width.]**

Ask: What is the area of the base of the pyramid? **[10 × 8 = 80 square centimeters]**

Ask: What is the height of the pyramid? **[7 centimeters]**

Ask: What equation can you write with the given information to find the volume of the pyramid? **[$V = \frac{1}{3}(10 \times 8) \times 7$]**

Ask: How is the volume of a pyramid similar to the volume of a prism with the same base area and height? **[The volume of a pyramid is $\frac{1}{3}$ the volume of a prism with the same dimensions.]**

Check
Problems 5–6

Ask: How is finding the volume of a triangular pyramid different than finding the volume of a rectangular pyramid? **[The area of the base is different. For a triangular pyramid, $B = \frac{1}{2}bh$. For a rectangular pyramid, $B = \ell w$.]**

Problem 7

Ask: What equation can you write with the given information to find the height of the pyramid? **[$112 = \frac{1}{3}\left(\frac{1}{2} \times 14 \times 8\right)h$]**

Problem 8

Ask: What equation can you write with the given information to find the width of the base of the pyramid? **[$320 = \frac{1}{3}(8 \times w)10$]**

Example 3

Say: A cylinder has two circular bases that are parallel. You find the volume of a cylinder in the same way as the volume for a prism by multiplying the area of the base by the height.

Ask: What is the shape of the base? **[circle]** What is the formula for the area of a circle? **[$A = \pi r^2$]**

Say: A cone has one circular base. The volume of a cone is $\frac{1}{3}$ the volume of a cylinder with the same radius and height.

Review the formulas for volume covered in the lesson. Point out that the figures that have two bases, prisms and cylinders, use the formula $V = Bh$. The figures that have one base, pyramids and cones, use the formula $V = \frac{1}{3}Bh$.

ALTERNATE STRATEGY

Strategy: Solve a simpler problem.

Problem 14

Since the cylinder and the cone have equal measures for the radius and height, you can simplify the expression for the volume of the compound figure. Some students may determine that since the cone is $\frac{1}{3}$ the volume of the cylinder, the volume of the composite figure is $1 + \frac{1}{3} = \frac{4}{3}$ times the volume of the cylinder. Show that this is true algebraically.

$$V = \pi r^2 h + \frac{1}{3}\pi r^2 h \qquad\qquad V_{cylinder} = \pi r^2 h \text{ and } V_{cone} = \frac{1}{3}\pi r^2 h$$

$$V = \pi r^2 h + \left(1 + \frac{1}{3}\right) \text{ or } \frac{4}{3}\pi r^2 h \qquad \text{Distributive Property}$$

Problem 15

Many students will solve this problem using two equations. Students will solve an equation to find the volume of the cone. Then use the value for the volume in another equation to find the height of the cylinder.

Show students how to write one equation to represent the problem. Since the figures have equal volumes, you can set the expressions for the volume of each figure equal to each other. Write the expression for the volume of the cone on one side of an equation and write the expression for the volume of the cylinder on the other side of the equation. Then solve for the height of the cone.

$$\frac{1}{3}\pi(6)^2 12 = \pi(4)^2 h$$

COMMON MISCONCEPTIONS

Problem 4

If students get a value of $x = 3$ instead of $x = 6$, they did not take into account that the area of the triangular base is $\frac{1}{2}bh$. The error is most likely a result of trying to do the problem quickly using mental math. They see that $66 \div 11 = 6$ and $6 \div 2 = 3$. Remind students to substitute the values into the formula for volume to avoid careless mistakes. A quick check of their work will also show them $\left(\frac{1}{2} \times 3 \times 2\right) \times 11 = 33$, which is not the correct volume.

Problem 14

Some students may try to quickly substitute the given values into a formula without thinking about the meaning of the variables.

Ask: What information are you given for the cone? **[the lengths of the diameter and the height]**

Ask: What information do you need to find the volume of the cone? **[the lengths of the radius and the height of the cone]**

Ask: What measure do you need to find before you can find the volume of the cone? **[the length of the radius]**

Ask: What information are you given for the cylinder? **[the lengths of the diameter and the height]**

Ask: Do you need to know the length of the diameter or the length of the radius to find the volume of the cylinder? **[the length of the radius]**

Error: The measure of the diameter was used instead of the radius.

Solution: The correct volume of the figure is $V = \pi(3)^2(6) + \frac{1}{3}\pi(3)^2 6 = 72\pi$.

ADDITIONAL ONLINE INTERVENTION RESOURCES

Use the following for students who have not mastered the concepts in Skill 27.

- Math on the Spot videos
- Personal Math Trainer with customized intervention
- Building Block worksheets (Skill 9: Area of Circles; Skill 10: Area of Polygons; Skill 11: Area of Squares, Rectangles, and Triangles; Skill 14: Circumference and Area of Circles; Skill 30: Exponents; Skill 31: Faces of Prisms and Pyramids; Skill 77: Round Decimals; Skill 83: Simplify Numerical Expressions; Skill 106: Volume)

SKILL 27 **Volume**

Vocabulary
Volume

Example 1

Volume is the amount of space inside a three-dimensional figure. Volume is measured in cubic units.

The volume V of a prism is the product of the base area B and the height h.

Volume of a prism: $V = Bh$

The rectangular prism has a base area of 14×8 or 112 square meters and a height of 5 meters. Find the volume.

$V = Bh$ Volume of a prism

$V = 112 \times 5$ $B = 112, h = 5$

$V = 560$ Multiply.

The volume is 560 cubic meters.

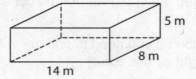

The triangular prism has a base area of $\frac{1}{2} \times 6 \times 7$ or 21 square inches and a volume of 252 cubic inches. Find the height.

$V = Bh$ Volume of a prism

$252 = 21 \times h$ $V = 252, B = 21$

$12 = h$ Divide each side by 21.

The height of the prism is 12 inches.

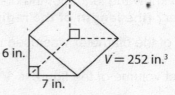

Check

Find the volume of each figure.

1.

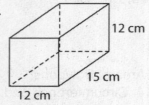

2.

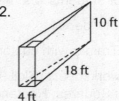

_____   _____

Find the missing dimension for each figure.

3.

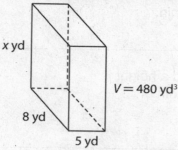

x yd

8 yd

5 yd

$V = 480 \text{ yd}^3$

4.

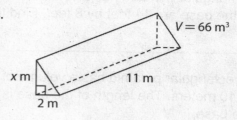

$V = 66 \text{ m}^3$

x m

11 m

2 m

Example 2

The volume V of a pyramid is $\frac{1}{3}$ times the product of the base area B and the height h.

Volume of a pyramid: $V = \frac{1}{3}Bh$

Find the volume of the square pyramid. Round to the nearest tenth.

$V = \frac{1}{3}Bh$ Volume of a pyramid

$V = \frac{1}{3}(10 \times 8) \times 7$ $B = 10 \times 8$, $h = 7$

$V \approx 186.7$ Simplify.

The volume is about 186.7 cubic centimeters.

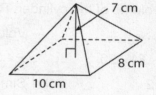

7 cm

8 cm

10 cm

Check

Find the volume of each figure. Round to the nearest tenth, if necessary.

5.

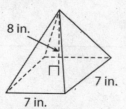

8 in.

7 in.

7 in.

6.

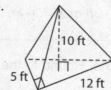

10 ft

5 ft

12 ft

---

7. A triangular pyramid has a volume of 112 cubic feet. The dimensions of the base are 14 feet by 8 feet. Find the height of the pyramid.

_____

8. A rectangular pyramid has a volume of 320 cubic meters and a height of 10 meters. The length of the base is 8 meters. Find the width of the base.

_____

9. The volume of a pyramid is 1000 cubic inches and a height of 15 inches. The dimensions of the base are 25 inches by 16 inches. What is the shape of the base of the pyramid?

_____

Example 3

The volume V of a cylinder is the product of the base area B and the height h, where $B = \pi r^2$.

Volume of a cylinder: $V = Bh$ or $V = \pi r^2 h$

Find the volume of the cylinder. Round to the nearest tenth. $V = \pi r^2 h$ Volume of a cylinder $V \approx 3.14 \times 8^2 \times 20$ $\pi \approx 3.14$, $r = 8$, $h = 20$ $V \approx 4019.2$ Simplify. The volume is about 4019.2 cubic centimeters.	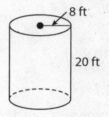

The volume V of a cone is $\dfrac{1}{3}$ times the product of the base area B and the height h.

Volume of a cone: $V = \dfrac{1}{3}Bh$ or $V = \dfrac{1}{3}\pi r^2 h$

Find the volume of the cone. Round to the nearest tenth. $V = \dfrac{1}{3}\pi r^2 h$ Volume of a cone $V \approx \dfrac{1}{3}(3.14 \times 7^2 \times 21)$ $\pi \approx 3.14$, $r = 7$, $h = 21$ $V \approx 1077.0$ Simplify. The volume is about 1077.0 cubic centimeters.	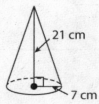

Check

Find the volume of each figure. Use 3.14 for π. Round to the nearest tenth, if necessary.

10.

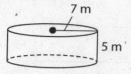

11.

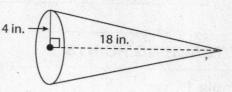

12.

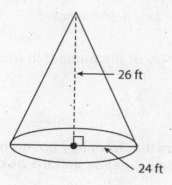

13.

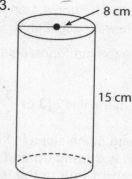

14. Explain the Error. Find the correct solution.

The total volume of the figure is the sum of the volume of the cylinder and the volume of the cone.

$$V = \pi(6)^2(6) + \frac{1}{3}\pi(6)^2 6 = 288\pi$$

_____

_____

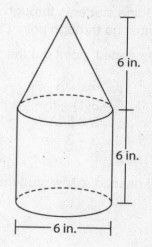

15. A cone and a cylinder have equal volumes. The cone has a radius of 6 inches and a height of 12 inches. The cylinder has a radius of 4 inches. Find the height of the cylinder.

_____

SKILL 27 VOLUME

Writing Equations of Parallel, Perpendicular, Vertical, and Horizontal Lines

KEY TEACHING POINTS

Example 1

Begin by reminding students that parallel lines have the same slope with a different *y*-intercept.

Direct students' attention to Example 1 and write the equation $y = 3x + 4$ on the board. Then review with the following questions:

Ask: Which part of the equation represents the slope of the line? **[*m* or the number in front of the *x*]**

Ask: What is the slope of the line? **[3 or $\frac{3}{1}$]**

Ask: What is the meaning of the slope in this equation? **[It means that from any point on the line, the next point is 3 units up and 1 unit to the right. It also means that the next point is 3 units down and 1 unit to the left.]**

Say: Remember that parallel lines have equal slopes.

Guide students through step 2 by pointing out which coordinates to substitute. The new line must go through point (1, 5) so $x = 1$ and $y = 5$ are substituted into the equation.

If needed, point out the steps taken when solving the equation for *b*.

$$y = mx + b$$
$$5 = 3(1) + b \qquad \text{Substitute } m = 3, x = 1, \text{ and } y = 5.$$
$$5 = 3 + b \qquad \text{Multiply.}$$
$$5 - 3 = 3 - 3 + b \qquad \text{Subtract 3 from both sides.}$$
$$2 = b \qquad \text{Simplify.}$$

If desired, show students a graph of the parallel lines.

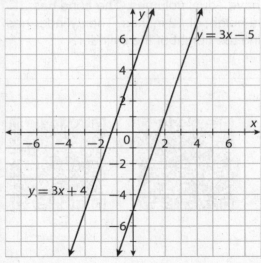

Check
Problems 1–3

Suggest to students that they write a small *x* and *y* above the ordered pair in each problem to help with substitution. Remind students to be mindful of negative numbers when performing operations. When each equation is written, suggest that students check their answers by verifying that the equation has the same slope but a different *y*-intercept.

Example 2

Tell students that they will now be writing equations for perpendicular lines.

Ask: How are parallel lines and perpendicular lines different? [**Parallel lines do not intersect but perpendicular lines do intersect.**]

Ask: What is special about the intersection of perpendicular lines? [**Perpendicular lines intersect at right angles.**]

In Example 2, slopes of perpendicular lines are said to be negative reciprocals of each other. Also point out that the product of the slopes of perpendicular lines is -1. In the example, the perpendicular slopes are 2 and $-\dfrac{1}{2}$. The product is $2\left(-\dfrac{1}{2}\right) = -\dfrac{2}{2} = -1$.

Work through the steps in Example 2, guiding students through the substitution, solving for *b*, and writing the equation. If desired, show students a graph of the perpendicular lines.

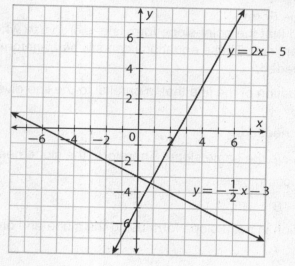

Check
Problem 5

Remind students that if there is no number in front of a variable, the coefficient is 1. Therefore, the equation $y = -x + 5$ has a slope of -1. Be aware that students might assume that lines with opposite slopes are perpendicular. Be sure to point out that because $-1 \cdot 1 = -1$, then -1 and 1 are negative reciprocals of each other.

Example 3

Review horizontal and vertical lines with students.

Ask: How can the horizontal line $y = 3$ be written in $y = mx + b$ form? [**$y = 0x + 3$**]

Ask: What is the slope of a horizontal line? [**0**]

Remind students that any line parallel to a horizontal line will have a slope of 0.

Point out that a vertical line cannot be written in $y = mx + b$ form because there is no y-value in the equation. The slope of a vertical line is undefined. Thus, a line parallel to a vertical line will also have an undefined slope.

Students may have trouble understanding how vertical and horizontal lines can be perpendicular because their slopes are not negative reciprocals. Point out that because horizontal and vertical lines intersect at right angles, they can be called perpendicular lines.

Check
Problems 7–10
If students have difficulty visualizing the graphs of the horizontal and vertical lines, remind them they can use ordered pairs to help. For example, the horizontal line given by $y = 6$ will go through points $(-3, 6)$, $(-2, 6)$, $(-1, 6)$, $(0, 6)$, $(1, 6)$, etc. Note that every y-coordinate is 6.

Problem 14
Remind students that the y-intercept represents the total cost when no movies are purchased. The slope represents the cost per movie.

ALTERNATE STRATEGY

Strategy: Use Point Slope Form
Some students might find that the point-slope form is easier to use when finding parallel and perpendicular lines. These equations can still be transformed into slope-intercept form if needed.

Example 1: Write the equation of the line that is parallel to the line given by $y = 4x - 6$ and goes through the point $(3, -8)$.

1. Determine the slope needed.

    Parallel lines have the same slope. Therefore, the slope needed is 4.

2. Identify the x- and y-coordinates.

    $x_1 = 3$ and $y_1 = -8$

3. Write the new equation in point slope form using the slope and ordered pair.
    $y - y_1 = m(x - x_1)$
    $y - (-8) = 4(x - 3)$

4. If desired, write the equation in slope intercept form.
    $y - (-8) = 4(x - 3)$
    $y + 8 = 4x - 12$
    $y + 8 - 8 = 4x - 12 - 8$
    $y = 4x - 20$

Repeat the point-slope strategy for finding perpendicular lines.

COMMON MISCONCEPTION

Problem 11

Ask: What is the slope of line given by the equation $y = \frac{1}{3}x + 2$? $\left[\frac{1}{3}\right]$

Remind students that they can check that equations represent perpendicular lines if the product of the slopes is –1. In the problem, $3\left(\frac{1}{3}\right) = 1$ so the lines are intersecting but not perpendicular.

Error: Students may determine the reciprocal but forget that slopes of perpendicular lines must be negative reciprocals. Have students check answers by multiplying the slopes to check that the product is –1.

Solution: The slope of the equation is $\frac{1}{3}$. The negative reciprocal of $\frac{1}{3}$ is –3 because $-3\left(\frac{1}{3}\right) = -1$. So,

$y = mx + b$

$1 = -3(6) + b$

$1 = -18 + b$

$19 = b$

The equation of the line perpendicular to $y = \frac{1}{3}x + 2$ and going through (6, 1) is $y = -3x + 19$.

ADDITIONAL ONLINE INTERVENTION RESOURCES

Use the following for students who have not mastered the concepts in Skill 28.

- Math on the Spot videos
- Personal Math Trainer with customized intervention
- Building Block worksheets (Skill 22 Connect Words and Algebra, Skill 23 Connect Words and Equations, Skill 42 Graph Equations, Skill 87 Slopes of Parallel and Perpendicular Lines)

SKILL 28 Writing Equations of Parallel, Perpendicular, Vertical and Horizontal Lines

Example 1

Lines that do not intersect are parallel lines. Parallel lines always have the same slope.

A line is given by the equation $y = 3x + 4$. Write a line parallel to this line going through point $(1, -2)$.

Step 1:	Identify the needed slope.	$m = 3$
Step 2:	Substitute the slope and coordinates of the point into $y = mx + b$. Then solve for b.	$y = mx + b$ $-2 = 3(1) + b$ $-2 = 3 + b$ $-2 - 3 = 3 - 3 + b$ $-5 = b$
Step 3:	Now write the equation of the parallel line.	$y = 3x - 5$

Vocabulary
Horizontal
Parallel
Perpendicular
Vertical

Check

Write the equation of the line that is parallel to the given line and goes through the given point.

1. Line given by $y = -4x + 5$ through the point $(-3, 0)$

2. Line given by $y = -2x - 4$ through the point $(1, -3)$

3. Line given by $y = \frac{1}{2}x + 2$ through the point $(8, -7)$

Example 2

Lines that intersect at right angles are called perpendicular lines. Perpendicular lines have slopes that are negative reciprocals.

A line is given by the equation $y = 2x - 5$. Write a line perpendicular to this line going through point $(2, -4)$.

Step 1:	Identify the needed slope.	$m = -\dfrac{1}{2}$
Step 2:	Substitute the slope and coordinates of the point into $y = mx + b$. Then solve for b.	$y = mx + b$ $-4 = -\dfrac{1}{2}(2) + b$ $-4 = -1 + b$ $-3 = b$
Step 3:	Now write the equation of the parallel line.	$y = -\dfrac{1}{2}x - 3$

Check

Write the equation of the line that is perpendicular to the given line and goes through the given point.

4. Line given by $y = \dfrac{1}{2}x + 4$ through the point $(-2, 9)$

_____

5. Line given by $y = -x + 5$ through the point $(4, 2)$

_____

6. Line given by $y = -3x + 9$ through the point $(6, -4)$

_____

Example 3

Different vertical lines are always parallel to each other. Different horizontal lines are always parallel to each other.

A vertical line and a horizontal line are always perpendicular to each other.

Name a line parallel to $y = 3$ that passes through the point $(4, -2)$.	Name a line parallel to $x = -2$ that passes through the point $(-3, 1)$.	Name a line perpendicular to the line $y = 3$ that passes through the point $(-2, -1)$.
Choose the y-coordinate of the ordered pair to create the parallel line.	Choose the x-coordinate of the ordered pair to create the parallel line.	The line given by $y = 3$ is horizontal. Choose the x-coordinate to create the perpendicular line.
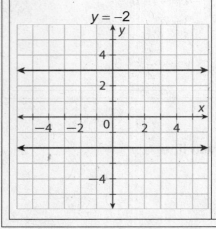	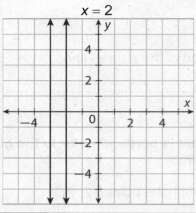	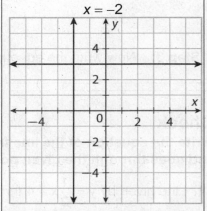

Check

Write the equation of the line that is parallel to the given line and goes through the given point.

7. Line given by $y = 6$ through the point $(-3, 0)$

    _____

8. Line given by $x = -1$ through the point $(4, 5)$

    _____

Write the equation of the line that is perpendicular to the given line and goes through the given point.

9. Line given by $y = 0$ through the point $(7, -8)$

    _____

10. Line given by $x = -3$ through the point $(4, 1)$

    _____

Name _____ Date _____ Class_____

11. Find the Error. Explain the solution.

   Question: Write the equation of the line
   that is perpendicular to $y = \frac{1}{3}x + 2$ and
   goes through (6, 1).

   _____

   _____

   Answer: The slope is $\frac{1}{3}$ so the

   _____
   perpendicular slope is 3. Substituting
   gives $1 = 3(6) + b$ or $b = -17$. The
   equation is $y = 3x - 17$.

12. Write an equation that is parallel to $y = -5x + 4$
    and goes through (10, 0).

    _____

13. Write an equation that is perpendicular to $y = -5x + 4$
    and goes through (1, 0).

    _____

14. A company rents movies that can be streamed online or downloaded
    to a computer. The company charges a one-time sign-up fee and a
    charge for each movie x. The equation to represent this is $y = 5x + 20$.

    What is the sign-up fee and cost per movie?

    _____

15. The owner is advertising a special in which the cost per movie stays
    the same but the sign-up fee decreases. For example, a customer will
    pay a total of $13 to rent two movies.

    A Write an equation that is parallel to $y = 5x + 20$
       and goes through point (2, 13).

    B What is the new sign-up fee?

    _____

SKILL 28 WRITING EQUATIONS OF PARALLEL, PERPENDICULAR, VERTICAL, AND HORIZONTAL LINES

Proportional Relationships

KEY TEACHING POINTS

Remind students that one way to show that two triangles are similar is to show that two pairs of the angles are congruent.

Ask: If two of the angles are congruent, can we be sure that the third is also congruent? Why or why not? **[Yes; If two are congruent, we can use the property that the measures of the angles must have a sum of 180° to find the third. The result would be the same when using the angles from either triangle.]**

Ask: Are there other ways to determine if two triangles are congruent? **[Yes; If the ratio between two sides in one triangle is the same as the ratio between two sides in the other triangle and the included angles are congruent, then the triangles are similar. Or, if all three pairs of sides are in the same ratio, then the triangles are similar.]**

Explain to students that in many of the following problems, they will be told if the triangles are similar and will have to use their understanding of these ideas to find missing values.

Example 1

If possible, draw both triangles on the board and mark corresponding sides with different colors. Stress to the students the importance of using corresponding sides and explain that they can be identified using the angles. For example, since $\overline{AB}$ and $\overline{DF}$ are both opposite the angle marked with three arcs, these are corresponding sides.

Write the given proportion on the board and work through the problem with the students.

Ask: Was that the only proportion that we could have used to find the value of x? **[No; The proportion $\dfrac{BC}{FE} = \dfrac{AC}{DE}$ could also be used.]**

Work through the problem again by substituting the known values into this proportion to show students that both will produce the same answer. Explain that when they are working through problems, they can use whichever pair of corresponding sides they prefer, but that there may not always be enough information to have a choice.

Check
Problem 2

Students may be tempted to decide that sides with lengths of 12 are corresponding sides. Point out that these are opposite non-corresponding angles and therefore cannot be corresponding sides.

Problem 3

Ask the students to use the given information to mark the congruent angles in the picture. This will help them easily identify corresponding sides.

Problem 4

Encourage students to sketch the two triangles to represent the situation. Explain that both triangles will be right triangles since the shadow is along the ground and that is at a right angle with a standing tree or person. Have them use a variable for the unknown height and write an equation. If they use x, the equation should be similar to $\dfrac{6.0}{x} = \dfrac{10.2}{68.0}$.

Problem 5

Students should recognize that the hypotenuse of one triangle corresponds with the hypotenuse of the other. However, they should also be able to explain why the sides of length x and 3.1 are corresponding.

Ask: What property allows us to say that the angles inside the triangles that are formed by the intersection of the two lines are congruent? **[They are vertical angles.]**

Problem 7

Ask: What are the measures of $\angle ABD$ and $\angle DBC$? **[50° and 70°]**

This calculation should help students see that there are not two pairs of congruent angles, and therefore the triangles cannot be similar. There are other ways to approach this problem.

Example 2

Review the basic statement of the triangle proportionality theorem with the students. Point out that when a line divides the triangle in this way, two triangles are actually created. Work through the example with students pointing out that this is a direct application of the triangle proportionality theorem.

Say: Let's look at the two similar triangles that are represented in this picture.

Draw triangles *ABC* and *MBN* on the board as shown below.

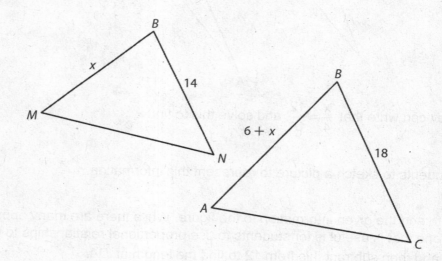

Ask: How can it be shown that the measures of angle *A* and *M* are the same? **[Since $\overline{MN} \parallel \overline{AC}$, $\overline{AB}$ is a transversal and these would be corresponding angles.]**

Ask: What allows us to say that the two triangles are similar? **[They have two pairs of congruent angles: the shared angle at *B* and the pairs of angles at *A* and *M*.]**

Say: Since the triangles are similar, we could have also found x using the proportion $\dfrac{MB}{AB} = \dfrac{NB}{CB}$.

Write this proportion on the board and the corresponding equation $\dfrac{x}{x+6} = \dfrac{14}{14+4}$. Solve this equation to show students that the solution is the same.

Say: As before, either approach will work, but there may not always be enough information to use both.

Check
Problem 8
This problem should not be too difficult for students. Ask them to first use an equation to find the value of x, but then also ask them to mentally determine the value of x. They should notice that 14 is twice as large as 7, so 8 must be twice as large as x.

Problem 10
This is a subtle problem since x is a side of the smaller triangle formed and not one of the proportionally divided sides. Encourage students to draw the triangles separately and use these to write an equation. Their picture should look similar to the image below.

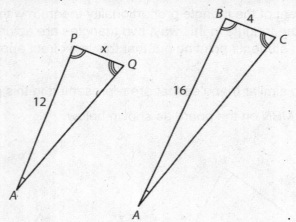

Using this, they can write that $\dfrac{x}{4} = \dfrac{12}{16}$ and solve this to find x.

Problem 11
Encourage students to sketch a picture to represent this information.

Problem 12
Ask students to add the given information to the figure. While there are many approaches to this problem, one that is useful is for students to use proportional relationships to find the length of $\overline{AF}$ and then subtract this from 12 to find the length of $\overline{DA}$.

ALTERNATE STRATEGY

Strategy: A Reasoning Approach to Problem 12

As mentioned before, there are other approaches to problem 12. The approach given below may be useful to students who are not completely comfortable with their algebra skills. Again, it is very important that students draw a diagram with the given lengths to better understand the problem and any of the valid approaches.

Since $EF = 9$ and $BF = 6$, it must be that $EB = 3$. This means that EB is one-third the length of EF. Since $\overline{AB}$ divides the triangle proportionally, DA must be one-third DF. Since $DF = 12$, $DA = 4$.

COMMON MISCONCEPTION

Problem 6

The error here results from not using corresponding sides and instead using their assumption of the orientation of the triangle or their impression of the relative lengths to write a proportion and then an equation. Based on the markings, $\overline{AB}$ and $\overline{DE}$ are opposite non-corresponding angles.

One correct proportion which could be used is $\dfrac{AB}{EF} = \dfrac{BC}{FD}$. The correct answer is found using the equation $\dfrac{16}{12} = \dfrac{x}{15}$. After cross multiplying, $x = 20$. Students could also use the proportion $\dfrac{AC}{ED} = \dfrac{BC}{FD}$.

ADDITIONAL ONLINE INTERVENTION RESOURCES

 Use the following for students who have not mastered the concepts in Skill 25.

- Math on the Spot videos
- Personal Math Trainer with customized intervention
- Building Block worksheets (Skill 63 Multiply Fractions, Skill 82 Simplify Fractions, Skill 90 solve for a Variable, Skill 95 Solve Proportions)

SKILL
29
Proportional Relationships

Example 1

If two triangles are similar, their corresponding side lengths are proportional. Using this property, it is possible to find the value of unknown side lengths.

Given that $\triangle ABC \sim \triangle DEF$, find the value of x.

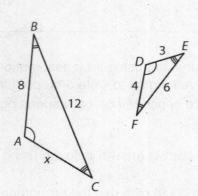

Write an equation using the property that corresponding side lengths are proportional

$$\frac{AB}{DF} = \frac{AC}{DE}$$

Substitute known values
$$\frac{8}{4} = \frac{x}{3}$$

Solve for x by cross multiplying
$$4x = 24$$
$$x = 6$$

Check
For each of the following, the given triangles are similar.
Find the value of x.

1.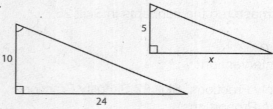

2.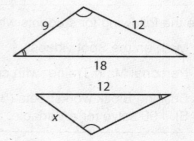

_____   _____

_____   _____

_____   _____

3. For the triangles below, $\triangle ABC \sim \triangle DEF$, $\angle A \cong \angle D$, and $\angle C \cong \angle E$.
   Use this information to find the value of x.

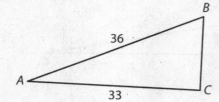

_____

_____

4. In the afternoon sun, Thomas casts a shadow that is 10.2 feet long while a
   nearby tree casts a shadow that is 68.0 feet long. If Thomas is 6.0 feet tall,
   use similar triangles to find the height of the tree to the nearest tenth of a foot.

_____

_____

5. Given the triangles below, find the value of x to the nearest tenth.

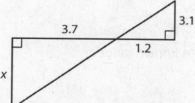

_____

_____

_____

_____

6. Explain the Error. Find the correct solution.

   Given that $\triangle ABC \sim \triangle DEF$, find the value of x to the nearest tenth.

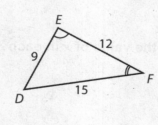

Since $\triangle ABC \sim \triangle DEF$, $\dfrac{AB}{DE} = \dfrac{BC}{DF}$.

Therefore

$$\dfrac{16}{9} = \dfrac{x}{15}$$

$$9x = 240$$

$$x = 26.7$$

_____

_____

7. In the below figure, is it possible to conclude that △ABD ~ △BDC? If not, why not? If so, what sides are corresponding sides?

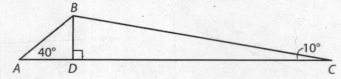

_____

_____

Example 2

The triangle proportionality theorem states that if a line intersects two sides of a triangle and is parallel to the third side, the sides are divided proportionally. This also implies that the resulting smaller triangle is similar to the original triangle.

In the triangle below, $\overline{MN} \parallel \overline{AC}$. Find the value of x.

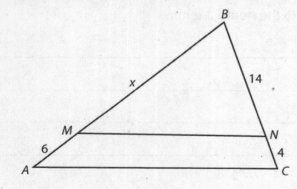

Write an equation
$$\frac{BM}{MA} = \frac{BN}{NC}$$

Substitute known values
$$\frac{x}{6} = \frac{14}{4}$$

Cross multiply and solve for x.
$$4x = 84$$

$$x = 21$$

Check
Given that the indicated lines are parallel, find the value of x in each of the triangles below.

8. $\overline{PQ} \parallel \overline{AC}$

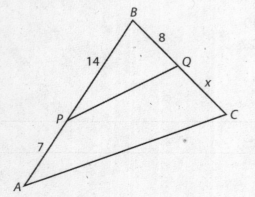

_____

_____

_____

9. $\overline{MN} \parallel \overline{DF}$

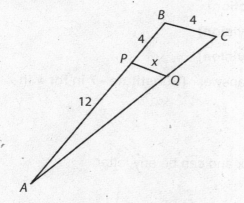

_____
_____
_____

10. $PQ \parallel BC$

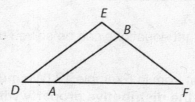

_____
_____
_____

11. Suppose that $\overline{PQ}$ intersects $\overline{AB}$ and $\overline{BC}$ in $\triangle ABC$. What statement must be true in order for the triangle proportionality theorem to apply?

_____
_____

12. In $\triangle DEF$ below, $\overline{DE} \parallel \overline{AB}$. If $BF = 6$, $EF = 9$ and $DF = 12$, what is the length of $\overline{DA}$?

_____
_____

SKILL 29 PROPORTIONAL RELATIONSHIPS

KEY TEACHING POINTS

Example 1

Ask: What is the variable in this equation? **[x]**

Ask: What can we move away from x in order to isolate it on one side of the equation? **[2]**

Ask: What is the inverse operation for addition? **[Subtraction]**

Ask: What is the inverse operation for multiplication? **[Division]**

Ask: What is the inverse operation for multiplication? **[Division]**

Ask: How can we check to make sure we have the right answer? **[Substitute –7 in for x in the original equation to see if it is equal to –54.]**

Check
Problem 1

Make sure students know that the variable is not always x and can be any letter.

Problem 2

Make sure students know that dividing by a fraction is equal to multiplying by its reciprocal.

Ask: How else can we represent one quarter of x? **[x multiplied by 1 and divided by 4.]**

Problem 3

Ask: How is this problem different from Example 1? **[The constant is listed first.]**

Ask: How can you isolate the variable on one side of the equation? **[Add 9 to both sides.]**

Problem 5

Ask: How do we divide decimals in this problem? **[Move the decimal place to the right one place in both the divisor and dividend.]**

Example 2

Make sure students understand that equations can be solved using either method and the answer is the same both ways.

Ask: How is this problem different from in Example 1? **[We must not only undo the four basic operations but now also the distributive property with parentheses.]**

Ask: What is the distributive property? **[$a(b + c) = ab + ac$ and $a(b - c) = ab - ac$]**

Ask: What is the second term inside the parentheses? **[Either that 3 is being subtracted from $6x$ or that it is the same as adding –3.]**

Ask: Why is multiplying a negative by a negative a positive number? **[When there is an even number of like signs, the result is positive.]**

Ask: Why do we have to multiply –4 by $6x$ and –3? **[Parentheses group terms together.]**

Ask: What is the opposite of multiplying by –4? **[Dividing by –4.]**

Ask: How can we check to make sure we have the right answer? **[Substitute 1 in for x in the original equation to see whether it is equal to –12.]**

Check

Problem 10

Ask: What is –2 multiplied by to distribute? [10 and –2g.]

Problem 11

Ask: What is the inverse operation of multiplying by $\frac{1}{2}$? [Dividing by $\frac{1}{2}$ or multiplying by 2.]

Problem 12

Ask: What is the first step to isolate the variable? [Distributing –2.5 or dividing both sides of the equation by –2.5.]

Problem 13

Ask: What is the coefficient that is being distributed? [–1.]

Example 3

Ask: What are some examples of like terms? [Answers may vary. Examples: –1 and 2 or 5x and –7x.]

Ask: What is the difference between coefficients and constants? [A coefficient is the number in front of a variable and is part of the term and a constant is a number without a variable or a variable to the zero power.]

Ask: Are there any like terms on the same side of the equal sign to combine? [3w and 5w.]

Ask: How can we get the variables on the same side of the equation? [Subtract w from both sides.] How can we get the constants on the same side of the equation? [Add 8 to both sides.]

Ask: Would we get the same answer if we subtracted 8w from both sides and added 1 to both sides? [Yes, we would get –7 = –7w, so w would still equal 1.]

Ask: How can we check to make sure we have the right answer? [Substitute 1 in for x in the original equation to see whether both sides are equal to each other.]

Check

Problem 16

Ask: Are there like terms that can be combined first? [Yes, 5 and –1.]

Problem 19

Ask: What number can we divide both sides of the equation by to eliminate the distributive property? [6.]

Problem 22

Ask: What coefficients are being distributed in this problem? [4 and –3.]

Ask: After distributing, what is the next step? [Combining like terms: 4 + (–9) and 24g + (12g).]

ALTERNATE STRATEGY

Strategy: Use models with positive and negative coefficients and constants.

1. Take the problem $-3x + 5 = 4x - 2$ and use any kinds of model in the classroom or on the board to take the place of the coefficient and constant values. These could include two-color counters or any other manipulatives. For instance, let **O** be equal to $-1x$, let ⊙ be equal to $1x$, let □ be equal to -1, and let ☑ be equal to 1.

2. Have students rewrite the equation with only addition. In this case, this means $-3x + 5 = 4x + (-2)$ using the definition of subtraction.

3. **Ask:** How can we represent $-3x$ with the symbols we just defined? **[OOO]** How can we represent 5? **[☑☑☑☑☑]** How can we represent $4x$? **[⊙⊙⊙⊙]** What about -2? **[□□]** How can we represent the entire equation? **[OOO + ☑☑☑☑☑ = ⊙⊙⊙⊙ + □□]**

4. **Ask:** How can we get all of the boxes to one side? **[Change them into the other type of box to bring them over to the same side of the equation.]** How can we get all of the circles to one side? **[Change them into the other type of circle to bring them over to the same side of the equation.]**

5. Show students how using the other type of box/circle cancels out the type of box/circle on the original side of the equation.

6. **Ask:** Is it easier or harder to have a positive coefficient of x when solving? **[Easier because then you do not have to divide by a negative to find the value of x.]**

7. **Ask:** How can we find the value of just one ⊙? **[OOO + ☑☑☑☑☑ = ⊙⊙⊙⊙ + □□, OOO + ⊙⊙⊙ + ☑☑☑☑☑ + ☑☑ = ⊙⊙⊙⊙ + ⊙⊙⊙ + □□ + ☑☑, ☑☑☑☑☑☑☑ = ⊙⊙⊙⊙⊙⊙⊙, ☑ = ⊙]**

8. Have students create and solve their own problems with coefficients that they create or get a random number generator.

COMMON MISCONCEPTION

Problem 15
Some students may incorrectly combine $8x + 4x$ as $12x^2$. Remind students that only the coefficients are combined when combining terms with the same variable and power. Since the both terms have x with an exponent of 1, the correct value is $12x$.

Problem 21
Some students will not divide all terms by 2 to eliminate the distributive property.

Ask: Dividing by what value will eliminate the distributive property? **[2.]** Name the terms that will be divided by 2. **[4, $2b$, $2(4b - 3)$, and -8.]**

Problem 22

Some students will either not distribute the −3 to the terms of 3 and 4g or will distribute 3 to both terms and not subtract the quantity of (9 + 12g).

Problem 23

Error: The −1 was not distributed to both terms in the quantity (1 + 7d), which results in an incorrect final solution for d.

Solution:

$$-6(-d-7)-(1+7d)=36$$
$$6d+42-(1+7d)=36$$
$$6d+42-1-7d=36$$
$$-d+41=36$$
$$-d=-5$$
$$d=5$$

ADDITIONAL ONLINE INTERVENTION RESOURCES

Use the following for students who have not mastered the concepts in Skill 30.

- Math on the Spot videos
- Personal Math Trainer with customized intervention
- Building Block worksheets

SKILL 30 Multi-step Equations

Example 1

To solve multi-step equations, first recall how to solve two-step equations using inverse operations.

$8x + 2 = -54$	Given equation.
$\underline{-2 = -2}$	The inverse operation for addition is subtraction.
$\dfrac{8x}{8} = \dfrac{-56}{8}$	Simplify.
	The inverse operation for multiplication is division.
$x = -7$	The value of x is -7.

Vocabulary

Inverse operations

Distributive property

Coefficient

Terms

Like terms

Constant

Check

Find the value of the variable in each two-step equation below using inverse operations.

1. $3y + 2 = 17$

2. $\dfrac{1}{4}x - 2 = 3$

3. $-9 + 14m = 33$

4. $54 = -\dfrac{2}{3}p - 12$

5. $-0.4q - 4 = 11.5$

6. $2 - 9k = 2$

7. $7r - 2 = -2$

8. $\dfrac{3}{2}w + 4 = 1.5w$

Example 2

The distributive property calls for distributing the coefficient to all terms within the parentheses. Multi-step equations can be solved either by distributing or using inverse operations to eliminate the coefficient.

<u>Method 1 – Distributing the Coefficient to All Terms Within the Parentheses</u>

$-12 = -4(6x - 3)$	Given equation.
$-12 = -24x + 12$	Distribute by multiplying the coefficient of -4 by the terms of $6x$ and -3
$\underline{-12} = \underline{-12}$	The inverse operation for addition is subtraction.
$\underline{-24} = \underline{-24x}$	Simplify.
$\underline{-24}\ \ \underline{-24}$	The inverse operation for multiplication is division.
$1 = x$	1 is the value of x.

<u>Method 2 – Use Inverse Operations to Eliminate the Coefficient</u>

$\underline{-12} = \underline{-4}(6x - 3)$	Given equation.
$-4\ \ \ \ -4$	The inverse operation for multiplication is division.
$3 = 6x - 3$	Simplify.
$\underline{+3}\ \ \ \ \ \underline{+3}$	The inverse operation for subtraction is addition.
$\underline{6} = \underline{6x}$	Simplify.
$6\ \ \ \ 6$	The inverse operation for multiplication is division.
$1 = x$	1 is the value of x.

The answer is the same using either method.

Check

Find the value of the variable in each equation below.

9. $7(b + 4) = 14$

10. $-2(10 - 2g) = -16$

_____

11. $-21 - \dfrac{1}{2}(4y - 6)$

12. $-2.5(-6 - 4h) = 12$

_____

13. $-(7 - 4x) = 33$

14. $-2 = 4(18.75 - 7y)$

_____

Example 3

To solve multi-step equations, it may be necessary to combine like terms first. Like terms can either be coefficients of the same variable or constants.

When like terms are on the same side of the equal sign, combine them. When **like terms** are on opposite sides of the equal sign, use **inverse operations** to bring them to the same side before combining.

$w - 1 = 3w + 5w - 8$	Given equation.
$w - 1 = 8w - 8$	Combine like terms on the same side of the equation.
$\underline{-w = -w}$	Inverse operations to combine like terms on one side of the equation.
$-1 = 7w - 8$	Simplify.
$\underline{+8 \qquad +8}$	Inverse operations to combine like terms on one side of the equation.
$\dfrac{7 = 7w}{7 \quad 7}$	Simplify.
	The inverse operation for multiplication is division.
$1 = w$	1 is the value of w.

Check
Find the value of the variable in each equation below.

15. $8x + 4x = 108$

16. $5 + 2p - 1 = -6$

17. $\dfrac{3}{8}r + 4 = \dfrac{1}{8}r - 14$

18. $11 - 16q + 2 = 15 - 20q$

19. $6(3y + 1) = -6y - 18$

20. $6.5 + 2.5h = 3h + 10.5$

21. $4 + 2b = 2(4b - 3) - 8$

22. $4(1 + 6g) - 3(3 + 4g) = 43$

23. Explain the Error. Find the correct solution.

When attempting to solve $-6(-d - 7) - (1 + 7d) = 36$, Danielle wrote out the following steps:

$$-6(-d - 7) - (1 + 7d) = 36$$

$$6d + 42 - (1 + 7d) = 36$$

$$6d + 42 - 1 + 7d = 36$$

$$13d + 41 = 36$$

$$13d = -5$$

$$d = \frac{-5}{13}$$

_____

_____

_____

SKILL 30 MULTI-STEP EQUATIONS

Characteristics of Quadratic Functions

KEY TEACHING POINTS

A quadratic equation is a second-order polynomial which means the greatest exponent of a variable in the equation is 2. For example, $y = ax^2 + bx + c$.

Ask: If $a = 0$, is the equation still a quadratic equation? **[No; If $a = 0$, the equation is $y = bx + c$. This is a first-order polynomial (linear) equation and not a second order polynomial (quadratic) equation.]**

Ask: If $b = 0$, is the equation still a quadratic equation? **[Yes; If $b = 0$, the equation is $y = ax^2 + c$. This is a second-order polynomial (quadratic) equation.]**

Ask: If $c = 0$, is the equation still a quadratic equation? **[Yes; If $c = 0$, the equation is $y = ax^2 + bx$. This is a second-order polynomial (quadratic) equation.]**

Quadratic equations are written using two different forms.

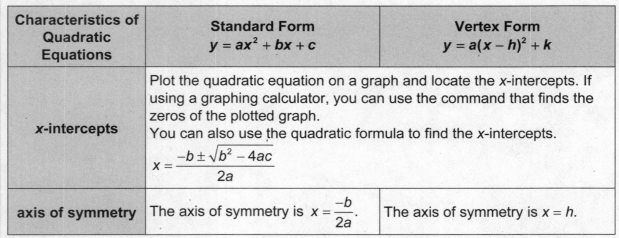

Standard Form	Vertex Form
$y = ax^2 + bx + c$	$y = a(x - h)^2 + k$

The graph of a quadratic equation is a parabola. A parabola is a U-shaped figure.

Both forms of quadratic equations give information about the graph of the equation.

The vertex is the minimum or maximum of the parabola.

The x-intercepts are the points where the parabola intersects the x-axis. A quadratic equation can have zero, one, or two x-intercepts.

The axis of symmetry is a vertical line. It divides the parabola into mirror images.

The y-intercept of the graph is the value of y when $x = 0$.

Characteristics of Quadratic Equations	Standard Form $y = ax^2 + bx + c$	Vertex Form $y = a(x - h)^2 + k$
x-intercepts	Plot the quadratic equation on a graph and locate the x-intercepts. If using a graphing calculator, you can use the command that finds the zeros of the plotted graph. You can also use the quadratic formula to find the x-intercepts. $x = \dfrac{-b \pm \sqrt{b^2 - 4ac}}{2a}$	
axis of symmetry	The axis of symmetry is $x = \dfrac{-b}{2a}$.	The axis of symmetry is $x = h$.

vertex	Use $x = \dfrac{-b}{2a}$ to find the vertex. $y = a(\dfrac{-b}{2a})^2 + b(\dfrac{-b}{2a}) + c$ $y = \dfrac{b^2}{4a} - \dfrac{b^2}{2a} + c$ $y = -\dfrac{b^2}{4a} + c$ The vertex is $\left(\dfrac{-b}{2a}, -\dfrac{b^2}{4a} + c\right)$.	Use the variable h and k to find the vertex. The vertex is (h, k).
y-intercept	Use $x = 0$ to find the y-intercept. $y = c$ The y-intercept is $(0, c)$.	Use $x = 0$ to find the y-intercept. $y = ah^2 + k$ The y-intercept is $(0, ah^2 + k)$.

Example 1

Let's look at a quadratic equation written in both standard form and vertex form,

Characteristics of Quadratic Equations	Standard Form $y = x^2 + 2x - 3$	Vertex Form $y = (x + 1)^2 - 4$
x-intercepts	$x = \dfrac{-2 \pm \sqrt{2^2 - 4(1)(-3)}}{2(1)} = \dfrac{-2 \pm 4}{2}$ $\dfrac{-2 + 4}{2} = 1$ $\dfrac{-2 - 4}{2} = -3$ The x-intercepts are $(1, 0)$ and $(-3, 0)$	
axis of symmetry	The axis of symmetry is $x = \dfrac{-2}{2(1)} = -1$	The axis of symmetry is $x = -1$.
vertex	Use $x = \dfrac{-b}{2a}$ to find the vertex. $x = \dfrac{-2}{2(1)} = -1$ $y = (-1)^2 + 2(-1) - 3 = -4$ The vertex is $(-1, -4)$.	Use the variables h and k to find the vertex. The vertex is $(-1, -4)$.
y-intercept	Use $x = 0$ to find the y-intercept. $y = (0)^2 + 2(0) - 3 = -3$ The y-intercept is $(0, -3)$.	Use $x = 0$ to find the y-intercept. $y = (0 + 1)^2 - 4 = -3$ The y-intercept is $(0, -3)$.

Ask: How can we check the answers? **[Graph the equation.]**

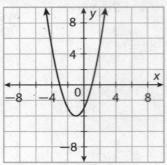

Check
Problem 1

Ask students to explain how they knew which form the equation is written in.

Problem 3

Ask students whether the graph is increasing or decreasing on each side of the axis of symmetry.

Problem 5

Ask students how they knew the vertex was the minimum or maximum. Students should compare the vertex to the *x*-intercepts. Also, students can look at the value of *a* to determine whether the parabola opens upward or downward.

Ask: Which way will the parabola open when the vertex is the minimum? **[opens upward]**

Ask: How can we check the answers? **[Graph the equation.]**

Check
Problem 8

Ask students to explain how they knew which form the equation is written in.

Problem 11

Ask students whether the graph is increasing or decreasing on each side of the axis of symmetry.

Problem 12

Ask students how it can be determined whether the vertex is the minimum or maximum without graphing the equation. Students should know that the value of *a* determines which way the parabola opens.

ALTERNATE STRATEGY

Strategy: Use a model.

You can graph any quadratic equation and find the *x*-intercept, axis of symmetry, vertex, and *y*-intercepts by locating them on the graph.

COMMON MISCONCEPTION

Problem 1

If this parabola were shifted downward 1 unit it would have only one x-intercept. If this parabola were shifted downward 2 units it would have no x-intercepts. Quadratic equations can have zero, one, or two x-intercepts, but never more than two. When a parabola's vertex is on the x-axis, there will only be one x-intercept for the quadratic equation. When a parabola opens upward and the vertex, or minimum is above the x-axis, there will be no x-intercept for the quadratic equation.

ADDITIONAL ONLINE INTERVENTION RESOURCES

Use the following for students who have not mastered the concepts in Skill 31.

- Math on the Spot videos
- Personal Math Trainer with customized intervention
- Building Block worksheets (Skill 45 Graph Ordered Pairs, Skill 97 Solve Quadratic Equations, Skill 102 Symmetry)

SKILL 31 — Characteristics of Quadratic Functions

When graphed, quadratic equations are called parabolas. All quadratic equations have a y-intercept, an axis of symmetry, and a minimum or maximum, which is also called the vertex. Parabolas can have zero, one, or two x-intercepts. Quadratic equations are written in either standard form or vertex form.

Example 1		Vocabulary
		Exponent

Example 1

The table shows how to find the characteristics of a quadratic equation written in standard form.

Characteristics	Standard Form $y = ax^2 + bx + c$
x-intercepts	Use the quadratic formula to find any x-intercepts, $(x, 0)$. $x = \dfrac{-b \pm \sqrt{b^2 - 4ac}}{2a}$
axis of symmetry	The axis of symmetry is $x = \dfrac{-b}{2a}$.
vertex	Use $x = \dfrac{-b}{2a}$ to find the vertex. Plug in $x = \dfrac{-b}{2a}$ and solve for y.
y-intercept	The y-intercept is at $(0, c)$.

Vocabulary
- Exponent
- Parabola
- Maximum
- Minimum
- Vertex
- y-intercept
- x-intercept
- Axis of symmetry

Find the characteristics for the standard-form quadratic equation $y = -x^2 + 2x + 3$.

Characteristics	Standard Form $y = -x^2 + 2x + 3$
x-intercepts	The x-intercepts are $(-1, 0)$ and $(3, 0)$.
axis of symmetry	The axis of symmetry is $x = 1$
vertex	The vertex is $(1, 4)$.
y-intercept	The y-intercept is $(0, 3)$.

Check

For Problems 1–5, use the quadratic equation $y = x^2 - 4x - 5$.

1. Which form is the quadratic equation written in?

   _____

2. Find the x-intercepts, if any, of the quadratic equation $y = x^2 - 4x - 5$.

   _____

3. Find the axis of symmetry and the vertex of the quadratic equation $y = x^2 - 4x - 5$.

   _____

4. Is the vertex of the quadratic equation $y = x^2 - 4x - 5$ a minimum or a maximum?

   _____

5. Find the y-intercept of the quadratic equation $y = x^2 - 4x - 5$.

   _____

6. Graph the quadratic equation $y = x^2 - 4x - 5$.

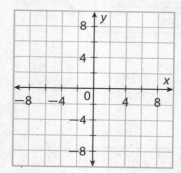

7. Jessica tossed a rock of a cliff that is 100 feet tall. The height of the rock can be modeled by the equation $h = -16t^2 + 32t + 100$, where h is the height in feet and t is time in seconds. What is the vertex of the parabola? What does it represent?

   _____

Example 2

The table shows how to find the characteristics of a quadratic equation written in vertex form.

Characteristics	Vertex Form $y = a(x - h)^2 + k$
x-intercepts	Plot the quadratic equation and locate the *x*-intercepts. If using a graphing calculator, you can use the command that finds the zeros of the plotted graph.
axis of symmetry	The axis of symmetry is $x = h$.
vertex	Use the variables h and k to find the vertex. The vertex is (h, k).
y-intercept	Use $x = 0$ to find the *y*-intercept. $y = ah^2 + k$ The *y*-intercept is $(0, \ ah^2 + k)$.

Find the characteristics for the vertex form-quadratic equation $y = 2(x + 1)^2 + 3$.

Characteristics	Vertex Form $y = 2(x + 1)^2 + 3$
x-intercepts	There are no *x*-intercepts.
axis of symmetry	The axis of symmetry is $x = -1$.
vertex	The vertex is $(-1, 3)$.
y-intercept	The *y*-intercept is $(0, 5)$.

Check

For Problems 8–12, use the quadratic equation $y = -\dfrac{1}{2}(x-5)^2 + 2.$

8. Which form is the quadratic equation written in?

_____

9. Graph the quadratic equation.

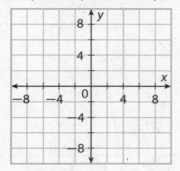

10. Find the x-intercepts, if any, of the quadratic equation
$y = -\dfrac{1}{2}(x-5)^2 + 2.$

_____

11. Find the axis of symmetry and the vertex of the quadratic equation
$y = -\dfrac{1}{2}(x-5)^2 + 2.$

_____

12. Find the y-intercept of the quadratic equation $y = -\dfrac{1}{2}(x-5)^2 + 2.$

_____

13. Explain the Error. Find the correct solution. When describing the graph
of $y = -(x-2)^2 + 3,$ Samuel said the axis of symmetry is at $x = -2.$

_____

SKILL 31 CHARACTERISTICS OF QUADRATIC FUNCTIONS

Solving Quadratic Functions

KEY TEACHING POINTS

Sketch any linear function and any quadratic function on the board (similar to those below) and ask students to identify which is which. Remind students that the graph of any quadratic function is a parabola.

Graph of $y = 2x + 4$

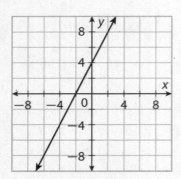

Graph of $y = x^2 - 4$

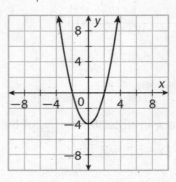

Ask: Will all graphs of quadratic functions look like this graph? **[No.]**

Ask: What might be different? **[The graph may open down, it may be more or less narrow, and it may or may not cross the x-axis.]**

Using both graphs, have students identify which points represent *y*-intercepts and which points represent *x*-intercepts.

Example 1
Ask: How do you find the *x*-intercept or intercepts of any function? **[Set y = 0 and solve for x.]**

Explain that when working with a quadratic function, setting $y = 0$ results in a quadratic equation. There are many methods for solving a quadratic equation.

Explain that this means that a graph can be used to solve an equation of the form $ax^2 + b + c = 0$.

Draw the graph from the example on the board being careful that the labels on the *x*-axis are clear.

Ask: What are the *x*-intercepts of this graph? **[–4 and 1]**

Explain that this means the solutions to the equation that result from setting $y = 0$ are –4 and 1.

Check
Problem 3
Students may be confused by the fact that this graph only touches the *x*-axis at one point. Explain that it is possible for a quadratic equation to have only one real solution and that this would be represented by this type of graph.

Problem 4

Make sure students understand that the same process applies whether the parabola opens up or down.

Problem 5

Ask students to sketch examples of parabolas with each of the given properties. If they have trouble, the following functions can be used. Students can graph each by hand or on a graphing calculator.

$y = x^2 - 9$ (crosses x-axis twice), $y = x^2 - 4x + 4$ (touches once), and $y = x^2 + 2x + 3$ (does not cross the x-axis)

Problem 6

Use problem 5 to help students understand the question. Use the last graph above as an example.

Ask: What are the x-intercepts of this function? **[There are no x-intercepts.]**

Remind students that the x-intercepts would represent the solution to the quadratic equation resulting from setting the function equal to zero. If there are no x-intercepts, there can't be any real-number solutions.

Example 2

Write the square root rule on the board so students can refer to it throughout the example. Stress that it only applies to equations where the squared term can be isolated.

Work through this example with the students step by step.

Ask: What are the x-intercepts of $y = 3x^2 - 12$? **[−2 and 2]**

Graph the equation (shown below) on the board so that students can see that the solutions found algebraically match the solutions found graphically.

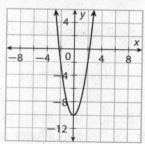

Check

Ask: If I know that the product of two factors is zero, what must be true? **[At least one of the factors is zero.]**

Explain to students that this is known as the "zero product rule" and that it can be applied to equations where factors are involved. Since quadratic equations can be written as a sum or difference of terms set equal to zero, this can be applied as long as those terms make up a factorable expression.

Example 3

Work through each step with the students. Explain that the goal of the first step is to set it up so that zero is on one side of the equation so that the zero product rule can be used.

Ask: What are the x-intercepts of $y = 2x^2 + x - 15$? [$\frac{5}{2}$ and 3]

Once again, have students verify their work with a graph. The graph of this function is shown below.

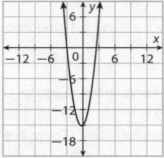

Check
Problem 20

Students may wish to move the squared term to the left side of the equation. This will result in a correct answer but students will then have a negative on that term to contend with. Encourage them instead to move terms in such a way that the squared term stays positive to minimize the chance for arithmetic errors.

Problem 21

Make sure that students understand that the coordinates will be ordered pairs.

Problem 22

This problem may be challenging for many students. Ask them to work backwards starting with the linear factors.

Ask: What equations of the form $x - c = 0$ would have solutions 5 and 9? [$x - 5 = 0$ and $x - 9 = 0$]

Ask: If these equations resulted from applying the zero product rule, what would have been the previous step? [$(x - 5)(x - 9) = 0$]

Now ask students to foil the left side. Explain that this is not the only possible equation since terms can be moved around and any non-zero multiplier could be placed in front of the expression.

Example 4

Work through each step with the students. Stress to students that the equation must be in the appropriate form before they can apply the formula.

Remind them that these solutions would represent the x-intercepts of the function $y = x^2 + 2x - 6$.

Have the students approximate these numbers to better understand the function.

ALTERNATE STRATEGY

Strategy: Matching

1. Place each of the graphs from questions on the board.

2. Write the following equations on the board in a random order: $x^2 = 1$, $x^2 - x = 6$, $0 = x^2 + 6x + 9$, $x^2 = 6x - 5$. (note: these are in order as the equations whose solutions are shown in graphs 1–4)

3. Ask the students to individually match the equation with the graph which could be used to solve it.

4. Once students have worked on their own, have them explain their answer and reasoning with their neighboring student.

5. Discuss the various methods with the students as a whole, stressing that they can always just solve the equation and use the x-intercepts but that there may be more efficient strategies.

COMMON MISCONCEPTION

Problem 27

The mistake shown in this problem is the result of not moving all terms to one side before applying the quadratic formula. Explain to students that this will result in a completely incorrect answer. Here, the correct steps would be to first write $x^2 - 7x - 10 = 0$ and then

solve it with the formula $x = \dfrac{7 \pm \sqrt{49 - 4(1)(-10)}}{2(1)} = \dfrac{7 \pm \sqrt{89}}{2}$.

ADDITIONAL ONLINE INTERVENTION RESOURCES

 Use the following for students who have not mastered the concepts in Skill 32.

- Math on the Spot videos

- Personal Math Trainer with customized intervention

- Building Block worksheets (Skill 34 Factor Trinomials, Skill 97 Solve Quadratic Equations)

| SKILL 32 | **Solving Quadratic Functions** |

Example 1

To find the x-intercepts of a quadratic function like $y = ax^2 + b + c$ (where a, b, and c are real numbers) using a graph, determine where the graph of the function crosses the x-axis.

These values are also the solution(s) to the quadratic equation $ax^2 + b + c = 0$.

The quadratic function $y = ax^2 + b + c$ is graphed below. What are the solutions to the equation $ax^2 + b + c = 0$?

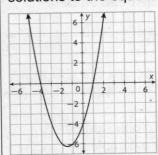

Since the graph crosses the x-axis at –4 and 1, the solutions are $x = -4$ and $x = 1$.

Vocabulary

Quadratic Function

Quadratic Equation

x-intercepts

Check

Each of the graphs below is of a quadratic function. Find the solution(s) to the equation resulting from setting the function equal to zero.

1.

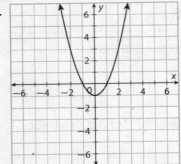

_____

2.

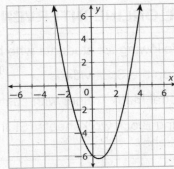

_____

3.

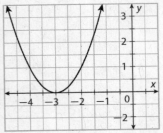

_____

4.

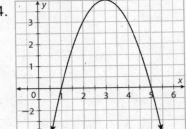

_____

5. There are three possibilities for how many times the graph of a quadratic function may cross the *x*-axis. What are they?

_____

6. If a quadratic function does not have any real number solutions, what property must its graph have? Explain.

_____

Example 2

If a quadratic equation can be written in the form $ax^2 = c$ for real numbers a and c, then the solution or solutions can be found using the square root. If $x^2 = c$, then $x = \pm\sqrt{c}$.

Find the solutions to the equation $3x^2 - 12 = 0$.

    Write the equation in $ax^2 = c$ form: $3x^2 = 12$

    Divide both sides by a: $x^2 = 4$

    Apply the square root rule: $x = \pm\sqrt{4} = \pm 2$

The solutions to the equation are $x = -2$ and $x = 2$.

Check

Solve each equation. Simplify the answer completely.

7. $4x^2 - 1 = 0$

    8. $5x^2 - 2 = 123$

    9. $8x^2 + 1 = 19$

_____

_____

_____

10. What are the *x*-intercepts of the quadratic function $y = 2x^2 - 10$? Explain.

_____

Example 3

Quadratic equations can also be solved using factoring.

Solve the equation $2x^2 + x = 15$.

Write the equation so that all terms are on one side: $2x^2 + x - 15 = 0$

Factor the quadratic expression: $(2x - 5)(x + 3) = 0$

Set each factor equal to zero: $2x - 5 = 0, \ x + 3 = 0$

Solve each linear equation: $x = \dfrac{5}{2}, \ x = -3$

The solutions to the equation are $x = \dfrac{5}{2}$ and $x = -3$.

Check

Solve each equation.

11. $x^2 + 3x - 4 = 0$

12. $x^2 - 10x + 21 = 0$

13. $x^2 = -3x - 2$

14. $3x^2 + 2x - 1 = 0$

15. $5x - 12 = -2x^2$

16. $10 = 2x^2 - x$

Example 4

The quadratic formula can be used to find the solutions to any quadratic equation $ax^2 + bx + c = 0$. Solutions found with this formula must be simplified.

Solve the equation $x^2 + 2x = 6$.

Write the equation so that all terms are on one side: $x^2 + 2x - 6 = 0$

Identify a, b, and c: $a = 1, \ b = 2, \ c = -6$

Apply the quadratic formula:
$$x = \dfrac{-b \pm \sqrt{b^2 - 4ac}}{2a}$$
$$= \dfrac{-2 \pm \sqrt{2^2 - 4(1)(-6)}}{2(1)}$$

$$= \frac{-2 \pm \sqrt{28}}{2}$$

Simplify the result completely:

$$= \frac{-2 \pm 2\sqrt{7}}{2}$$

$$= -1 \pm \sqrt{7}$$

The solutions to the equation are $x = -1 + \sqrt{7}$ and $x = -1 - \sqrt{7}$.

Check

Solve each equation. Simplify the answer completely.

17. $x^2 + 3x = 2$

18. $6x^2 - 5x + 1 = 0$

19. $x^2 - 6x - 3 = 0$

20. $x^2 - 2x = 44$

21. Explain the Error. Find the correct solution.

A student solves the equation $x^2 = 7x + 10$ using the following steps.

$$x = \frac{-7 \pm \sqrt{49 - 4(1)(10)}}{2(1)} = \frac{-7 \pm \sqrt{9}}{2} = \frac{-7 \pm 3}{2}$$

$$x = \frac{-7 + 3}{2} = \frac{-4}{2} = -2, \ x = \frac{-7 - 3}{2} = \frac{-10}{2} = -5$$

Solutions are $x = -2$ and $x = -5$.

SKILL 32 SOLVING QUADRATIC FUNCTIONS

Answer Key

Module Pre-Tests

Pre-Test Module 1

1. $A'(3, 2)$, $B'(6, 6)$, $C'(6, 1)$.

2. $A'(1, -2)$, $B'(4, -6)$, $C'(4, 3)$.

3. Quadrant IV

4. $(2, -5)$

5. complementary, adjacent angles

6. vertical angles

7. supplementary, adjacent angles

8. adjacent angles

9. 6 units; $\overline{AB}$ is a vertical line segment with endpoints at $(-5, 5)$ and $(-5, -1)$. Therefore, the length is determined by finding the difference between the y-coordinates. So, $5 - (-1) = 6$ units

10. Using the midpoint formula with endpoints $(-3, 4)$ and $(6, 3)$:

$$\left(\frac{x_1 + x_2}{2}, \frac{y_1 + y_2}{2}\right)$$

$$\left(\frac{-3 + 6}{2}, \frac{4 + 3}{2}\right)$$

$$\left(\frac{3}{2}, \frac{7}{2}\right) \text{ or } (1.5, 3.5)$$

Pre-Test Module 2

1. $P'(5, 6)$

2.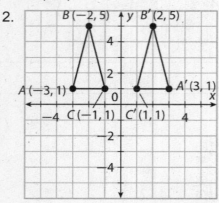

3. $P'(-9, 3)$

4. Quadrant III

5. $(x, y) \rightarrow (x + 3, y - 4)$

6. $A'(1, -1)$, $B'(4, -2)$, $C'(1, -3)$

7. $A'(1, 1)$, $B'(4, 2)$, $C'(1, 3)$

8. $A'(-1, 4)$, $B'(0, 7)$, $C'(1, 4)$

9. A True B False C False D True
   E False

Pre-Test Module 3

1. A False B True C False D False

2. $(x, y) \rightarrow (x - 1, y + 4)$

3.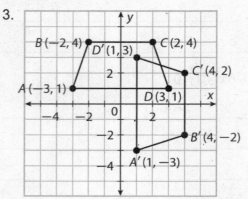

4. Yes; a rotation does not change the side lengths or the angle measures of the triangle.

5. $P'(-2, 7)$

6. $P'(7, 2)$

7. $62°$

8. $28°$

9. 4

10. 2

Pre-Test Module 4

1. $y = -5x + 3$

2. 62

3. $56°$

4. $124°$

5. Supplementary

6. $x = 3$

7. Neither; the slope of the first line is $\frac{1}{2}$ while the slope of the second is 3. These are not the same and do not have a product of –1.

8. 65

9. 125

10. 50

11.

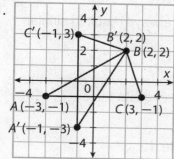

Pre-Test Module 5

1. A False B True C True D False

2.

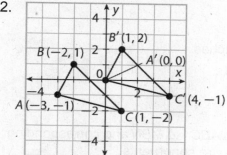

3. $P'(5, -1)$

4. A False B True C True D True

5. $(x, y) \rightarrow (x - 1, y - 4)$

6. Quadrant III

7. Yes; a rotation will not change the side lengths or the angle measurements of the triangle.

Pre-Test Module 6

1. 80°

2. 20

3. 40°

4. 40°

5. 160°

6. 20°

7. 160°

8. supplementary

9. 25

10. 20

11. A True B False C True D True

Pre-Test Module 7

1. 30°

2. 20

3. 5

4. $\left(1, \dfrac{5}{2}\right)$

5. A False B True C False D True

6. $\sqrt{29}$

7. No; the sum of the measures of the interior angles must be 180.

8. 12

9. 132°

10. 55°

Pre-Test Module 8

1. A True B False C True D True

2. $\sqrt{29}$

3. $\left(-\dfrac{3}{2}, -2\right)$

4. 90°

5. 9

6. 30°

7. 60°

8. 120°

9.

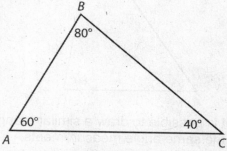

10. No; it is possible to draw the triangle with different side lengths (although they will always be proportional to the one drawn).

Pre-Test Module 9

1. A False B True C True D False

2. 40°

3. 8

4. 115°

5. 4

6. 70°

7. 110°

8. 15

9. A False B True C False D True

10. 10

Pre-Test Module 10

1. y-intercept 2; slope $-\dfrac{5}{2}$

2. −1

3. $4\sqrt{2}$

4. (0, 2)

5. A True B False C False D False

6. $y = 2x - 1$

7. 52 ft²

8. $y = -4x + 5$

9. 23.1 ft²

10. For each additional minute of talk time used, the total cost increases by 10 cents.

Pre-Test Module 11

1. A True B False C False D True

2. Sample answer:

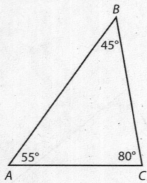

3. No; it is possible to draw a similar triangle with the same angle measurements.

4.

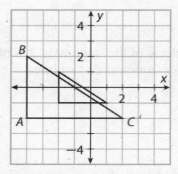

5. Yes; dilations always result in similar figures.

6. 3.2

7. No; under a dilation, every coordinate is multiplied by the scale factor.

8. (1, 7)

Pre-Test Module 12

1. $2\sqrt{10}$

2. 2

3. 4

4. $\sqrt{13}$

5. 24.2 inches

6. 60 feet

7. 4

8. 7.5

9. 60°; $\triangle ABC \sim \triangle MBN$ and corresponding angles are congruents.

10. No; $2^2 + 6^2 \neq 10^2$

11. 1.5 centimeters

Pre-Test Module 13

1. A True B False C True D True

2. 30

3. 150

4. 30

5. 3

6. $5\sqrt{3}$

7. 16

8. 35

9. 20

10. 70

Pre-Test Module 14

1. $\overline{EF}$
2. $\triangle TBM \sim \triangle FWL$
3. 12 in.
4. $x = \dfrac{3}{5}$
5. $x = 9$

Pre-Test Module 15

1. A True B False C True D False
2. 40°
3. 14; opposite sides of a parallelogram are congruent
4. 70°
5. 110°
6. 10
7. 57
8. 40
9. 70°
10. The sum of their measures is 90°.
11. 20

Pre-Test Module 16

1. 4π
2. 2 and −1; These are the points at which the graph crosses the x-axis.
3. No; since the graph is a parabola opening up, it will never reach a maximum value.
4. Yes; since its graph is a parabola opening up, it will reach a minimum value at the vertex.
5. 25.1 ft
6. 63.6 ft^2
7. The parabola will open down. When the coefficient of the squared term is negative, the parabola will open down.
8. One; it only touches the x-axis at one point
9. $x = 4$
10. 0
11. 3π

Pre-Test Module 17

1. 31.4 cm
2. $\left(\dfrac{3}{2}, \dfrac{1}{2}\right)$
3. $7\sqrt{2}$ units
4. The graph is a parabola that opens downward; it has a maximum value.
5. The graph is a parabola that opens upward; it has a minimum value.
6. $x = -3$ and $x = 2$

Pre-Test Module 18

1. volume: 48 in^3; surface area: 92 in^2
2. volume: 75.4 m^3; surface area: 100.5 m^2
3. 64 ft^3
4. 42.7 in^3
5. 87.2 in^2
6. 5 ft
7. 240 in^3

Pre-Test Module 19

1. a triangle
2. a rectangle
3. 96 in^2
4. 182π in^2
5. 452.4 m^2
6.

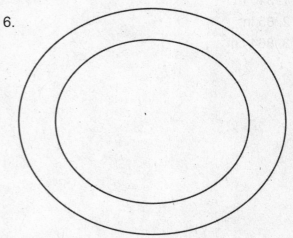

Pre-Test Module 20

1. 28 m^2
2. 16.5 ft
3. 288 in^3
4. 113.1 ft^3

5. 30 ft^3 of sand

6. 180.5 cm^2

7. 1 in. : 5 ft

8. 25.3 in.

9. 44.0 in.

Pre-Test Module 21

1. 0.429

2. 0.643

3. 0.238

4. No; the two events can occur at the same time. There are freshmen who preferred 2nd period study hall.

5. HH, TT, HT, TH

6. $\dfrac{2}{5}$

7. $\dfrac{7}{10}$

8. $\dfrac{3}{10}$

9. 20%

10. 80%

11. sample answer: a number less than 3 is rolled

Pre-Test Module 22

1. 340 m^2

2. 85 in^2

3. 864 cm^2

4. 0.55

5. 87.5%

6. 12.5%

7. No; the events can occur at the same time because there are full time employees working at location A.

8. 0.2

Pre-Test Module 23

1. $\dfrac{6}{13}$

2. 0.22

3. 0.36

4. 9

5. A False B False C True D True

6. 0.35

7. Spanish; the largest group is Spanish speakers, so the most likely outcome is that a randomly selected person speaks Spanish.

8. 24; since the probability that a person works full-time is $\dfrac{4}{5}$, and the group is randomly selected, then $\dfrac{4}{5} \times 30$, or 24 out of 30, people should work full-time, although it may not be exact because of randomness.

Answer Key

Post-Test: Skill 1

1. $D'(4, -1)$, $E'(5, 2)$, $F'(8, 0)$
2. 5 units left and 3 units up
3. $D'(3, 1)$
4. $\dfrac{1}{2}$
5. A True B False C False D True
6. $H(-5, 2)$, $I(-3, 2)$, $J(-3, 6)$, $K(-5, 5)$
7. 270° clockwise rotation or 90° counter clockwise rotation
8. point C'
9. $a = 2$, $b = -5$
10. A True B False C True D False

Post-Test: Skill 2

1. neither
2. $\angle 5$ and $\angle 6$
3. 30°
4. 60°
5. 90°
6. 104°
7. A False B True C False D True
8. 21
9. 35
10. 52°
11. 53°
12. A False B True C True D False

Post-Test: Skill 3

1. 70
2. 93°
3. 61°
4. 45
5. 45°, 45°, 90°
6. 122°
7. 70°
8. 40°, 60°, 80°
9. $\angle 1$ and $\angle 3$
10. $\angle 4$

11. 88°
12. $x = 40°$, $y = 36°$
13. A True B True C False D True

Post-Test: Skill 4

1. diameter
2. 4 in.
3. 49π in^2
4. A. 9 ft; B. 18 ft
5. 78.5 in^2
6. 200.96 ft^2
7. 50π cm^2
8. 1 mm
9. 197.82 mm^2
10. A. 12 cm; B. 113.04 cm^2
11. 4 ft

Post-Test: Skill 5

1. a rectangle and a triangle
2. 24 m
3. 96 m^2
4. 240 m^2
5. 336 m^2
6. 4 in.
7. 16 in^2
8. 64 in^2
9. 48 in^2
10. 2 ft
11. 6.28 ft^2
12. 5 ft
13. 20 ft^2
14. 26.28 ft^2

Post-Test: Skill 6

1. 31.4 cm
2. 50.2 in
3. 66 m
4. 220 yd
5. 20.6 ft
6. 3 in

7. 5.1 ft

8. No the circumference of a cake with a diameter of 8 inches is 24π inches. This cake is larger than a cake with a circumference of 24 inches. The diameter of a cake with a circumference of 24 inches has to be less than 8 inches, so the writing will not fit.

9. 122.5 mm

Post-Test: Skill 7

1. $\angle F \cong \angle U$, $\angle H \cong \angle T$, $\angle G \cong \angle V$

2. $\overline{FH} \cong \overline{UT}$, $\overline{HG} \cong \overline{TV}$, $\overline{GF} \cong \overline{VU}$

3. $\triangle FHG \cong \triangle UTV$

4. 86°

5. 25 in

6. A False B True C True D True

7. 4.5 m

8. $\angle Q$

9. side QR

10. 40°

11. 107°

12. 8 cm

13. 20 cm

Post-Test: Skill 8

1. triangular prism

2. ABC and EFD

3. ABC, EFD, $ABFE$, $BCDF$, $CDEA$

4. $\overline{AB}$, $\overline{BC}$, $\overline{CA}$, $\overline{EF}$, $\overline{FD}$, $\overline{DE}$, $\overline{AE}$, $\overline{BF}$, $\overline{CD}$

5. A, B, C, D, E, F

6. cylinder

7. angled slice

8. trapezoid

9. triangle

10. circle

11. pentagons and rectangles

12. pentagon

13. rectangle

14. triangular pyramid

15. A True B False C False D False

Post-Test: Skill 9

1. (−3, 5)

2. (−2, 1.5)

3. (−4.5, −4)

4. (6, 0)

5. (−2, 8)

6. (8, −0.5)

7. (−3, −6)

8. (−1.5, −4.5)

9. $\sqrt{104} \approx 10.2$ miles

10. $\sqrt{50} \approx 7.1$ miles

11. Answers will vary. Possible answers: (13, −6), (−7, −6), (3, 4), (3, −16)

Post-Test: Skill 10

1. one

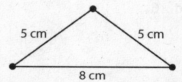

2. No. If 20 meters is the base side, then the sides measuring 7 meters and 10 meters are not long enough to intersect.

3. 80°

4. many

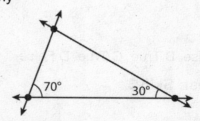

5. A Yes B No C Yes

6. A No B Yes C Yes

7. Possible answers: any segment greater than 23 cm or less than 7 cm will result in no triangle

8. Possible answers: 8 cm or 15 cm

9. Possible answers: any length between 7 cm and 23 cm inclusive

10. one

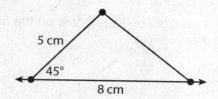

5 cm
45°
8 cm

Post-Test: Skill 11

1. choosing a "Lose a Turn" card
2. choosing a "Lose a Turn" card and not choosing a "Lose a Turn" card
3. 6 times
4. 260 cards
5. 24 phones
6. 2040 people
7. 18 times
8. 100 people
9. $\frac{3}{10}$
10. 288 people
11. 2 foul shots
12. 20 green mints, 50 pink mints, 80 yellow mints

Post-Test: Skill 12

1. corresponding angles
2. alternate interior angles
3. alternate exterior angles
4. same-side interior angles
5. corresponding angles
6. $x = 62$; corresponding angles are congruent; $y = 65$; supplementary angles have a sum of 180°
7. $y = 118$; supplementary angles have a sum of 180°
8. corresponding angles; ∠3 is not congruent to ∠7 because line c is not parallel to line d.
9. m∠4 = 108°
10. m∠3 = 72°
11. $x = 96$; $y = 60$

Post-Test: Skill 13

1. $\overline{AB} \cong \overline{CD}$ and $\overline{AD} \cong \overline{BC}$
2. ∠A ≅ ∠C and ∠B ≅ ∠D
3. ∠B and ∠C , ∠C and ∠D
4. $x = 31$
5. $y = 7$
6. m∠E = 129°, m∠F = 51°, m∠H = 129°
7. $RS = 4$ in, $UR = 9$ in
8. $x = 28$
9. m∠J = 124°, m∠K = 56°, m∠L = 124°, m∠M = 56°
10. $x = 4$, $y = 2$
11. $EC = 16$
12. $AC = 32$
13. $ED = 9$

Post-Test: Skill 14

1. $\frac{2}{8} = \frac{1}{4}$
2. $\frac{5}{8}$
3. $\frac{11}{26}$
4. Yes, it is not possible to get one prize that is both medium and large.
5. $\frac{29}{37}$
6. 70%
7. 68%
8. 63%
9. 31–50 year olds or over 50
10. A No B Yes C No

Post-Test: Skill 15

1. 15, 16, 17, 18, 19, 20
2. $\frac{3}{6} = \frac{1}{2}$
3. $\frac{2}{6} = \frac{1}{3}$

4. $\frac{2}{11}$

5. $\frac{4}{11}$

6. A $\frac{2}{30} = \frac{1}{15}$ B $\frac{8}{30} = \frac{4}{15}$ C $\frac{4}{30} = \frac{2}{15}$

   D $\frac{16}{30} = \frac{8}{15}$

7. $\frac{3}{30} = \frac{1}{10}$

8. $\frac{6}{30} = \frac{1}{5}$

9. $\frac{8}{100} = 0.08 = 8\%$

10. $\frac{3}{60} = \frac{1}{20} = 0.05 = 5\%$

11. Because the percent probability of getting a leaky pen was lower after the machine adjustment was made, the company's improvement worked.

12. A Yes B No

Post-Test: Skill 16

1. $\frac{A'B'}{AB} = \frac{17}{13}$, $\frac{B'C'}{BC} = \frac{8}{5}$, $\frac{C'A'}{CA} = \frac{15}{12} = \frac{5}{4}$

2. No; the ratios of the corresponding side lengths are not equal.

3. $k = 3$

4. Yes; $\frac{4}{6} = \frac{2}{3}$ and $\frac{6}{9} = \frac{2}{3}$, so the ratios of the corresponding side lengths are equal and the image is a dilation.

5. $A''(10, 15)$

6. Isosceles triangle

7. $F'(0, 6)$, $G'(6, -3)$, $H'(-6, -3)$

8. reduction

9. $P(4, 12)$, $Q(4, 20)$, $R(16, 32)$

10. A False B False C True D False

Post-Test: Skill 17

1. The image is itself since it is on the line of reflection.

2. 90°

3.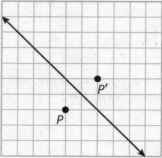

4.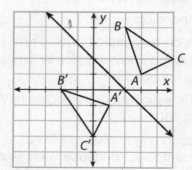

5. $A'(1, -1)$, $B'(1, -4)$, $C'(3, -1)$

6. $A'(-1, 1)$, $B'(-1, 4)$, $C'(-3, 1)$

7. $A'(1, 1)$, $B'(4, 1)$, $C'(1, 3)$

8. Three points: $(2, 0)$, $(0, 2)$, $\left(\frac{5}{2}, -\frac{1}{2}\right)$

Post-Test: Skill 18

1.

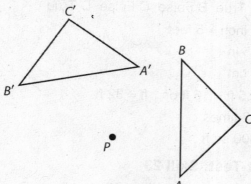

2. 130°

3. 5 units

4. (5, 3)

5.

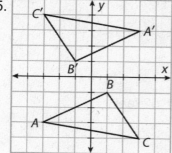

6. Sample answers: 360°, 720°, 1080°, and any other multiple of 360°

7. Quadrant III

8. Quadrant I

Post-Test: Skill 19

1. A translation is a shift or slide of a figure up or down, left or right.

2. A translation changes only the location of the figure. It does not change the size or shape.

3. Yes. Shift a figure diagonally by shifting right or left, then up or down.

4. $(x + 6, y + 3)$

5. $(x - 9, y - 2)$

6. translate 4 units right and 7 units down

7.

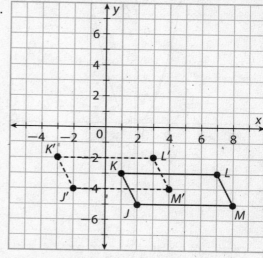

8. $D'(-3, 5)$; $E'(2, 5)$; $F'(2, 4)$

9.

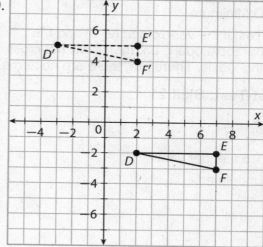

Post-Test: Skill 20

1. Answers will vary. Sample response: $y = x^2 + 4x + 5$.

2. Because $a = -1$ which is less than 0, the parabola opens down.

3. maximum

4. 12

5. (2, 12)

6. 0 and 4

7. $x = 2$

8. Answers will vary. Sample response:

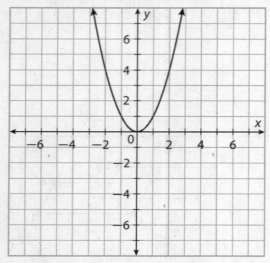

9. $x = 5$

10. A Minimum B Maximum C Maximum
    D Minimum

11. Yes, if the vertex is at (2, 3) and the
    parabola opens up, then it will not cross
    the x-axis. Therefore, there are no zeros.

Post-Test: Skill 21

1. $\frac{2}{4} = \frac{1}{2}$

2. 1.5 feet per year

3. undefined

4. $\frac{7}{3}$

5. $-\frac{2}{6} = -\frac{1}{3}$

6. 0

7. $\frac{5}{8}$

8. $\frac{4}{11}$

9. undefined

10. A True B False C False D True
    E True

Post-Test: Skill 22

1. 150 mi

2. 600 mi

3. 9 in

4. 1 inch = 10 feet

5. length: 12.6 in; width: 7.5 in

6. A True B False C False D True

7. 1 inch = 5 feet

8. 15 in

9. 6 cm

10. 0.5 ft = 16 ft or 1 ft = 32 ft

11. 32 times

12. 600 sq ft

Post-Test: Skill 23

1. Yes; the arcs indicate that $\angle J \cong \angle R$,
   $\angle K \cong \angle S$, $\angle L \cong \angle T$

2. $\frac{RS}{JK} = \frac{12}{15} = \frac{4}{5}$, $\frac{ST}{KL} = \frac{16}{20} = \frac{4}{5}$,
   $\frac{TR}{LJ} = \frac{20}{25} = \frac{4}{5}$

3. Yes; $\frac{4}{5}$

4. $QR = 5$

5. 20 feet, 48 feet, 52 feet

6. $\frac{3}{2}$

7. $x = 8$

8. $y = 18$

9. 24 inches

10. A True B True C False

Post-Test: Skill 24

1. 504 in^2

2. 88π ft^2

3. 144 in^2

4. 65 cm^2

5. 122 in^2

6. 64π ft^2

7. 305 in^2

Post-Test: Skill 25

1. $3\sqrt{10}$

2. 4

3. No; The triangle is not a right triangle and
   the Pythagorean Theorem only applies to
   right triangles.

4. No; $16^2 + 30^2 \neq 31^2$

5. 72.2 miles

6. Sample answer: 3, $\sqrt{13}$

7. $\sqrt{3}$

Post-Test: Skill 26

1. $-\dfrac{1}{2}$

2. 3

3. $y = 5x - \dfrac{1}{5}$

4. slope: -1; y-intercept: 4

5. A False B True C False D True

6. $y = -2x + 3$

7. slope: $\dfrac{2}{3}$; y-intercept: $\dfrac{1}{3}$

8. $y = \dfrac{3}{4}x + 2$

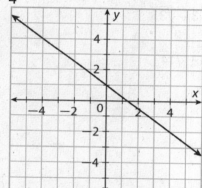

9. 15; the cost in dollars per ticket

10. 5; the cost for parking

Post-Test: Skill 27

1. 220 cm^3

2. 360 in^3

3. $w = 3$ m

4. $h = 22.5$ in

5. $V = 37.7$ ft^3

6. $h = 5.7$ cm

7. 37,500 cm^3

8. Cylinder A: 32π; Cylinder B: 64π;
   Cylinder B has a greater volume.

9. 36 cm

10. 77.7 ft^3

11. A True B False C True D False

Post-Test: Skill 28

1. A parallel B perpendicular C neither
   D perpendicular E parallel

2. $y = -4$

3. $y = 2x - 1$

4. $y = -\dfrac{1}{5}x - \dfrac{22}{5}$

5. $y = -x - 8$

6. $y = -3$

7. $x = 6$

8. $y = -3x - 3$

9. A False B True C True D False
   E True F False (sometimes they are the
   same line) G True

Post-Test: Skill 29

1. $\dfrac{BC}{DE} = \dfrac{AB}{DF}$, $\dfrac{EF}{CA} = \dfrac{DF}{BA}$

2. $\dfrac{MN}{PR} = \dfrac{QM}{QP}$, $\dfrac{QM}{MP} = \dfrac{QN}{NR}$

3. No; $\overline{MN}$ is not parallel to $\overline{AC}$, so the
   triangle proportionality theorem does not
   apply.

4. 40 feet

5. 12

6. 10

7. Sample answer: 4, 14, 16.

Post-Test: Skill 30

1. $z = -1$

2. $y = 7$

3. $n = -8$

4. $m = 0$

5. no solution

6. $x = 8$

7. $a = 3$

8. $k = 1$

9. $r = 9$

10. $f = -0.5$

11. $w = -0.25$

12. $b = -3$

13. $p = -0.2$

14. $g = -20$

Post-Test: Skill 31

1. (1, 0), (3, 0)
2. $x = 2$
3. (2, 1)
4. maximum
5. (0, –3)
6.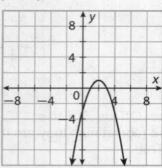
7. (–1, 0), (–7, 0)
8. $x = -4$
9. (–4, –9)
10. minimum
11. (0, 7)
12.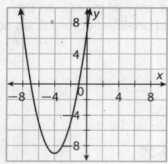

Post-Test: Skill 32

1. $x = -2$ and $x = 3$
2. $x = \pm 6$
3. $x = \pm 4$
4. $x = -3$ and $x = 6$
5. $x = -1$ and $x = \dfrac{3}{2}$
6. $x = -\dfrac{5}{2}$ and $x = \dfrac{4}{3}$
7. $x = \dfrac{1}{8}$ and $x = 2$
8. $x - 2$ and $x - 7$
9. $x^2 - 9x + 14 = 0$
10. 2 solutions
11. $x = \dfrac{1 \pm \sqrt{3}}{2}$
12. $x = \dfrac{-3 - \sqrt{33}}{2}$
13. $x = 3 \pm \sqrt{14}$

Answer Key

Reteach 1-1

1. $3\sqrt{2}$

2. $\sqrt{34}$

3. $\sqrt{17}$

4. $(4, 2)$

5. $\left(-\dfrac{9}{2}, -1\right)$ or $(-4.5, -1)$

6. $\left(\dfrac{1}{2}, 0\right)$ or $(0.5, 0)$

Reteach 1-2

1. $\angle ACB$; $\angle BCA$; $\angle C$; $\angle 4$

2. $\angle EDF$; $\angle FDE$; $\angle D$; $\angle 2$

3. straight

4. obtuse

5. acute

6. right

Reteach 1-3

1. rotation; rigid motion

2. dilation; not a rigid motion

3. reflection; rigid motion

4. translation; rigid motion

Reteach 1-4

1. Hypothesis: Angles are vertical.

   Conclusion: Angles are congruent.

2. Hypothesis: An angle measures 90°

   Conclusion: An angle is a right angle.

3. False. $\left(\dfrac{1}{2}\right)^2 = \dfrac{1}{4}$

Reteach 2-1

1. shift 3 units left and 1 unit up

2. shift 6 units right and 2 units down

3.

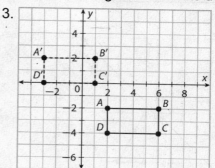

Reteach 2-2

1.

pre-image	image
(−4, 5)	(−4, −5)
(−2, −1)	(−2, 1)
(2, −2)	(2, 2)
(5, 5)	(5, −5)

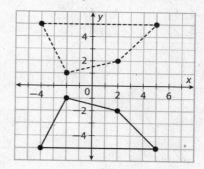

2.

pre-image	image
(1, 0)	(0, 1)
(3, −4)	(−4, 3)
(1, −4)	(−4, 1)

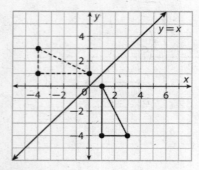

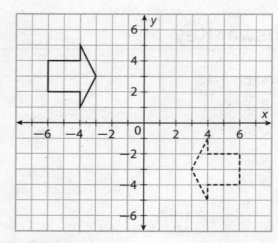

Reteach 2-3

1.

pre-image	image
(−6, 2)	(−2, −6)
(−6, 4)	(−4, −6)
(−4, 4)	(−4, −4)
(−4, 5)	(−5, −4)
(−3, 3)	(−3, −3)
(−4, 1)	(−1, −4)
(−4, 2)	(−2, −4)

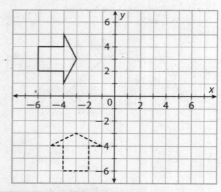

2.

pre-image	image
(−6, 2)	(6, −2)
(−6, 4)	(6, −4)
(−4, 4)	(4, −4)
(−4, 5)	(4, −5)
(−3, 3)	(3, −3)
(−4, 1)	(4, −1)
(−4, 2)	(4, −2)

Reteach 2-4

1.

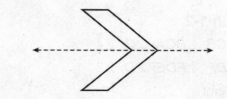

2.

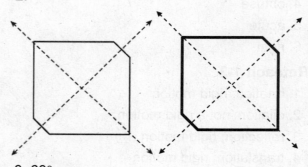

3. 60°

4. no rotational symmetry

Reteach 3-1

1.

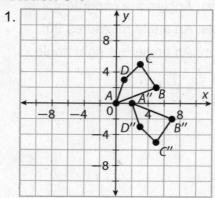

2.

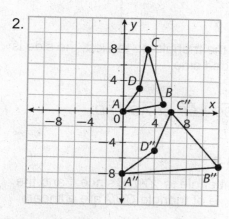

Reteach 3-2

1. not congruent

2. congruent (reflection across *y*-axis and translation 2 units up)

Reteach 3-3

1. $\overline{FG} \cong \overline{LM}$, $\overline{GH} \cong \overline{MN}$, and $\overline{HF} \cong \overline{NL}$

   $\angle F \cong \angle L$, $\angle G \cong \angle M$, and $\angle H \cong \angle N$

2. $\overline{ST} \cong \overline{WX}$, $\overline{TU} \cong \overline{XY}$, $\overline{UV} \cong \overline{YZ}$,

   and $\overline{VS} \cong \overline{ZW}$, $\angle S \cong \angle W$,

   $\angle T \cong \angle X$, $\angle U \cong \angle Y$, and $\angle V \cong \angle Z$

Reteach 4-1

1. 50°

2. 130°

3. 50°

4. $\angle BFC$ and $\angle DFC$

5. Answers may vary and may include any pair of angles that make up a linear pair or any pair of vertical right angles.

   Sample answers include:

   $\angle AFC$ and $\angle DFC$

   $\angle AFE$ and $\angle DFE$

6. 30°

Reteach 4-2

1. $\angle 2$ and $\angle 7$; $\angle 3$ and $\angle 6$

2. $\angle 2$ and $\angle 3$; $\angle 6$ and $\angle 7$

3. $\angle 1$ and $\angle 3$; $\angle 2$ and $\angle 4$;

   $\angle 5$ and $\angle 7$; $\angle 6$ and $\angle 8$

4. $\angle 5$ and $\angle 4$; $\angle 1$ and $\angle 8$

5. 65°

6. 80°

7. Any two of $\angle 7$, $\angle 2$, $\angle 5$

Reteach 4-3

1. No, because the corresponding angles that measure 75° and 68° are not congruent.

2. Yes, because the same side interior angles that measure 75° and 105° are supplementary.

3. 85°

4. 85°

Reteach 4-4

1. 90

2. 40

3. 30

4. 90°

5. 4 cm

Reteach 4-5

1. −5

2. $y = 5x - 12$

3. $\dfrac{3}{2}$

4. $y = 2x - 2$

Reteach 5-1

1. $\overline{PQ} \cong \overline{ST}$ and $\overline{PR} \cong \overline{SU}$

2. $\angle Q \cong \angle T$ and $\angle P \cong \angle S$

3. 20°

4. 4 cm

5. 60°

Reteach 5-2

1. $\angle C \cong \angle F$

2. $\overline{AB} \cong \overline{DE}$

3. $\angle 1 \cong \angle 2$; right

4. $\overline{JK}$; $\overline{LK}$

5. $\triangle JKM \cong \triangle LKM$; ASA

Reteach 5-3

1. 5 cm

2. 90°

Statements	Reasons
1. $\angle 1 \cong \angle 2$; $\overline{AB} \cong \overline{BC}$	1. Given
2. $\overline{DB} \cong \overline{DB}$	2. Reflexive Property of Equality
3. $\triangle ABD \cong \triangle CBD$	3. SAS

Reteach 5-4

1. 5 cm

2. 8 cm

Statements	Reasons
1. $\overline{RU} \cong \overline{TU}$; $\overline{US}$ bisects $\overline{RT}$	1. Given
2. $\overline{RS} \cong \overline{TS}$	2. Definition of bisect
3. $\overline{US} \cong \overline{US}$	3. Reflexive property of equality
4. $\triangle RSU \cong \triangle TSU$	4. SSS

Reteach 6-1

1. 6

2. 36°

3. 35°

4. 145°

5. 4 units

Reteach 6-2

1. No. For the triangle on the left, the side is an included side.

2. Yes.

3. Either $\overline{BC} \cong \overline{EF}$ or $\overline{AC} \cong \overline{FD}$.

4. $\angle B \cong \angle D$

Reteach 6-3

1. The right angle is $\angle ADB$ since it and the right angle of triangle CBD are a linear pair.

2. $\overline{BD} \cong \overline{BD}$ by the Reflexive Property of Equality

3. Yes, since one leg and the hypotenuses are congruent, they are congruent by HL.

4. 5

5. 5

6. No, because we only have one corresponding leg that is congruent.

Reteach 7-1

1. 100

2. 20

3. 30

4. 80

Reteach 7-2

1. 32

2. 15

3. 5

4. 9

Reteach 7-3

1. possible

2. not possible

3. possible

4. possible

5. Longest: $\overline{AB}$, Shortest: $\overline{BC}$

6. Longest: $\overline{BC}$, Shortest: $\overline{AB}$

7. Longest: $\overline{AC}$, Shortest: $\overline{AB}$

Reteach 8-1

1. 90°
2. 12
3. 12
4. 8
5. 10

Reteach 8-2

1. $\angle ZWY$
2. 9 cm
3. 50°
4. 15°
5. 20°
5. 3 cm

Reteach 8-3

1. 5 m
2. 8 ft.
3. 24 cm
4. Answers may vary. Any pair of right angles in the figure are correct.

Reteach 8-4

1. $\overline{QP}$
2. 8
3. 18
4. 4
5. 8

Reteach 9-1

1. $\angle HGF$
2. $\overline{GD}$
3. $\overline{EF}$
4. $\overline{EG}$
5. 16
6. 95°
7. 4
8. 10

Reteach 9-2

1. $\angle WXY; \angle ZYX$
2. $\overline{YZ}, \overline{YX}$

3. bisect each other
4. 12; GH
5. 100°; GFE

Reteach 9-3

1. $\overline{FH}$
2. 90°
3. $\overline{FG}$
4. 32
5. 90°
6. $\overline{TS}, \overline{SR}, \overline{QR}$

Reteach 9-4

1. *PQRS* is a rhombus, because consecutive sides are congruent.
2. *ABCD* is a rectangle because it contains a right angle.
3. *QRST* is a rhombus. Consecutive sides are congruent, and the diagonals are perpendicular.

Reteach 9-5

1. 90°
2. 9
3. $\angle D$ and $\angle C$
4. $\overline{SB}, \overline{XY}$, and $\overline{DC}$
5. 10

Reteach 10-1

1. $\overline{AB} \parallel \overline{DC}$ and $\overline{AD} \parallel \overline{BC}$
2. $A(-2, 1); B(1, 3); C(4, 1); D(1 -1)$
3. $\dfrac{2}{3}$
4. $-\dfrac{2}{3}$
5. $\dfrac{2}{3}$
6. $-\dfrac{2}{3}$
7. Yes, *ABCD* is a parallelogram. Since both pairs of opposite sides have the same slope, they are parallel. So, the quadrilateral is a parallelogram.

Reteach 10-2

1. $W(-2, -2)$; $X(4, 2)$; $Y(2, 5)$; $Z(-4, 1)$

2. $m\overline{WX} = \dfrac{2}{3}$

   $m\overline{XY} = -\dfrac{3}{2}$

   $m\overline{YZ} = \dfrac{2}{3}$

   $m\overline{ZW} = -\dfrac{3}{2}$

3. Each product is −1.

4. Yes. Since the product of the slopes of the consecutives sides is −1, the sides are perpendicular. Therefore, $WXYZ$ is a rectangle.

Reteach 10-3

1. $AB = \sqrt{8}$, $BC = \sqrt{26}$, and $CA = \sqrt{10}$

   $XY = \sqrt{8}$, $YZ = \sqrt{26}$, and $ZX = \sqrt{10}$

2. $\overline{AB} \cong \overline{XY}$, $\overline{BC} \cong \overline{YZ}$, $\overline{CA} \cong \overline{ZX}$

3. SSS

4. $\angle C \cong \angle Z$ by CPCTC

Reteach 10-4

1. $D(-2, 3)$, $E(3, 3)$, $F(3, -1)$, $G(-2, -1)$

2. $DF = \sqrt{41}$; $EG = \sqrt{41}$

3. Yes, because its diagonals are congruent.

Reteach 10-5

1. $4 + 2\sqrt{10}$ units

2. 6 square units

3. $4 + \sqrt{13} + \sqrt{5}$ units

4. 4 square units

Reteach 11-1

1. 80°

2. 15

3. 21

4. 3

5. No. The corresponding angles of the two triangles are not congruent.

Reteach 11-2

1. y-axis

2. 2 units down and 1 unit left

3. 2

4.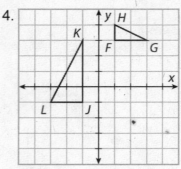

Reteach 11-3

1. $\angle F$

2. $\dfrac{AB}{EF} = \dfrac{DC}{HG} = \dfrac{CB}{GF} = \dfrac{AD}{EH}$

3. 70°

4. 12

5. 5

Reteach 11-4

1. $\overline{AB} \parallel \overline{DE}$

2. $\angle 2 \cong \angle 3$

3. $\angle 1 \cong \angle 4$

4. AA

5. 5

6. 12

Reteach 12-1

1. 6

2. 8

3. No, because $\dfrac{YZ}{ZV} \neq \dfrac{XW}{WV}$

Reteach 12-2

1. $(-4, -4)$

2. $(2, 5)$

3. 9

4. 6

5. $\dfrac{2}{3}, \dfrac{2}{3}$

6. 4, 6

7. (0, 2)

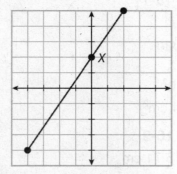

Reteach 12-3

1. $\overline{PT}$

2.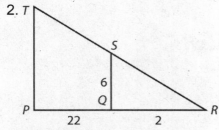

3. $\triangle QRS \sim \triangle PRT$

4. $\dfrac{PT}{QS} = \dfrac{PR}{QR}, \dfrac{PT}{6} = \dfrac{24}{2}$

5. 72 feet tall

Reteach 12-4

1. 10

2. 30

3. $\sqrt{96} = 4\sqrt{6} \approx 9.8$

4. $\sqrt{18} = 3\sqrt{2} \approx 4.2$

5. 3

6. $\sqrt{60} = 2\sqrt{15} \approx 7.7$

Reteach 13-1

1. $\dfrac{5}{12}$

2. $\dfrac{12}{5}$

3. $36.9°$

4. $29.1°$

Reteach 13-2

1. $\dfrac{4}{5}, \dfrac{3}{5}$

2. $\dfrac{3}{5}, \dfrac{4}{5}$

3. $\dfrac{15}{17}$

4. $28.1°$

5. $\dfrac{15}{17}$

6. $61.9°$

Reteach 13-3

1. 6

2. $6\sqrt{2}$

3. $45°$

4. 8

5. $4\sqrt{3}$

6. $\dfrac{1}{2}$

7. $\dfrac{\sqrt{3}}{2}$

8. $\dfrac{\sqrt{3}}{2}$

9. $\dfrac{1}{2}$

10. $\dfrac{\sqrt{3}}{3}$

11. $\sqrt{3}$

Reteach 13-4

1. $16.3°$

2. $73.7°$

3. 25

4. 57.8 cm^2

Reteach 14-1

1. $n \approx 8.5$, $p \approx 6.1$, $m\angle P = 41°$

2. $d \approx 11.5$, $m\angle D \approx 35.9°$, $m\angle F \approx 19.1°$

3. $g \approx 11.8$ in., $k = 13$ in., $m\angle K = 63°$

Reteach 14-2

1. $y \approx 7.5$, $m\angle X \approx 68°$, $m\angle Z \approx 31.7°$

2. $m\angle J \approx 36.9°$, $m\angle K \approx 106.2°$, $m\angle L \approx 36.9°$

3. $d \approx 5.5$ m, $m\angle E \approx 128.7°$, $m\angle F \approx 23.8°$

Reteach 15-1

1. $\angle SZT$
2. $\overline{PR}$ or $\overline{PQ}$
3. $\angle RPQ$
4. Answers will vary—some examples include $\overset{\frown}{DE}$, $\overset{\frown}{EA}$, and $\overset{\frown}{BC}$
5. $85°$
6. $\angle DEC$
7. $20°$

Reteach 15-2

1. SRQ
2. SPQ
3. $360°$
4. $180°$
5. $m\angle SRQ + m\angle SPQ = 180°$
6. $95°$
7. $85°$

Reteach 15-3

1. Y
2. $90°$
3. $\angle B$ or $\angle ABC$
4. $90°$
5. $135°$

Reteach 15-4

1. 4
2. 9
3. 16
4. 8

Reteach 15-5

1. $45°$
2. $20°$
3. $80°$
4. $184°$
5. $20°$
6. $80°$

Reteach 16-1

1. 37.68 in.
2. 37.68 cm
3. 31.40 ft.
4. 50.24 ft^2
5. 113.04 cm^2

Reteach 16-2

1. $5\pi \approx 15.71$ cm
2. $5\pi \approx 15.71$ cm
3. $\dfrac{5\pi}{4} \approx 3.93$ ft.
4. $\dfrac{\pi}{2}$ rad
5. $\dfrac{2\pi}{3}$ rad
6. $\dfrac{13\pi}{36}$ rad
7. $60°$
8. $135°$
9. $180°$

Reteach 16-3

1. $\dfrac{1}{12}$
2. $25\pi \approx 78.54$ cm^2
3. $\dfrac{1}{12} \times \pi \times 5^2$; 6.54 cm^2
4. $16\pi \approx 50.27$ cm^2
5. $18\pi \approx 56.55$ in^2
6. $50\pi \approx 157.08$ ft^2

Reteach 17-1

1. $(x-2)^2 + (y+2)^2 = 36$
2. $x^2 + y^2 = 100$
3. $(x+4)^2 + (y+2)^2 = 5$
4. $(x-2)^2 + (y-3)^2 = 5$
5. $(x+3)^2 + (y-4)^2 = 16$

Reteach 17-2

1. $x^2 = 16y$; $y = \frac{1}{16}x^2$

2. $x^2 = -4y$; $y = -\frac{1}{4}x^2$

3. $(x - 3)^2 = -4(y - 1)$

Reteach 18-1

1. 240 in^3
2. 288 ft^3
3. 625 cm^3
4. 2010.62 cm^3
5. 27 ft^3

Reteach 18-2

1. 80 in^3
2. 128 in^3
3. 41.67 m^3
4. two pyramids and a rectangular prism
5. $V_{prism} = 8$ m^3; $V_{pyramids} \approx 26.67$ m^3.
6. V = 61.34 m^3

Reteach 18-3

1. 113.10 ft^3
2. 10,857.34 cm^3
3. 5,428,672.10 mm^3
4. cylinder; cone
5. 804.25 cm^3
6. 1072.33 cm^3
7. 1876.58 cm^3

Reteach 18-4

1. 904.78 cm^3
2. 2144.66 ft^3
3. 523.60 in^3
4. cone; sphere
5. 33.51 in^3
6. 16.76 in^3
7. 50.27 in^3

Reteach 19-1

1. cylinder
2. pyramid

3. rectangle

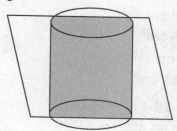

4. triangle

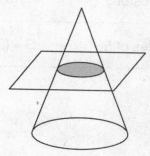

5. circle

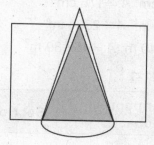

Reteach 19-2

1. 54 cm^2
2. 108 cm^2
3. 252 in^2
4. 502.65 in^2
5. 942.48 cm^2
6. 150.80 ft^2

Reteach 19-3

1. 48 ft^2
2. 252 cm^2
3. 400 ft^2
4. 301.59 ft^2
5. 763.41 m^2
6. 703.72 in^2

Reteach 19-4

1. 804.25 in^2
2. 1809.56 cm^2
3. 1256.64 ft^2

4. Two hemispheres and a cylinder
5. 508.94 cm^2
6. 904.78 cm^2
7. 508.94 cm^2
8. 1922.66 cm^2

Reteach 20-1
1. $P = 72$ ft. $A = 216$ ft^2
2. $P = 64$ cm $A = 176$ cm^2
3. $P = 192$ in. $A = 2304$ in^2
4. $C = 75.40$ m $A \doteq 452.39$ m^2

Reteach 21-1
1.

Description of Subset	Set Notation	Number of Elements in Subset	Number of Elements in Universal Set
Multiples of 3	$A = \{3, 9, 15\}$	$n(A) = 3$	$n(U) = 7$
Multiples of 5	$B = \{5, 15\}$	$n(B) = 2$	$n(U) = 7$

2. $\dfrac{3}{7}$

3. $\dfrac{2}{7}$

4.
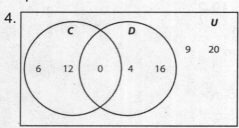

Reteach 21-2
1. a–d. $\boxed{8}$ $\boxed{7}$ $\boxed{6}$ $\boxed{5}$

   e. $8 \cdot 7 \cdot 6 \cdot 5 = 1680$
2. a. 120

   b. $\dfrac{1}{14}$

Reteach 21-3
1. permutation
2. combination

5. $C = 628.32$ ft $A = 31{,}415.93$ ft^2
6. $C = 3926.99$ cm $A = 1{,}227{,}184.63$ cm^2

Reteach 20-2
1. 750 square feet
2. 15 people
3. 0.02 people per square foot

Reteach 20-3
1. 4 feet
2. 2 feet
3. 4 feet

3. a. 990

   b. 6

   c. $\dfrac{990}{6} = 165$

4. a. $\dfrac{60}{6} = 10$

   b. $\dfrac{2}{33}$

Reteach 21-4
1. overlapping
2. mutually exclusive
3. mutually exclusive
4. overlapping
5. $\dfrac{1}{2}$

6. $\dfrac{2}{3}$

7. $\dfrac{4}{13}$

Reteach 22-1

1. a. 55
   b. 35
   c. about 64%
2. a. 45
   b. 25
   c. about 56%

Reteach 22-2

1. a. $\dfrac{2}{3}$

   b. $\dfrac{2}{3}$

   c. yes

2. a. $\dfrac{2}{3}$

   b. $\dfrac{4}{5}$

   c. $\dfrac{8}{15}$

   d. yes

3. $\dfrac{1}{5}$

Reteach 22-3

1. independent
2. dependent
3. a. $\dfrac{4}{52}$ or $\dfrac{1}{13}$

   b. $\dfrac{3}{51}$ or $\dfrac{1}{17}$

   c. $\dfrac{1}{221}$

Reteach 23-1

1. true
2. Sample answer: Each player's section is the same size, which means each section has the same probability of the spinner landing on it.
3. false
4. Each player's section is not the same size. Each section does not have the same probability of the spinner landing on it.
5.

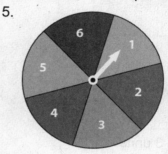

Reteach 23-2

1. about 113 P(Positive) = 2% × 87% + 98% × 9.8% = 11.3%. That means that out of 1000 people, roughly 113 people would test positive for Perform X.

2. about 17 P(PerformX|Positive) = 15.3%. That means the answer would be 113 × 15.3% = 17.3 or roughly 17 people. If the question was "how many people tested positive for Perform X?" then it would be 1000 × 2% = 20 but this is a conditional probability problem based on the condition that they already tested positive.

Answer Key

Skill 1: Algebraic Relationships of Transformations

1. $D'(4, 3)$, $E'(5, 6)$, $F'(8, 4)$

2.
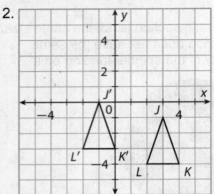

3. right 5 units, up 3 units

4. $L'(-1, -3)$, $M'(2, -5)$, and $N'(2, -2)$

5. $E'(4, 2)$, $F'(1, 1)$, $G'(1, -2)$, $H'(3, -3)$

6. y-axis

7. x-axis

8. $Q'(5, -1)$, $R'(1, -1)$, $S'(1, -3)$, $T'(5, -3)$;
   $Q''(5, 1)$, $R''(1, 1)$, $S''(1, 3)$, $T''(5, 3)$;

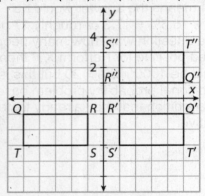

9. $A'(1, 3)$, $B'(-2, 1)$, $C'(-4, 1)$, $D'(-4, 5)$, $E'(-2, 5)$

10. $A'(3, -1)$, $B'(1, 2)$, $C'(1, 4)$, $D'(5, 4)$, $E'(5, 2)$

11. $A'(-1, 3)$, $B'(2, 1)$, $C'(4, 1)$, $D'(4, 5)$, $E'(2, 5)$

12. $X(-4, -1)$, $Y(-6, -5)$, $Z(-1, -2)$

13.
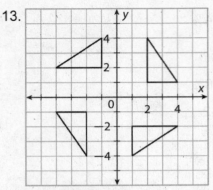

14. Triangle XYZ has coordinates $X(1, 6)$, $Y(5, 6)$, $Z(5, 2)$ and its image has coordinates $X'(1, 3)$, $Y'(3, 3)$, $Z'(3, 1)$. The coordinates of the image are not multiplied by the scale factor $\frac{1}{2}$. Triangle $X'Y'Z'$ is the image of a triangle with vertices $X(2, 6)$, $Y(6, 6)$, $Z(6, 2)$ that has been dilated by a scale factor of $\frac{1}{2}$.

15. $\frac{2}{3}$

Skill 2: Angle Relationships

1. Sample answer: $\angle 1$ and $\angle 3$ or $\angle 2$ and $\angle 4$

2. Sample answer: $\angle 1$ and $\angle 2$, $\angle 2$ and $\angle 3$, $\angle 3$ and $\angle 4$, or $\angle 4$ and $\angle 1$

3. $80°$

4. $100°$

5. neither

6. supplementary

7. complementary

8. $130°$

9. $52°$

10. Sample answer: The sum of the angles is $90° + 90° = 180°$, so the angles are supplementary.

11. $m\angle 1 = 18°$; Sample answer: $\angle 1$ and $\angle 6$ are complementary.

12. $m\angle 2 = 90°$; Sample answer: $\angle 2$ is a right angle.

13. $m\angle 3 = 72°$; Sample answer: $\angle 3$ and $\angle 6$ are vertical angles.

14. m∠4 = 18°; Sample answer: ∠1 and ∠4 are vertical angles.

15. m∠5 = 90°; Sample answer: ∠2 and ∠5 are vertical angles.

16. $40 + x + 25 = 180$; m∠BCD = 115°

17. 15°

18. 90°

19. m∠S = 40°, m∠T = 50°

Skill 3: Angle Theorems for Triangles

1. $x = 40$
2. $x = 50$
3. $x = 82$
4. $x = 65$
5. 62°
6. 64°
7. 50°, 50°
8. 35°, 35°
9. 32°, 56°
10. 50°, 60°, 70°
11. 42°, 48°
12. $x = 15$
13. 36°, 54°, 90°
14. ∠1 and ∠2
15. ∠2 and ∠3
16. ∠1 and ∠3
17. $x = 25$
18. $x = 63$
19. $x = 98$
20. $x = 64$

21. These are the measures of the two remote interior angles and the exterior angle. The measures of the interior angles of the triangle are 20°, 70°, and 90°.

22. 24°, 36°, 120°

23. $x = 58$; The measure of the exterior angle is 100° and its two remote interior angles measure $x°$ and 42°, so $x + 42 = 100$.

24. 43°

25. $x = 38$, $y = 72$; In the first triangle, $x + 60 + 82 = 180$, so $x = 38$. Use the value for x in the second triangle, $38 + 70 + y = 180$, so $y = 72$.

Skill 4: Area of a Circle

1. 8 cm; 4 cm
2. 10 m; 5 m
3. 11 ft; 5.5 ft
4. $\dfrac{x}{2}$
5. $A = \pi(12)^2 = 144\pi$ m²
6. $A = \pi(2)^2 = 4\pi$ cm²
7. $A = \pi(3.5)^2 = 12.25\pi$ ft².

8. To calculate half of a circle, I can use half of the circle area formula. The area of a half-circle is $A = \dfrac{1}{2}\pi r^2$.

9. The diameter was used instead of the radius. The area of the circle is $A = \pi(2.5)^2 = 6.25\pi$ in.².

10. The diameter is 12 m so the radius is 6 m. $A = \pi(6)^2 = 36\pi \approx 36(3.14) = 113.04$ m².

11. The radius is 3 m. $A = \pi(3)^2 = 9\pi \approx 9(3.14) = 28.26$ cm².

12. A. Because the line is horizontal and the difference of the x-coordinates is $6 - (-2) = 8$ units.

    B. 4

    C. $A = \pi(4)^2 = 16\pi$

    D. 50.24 units²

13. A. $\pi(8)^2 = 64\pi$ ft²

    B. $\pi(6)^2 = 36\pi$ ft²

    C. 64π ft² $- 36\pi$ ft² $= 28\pi$ ft²

    D. about 87.92 ft²

14. The student forgot that when calculating the area of a circle, the radius is squared. To calculate the difference, you must square the radius first and then determine the difference.

Skill 5: Area of Composite Figures

1. rectangle and triangle

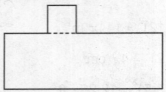

2. Two rectangles

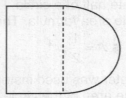

3. rectangle and half circle

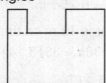

4. three rectangles

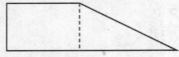

5. rectangle length = 7 cm; rectangle width = 2 cm; rectangle area = 14 cm; triangle base = 4 cm; triangle height = 3 cm; triangle area = 6 cm; Total area = 14 cm + 6 cm = 20 cm^2.

6. triangle base = 4 cm; triangle height = 4 cm; triangle area = 8 cm^2; circle radius = 2 cm; half circle area ≈ 6.3 cm^2; total area = 8 cm^2 + 6.3 cm^2 = 14.3 cm^2

7. The area of the rectangle is 6 × 4 = 24 m^2. The area of the triangle is $\frac{1}{2}$ × 8 × 4 = 16 m^2.

8. The area of the small rectangle is 4 × 5 = 20 cm^2. The area of the medium rectangle is 8 × 5 = 40 cm^2. The area of the large rectangle is 20 × 11 = 220 cm^2. The total area is 20 + 40 + 220 = 280 cm^2.

9. The circular part shown is only a half circle. So, the diameter of the circle is 8 m and the radius is 4 m. Therefore, the area of the half-circle is

$\frac{1}{2}\pi(4)^2 = 8\pi \approx 25.1\,\text{m}^2$. The total area is 40 m^2 + 25.1 m^2 = 65.1 m^2.

10. Sample answer: I will subtract the area of the square from the area of the circle. The area of the circle is

$\pi(4)^2 = 16\pi \approx 50.3\,\text{ft}^2$. The area of the square is 5 × 5 = 25 ft^2. The shaded area is 50.3 ft^2 − 25 ft^2 = 25.3 ft^2.

11. Sample answer: I will subtract the area of the small triangle from the area of the large triangle. The area of the large triangle is $\frac{1}{2}$ × 12 × 12 = 72 cm^2. The area of the small triangle is $\frac{1}{2}$ × 6 × 6 = 18 cm^2. The shaded area is 72 cm^2 − 18 cm^2 = 54 cm^2.

12. Sample answer: I will subtract the area of the circle from the area of the square. The area of the circle is $\pi(3)^2 = 9\pi \approx 28.3\,\text{ft}^2$. The area of the square is 6 × 6 = 36 ft^2. The shaded area is 36 − 28.3 = 7.7 ft^2.

13. The grid shows the diameter of the circle is 10 units so the radius is 5 units. The base of the triangle is also 10 units and the height is 5 units. Therefore, the shaded area is

$\pi(5)^2 - \frac{1}{2}(10)(5) = 25\pi - 25 \approx$ 78.5 − 25 = 53.5 units^2

14. Yes; The length of the figure is 15 and there are 3 circles end to end. Therefore, the diameter of each circle must be 15 divided by 3 or 5 m. Note that the width of the rectangle is the same as the diameter, which is 5 meters. The area of the rectangle is 15 × 5 = 75 m^2. The area of each circle is $\pi(2.5)^2$ so the area of three circles is $3\pi(2.5)^2$. Subtract the area of the three circles from the area of the rectangle to get the shaded area.

15. A 30 ft; B 706.9 ft^2; C 20 ft; D 314.2 ft^2; E 392.7 ft^2

16. Answers will vary: Method 1 divides the shape into two trapezoids. The area of one can be calculated and then doubled to determine the total area. Method 2 divides the shape into a triangle and a rectangle. The area of these shapes might be simpler to calculate.

Skill 6: Circumference

1. 94.2 cm
2. 62.8 in.
3. 25.1 ft
4. 56.5 yd
5. 37.7 m
6. 34.5 mm
7. 40.8 ft
8. 50.2 in.
9. 176 yd
10. 132 cm
11. 220 in.
12. 44 in.
13. 154 in, 153.9 in, 153.9 in
14. 4.8 yd
15. 1.3 ft
16. 5.7 in.
17. 263.8 mm
18. 21.4 ft
19. 13.1 cm
20. 2.5 ft
21. 1.5 in.
22. The value for circumference is 100π, not 100, so $r = \dfrac{100\pi}{2\pi}$ or 50 cm
23. 1,256 yd
24. 205.6 m
25. 69.1 in.
26. 26.5 in.

Skill 7: Congruent Figures

1. $\angle G \cong \angle K$, $\angle H \cong \angle L$, $\angle I \cong \angle J$; $\overline{GH} \cong \overline{KL}$, $\overline{HI} \cong \overline{LJ}$, $\overline{IG} \cong \overline{JK}$; $\triangle GHI \cong \triangle KLJ$
2. $\angle T \cong \angle Y$, $\angle U \cong \angle X$, $\angle V \cong \angle W$; $\overline{TU} \cong \overline{YX}$, $\overline{UV} \cong \overline{XW}$, $\overline{VT} \cong \overline{WY}$; $\triangle TUV \cong \triangle YXW$
3. Corresponding parts are not listed in the correct order. The congruence statement should be $\triangle JKL \cong \triangle MNL$.
4. $\angle C \cong \angle Q$, $\angle D \cong \angle R$, $\angle E \cong \angle S$; $\overline{CD} \cong \overline{QR}$, $\overline{DE} \cong \overline{RS}$, $\overline{EC} \cong \overline{SQ}$; $\triangle EDC \cong \triangle SRQ$

5. $\angle B \cong \angle M$, $\angle A \cong \angle N$, $\angle C \cong \angle P$; $\overline{BA} \cong \overline{MN}$, $\overline{AC} \cong \overline{NP}$, $\overline{CB} \cong \overline{PM}$; $\triangle ABC \cong \triangle NMP$
6. $\angle U \cong \angle F$, $\angle V \cong \angle G$, $\angle T \cong \angle H$; $\overline{UV} \cong \overline{FG}$, $\overline{VT} \cong \overline{GH}$, $\overline{TU} \cong \overline{HF}$; $\triangle UTV \cong \triangle FHG$
7. $\angle K \cong \angle W$, $\angle I \cong \angle Z$, $\angle J \cong \angle X$; $\overline{KI} \cong \overline{WZ}$, $\overline{IJ} \cong \overline{ZX}$, $\overline{JK} \cong \overline{XW}$; $\triangle IJK \cong \triangle ZXW$
8. not congruent
9. trapezoid $ZWXY \cong KLMN$
10. $\triangle CDE \cong \triangle FHG$
11. $\triangle PQR \cong \triangle STU$
12. $x = 32$ mm, $y = 60°$
13. a. 48°; b. 20 in
14. a. 110°; b. 108 cm
15.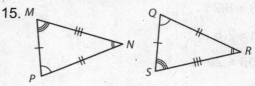

Skill 8: Cross Sections

1. rectangular prism; bases: PQRS and VWTU or SRTU and PQWV or PSUV and QRTW; faces: PQRS, VWTU, SRTU, PQWV, PSUV, QRTW; edges: $\overline{PQ}$, $\overline{QW}$, $\overline{WV}$, $\overline{VP}$, $\overline{SR}$, $\overline{RT}$, $\overline{TU}$, $\overline{US}$, $\overline{QR}$, $\overline{PS}$, $\overline{VU}$, $\overline{WT}$; vertices: P, Q, R, S, T, U, V, W
2. square pyramid; base: MNKL; faces: JKL, JLM, JNM, JKN, MNKL; edges: $\overline{JK}$, $\overline{JL}$, $\overline{JM}$, $\overline{JN}$, $\overline{KL}$, $\overline{LM}$, $\overline{MN}$, $\overline{NK}$; vertices: J, K, L, M, N
3. cone; base: circle H; face: circle H; edges: none; vertex: G
4. cylinder; bases: circle Y and circle Z; faces: circle Y and circle Z; edges: none; vertices: none
5. 2 pentagons and 5 rectangles
6. a. Figure B
   b. Figure A and Figure C
   c. Figure A
   d. Figure B and Figure C
7. rectangle
8. circle

9. triangle

10. rectangle

11. rectangle

12. triangle

13. The angled cross section of a cube always results in a rectangle. The horizontal and vertical cross sections of a cube always result in a square.

Skill 9: Distance and Midpoint Formula

1. (2, 0)

2. (−3.5, −0.5)

3. (−5, 4)

4. (1, 7.5)

5. (0, −4)

6. $\sqrt{37} \approx 6.1$

7. $\sqrt{68} \approx 8.2$

8. $\sqrt{61} \approx 7.8$

9. $\sqrt{405} \approx 20.1$

10. 13

11. $\sqrt{314} \approx 17.7$

12. The student found the difference of the x- and y-values instead of just the x-values and then just the y-values.

$$d = \sqrt{(3-(-5))^2 + (-8-1)^2}$$
$$d = \sqrt{8^2 + (-9)^2}$$
$$d = \sqrt{64+81}$$
$$d = \sqrt{145}$$
$$d \approx 12.0$$

13. A 5 units B $\sqrt{20} \approx 4.5$ units C 5 units
    D isosceles

14. $\sqrt{101} \approx 10.0$

15. (10)(5) = 50 miles

Skill 10: Geometric Drawings

1. many triangles

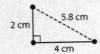

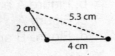

2. one triangle

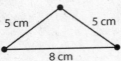

3. many

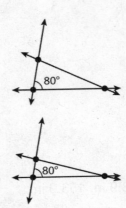

4. many

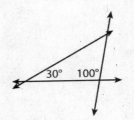

5. one triangle

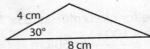

6. one triangle

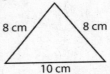

7. The student forgot to check that the sum of the interior angles is 180°. The correct solution is that there is no way to draw a triangle with angle measures of 20°, 40°, 60° because they do not sum to 180°. Therefore, no triangle exists.

8. A. Answers will vary. Sample answer: Triangles can be drawn with 4 cm, 4 cm and 5 cm.

   B. Answers will vary. Sample answer: A triangle can have side lengths 4 cm, 5 cm, and 8 cm.

9. This statement is not true because a triangle cannot be drawn with side lengths 4 cm, 4 cm, and 12 cm because the two shorter sides will not reach.

Skill 11: Making Predictions with Probability

1. 450 people

2. 840 people

3. 36 students

4. $\dfrac{1}{15}$

5. about 14 shots

6. 112 people

7. $\dfrac{1}{50}$ or 2%

8. 20 toothbrushes

9. 10 times

10. about 3 apricots

11. There were predicted to be 16 monkeys that were given away, so there should be about 9 monkeys left in the box.

12. 150 more birthday cards; $\dfrac{30}{60}$ or 50% of the cards should be birthday cards and $\dfrac{12}{60}$ or 20% of the cards should be thank you cards.
$0.5(500) - 0.2(500) = 250 - 100$ or 150 cards

Skill 12: Parallel Lines Cut by a Transversal

1. corresponding

2. alternate exterior

3. alternate interior

4. same-side interior

5. corresponding

6. $m\angle 3 = 82°$; $\angle 1$ and $\angle 3$ are corresponding angles.

7. $m\angle 4 = 98°$; $\angle 2$ and $\angle 4$ are corresponding angles.

8. $m\angle 5 = 82°$; $\angle 1$ and $\angle 5$ are alternate exterior angles.

9. $m\angle 6 = 98°$; $\angle 2$ and $\angle 6$ are alternate interior angles.

10. Lines v and w are not parallel, so corresponding angles are not congruent.

11. $m\angle 2 = 68°$

12. $m\angle 3 = 68°$

13. $m\angle 4 = 112°$

14. $m\angle 5 = 112°$

15. $m\angle 6 = 68°$

16. $m\angle 7 = 68°$

17. $m\angle 8 = 112°$

18. $m\angle 9 = 78°$

19. $m\angle 10 = 102°$

20. $m\angle 11 = 102°$

21. $m\angle 12 = 78°$

22. $m\angle 13 = 78°$

23. $m\angle 14 = 102°$

24. $m\angle 15 = 102°$

25. $x = 115$; corresponding angles are congruent; $y = 65$; supplementary angles have a sum of $180°$

26. Yes; line s is a transversal and $\overline{CD} \parallel \overline{EF}$. $\angle ACD$ and $\angle AEF$ are corresponding angles, so the angles are congruent.

27. No; the angles are not formed by the same transversal, so you cannot determine whether the angles are congruent.

28. $116°, 64°, 116°, 64°$

Skill 13: Parallelograms

1. $x = 3$

2. $x = 11$

3. 28 meters

4. Opposite sides should be congruent. Since $\overline{DE} \parallel \overline{FG}$ and $\overline{EF} \parallel \overline{DG}$, $\overline{DE}$ and $\overline{FG}$ are opposite sides, and $\overline{EF}$ and $\overline{DG}$ are opposite sides. So, $DE = FG = 11$ ft and $DG = EF = 14$ ft.

5. 14 in

6. $123°$

7. $57°$

8. 24 cm

9. 20 cm

10. $x = 26$

11. $x = 30$

12. $x = 22$, $y = 10$

13. $x = 24$

14. $y = 5$

15. $\angle S$ and $\angle T$, $\angle S$ and $\angle V$

16. $\angle T$ and $\angle S$, $\angle T$ and $\angle U$

17. $\angle U$ and $\angle T$, $\angle U$ and $\angle V$

18. $\angle V$ and $\angle U$, $\angle V$ and $\angle S$

19. $123°$

20. $m\angle P = 52°$, $m\angle Q = 128°$, $m\angle S = 128°$

21. $m\angle E = 107°$, $m\angle F = 73°$, $m\angle H = 73°$

22. $x = 54$, $m\angle K = 126°$, $m\angle L = 54°$, $m\angle M = 126°$, $m\angle N = 54°$

23. $x = 1$, $y = 8$

24. $GI = 34$; $HJ = 40$

25. $x = 7$, $y = 4$

26. $GD = 10$

27. $CE = 28$

Skill 14: Probability of Compound Events

1. $\dfrac{14}{18} = \dfrac{7}{9}$

2. $\dfrac{15}{27} = \dfrac{5}{9}$

3. $\dfrac{12}{20} = \dfrac{3}{5}$

4. $\dfrac{5}{6}$

5. 85%

6. The student did not subtract the probability of a number being even and less than 6. The solution is, P(even or less than 6) $= \dfrac{5}{10} + \dfrac{5}{10} - \dfrac{2}{10} = \dfrac{8}{10} = \dfrac{4}{5}$.

7.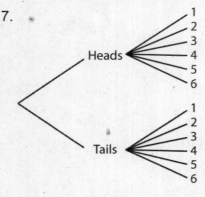

8. $\dfrac{7}{12}$

9. $\dfrac{9}{12} = \dfrac{3}{4}$

10. $\dfrac{56}{100} = 56\%$

11. $\dfrac{60}{100} = 60\%$

12. $\dfrac{69}{100} = 69\%$

13. The mutually exclusive event is the probability of the student being from 11th or 12th grade because a student cannot be in both grades at the same time.

Skill 15: Probability of Simple Events

1. Possible event: H; Sample Space: H, T

2. Possible event: HH; Sample Space: HH, HT, TH, TT

3. Possible event: C; Sample Space: A, B, C, D, E

4. Possible event: 2; Sample Space: 1, 2, 3, 4

5. $\dfrac{15}{35} = \dfrac{3}{7}$

6. $\dfrac{5}{10} = \dfrac{1}{2}$

7. $\dfrac{3}{12} = \dfrac{1}{4}$

8. The student forgot to include all the events in the sample space. P(yellow) $= \dfrac{20}{50} = \dfrac{2}{5}$

9. $\dfrac{5}{200} = \dfrac{1}{40} = 0.025 = 2.5\%$

10. $\dfrac{1}{4} = 0.25 = 25\%$

11. $\dfrac{1}{6}$

12. P(rose) $= \dfrac{9}{20}$; P(tulip) $= \dfrac{5}{20}$; P(carnation) $= \dfrac{3}{20}$; P(lily) $= \dfrac{3}{20}$

13. $P(\text{crash}) = \dfrac{3}{30} = \dfrac{1}{10} = 0.1 = 10\%$

14. $P(\text{not crashing}) = \dfrac{27}{30} = \dfrac{9}{10} = 0.9 = 90\%$

15. They both add to 1 because the software will either crash or not crash.

Skill 16: Properties of Dilations

1. $\dfrac{D'E'}{DE} = \dfrac{10}{15} = \dfrac{2}{3}$, $\dfrac{E'F'}{EF} = \dfrac{6}{9} = \dfrac{2}{3}$, $\dfrac{F'D'}{FD} = \dfrac{8}{12} = \dfrac{2}{3}$

2. $\dfrac{2}{3}$

3. Dilation; $\dfrac{1}{2}$

4. Not a dilation.

5. The ratios of corresponding sides are not equal since $\dfrac{Q'R'}{QR} = \dfrac{12}{4} = 3$ and $\dfrac{R'S'}{RS} = \dfrac{8}{6} = \dfrac{4}{3}$. $Q'R'S'T'$ is not a dilation of rectangle $QRST$.

6. No; $\dfrac{2}{4} \neq \dfrac{5}{8}$

7. Yes; the ratios of corresponding sides are equal. The scale factor is $\dfrac{15}{4}$ or $3\dfrac{3}{4}$.

8. $A'(0, 5)$, $B'(10, 0)$, $C'(10, -10)$, $D'(-10, -10)$, $E'(-10, 0)$

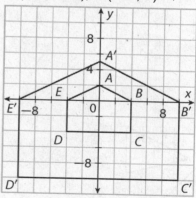

9.

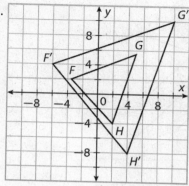

10.

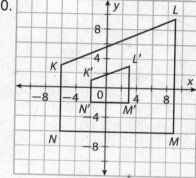

11. A. $P'(12, 4)$, $Q'(0, -8)$, $R'(-8, 16)$
    B. Enlargement

12. $\dfrac{1}{4}$

13. $W(-15, 10)$, $X(5, 10)$, $Y(5, -25)$, $Z(-10, -15)$

14. $A''(4, 8)$

Skill 17: Properties of Reflections

1.

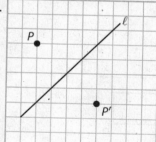

2.

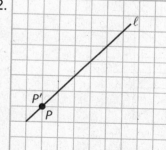

3.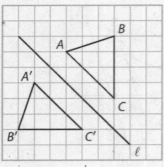

4.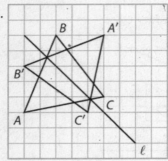

5. 4 units

6. 2.5 units

7.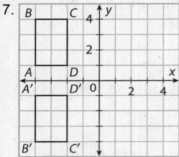

8.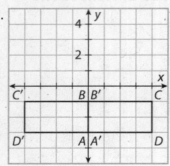

9.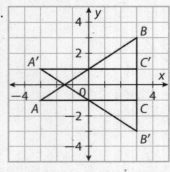

10.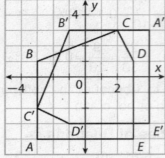

11.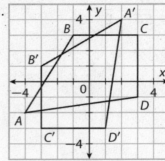

12.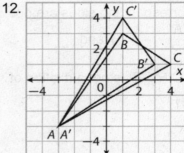

13. $A'(-1, -1)$, $B'(0, -1)$, $C'(-1, 4)$

14. The image of the point B is incorrect. If the figure is reflected across this line, then the coordinates of B' should be $(3, 2)$

15. $\left(-\dfrac{1}{2}, \dfrac{13}{2}\right)$

16. $\left(5, \dfrac{5}{2}\right)$

17. $(-2, 1)$

18.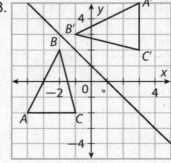

19.

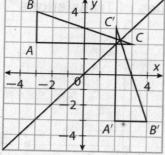

20.

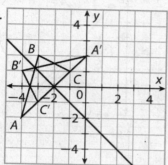

21. The correct answer will include two of the following three points.

$$\left(-\frac{3}{2}, -\frac{3}{2}\right), \ (0, 0), \text{ or } (1,1)$$

22. Line m must connect the midpoints of $\overline{AB}$ and $\overline{CD}$.

Skill 18: Properties of Rotations

1.

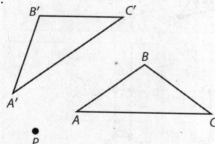

2.

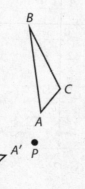

3.

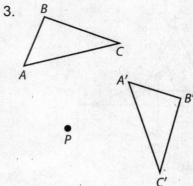

4.

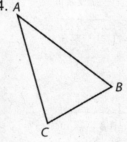

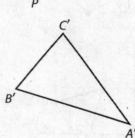

5. 195°

6. 100°

7. 160°

8.

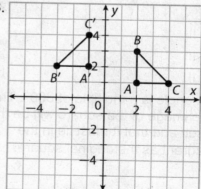

9.

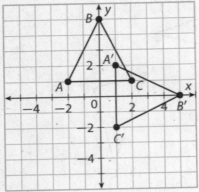

10.

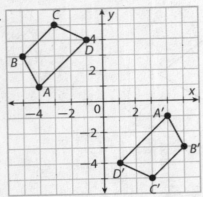

11.

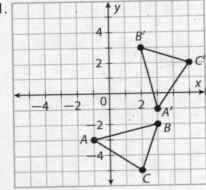

12. Quadrant III

13. Quadrant III

14. Quadrant II

15. The given angle is a multiple of 360°. This means the image of the square will be the square itself and that it must lie in the same quadrant as the original square: Quadrant I.

Skill 19: Properties of Translations

1.

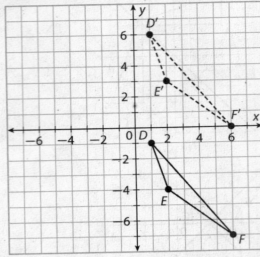

2.

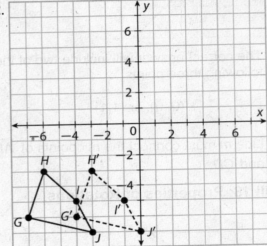

3.

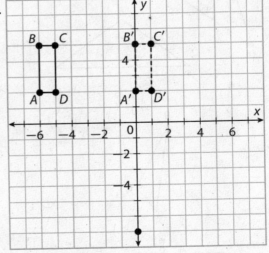

4.

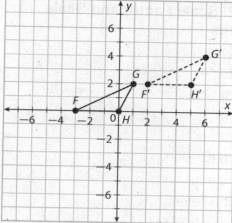

5. $(-2, 1) \rightarrow (-2 + 2, 1 - 3) \rightarrow (0, -2)$

$(-3, 3) \rightarrow (-3 + 2, 3 - 3) \rightarrow (-1, 0)$

$(3, 3) \rightarrow (3 + 2, 3 - 3) \rightarrow (5, 0)$

$(4, 1) \rightarrow (1 + 2, 2 - 3) \rightarrow (3, -1)$

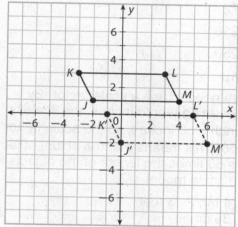

6. The error shows the student added 4 units to each of the coordinates, thereby shifting the figure to the right. In fact, the figure should be shifted to the left by 4 units and up by 3 units.

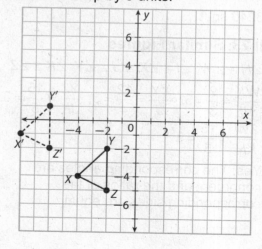

7. A. $(x + 5, y - 8)$

   B. $A'(-1, -6)$

     $B'(-1, -4)$

     $C'(3, -4)$

     $D'(3, -6)$

Skill 20: Quadratic Functions

1. Yes; $a = 3$, $b = 5$, $c = -8$

2. No

3. Yes; $a = 1$, $b = 6$, $c = 5$

4. Yes; $a = -2$, $b = 4$, $c = 0$

5. A down; B $(-3, 9)$; C maximum; D 9

6. A down; B $(1, 4)$; C maximum; D 4

7. A up; B $(-2, -4)$; C minimum; D -4

8. Graph opens down because $a = -1$ which is less than zero. The graph has a maximum.

9. Graph opens up because $a = 7$ which is less than zero. The graph has a maximum.

10. 2; -1 and 3

11. 0

12. $x = -2$

13. $x = 1$

14. **A.** The number in front of t^2 is -16 so this means the graph will open down.

   B. $(2, 65)$

   C. maximum at 65

   D. $x = 2$

   E. The ball is on the ground when the height is zero. That happens when $t = 0$ and $t = 4$. So, the ball hits the ground after 4 seconds.

15. The error is that a graph that opens up extends up infinitely. Therefore, the graph has a minimum.

Skill 21: Rate of Change and Slope

1. A $\dfrac{6.75}{3}$ B 2.25

2. A $\dfrac{-2}{5}$ B -0.4

3. $\dfrac{5}{9}$

4. $-\dfrac{2}{3}$

5. $\dfrac{1}{10}$

6. -6

7. $-\dfrac{3}{5}$

8. $\dfrac{4}{5}$

9. horizontal, slope is $\dfrac{0}{6} = 0$

10. vertical, slope is $\dfrac{0}{6}$ which is undefined

11. The x- and y-coordinates were not kept in the same order. The slope of the line through points (4, 7) and (2, 9) is $\dfrac{9-7}{2-4} = \dfrac{2}{-2} = -1$.

12. A. Plant B $\dfrac{3}{6} = \dfrac{1}{2}$

　　B. Plant C: $\dfrac{4}{6} = \dfrac{2}{3}$

　　C. Plant D: $\dfrac{10}{6} = \dfrac{5}{3}$

　　D. Plant B unit rate is $\dfrac{0.5}{1}$. Plant C unit rate is about $\dfrac{0.67}{1}$. Plant D unit rate is $\dfrac{1.67}{1}$. So, each week, Plant B grows 0.5 inches, Plant B grows 0.67 inches, and Plant D grows 1.67 inches. Therefore, Plant D has the fastest growth. I also know this is true by looking at the graph and seeing that Plant D has the steepest slope.

　　E. If a plant has a 0 slope growth rate, that means the plant does not grow at all. It just stays the same height. So, it is possible for a plant growth rate to be 0. If a plant growth rate is undefined, this means the plant grows infinitely with no passage of time. This is not possible. Therefore, it does not make sense for a plant growth rate to be undefined.

Skill 22: Scale Factor and Scale Drawings

1. 32 ft
2. 80 ft
3. 104 ft
4. 132 ft
5. 252 ft
6. 393.6 ft
7. 360 yards
8. 8 centimeters
9. 1 inch = 0.75 mile
10. A. 12 ft
　　B. 96 ft long and 72 feet wide
11. length: 12.5 in.; width: 4.5 in.; wingspan: 12 in.
12. 1:72
13. 1:216
14. 1:2500
15. 1:16
16. You need to use a scale factor. By converting feet to inches, the scale is 1 inch = 60 inches, so the scale factor is 1:60. This means that the actual objects are 60 times the length of the objects in the scale model.
17. A. 1 inch = 3 feet
　　B. 36 times
18. 32 mm
19. 3 in
20. 10 in
21. decrease
22. 3240 sq ft

Skill 23: Similar Figures

1. $\angle H \cong \angle W$, $\angle I \cong \angle X$, $\angle J \cong \angle Y$, $\angle K \cong \angle Z$

2. $\dfrac{WX}{HI} = \dfrac{9}{3} = 3$, $\dfrac{XY}{IJ} = \dfrac{12}{4} = 3$, $\dfrac{YZ}{JK} = \dfrac{15}{5} = 3$, $\dfrac{ZW}{KH} = \dfrac{15}{5} = 3$

3. Yes; The corresponding angles are congruent and the ratios of the corresponding sides are equal.

4. Yes; The corresponding angles are congruent and $\dfrac{7}{28} = \dfrac{8}{32} = \dfrac{6}{24}$. The ratio of corresponding sides is $\dfrac{1}{4}$.

5. Yes; The corresponding angles are congruent and $\dfrac{8}{6} = \dfrac{12}{9}$. The ratio of corresponding sides is $\dfrac{4}{3}$.

6. Yes; The corresponding angles are congruent and $\dfrac{9}{12} = \dfrac{12}{16} = \dfrac{15}{20}$. The ratio of corresponding sides is $\dfrac{3}{4}$.

7. No; The corresponding angles are congruent, but the ratios of corresponding sides are not equal. $\dfrac{6}{6} = \dfrac{5}{5}$ and $\dfrac{5}{4} = \dfrac{10}{8}$, but $1 \neq \dfrac{5}{4}$.

8. Since $\dfrac{3}{9} \neq \dfrac{4}{16}$, the ratios of corresponding sides are not equal. Rectangle $ABCD$ is not similar to rectangle $PQRS$.

9. Yes; A square has four 90° angles, so all angles are congruent. The ratios of corresponding sides all equal $\dfrac{9}{8}$.

10. No; A rectangle has four 90° angles, so all angles are congruent. However, the ratios of corresponding sides are not equal since $\dfrac{240}{200} \neq \dfrac{170}{135}$.

11. A $\dfrac{25}{10} = \dfrac{20}{x}$; $x = 8$

   B $\dfrac{25}{10} = \dfrac{y}{6}$; $y = 15$

12. A. 4

   B. Since DG = 3, perimeter of $DEFG$ = 16; perimeter of $RSTU$ = 64; The scale factor is 4 and the ratio of the perimeters is $\dfrac{64}{16} = 4$.

   C. area of $DEFG$ = 15; area of $RSTU$ = 240; The scale factor is 4 and the ratio of the areas is $\dfrac{240}{15} = 16$.

Skill 24: Surface Area

1. $B = 40$ cm^2; $P = 28$ cm; $L = 84$ cm^2; $S = 164$ cm^2

2. $B = 24$ cm^2; $P = 24$ cm; $L = 144$ cm^2; $S = 192$ cm^2

3. 460 in^2

4. 37.9 in^2

5. $B = 100\pi$ m^2; $L = 80\pi$ m; $S = 280\pi$ m^2

6. $B = \pi$ in^2; $L = 8\pi$ in; $S = 10\pi$ in^2

7. 2513.3 ft^2

8. The diameter was used instead of the radius. The correct surface area is 240π cm^2.

9. $B = 4$ in^2; $P = 8$ in; $L = 20$ in^2; $S = 24$ in^2

10. $B = 144$ in^2; $P = 48$ in; $L = 240$ in^2; $S = 384$ in^2

11. 97.6 in^2

Skill 25: The Pythagorean Theorem

1. $\sqrt{13}$

2. $\sqrt{17}$

3. $7\sqrt{2}$

4. $3\sqrt{10}$

5. 6.7 feet

6. 12

7. 20

8. 3

9. 4 units

10. 4 units

11. 8 feet

12. Error: Treating 5 as a leg length instead of the hypotenuse. Correct solution is $x = 3$.

13. No; The Pythagorean Theorem only applies to right triangles.

14. Yes; $9^2 + 12^2 = 15^2$.

15. No; $5^2 + 12^2 \neq 14^2$.

16. Yes; $8^2 + 8^2 = \left(8\sqrt{2}\right)^2$.

17. Sample Answer: 3, 4, 5. The justification should show that the Pythagorean Theorem holds for the given 3 numbers; in this case $3^2 + 4^2 = 5^2$

Skill 26: Using Slope and y-intercept

1. slope: 2; y-intercept: –3

2. slope: $\frac{1}{2}$; y-intercept: 2

3. slope: $-\frac{2}{3}$; y-intercept: 4

4. slope: –1; y-intercept: –1

5. A 5; The slope represents the cost in dollars per class.

   B 10; The y-intercept represents the registration fee.

6. $y = 3x - 1$

7. $y = -4x + 5$

8. $y = \frac{3}{4}x + 2$

9. $y = -\frac{4}{5}x - 3$

10. slope: –3; y-intercept: 1

11. slope: $\frac{1}{4}$; y-intercept: –5

12. $y = -2x + 3$;

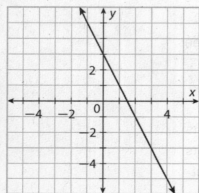

13. $y = \frac{3}{4}x + 2$

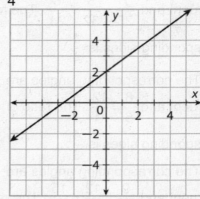

14. The variables x and y were transposed. The given slope and y-intercept is for the equation $2x + y = 4$. For the equation $x + 2y = 4$, the slope is $-\frac{1}{2}$ and the y-intercept is 2.

15. slope: 20; the cost in dollars per hour of the repair; y-intercept: 30; the cost of the parts

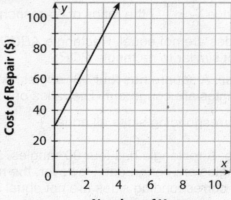

Skill 27: Volume

1. 2160 cm^3

2. 360 ft^3

3. 12

4. 6

5. 130.7 in^3

6. 100 ft^3

7. 6 ft

8. 12 m

9. triangle

10. 769.3 m^3

11. 301.4 in^3

12. 3918.7 ft³

13. 753.6 cm³

14. The measure of the diameter was used instead of the radius. The correct volume of the figure is

$$V = \pi(3)^2(6) + \frac{1}{3}\pi(3)^2 6 = 72\pi.$$

15. 9 in.

Skill 28: Writing Equations of Parallel, Perpendicular, Vertical, and Horizontal Lines

1. $y = -4x - 12$

2. $y = -2x - 1$

3. $y = \frac{1}{2}x - 11$

4. $y = -2x + 5$

5. $y = x - 2$

6. $y = \frac{1}{3}x - 6$

7. $y = 0$

8. $x = 4$

9. $x = 7$

10. $y = 1$

11. The slope of the equation is $\frac{1}{3}$. The negative reciprocal of $\frac{1}{3}$ is -3 because $-3\left(\frac{1}{3}\right) = -1$. So, the equation of the line perpendicular through point (6, 1) is $y = -3x + 19$.

12. $y = -5x + 50$

13. $y = \frac{1}{5}x - 2$

14. Sign-up fee: $20; cost per movie: $5

15. A $y = 5x + 3$; B new sign-up fee is $3

Skill 29: Proportional Relationships

1. 12

2. 8

3. 22

4. 40.0 feet

5. 9.6

6. The proportion written is correct since it is not using corresponding sides. The correct answer is $x = 20.0$.

7. No; There is only one pair of congruent angles, the triangles cannot be similar.

8. 4

9. 10

10. 3

11. $\overline{PQ} \parallel \overline{AC}$

12. 4

Skill 30: Multi-step Equations

1. $y = 5$

2. $x = 20$

3. $m = 3$

4. $p = -99$

5. $q = -38.75$

6. $k = 0$

7. $r = 0$

8. no solution

9. $b = -2$

10. $g = 1$

11. $y = -9$

12. $h = -0.3$

13. $x = 10$

14. $y = 2.75$

15. $x = 9$

16. $p = -5$

17. $r = -72$

18. $q = 0.5$

19. $y = -1$

20. $h = -8$

21. $b = 3$

22. $g = 4$

23. Danielle forgot to multiply 7d by -1 when distributing the coefficient to remove the parentheses. $d = 5$

Skill 31: Characteristics of Quadratic Functions

1. standard form

2. (−1, 0) and (5, 0)

3. $x = 2$; (2, −9)

4. minimum

5. (0, −5)

6.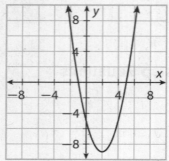

7. (1, 116); the maximum, or the highest point the rock reaches during flight

8. vertex form

9.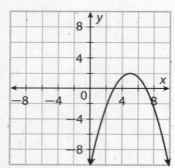

10. (3, 0) and (7, 0)

11. $x = 5$; (5, 2)

12. (0, −10.5)

13. Samuel confused the sign of h.

Skill 32: Solving Quadratic Functions

1. ±1

2. −2, 3

3. −3

4. 1, 5

5. none, one time, two times

6. The graph does not cross the x-axis.

7. ±3

8. ±2

9. $\pm\sqrt{3}$

10. $\pm\dfrac{1}{2}$

11. ±5

12. $\pm\dfrac{3}{2}$

13. $\pm\sqrt{5}$, The x-intercepts are found by setting the equation equal to zero. The solutions to $y = 2x^2 - 10$ are $\pm\sqrt{5}$.

14. The student did not include the negative square root. The last step should be $x = \pm\sqrt{24} = \pm 2\sqrt{6}$.

15. −4, 1

16. 3, 7

17. −2, −1

18. $-1, \dfrac{1}{3}$

19. $-4, \dfrac{3}{2}$

20. $-2, \dfrac{5}{2}$

21. (−6, 0) and (5, 0); the solutions to the equation formed by setting $y = 0$ are −6 and 5. These indicate the location of the x-intercepts.

22. For the solutions to be 5 and 9, the factors had to be $x - 5$ and $x - 9$. Therefore, one possible equation would be $x^2 - 14x + 45 = 0$.

23. $\dfrac{-3 \pm \sqrt{17}}{2}$

24. $\dfrac{1}{3}, \dfrac{1}{2}$

25. $3 \pm 2\sqrt{3}$

26. $1 \pm 3\sqrt{5}$

27. The student did not move all terms to one side before applying the formula.
If $x^2 = 7x + 10$, then $x^2 - 7x - 10 = 0$ and $x = \dfrac{7 \pm \sqrt{49 - 4(1)(-10)}}{2(1)} = \dfrac{7 \pm \sqrt{89}}{2}$.